The

CAUDILLS

∞ THE LOCHLAINN SEABROOK COLLECTION ∞

CONSTITUTIONAL HISTORY
America's Three Constitutions: Complete Texts of the Articles of Confederation, Constitution of the United States of America, and Constitution of the Confederate States of America
The Articles of Confederation Explained: A Clause-by-Clause Study of America's First Constitution
The Constitution of the Confederate States of America Explained: A Clause-by-Clause Study of the South's Magna Carta

VICTORIAN CONFEDERATE LITERATURE
Rise Up and Call Them Blessed: Victorian Tributes to the Confederate Soldier, 1861-1901
Support Your Local Confederate: Wit and Humor in the Southern Confederacy
The God of War: Nathan Bedford Forrest As He Was Seen By His Contemporaries
The Old Rebel: Robert E. Lee As He Was Seen By His Contemporaries
Victorian Confederate Poetry: The Southern Cause in Verse, 1861-1901

ABRAHAM LINCOLN
Abraham Lincoln: The Southern View - Demythologizing America's Sixteenth President
Lincolnology: The Real Abraham Lincoln Revealed in His Own Words - A Study of Lincoln's Suppressed, Misinterpreted, and Forgotten Writings and Speeches
Lincoln's War: The Real Cause, the Real Winner, the Real Loser
The Great Impersonator! 99 Reasons to Dislike Abraham Lincoln
The Unholy Crusade: Lincoln's Legacy of Destruction in the American South
The Unquotable Abraham Lincoln: The President's Quotes They Don't Want You To Know!

NATURAL HISTORY
North America's Amazing Mammals: An Encyclopedia for the Whole Family
The Concise Book of Owls: A Guide to Nature's Most Mysterious Birds
The Concise Book of Tigers: A Guide to Nature's Most Remarkable Cats

PARANORMAL
Carnton Plantation Ghost Stories: True Tales of the Unexplained from Tennessee's Most Haunted Civil War House!
UFOs and Aliens: The Complete Guidebook

FAMILY HISTORIES
The Blakeneys: An Etymological, Ethnological, and Genealogical Study - Uncovering the Mysterious Origins of the Blakeney Family and Name
The Caudills: An Etymological, Ethnological, and Genealogical Study - Exploring the Name and National Origins of a European-American Family
The McGavocks of Carnton Plantation: A Southern History - Celebrating One of Dixie's Most Noble Confederate Families and Their Tennessee Home

MIND, BODY, SPIRIT
Autobiography of a Non-Yogi: A Scientist's Journey From Hinduism to Christianity (Dr. Amitava Dasgupta, with Lochlainn Seabrook)
Britannia Rules: Goddess-Worship in Ancient Anglo-Celtic Society - An Academic Look at the United Kingdom's Matricentric Spiritual Past
Christ Is All and In All: Rediscovering Your Divine Nature and the Kingdom Within
Christmas Before Christianity: How the Birthday of the "Sun" Became the Birthday of the "Son"
Jesus and the Gospel of Q: Christ's Pre-Christian Teachings As Recorded in the New Testament
Jesus and the Law of Attraction: The Bible-Based Guide to Creating Perfect Health, Wealth, and Happiness Following Christ's Simple Formula
Seabrook's Bible Dictionary of Traditional and Mystical Christian Doctrines
The Bible and the Law of Attraction: 99 Teachings of Jesus, the Apostles, and the Prophets
The Book of Kelle: An Introduction to Goddess-Worship and the Great Celtic Mother-Goddess Kelle, Original Blessed Lady of Ireland
The Goddess Dictionary of Words and Phrases: Introducing a New Core Vocabulary for the Women's Spirituality Movement
Vintage Southern Cookbook: Delicious Dishes From Dixie

WOMEN
Aphrodite's Trade: The Hidden History of Prostitution Unveiled
Princess Diana: Modern Day Moon-Goddess - A Psychoanalytical and Mythological Look at Diana Spencer's Life, Marriage, and Death (with Dr. Jane Goldberg)
Women in Gray: A Tribute to the Ladies Who Supported the Southern Confederacy

REPRINTS
A Short History of the Confederate States of America (author Jefferson Davis; editor Lochlainn Seabrook)
Prison Life of Jefferson Davis (author John J. Craven; editor Lochlainn Seabrook)
Life of Beethoven (author Ludwig Nohl; editor Lochlainn Seabrook)
The New Revelation (author Arthur Conan Doyle; editor Lochlainn Seabrook)

Lochlainn Seabrook does not author books for fame and fortune, but for the love of writing and sharing his knowledge.

❦ SeaRavenPress.com ❦

Warning: SEA RAVEN PRESS BOOKS WILL EXPAND YOUR ★ MIND!

The

CAUDILLS

AN ETYMOLOGICAL, ETHNOLOGICAL, AND GENEALOGICAL STUDY

Exploring the Name and National Origins of a European-American Family

---•———

BY "THE VOICE OF THE TRADITIONAL SOUTH," COLONEL

LOCHLAINN SEABROOK

JEFFERSON DAVIS HISTORICAL GOLD MEDAL WINNER

Diligently Researched and Generously Illustrated
by the Author for the Elucidation of the Reader

2003

SEA RAVEN PRESS, NASHVILLE, TENNESSEE, USA

THE CAUDILLS

Published by
Sea Raven Press, Cassidy Ravensdale, President
Nashville, Tennessee, USA
SeaRavenPress.com • searavenpress@gmail.com

Sea Raven Press

Enlightening, educational, & entertaining books for the whole family!

1st SRP paperback edition, 1st printing, April 2003 • ISBN: 978-0-9821899-9-3
2nd SRP paperback edition, 1st printing: April 2010 • ISBN: 978-0-9821899-9-3
3rd SRP paperback edition, 1st printing: October 2021 • ISBN: 978-0-9821899-9-3
1st SRP hardcover edition, 1st printing: January 2016 • ISBN: 978-1-943737-23-9
2nd SRP hardcover edition, 1st printing, October 2021 • ISBN: 978-1-943737-23-9

ISBN: 978-0-9821899-9-3 (paperback)
Library of Congress Control Number: 2010922902

The Caudills: An Etymological, Ethnological, and Genealogical Study, by Lochlainn Seabrook. Contains a foreword, introduction, index, bibliography, appendices, and genealogical material.

ARTWORK
Front & back cover design & art, book design, layout, & interior art by Lochlainn Seabrook
All images, image captions, graphic design, & graphic art copyright © Lochlainn Seabrook
All images selected, placed, manipulated, and/or created by Lochlainn Seabrook
Image cleaning, coloration, & tinting by Lochlainn Seabrook
Cover photo: Faro & Doris Caudill, homesteaders, Pie Town, NM, 1940, by Russell W. Lee
(For Faro's genealogy see page 124)

All persons who approve of the authority and principles of Colonel Lochlainn Seabrook's literary work, and realize its benefits as a means of reeducating the world concerning important facts left out of our history books, are hereby requested to avidly recommend his books to others and to vigorously cooperate in extending their reach, scope, and influence around the globe.

The views on the South & the American "Civil War" documented in this book are those of the publisher.

PRINTED & MANUFACTURED IN OCCUPIED TENNESSEE, FORMER CONFEDERATE STATES OF AMERICA

SEA RAVEN PRESS

DEDICATION

To the teetotaling Danish de Caudella families

of Normandy, France

EPIGRAPH

People will not look forward to posterity who never look backward to their ancestors.

Edmund Burke (1729-1797)

CONTENTS

GENERAL EXPLANATIONS
for items used in this book

ABBREVIATIONS

abt. = 'about'

aft. = 'after'

b. = 'born'

b. c. = 'born circa' (i.e., born around)

BCE = 'Before Common Era' (in the Gregorian Calendar, preceding the year 0)

bef. = 'before'

c. = 'circa' (i.e., around or about)

CE = 'Common Era' (in the Gregorian Calendar, beginning in the year 0)

d. = 'died'

ed. = 'editor'

f. = 'flourished' (i.e., lived)

(fn) = 'footnote'

r. = 'reigned' or 'ruled'

DATES OF INDO-EUROPEAN LANGUAGES AND BRANCHES

UNRECORDED
Prehistoric language: 10,000 to 7000 BCE

Proto-Indo-European: 7000 to 3000 BCE

Old European: 1st Millennium to about Common Era; a pre-Celtic, non-Germanic, Neolithic language spoken in the British Isles c. 4th Century BCE

INDO-IRANIAN
Sanskrit: pre-1000 BCE; oldest known member of the Indo-European languages

GERMANIC

Old Teutonic: identical to Old German
Old Saxon: to 12th Century
Old German: to 12th Century
Old High German: 750 to 1150
Middle High German: 1150 to 1350
Middle Low German: 12th to 16th Centuries
Early New High German: 1350 to 1650
New High German: 1650 to present

Old Scandinavian: to 1350 (can also include both Old Norse and Old
    Danish, as well as Anglo-Scandinavian languages, such as Anglo-
    Danish)
Old Norse: to 1350 (similar, and perhaps nearly identical to, Old
    Danish)
Old (or Early) Danish: 9th to 11th Centuries (similar, and perhaps nearly
    identical to, Old Norse)
Anglo-Danish: 9th to 11th Centuries

Early English: 450 to 7th Century (began with the Jute, Angle, and Saxon
    Invasion of England in the 5th Century)
Old English (also known as Anglo-Saxon): 7th to 12th Centuries (can
    include dialects such as Anglian and West Saxon)
    Four Dialects:

    1. Northumbrian
    2. Mercian
    3. West Saxon (spoken in Wessex, and referred to as "standard
        Old English"; *Beowulf* and the *Anglo-Saxon Chronicle*
        written in this dialect)
    4. Kentish Middle English: 12th to 15th Centuries (held by some
        to begin with the Norman Invasion in the 11th Century,
        and end with the death of Chaucer in the year 1400)

Modern English: 15th Century to present
American English: from 17th Century

CELTIC
Old Irish: 7th to 11th Centuries
Middle Irish: 11th to 15th Centuries
Modern Irish: 15th Century to present

Middle Scots: 1474 to 1730

Old (or Primitive) Welsh: to 1150
Middle Welsh: 1150 to 16th Century
Modern Welsh: 16th Century to present

ITALIC
Old Latin: prior to Classical Period
Late Latin: 3rd to 6th Centuries
New Latin: 15th Century to present

Old French: 9th to 13th Centuries, and sometimes to the 16th Century
　　　　(can also include Norman French and Anglo-Norman)
Middle French: 14th to 16th Centuries
Modern French: 16th Century to present
Norman French: 9th to 11th Centuries
Anglo-Norman: 11th to 13th Centuries

BRANCH UNKNOWN
Late Greek: 3rd to 6th Centuries
Middle Greek: 7th to 15th Centuries
Modern Greek: 15th Century to present

NOTES TO THE READER

☞ Throughout this book, I use 'single quote' marks for definitions and meanings, and "double quote" marks for actual quotations.

☞ While there are dozens of spelling variations of the name Caudill, I have chosen to use this particular one in my book. Not only for simplicity's sake, but also because this is the one most commonly used among my own Appalachian Caudill ancestors.

☞ There is an impression among the general populace that all of the scholarly research into surnames has been done, and that we know all there is to know about most names.

Actually, nothing could be further from the truth. We have examples of thousands of surnames whose birth, development, and nationality are still not known with any certainty. Even many of those surnames which seem to have a solid provenance continue to be held suspect by some linguistic researchers (I am among them).

Second, *onomastics*, the scientific study of proper names, is more vital today than ever before. Experts all over the world continue to probe into the many mysteries of surnames, with new findings emerging and new theories being postulated on a regular basis.

Onomastics includes the fields of *toponymy*, the study of place-names, and *anthroponymy*, the study of personal names. An associated field, *etymology*, the study of the origins and history of words, also plays an important role in surname research.

The book you now hold in your hand represents one researcher's current work on the surname Caudill (and its many variant spellings) utilizing these sciences. Though there is still much to learn, and though etymology, like genealogy, is an open-ended, ever-growing field, I am quite confident that this book will not only add much that is new to the study of the Caudill name, but that it will also take the reader beyond nearly all current knowledge on this topic.

L. S.

Caudill Coat of Arms, Shield, Crest, & Motto

(Caudill Coat of Arms kindly donated by Mark Carroll)

CAUDILL CREST: A royal crown sitting on top of a Knight's helmet, out of which a red-gloved hand holding a sword emerges.

CAUDILL SHIELD: A base of green, with four red serpentine bars running horizontally, and three black pennants hanging vertically.

CAUDILL MOTTO: *Fac et Spera* (Latin for 'Do and Hope')

FOREWORD

This wonderfully written and meticulously researched book is a treasure-trove of intriguing Caudill information, which includes everything from maps to the Cawdor Castle in Scotland, useful Websites, and an extensive Caudill family tree, to our family Coat of Arms, a list of Caudill researchers, and lovely old-fashioned illustrations of down-home country life!

Within these pages the author, Lochlainn Seabrook, himself a Caudill descendant, has lovingly shared the benefit of his background in etymology and his extensive scholarly research into the origins and meaning of the Caudill surname. Who knew, for example, that its roots lie in ancient India, or that in Medieval Europe it was an everyday word connected with witches, healing, and teetolalism?

This is an important and unique book that each and every person with an interest in the Caudills will be proud to have in their library. With its wealth of helpful research data on not only the Caudills, but on allied families as well, this is a "must have" for all family members and researchers.

DELMERENE CAUDILL
Letcher County, Kentucky
Spring 2003

Highway near Neon, Letcher Co., KY, named after famed early country music singer Martha Carson (1921-2004), a close cousin of the author. Martha, born Irene Ethel Amburgy in Neon, later became the reigning queen of Gospel music in the 1950s, after which she was known as "The First Lady of Gospel Music." She was a member of the Grand Ole Opry, sold millions of records, and toured with Patsy Cline, Little Jimmy Dickens, Del Reeves, and many others. She was closely related to many of the Caudills of Letcher Co. The author attended Martha's funerary memorial in Nashville, December 2004. (Photo courtesy Tean Caudill)

INTRODUCTION

Many theories on the origins and meaning of the surname Caudill have been proposed, most of which I have found to be quite erroneous, being based on speculation, subjective opinion, misinformation, and a lack of knowledge of both onomastics and history. This book seeks to address this topic from a more impartial point of view, using chiefly the sciences of etymology and ethnology.

Although the origins of some ancient surnames will probably never be known with complete certainty, etymological methodologies can often succeed in doing what other approaches fail to do: trace such names back to their earliest beginnings, and in doing so determine, not only the true meaning of the name itself, but also uncover the original nationality of the families bearing this name. Etymology is able to achieve this because, as a science, it is based on objective data rather than on personal sentiment, on facts and evidence rather than on biases and hearsay. Unfortunately, many a family's genealogical history has been unwisely written using the latter.

Just as modern science has illuminated the dark corners of Medieval science, modern etymology too often reveals new information about families and their names, information that may have seemed hopelessly misplaced for centuries. Obstacles such as lost civil records, family skeletons, spurious family traditions, disinformation, and personal prejudices—not to mention the linguistic entropy that inevitably bears upon surnames due to the passage of time—all fall before the bright and guiding light of etymology. Throughout this book, it is this beacon I will follow in an effort to correct the current fallacies surrounding the origins of the Caudill name and family.

There is another reason I wrote this book, however, one of a more personal nature. I am a direct descendant of the Caudills of Virginia and Kentucky, a line that can be tenuously traced back to my 11th great-grandfather, William Caudill, possibly born in Scotland around 1585.

I descend from the Caudills twice, through two children of Stephen James Caudill (b. c. 1685 in Scotland) and his wife Mary Elizabeth "Betsy" Fields (b. 1698 in Scotland). Stephen and Mary are my 8th great-grandparents.

My closest Caudill ancestor is Henrietta "Henny" Caudill, born in 1753 in Sussex, Stafford County, Virginia. Henrietta—who married Benjamin Adams, Jr. (1749-1824), the son of John Hobbs Adams, Sr. (1729-1815)—is my 6th great-grandmother.

I am honored to be a blood descendant of this very interesting Southern and Appalachian family, one associated, by tradition at least, with Clan Campbell (Gaelic for 'crooked mouth')—which dates from Strathclyde in the year 1263.

The Campbell motto is: *Ne obliviscaris* ('Do Not Forget'). I for one will not forget that the early Campbells supported my 23rd great-grandfather, the great Scottish King, Robert the Bruce (1274-1329), who, with undying fidelity to his land and his people, fought and won Scottish independence from England on 23 June, 1314.

It is my hope that this book will increase appreciation, pride, wonderment, and knowledge of the Caudill family, among all its descendants, friends, and researchers.

LOCHLAINN SEABROOK
Franklin, Williamson County, Tennessee, USA
Spring 2003

The
CAUDILLS

An Etymological, Ethnological, and Genealogical Study

SEA RAVEN PRESS
NASHVILLE ✦ TENNESSEE
EST. 1995

"Books invite all; they constrain none."
Hartley Burr Alexander (1873-1939)

1

ORIGINS: AN ANCIENT HINDU GODDESS NAMED KALI

WHAT ARE THE ORIGINS OF the surname Caudill? What is its history, and what does it mean? What is the nationality of those who bear this name, and where and when did the earliest known Caudill live? The purpose of this book is to answer these questions, and while doing so, correct the many misconceptions surrounding these topics.

To begin our quest, we must travel back in time at least 3,500 years to Asia, and more specifically to the land of ancient India. Here, in Sanskrit, the classical language of the Hindu peoples, we find the etymon, or earliest true base-word, out of which the surname Caudill would later form.

This word was *kal*, and would have meant 'dark,' 'hot,' 'burning,' or 'scorched.' While we have no written record of the word *kal* (this is my hypothetical word), we can postulate its existence from recorded words that subsequently emerged from it.

The earliest of all such words is *Kali*, the name of the prehistoric Hindu Triple-Goddess in her "dark" underworld aspect. Kali's very name means 'burning' or 'dark,'[1] and it is her name which forms the base for such words as: *calamity*, meaning 'misery,' 'misfortune,' or 'disaster'; *calamari*, the black "inky" substance that squids eject when

---

1. One of Kali's more violent groups of devotees was known as the *Thuggee*, which gives us the Modern English word thug, an 'assassin,' 'killer,' or 'gangster.' *Thuggee* in turn derives from the Hindi word *thag*, 'thief,' which comes from the Sanskrit word *sthaga*, 'rogue,' which derives from the Sanskrit word *sthagati*, 'one who covers,' or 'one who conceals.'

threatened; *calcine*, heating to a high temperature in order to eliminate volatile matter; and *calx* (i.e., 'limestone'), the calcium-like material left after a mineral has been exposed to extreme heat (the immediate parent of the Latin *calx* is probably the Greek *khalix*, meaning 'limestone,' a word that also derives from the name of the "hot" ancient Destroying Goddess of the Underworld, Kali).

2

BLACK ANNIS, CALLY BERRY, & THE HAG OF WINTER: KALI'S MIGRATION INTO EUROPE

A S KALI'S RELIGION AND MYTHS spread westward across Asia and into Europe, her name was adopted and transformed by each subsequent culture and society. In England, for example, the dark Kali became known as both the *Black Queen* and as *Black Annis* ('Dark Grandmother'), a deity still believed by some to live in a cave in the Dane Hills of Leicester.

Kali's Roman spelling, *Cale*, however, also must have entered England early on, for it has been preserved in the name of both the English River Cale (Dorset, Somerset County) and in the English town of Wincanton (Somerset County), whose original spelling (in King William's *Domesday Book*, 1086)[2] was *Wincaletone*, loosely meaning: 'Farm on the White River belonging to the Goddess Cale.'

In England, Cale's/Kali's name may have also been confused with an ancient Scandinavian man's name, *Kali*, which itself probably has early linguistic links with this Goddess. We have record, from the year 1044, of an English town called *Calethorp*, which some anthroponymists translate, in Old Norse, as 'outer farm of a Scandinavian man known as Kali.'

I would suggest an alternate, perhaps more accurate, translation: 'outer farm of a family of followers of the Goddess Cale.' We will note here that early Scandinavians did indeed worship their own version of the great Indo-European underworld Triple-Goddess, a belief not yet extinct

---

2. King William I "the Conqueror" (1024-1087) is my 26th great-grandfather.

in that region.[3]

In this same sense, Cale's name may have also been used in the formation of such English place-names as: Calmsden (Gloucestershire County), spelled *Kalemundesdene* in 852; Calow (Derbyshire County), spelled *Calehale* in the *Domesday Book* (1086); Calstock (Cornwall County), spelled *Kalestoc* in the *Domesday Book* (1086); and Calstone Wellington (Wiltshire County), spelled *Calestone* in the *Domesday Book* (1086).[4]

In Ireland, the great female Indian deity Kali became the Goddess *Cally Berry* ('Old Gloomy Woman'), also known as *Kilda*, or more commonly, *Kelle* (in ancient Irish, perhaps spelled *Ceallai*).[5]

Kali's absorption into Irish culture and language was an easy one, not only because the ancient Irish were enthusiastic Goddess worshippers,[6] but also because Sanskrit is a distant ancestor of the Celtic languages (these include the now extinct Gaulish branch, as well as the modern Insular branch, the latter being comprised of both *Gaelic* [Irish, Manx, and Scottish] and *Brythonic* [Breton, Cornish, Welsh]).[7]

An entire civilization—Kelle's devoted northern European followers, named themselves after her, a name their descendants still bear to this day: the Kelts or Celts.

One of their earlier names, the Gauls or Gaels, derives from an even older version of Kelle, namely the Old European Mother-Goddess, *Gala*, whose name gives us the words "gal," "gala," "galaxy," and "galactic" (ga-lactic, i.e., 'Gala's milk'),[8] and whose name was given to

---

3. In Scandinavia the Triple-Goddess Kali is still known as the Norns ('Fates'), whose three Goddesses are named Urda, Verdandi, and Skuld, respectively governing the past, present, and future of each person's life. Urda the Earth-Goddess has given us the modern English word "earth," while the Goddess Skuld is identical to Scota, the Goddess after whom Scotia, or Scotland, is named.

4. Despite the similarities between these old spellings and the Goddess name Kale/Cale, the relationship here remains questionable since such place-names may also possesses meanings unrelated to her. The names are so old, in fact, it is impossible to know with any certainty. Based on etymology alone, however, a distant link seems likely.

5. For more on the Irish Goddess Kelle, the original "Blessed Lady of Ireland," see my book, *The Book of Kelle*.

6. For more on Goddess worship among the early Celts and Anglo-Saxons, see my book *Britannia Rules*.

7. Note that Ireland was named after the Irish Earth-Goddess *Eriu*; hence the Irish Gaelic name for Ireland, *Erin*, meaning the "Land of [the Goddess] Eriu."

8. The ancients thought that the nighttime galaxy looked like the Goddess Gala's breast milk, which she pours forth to feed her star-children (the constellations). Hence they named it *galakt* (in Greece), or *galaxias* (in Rome), 'Gala's milk', in Modern English, "galaxy."

the ancient lands of the freedom-loving Celts: Galatia, meaning 'the land of the Goddess Gala' (in ancient Greece, Kali/Kelle/Gala was sometimes known as the Earth-Goddess Gaea, Gaia, or Galatea).[9]

One ancient Irish family even adopted Kelle's name as both its personal clan name and its surname: the *Ó Ceallaighs*—in English, the Kelleys, Kellys, McKellys, MacKellys, O'Kelleys, etc., modern day families that may thus claim descent from this prehistoric Celtic Goddess.[10] Kelle's ancient temple sites still carry her memory in the names of the places built over them, two examples being the Irish city of Kildare and Saint Kilda's Isle.[11]

Kelle's connection to both the cauldron (an archetypal womb symbol of birth, death, and rebirth) and families named Kell and Kells is evident in these very surnames, for both are sometimes shortened forms of the Old Norse word *ketill*, which means 'cauldron,' and which gives us the English word "kettle." To this day, in Ireland and Scotland, the Kells place-name continues to mark one of Kelle's ancient holy sites (e.g., *Ceanannus Mór, Eire*).

In Scotland, Kali/Cale/Kelle became the Dark Earth-Goddess *Carlin* ('Old Woman'), or *Cailleach Bheur* ('Hag of Winter'),[12] which is why the ancient Romans named Scotland *Caledonia*, meaning 'the Land Given by Cale.'[13]

The Scots (or more accurately, the *Scoti*) themselves took their name from the Scandinavian version of this very same ancient Roman dark underworld-goddess, a female deity known as *Skadi* (or *Skuld*). Her

---

9. Saint Paul's argumentative New Testament letter to his new Celtic converts in Galatia (the book of *Galatians*) reveals the fiery independence of the ancient Goddess worshipping Celts, a trait for which their descendants are still known to this day. Goddess worship itself is still practiced throughout the Emerald Isle, while it has been subsumed into Celtic Christianity in a thousands different ways.

10. Kelly is the second most common name in Ireland today.

11. It is interesting to note the connection between the Christian "Saint Kilda" and the great Irish Pagan Goddess Kelle/Kilda. *The Oxford Dictionary of Saints* maintains that Saint Kilda "never existed." If true, then who was he? Masculinizing and christianizing Pagan female deities has long been a tradition in the Catholic Church, so we can be quite sure that Saint Kilda is a disguised version of the great Irish Pagan Goddess Kelle/Kilda/Kali, whose name, figure, and legends he accrued over the centuries.

12. The word *cailech* is still used throughout the Celtic lands as a synonym for 'old woman.'

13. According to Scottish mythology, Loch Awe, Argyll, Scotland, was accidentally created by *Cailleach Bheur*, who felt so guilty for flooding the area that she turned herself to stone. Prehistoric standing stones, or *menhirs*, which still dot the landscape of Scotland and Ireland, are said to be manifestations of *Cailleach Bheur*, and are still worshipped in her honor by modern Celtic Pagans.

gaelicized name became *Scota* or *Scotia*, the earliest known name of both Scotland and Ireland.

So great was her importance in the ancient world that the Goddess Skadi—whom the Goths knew as *Skadus*, the Irish knew as *Scatha*, and the early English knew as *Sceadu*—also gave her name to the Isle of Skye, to the ancient nation of Scythia, and even to Scandinavia itself.

3

THE TRIPLE-GODDESS, WINE, & THE BLOOD OF LIFE

EVERY EARLY EASTERN AND EUROPEAN nation and people had its dark Triple-Goddess, most whose names can be traced back to the Sanskrit etymon *kal*, out of which the Caudill surname itself arose.

This all-powerful deity not only personifies the three stages of life (*youth*, represented by the Virgin; *parenthood*, represented by the Mother; and *old age*, represented by the Crone), but in mythology she also represents the subconscious mind, the "dark" side of human nature, nighttime, inner and outer darkness, and, in essence, the triads of birth, death, and rebirth, and the mind, body, and soul complex.

In Phoenicia, for instance, the dark Triple-Goddess was known as *Calpe*; in Palestine she was *Kalu*; and in ancient Greece she was *Kalli* (her name was also given here to the Goddesses *Caligo*, *Callisto*, and *Calypso*). To the early German Saxons she was *Kale*; to the ancient Gypsies she was *Kalika*; in early Malaysia she was *Kari*; and in old Finland she was called *Kalma*. Hindus assert that the word *karma* comes from one of Kali's titles, *Kauri-Ma* ('Brilliant Mother'), and that she invented the Sanskrit language itself as well.[14]

Kali probably arrived in what is now Italy sometime in the 3rd Millennium BCE, where she became the Goddess *Cale* (later subsumed

---

14. By extension of Kali's title, *Kauri-Ma*, she is also the mother of hundreds of other later emerging Goddesses, such as *Ker*, *Car*, *Q're*, *Cae-Dia*, and *Kore*, whose sacred symbol, the five-pointed pentacle (the holy emblem of human life), is found in the center of the sliced apple. Long one of Kali-Kore's most sacred fruits, to this day the apple's heart bears the Goddess' name: 'core,' a word that still literally means 'heart' in many languages. For example, in Spanish heart is *corazón*'; in French, *coeur*; in Italian, *cuore*; and in Portuguese, *coração*. All derive from the Latin word *cor*, 'heart.' (See the following footnote.) Concerning the number five, this number (and its holy symbol, the pentagram) has always been sacred in native Celtic religion, and for many reasons; among them because it represents the north, south, east, west, and center. The five Provinces of Ireland were created based upon this sacred numerology. The sacrality of the number five of course derives from the five points of the human body: the head, two hands, and two feet, an image made famous by the Italian Renaissance man, Leonardo da Vinci (1452-1519), in his sketch the "Vitruvian Man": an unclothed male standing outstretched as a five-pointed star, the pentacle.

into various Roman female deities, such as the Fate-Goddess *Cale* ('fair') and the great Latin Triple-Goddess, *Diana* (Dea-Anna, literally 'Goddess-Grandmother'). Cale's holiest day fell on the first day of each month of the Roman Lunar Year, a day known after her name as the *Calendae*, or the *Kalends* (i.e., 'Kali's Time System'), from which we derive the modern English word "calendar."[15]

Throughout pre-Christian Italy, wine was held to be a symbol of Cale's sacred "Blood of Life," which when imbibed during temple sacraments, purified the soul of sin and bestowed immortality. Later these beliefs and rituals were passed on to the Roman Wine-Goddess *Libera*, the consort of the Wine-God *Bacchus Liber*, whose names give us the words "liberal" and "liberate," and whose boisterous and licentious festivals, the *Bacchanalia*,[16] give us the words "bacchanalian" ('a drunken feast'), and "bachelor" (originally meaning 'a bucolic man'; that is, a 'shepherd, farmer, or peasant').[17]

It is no accident that Cale also gave her name to both the Latin word *calixicis*, meaning a 'cup,' 'pot,' or 'wine,' and to the Italian Campanian town of Cale (in Latin, *Calesium*), famed around the Mediterranean for its wine, associations that lead us one step closer to understanding the development of the surname Caudill.

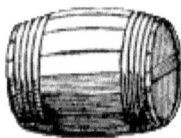

15. The name of the European Goddess Kali/Cale/Cor also contributed to many surnames as well as everyday words. One example is the surname Corderoy (after which the cloth is named), from the French *cœur de roi*, 'heart of [the] king.' In the Medieval period, one bearing the Corderoy surname was no doubt thought to be "courageous," a word that derives from the Old French word *cuer*, 'heart.'

16. Early on, aspects of the Bacchanalia were incorporated into the Christian holy day we call Christmas, such as the word "merry" in the phrase "Merry Christmas." For more on the Pagan foundations of Christmas, see my book *Christmas Before Christianity*.

17. Both Judaism and the early Christian Church adopted Kali's/Cale's symbol of wine as the "Blood of Life," which is one reason biblical texts refer to Jesus as the "true vine" (e.g., John 15:1-11). Jesus himself speaks more plainly on the subject. At the Last Supper, he blessed a cup of wine and referred to it as "my blood of the New Testament, which is shed for many (Mark 14:23-25)." Wine continues to play an integral and purifying role in the holy sacraments of both Christian and Pagan denominations and sects around the world.

4

HOT ALE & THE WITCHES' CAULDRON

BY THE EUROPEAN MIDDLE AGES (c. 500 to c. 1500) the religion and figure of the Goddess Cale had moved north out of Italy into France, where she left a mark of her presence upon the city that still bears her name: Calais.[18]

Though by this time Christianity had temporarily succeeded in suppressing the public worship of the Goddess Cale, Latin, the language of her Pagan Italian followers, was enthusiastically adopted by both French and Norman scribes and scholars. In our study of the origins of the Caudill name, it is important to note here that it was at this time, the early Medieval period, that Latin became the documentary language of the French and Norman people.[19]

Despite the largely academic usage of Latin, however, some Latin words inevitably filtered down into the lower strata of Norman society, where they began to be used in everyday speech. One of these words was *caldellum*, the Middle Latin word for a popular gruel made with fermented hops, malt, spices, and sugar.

Caldellum literally means a 'warm libation,' or a 'hot beverage,' and derives from the Latin *caldus*, 'hot,' which derives from the Latin adjective *calidus*, essentially meaning 'warm,' but also more generally meaning 'hot,' 'rash,' 'hot-headed,' or 'a warm drink.'

Calidus in turn comes from an even older Latin word, *calere*, 'to be warm' or 'to be hot,' a word derived from the name of the Underworld-Goddess Cale (Kali), the ruler of pots, heat, wine, and darkness (i.e., the subconscious side of life).

---

18. Though some claim that Calias, France, derives its name from the Greek God Calias (one of the twin sons of the Greek God Boreas and the Greek Goddess Orithyia), it is my belief that both the city and the God derive their names from the Goddess Cale, as the Divine Feminine preceded the Divine Masculine.

19. Modern scientists around the world have continued this tradition into the present day, using a classification system called taxonomy. The inventor, the "Father of Taxonomy," is the Swedish botanist, Carl von Linné (1707-1778), who latinized his own name to Carolus Linnaeus.

Caldellum, actually a type of light but thick ale, was often used as a substitute for strong alcoholic drinks in the treatment of the sick and dying, or for aiding women in the throes of labor. Because of this, *caldellum* developed—quite unjustly—a reputation for being a beverage fit only for the weak, the fragile, and the infirm; in other words, a "prissy's drink." Conversely, though far more rarely, *caldellum* also came to be used for someone who refused anything but the strongest drink.

Cale's word *calere*, the root of *caldellum*, also gives us the Latin words *calor* (in English and French, "calorie"), meaning 'heat'; *caleo*, 'to feel warm with passion'; *calesco*, 'to become excited or inflamed'; *calida*, 'warm water'; *calefacio*, 'to warm,' 'to arouse'; *calefactare*, 'to heat'; and *caldarius*, 'hot bath.' All of these words have associations with the caldron, and hence not only with both feminine Pagan religion and traditional medicinal drinks, but also with the surname Caudill, as we are about to see.

The English word "caldron" derives from the Latin feminine word *caldaria,* 'pot of warm water' (identical to *calidarium*, 'hot bath'), a derivative of *calidus*, 'warm.' In Spanish, *calidaria* became *caldera* (the scientific name for large volcanic craters formed by violent explosions), and then *calderon* ('caldron'), while in Italian *calidaria* became *calderone* (also meaning 'caldron').

A Vulgar Latin form of *caldaria*, written *caldario*, gave rise, in Old French, to *chauderon* (in Modern French, *chaudron*). This in turn gave rise, in Anglo-Norman, to a more softened form, *caudron*; which in Middle English, became *cauderon*. In the 15th Century, the Old Latin "l" (i.e, the letter "L") was re-inserted back into the word, creating, in Modern English, the word "caldron," 'a large cooking kettle.'

In the Old Religion, that is, the original feminine based Earth-worshipping Religions—of which modern Wicce (i.e., 'Witchcraft,' or the Craft) is a remnant, the *caldaria*, or caldron, has long been a symbol of the 'hot,' 'dark,' 'boiling,' life-giving, womb of the great Mother-Earth Goddess, out of which all souls are born, die, and are born again. Hence Wiccens, from prehistoric to modern times, have used the cauldron in the preparation (usually by boiling) of curative potions, rejuvenating drinks, rehabilitative medications, and healing ointments, balms, lotions, unctions, and salves.[20]

Once again, here we see the ancient associations between the Goddess Kali, female-based religion, the caldron, darkness, hot healing drinks, and the surname Caudill.

---

20. The age-old connection between hot medicinal drinks, wine, and the reproductive aspects of the Great Goddess can be seen in the Old English word *bytt* (in Modern English, butt), which means both 'cask' and 'womb.'

5

VIKINGS IN NORMANDY: FROM NICKNAME TO SURNAME

THE MEDIEVAL NORMANS, WHO BEGAN life in France in the year 845 as Danish Viking raiders,[21] adopted most of these Latin words, along with their French counterparts. Following a common custom of modifying foreign words to suit one's own language, the Normans altered *caldaria* to *caudiere*, the Old Norse French word for caldron. We will note here that *caudiere* is in turn related to the Latin word *cadus* ('barrel'), the Greek *kadus* ('jar'), the Hebrew *kad* ('pail'), and the French *cade* ('cask'), i.e., a container for holding wine.[22]

It was at this time, between the 9th and 10th Centuries, that the Normans also normanized the Latin cousin of the word caldron, *caldellum* (a hot recuperative ale) which became, in Old Norse French, *caudel.*

By now, however, the definition of the word *caudel* had begun to change. No longer merely the name of a rejuvenating but mild ale or gruel for the infirm, the word *caudel* began to be used as a disparaging nickname for a woman or man who abstained from alcoholic beverages. Thus anyone who did not like strong drink, or who could not hold their liquor, was known as a caudel.

Shortly after this, perhaps by around 911—the year the Danes founded the Province of Normandy in northwestern France—this nickname began to be accepted as an actual surname; a surname that in the Norman French language[23] of the day was no doubt written with the prepositions *le* or *de* ('the'), making *de Caudella*, or perhaps *de Cadouel;*

---

21. For more on this subject, see my book, *The Blakeneys: An Etymological and Ethnological Study*.

22. French-speaking peoples, in general, dislike harsh consonants, such as the hard 'l' and 'r' in *caldaria*; thus foreign words with such elements are inevitably softened and smoothed over through linguistic francicization. This is precisely what occurred in Normandy with the word *caldaria*, which was here normanized to *caudiere*.

23. Norman French was the language spoken by the Danish Normans in France between the 9th and 11th Centuries.

that is, 'the Caudel,' or more freely, 'one who abstains from hard drink.'

6

THE NORMAN INVASION: BIRTH OF THE CAUDILL NAME

W E HAVE RECORDS OF NORMAN Caudills in Scotland prior to the Norman Invasion of England in 1066 (note that the name was not spelled "Caudill" at this time). Hence, it is apparent early on that many ancient Norman Caudill families inherited the restless nomadic energies of their Danish Viking ancestors. For sometime between the years 900 and 1000, they had already migrated hundreds of miles to the north to Scotland.

Despite these rare pre-Conquest migrations of the Norman surname *de Caudella* (pronounced "du caw-DEE-yah") out of Medieval France into the British Isles, when the Norman Conquest finally came, it only accelerated this process, as thousands of Normans began crossing the English Channel. Among these would have been dozens, perhaps hundreds, of Norman *de Caudella* families, all seeking a new life in their latest conquest, the nation of Anglo-Saxon England.

It was here, in mid-11th-Century England, that the Norman surname, *de Caudella*, became an "English" surname which, after anglicization and without the preposition, was written (in Middle English) *Cadel*.

The emergence of a host of other Anglo-Saxon spelling variations of this surname were to quickly follow (in alphabetical order): Caddell, Cadell, Cadle, Cadwal, Caudell, Caudill, Caudle, Cawdell, Cawdle, Cawdor, Codill, Cordall, Cordell, Cordial, Cordill, Cordle, and Kaldel. (Note the overt vestiges of the ancient Triple-Goddess Kali's/Cor's name in many of these spellings.)

7

WELLS, SPRINGS, & BOILING POOLS: NAMES RELATED TO CAUDILL

OTHER CLOSELY RELATED ENGLISH SURNAMES arose at this time as well, such as Caldwell, which was written *Caldeuuella* by Norman scribes in the 11ᵗʰ Century; *Kadewelle* in the 13ᵗʰ Century; and *Cadwel* in the 14ᵗʰ Century. Each of these forms stem from the earlier Old English toponym (i.e., a place-name), *Ceald Wielle* (in Modern English, "Cold Well"), meaning 'cold spring.'

From Caldwell itself many variations emerged (in alphabetical order): Cadwall, Cadwell, Calwell, Caldwill, Cardwell, Caudwell, Cauldwell, Cauldwill, Chadwell, Cholwell, Coddle, Coldwell, Cottle, and Couldwell.

Here we can see the linguistic "watery" ties which connect the surname Caudill (two early forms of which were *Cadella* and *Caudella*) with the surname Caldwell (two early forms which were *Kadewelle* and *Cadwel*). The *-ill* or *-ella* element in the Caudill spelling variations means 'beverage' or 'liquid,' while the *-wella* or *-well* (in Old English, *wællen*) element in Caldwell means 'stream' or 'spring.'[24]

The pedigree of these affixal elements begins with the Latin word *volvere*, meaning 'to roll' (as in voluble, 'to seethe,' or 'to fume'), which gave rise to the Old High German word *wella*, 'wave,' which gave rise to the Old English word *weallan*, 'to boil,' which gave rise to the Middle English word *welle* (in Modern English, "well"), meaning 'a small body of water fed by a spring.'

We thus have the complete meaning here of 'water boiling up

---

24. Note, however, that the Old English word *cald*, meaning 'cold' (as in Caldwell/Coldwell) has the opposite meaning of the Latin words *calidus* and *calere*, which mean 'warm' or 'hot' (as in Caudill/Cordill).

to form a pool,' a definition that accurately resonates with all of the ancestor-words of the Caudill names, from the prehistoric etymon *kal* ('dark,' 'hot,' 'burning,' 'scorched') to the name of the Underworld Wine-Goddess, *Kale/Cale* ('dark,' 'burned,' 'cask,' 'pot,' 'hot'); from the Latin *calere* ('to be warm') and *calidus* ('a warm drink'), to the Latin *caldellum* ('hot beverage') and the English caldron ('kettle for cooking').

As time passed, many villages and regions throughout England were eventually named after *cadel*, the "prissy's drink" (most probably by conservative Christian preachers, prohibitionists, and strict teetotalers), and after its linguistic cousin, *ceald wielle* (that is, Caldwell, 'cold spring').

Among such English toponyms we have: *Cawdle Fen* (Cambridgeshire County), *Caudle Green* (Gloucestershire County), *Chadwell* (Essex, Hertfordshire, Leicestershire, and Wiltshire Counties), *Caldwall* (Worcestershire), *Chardwell* (Essex County), *Chardle Ditch* (Cambridgeshire County), and *Caldwell* (in Scotland and England), just to name a few.

Bearing these place-names in mind, there can be little doubt that many modern day Caudills are not direct descendants of the Norman *de Caudellas*, whose own Danish ancestors had coined the derogatory surname *Caudel* in Normandy between the 9th and 10th Centuries. Instead, following the most common method of acquiring a surname, many Medieval English and Scottish families adopted the name Caudill from one of the many Caudill toponyms that have dotted England's and Scotland's landscapes for nearly 1,000 years.

Caudill is a word-name with many other associations and spellings as well, and so also has linguistic connections with the following surnames: Calder and Caulder (that is, 'one who drinks *cadel*,' and so perhaps meaning 'a teetotaler');[25] Calderon, Coldron, Cauldron (probably a metonymic for one who cooks or makes cauldrons), and Cawdron (from the Anglo-French word *cauderon* and the Old French word *chalderonnier*, both meaning 'a maker of caldrons'); and Caldecot, Caldecote, Caldecott, Caldecourt, Caldicot, Calidcott, Callicott, Calcott, Calcut, Calcutt, Callcott, Caulcott, Caulcutt, Caulkett,

---

25. The name *Calder* has other ancient Celtic meanings, such as 'rapid stream.'

Cawcutt, Corcut, Corkett, Corkitt, Coldicott, Colicot, Collacot, Collacutt, Collecott, Collicutt, Colcott, Colcutt, Collcott, Collkutt, Colkett, Colocott, Chaldecott, and Chalcot (all of these from the Old English, *ceald cote*, meaning 'cold cottage'; i.e., a drafty or inhospitable dwelling).

8

VIKING RAIDERS & ENGLISH PLACE-NAMES: TRACING THE NATIONALITY OF THE CAUDILLS

HAVING THUS ESTABLISHED THE ETYMOLOGY of the surname Caudill, we are now prepared to trace the ethnology, or nationality, of the name as well.

The earliest use of the word *cadel*, as both a nickname and a surname, emerged from early Normandy, which was founded by the Danish chieftain and Viking leader, *Hrolf the Ganger* (c. 860-c. 931), in the year 911.[26] It is here, in this exact time and place (i.e., in early 10th-Century Danish France), that we find *caudel*, the Old Norse French variation of *caldellum*.

Based on this fact alone, it is obvious that the original nationality of Caudill can be none other than Danish, since the founders of Normandy were Viking raiders from 8th-Century Denmark.

Technically speaking, however, the Normans—the people who actually coined the surname Caudill—were a hybrid race, a restless nomadic people comprised of Danes and French who early on joined themselves culturally and consanguineously (through marriage).

Hence, a more detailed genetic ethnology of the name would begin with Caudill rooted in 1. Danish; then, in order of geographical and national dissemination, 2. French; 3. Norman; 4. English (i.e., Anglo-Saxon, and thus German); 5. Welsh; 6. Scottish; and 7. Irish. The name (and its many variant spellings) then migrated from Europe to the Americas.

Still, not all American Caudills can trace their genetic heritage to Normandy. As mentioned earlier, in the Medieval period, some

---

26. Hrolf the Ganger (i.e., 'Rollo the Rover or Walker') is my 30th great-grandfather.

purely English and Scottish families simply adopted the name Caudill from local place-names, such as *Caudle Green* (Gloucestershire County, England), *Cawdle Fen* (Cambridgeshire County, England), and *Caldwell* (found in both Scotland and England).

For now though, we can safely say that most of those possessing the Caudill surname are ultimately of Norman (i.e., Danish and French) heritage. Some however—those who took their surname from nearby toponyms—must certainly be of English, and far more rarely, of Scottish heritage. Only an in-depth study, tracing one's Caudill ancestors back to at least the Middle Ages, could determine, with any accuracy, which is the correct heritage (not always an easy task).

9

LATIN TAILS & SPANISH SHIPWRECKS: ALTERNATIVE THEORIES

N O STUDY OF THE CAUDILL surname would be complete without considering other theories of origin. Since these thoroughly contradict my views on the matter, I would like to address them here and eliminate them one by one.

Some have suggested, for instance, that Caudill derives from the English word caudal, meaning 'situated or directed toward the hind part of the body.' Actually, this is a case of misunderstanding and false association.

As we have seen, Caudill comes from the Old Norse French word *caudel,* meaning a 'warm drink.' The English caudal, on the other hand, is a zoological term deriving from the Latin word *cauda* ('tail'), and thus means 'of or belonging to the tail.'[27] The similarities between these two words then are coincidental, and are the linguistic equivalent of convergent, or more accurately, parallel evolution in biology.[28]

---

27. The Latin *cauda* also gave rise to both the Italian word *coda*, a 'tail'-piece, and the French word *queue*, 'tail.' The latter word gave rise to both the metaphorical English word of the same spelling, *queue*, meaning a 'line of people waiting,' and *cue*, a 'billiard stick.'

28. What I call *linguistic parallel evolution* (in which two words of unrelated etymological ancestry arise and evolve independently, but end up sharing the same or similar spelling and/or meaning) is very common. For example, we have the Welsh forename *Cain* and the Hebrew forename *Cain*. Both are spelled the same in Modern English, but have completely separate and dissimilar etymologies. The Welsh Cain (as a surname, also spelled Caine, Cane, Kain, Kaine, Kane, Kayne, and O'Kane) is an abbreviated form of the Welsh women's names, *Ceindrych* and *Ceinwen* (in the 13th Century, written *Keina*), all which derive from the feminine Welsh word *cain*, meaning 'beautiful.' One of the more familiar people with this, the Anglo-Celtic version of the name, is the English film actor, Maurice Micklewhite, better known as Michael Caine (b. 1933). Other notable Cains include the American writer, James M. Cain (1892-1977), and the English novelist, Sir Thomas Henry Hall Caine (1853-1931). The Hebrew form of Cain, however, is from the Hebrew word *qayin*, meaning a 'lance' or 'spear,' and derives from the related primitive root-word *qanah*, meaning 'to erect,' 'to create,' 'to possess,' or 'provoke to jealousy.' In the Old Testament, the name was given to the first-born son of Adam and Eve: *Qayin*, that is, Cain (see Genesis 4:1). An early Near-Eastern town, inhabited by a tribe called the Kenites (Cainites), was also named Cain or *Qayin* (Joshua 15:57). Located about 3 miles south-east of modern-day Hebron, Jordan, it is now spelled Yekin. In England, both

Another prevalent theory asserts that the surname Caudill is of Spanish derivation, based on the fact that a number of men from Madrid, possessing the surname Cordillo, shipwrecked off the coast of Scotland in 1588 during a brief military skirmish between Spain and England. According to this theory, either the name Cordillo was then adopted by the Scottish natives, or those Spanish sailors who were named Cordillo settled in Scotland. Either way, so it is claimed, Cordillo was celticized, becoming, presumably, Caudillo, then Caudill (or Caudle).

There are several problems with this view, however, all which prove to be insurmountable.

To begin with, while we know that a Spanish armada was indeed defeated by the English off Scotland in the late 16th Century, there is currently no known record of any men by the name of Cordillo from this fleet. Hence, at this point the entire idea is purely conjectural.

Second, the surname Cordillo would not have been celticized by the Scots to "Caudillo" and then "Caudill," even if Spaniards with this name were in Scotland in the 16th and 17th Centuries. Caudill, is a relatively modern Anglo-Celtic spelling variation of the Middle English spelling Cadel, which derives from the Anglo-Norman spelling Caudle, which derives from Norman spelling de Caudella, which derives from the Old Norse French word caudel. In short, Cordillo would not, and could not, have been celticized to Caudill, as the common—or perhaps, the only known—form in Scotland at that time was Caudle.

Third, as etymology shows, the names Cordillo and Caudillo are related in appearance only, with no direct linguistic links. Let us examine this more closely.

Cordillo is the masculine form of the Old Spanish feminine word, cordilla, which is a diminutive of cuerda, a Spanish word meaning

---

the Welsh word-name Ceinwen and the Hebrew word-name Qayin were anglicized to "Cain" and were eventually adopted as surnames, masking their very disparate backgrounds in two different lands and two different language groups. (Welsh, like Irish and Scottish, is a Celtic language and belongs to the Indo-European Language Family. Hebrew, like Arabic and Ethiopic, is a Semitic language that belongs to the Afro-Asiatic Language Family.) Another example of this problematic phenomenon concerns the Old French word maire ('mayor'). the Middle English word mire ('physician'). and the German word meier ('bailiff' or 'farmer'). In England all three words eventually became surnames, which in Modern English, were typically spelled one way: Mayor (though other variations arose: Mayer, Mayers, Meier, Meyer, Meyers, and most commonly, Myer). Thus the eponymous ancestor (i.e., the original owner) of this family name may have been a French mayor, a German farmer, or an English doctor! This perfectly illustrates that only a careful genealogical study of one's Mayor family history could determine its true nationality.

a 'cord' or 'rope' (similarily, *cordillera* is the generic Spanish term for a chain of mountains, which often have a 'rope-like' or 'chain-like' appearance).[29] Thus, the family name Cordillo, no doubt, began as an *occupation name* for a small, or loveable, woman or man who made cord, or worked with rope.

Cordillo then is not only related to the English word "cord," it is also the Spanish version of the English occupation surname, Corder (in Old French, *Cordier*): 'a maker of cords.' As such, Cordillo and Caudill cannot, and do not, have any direct relationship with one another, for the former is entirely Spanish in character, while the latter is entirely Danish-French (Norman) in character.

It is true that one can still distinguish Caudill's roots in the Latin word *caldellum*, and that Latin is one of the ancient foundation languages of Spanish. However, this does not in anyway connect Caudill with Cordillo. For an objective linguistic examination of the birth, evolution, and geographical movement of the surname Caudill clearly reveals that it did not pass through Spain before migrating north to the British Isles. Instead, it traveled directly from Normandy, France, as *caudel*, to England, where it became *cadel*, or as a surname, *de Cadella*, in the 11th Century.

---

29. Intriguingly, there is a 'chain' of hills in Dorset County, England, that seems to have been known in ancient times as "the Caundle" (recorded in the *Domesday Book* as *Candel* by Norman scribes in 1086). The similarities in spelling and meaning between the Spanish word *cordillera* (or *cuerda*) and the English word *caundle* may be accidental. Or they may reflect a common ancestry in ancient Latin.

10

A HYBRID-NAME: GERMANIC & ITALIC INFLUENCES

SO MUCH FOR THE VIEW that Caudill derives from the surname Cordillo. But what about the surname *Caudillo*?

Caudillo does have linguistic connections to the surname Caudill, though these links are ancient and indirect. Above all, neither one derives from the other. Before we discuss this topic, let us first look at why the Spanish Caudillo is *not* directly related to the Norman Caudill.

Caudillo is the Spanish word for 'leader,' 'commander,' or 'chief,' and is thus not only related to the Spanish word *caudillaje*, meaning 'military leaders' or 'political leadership,' but also to the Spanish word *alcalde* (from the Arabic *cadi*, *al-qadi*, or *al-cadi*), meaning 'the judge' (in English "alcayde," or simply "cadi"); the Spanish *alcaide* (from the Arabic *al-qaid*), 'the captain' or 'commander of a castle'; and the Spanish *alcazar* (from the Arabic *al-qasr*), a 'castle,' 'fortress,' or 'palace.' These words in turn are related to the Spanish word *caudal*, meaning 'fortune,' 'wealth,' and 'property.'

From these meanings alone it is clear that the Norman surname Caudill ('hot liquid') simply has no direct linguistic connection with the Spanish word *caudillo* ('military leader').

As for the *indirect* linguistic connection between Caudill and *caudillo*, this is to be found in the second definition of *caudillo's* cousin word, *caudal*: 'volume' (of fluids), a meaning that also shows affinities with the Spanish word *caudaloso*, 'containing water.' Even here though, such similarities in meanings merely show a common ancestry in the Old Latin words *calere* ('to be hot') and *calidus* ('hot'), and not any type of direct or recent connection between the Norman surname Caudill and the Spanish word *caudillo*.

But, some might argue, what of the shared Latin foundation that both Caudill and *caudillo*, and even the Italian-Spanish surname Cordillo, have in the Italic language group, which includes French, Spanish, and Italian (as well as Portuguese, Judeo-Spanish [called "Ladino"], Catalan, Haitian Creole, Rhaeto-Romanic, Sardinian, Dalmation, Rumanian, and Provençal)? Does this not indicate familial affinities, making the British Caudills and the Spanish Cordillos distant relatives?

In truth, Caudill is only a *partial*, not a complete, member of the Italic language group. Why? Because it is what is known as a hybrid-name; that is, it is a surname made up of elements or words from two or more different languages.

While Caudill's French elements do indeed make it 50 percent Italic, its Norman elements make it 50 percent Germanic as well. For the surname is a creation of one group from among the Norsemen, the Danish Vikings,[30] who originally spoke Old Norse, a Scandinavian language that belongs to the Germanic language group and which is primarily Danish in character. After establishing Normandy, the Norsemen ('North men,' i.e., 'people from the north') became the Normans, and began speaking a blend of Old Norse and French known as "Norman French," the Germanic-Italic language out of which both the nickname *caudel* and the surname Cadel/Caudill were born.

Yet even the 50 percent of the Caudill name that contains Italic elements does not demonstrate Spanish origins for the surname, for this particular linkage dates from a period long before the rise of the Normans, or even of the nations of France and Spain themselves. Indeed, to find even this fragile connection we would have to travel back to prehistory and the origins of the name of the Indo-European Triple-Goddess, Kali ('dark,' 'hot'), whose name later emerged in ancient Rome as the Goddess Cale.

From this, the Latin connection between the Old Norse French word *caudel*, the Norman surname *Caudel*, and the Spanish word *caudillo*, as well as the surname *Caudillo*, is obvious, for Latin is an ancient language that aided in the development of both French and Spanish. The Goddess Cale's name is even found in both cultures: in France, as the name of the city of Calais or *Calaisis* (meaning 'the territory of [the

---

Goddess] Cale'),[31] and in Spain as the Dark-Goddess *Califia*, after whom the American state of California was named.[32]

It is vitally important to stress here though that these ties do not indicate a *genetic* relationship between the bearers of the surnames Caudill and Caudillo. Rather they reveal a shared common, and extremely ancient, *linguistic* ancestry, one rooted in the prehistoric Proto-Indo-European language that emerged thousands of years before Europe was divided into separate nations.

---

31. The legend that the French city of Calais was named after the Greek God *Calais* (one of the winged twin sons of the Goddess *Oreithyia* and the God *Boreas*) is no doubt a late patriarchal fabrication, invented to obfuscate its feminine origins in the name of the Goddess Cale. Indeed, both archaeology and etymology show that a belief in female deities precedes that of male deities by hundreds of thousands of years. For example, while fossils and artifacts showing Goddess worship date from at least 500,000 years ago, the earliest evidence showing God worship dates from only between 6,000 and 10,000 years ago. We also know now that most of the names of male deities derive from the names of far earlier female deities. The Greek God Heracles (in Latin, Hercules), for example, took his name from the older Greek Goddess Hera. Heracles, in fact, means 'Glory of Hera'. Another example: the Roman War-God Mars arose *after* the Goddess he derived his name from, namely the Mother-Moon-Sea-Goddess Mari, who rules both the Moon and the Sun, as well as the 12 astrological Star-signs of the Zodiac. Pre-Christian images of Mari often portray her standing on her sacred symbol, the lunar crescent, wearing a crown of 12 stars. An archetypal female deity, Mari is also known throughout the world's religions and mythologies as Ma, Maerin, Maid Marian, Mama, Mar, Mara, Marah, Mare, Mari, Marica, Mariam, Marian, Marie, Mari-El, Mariham, Marina, Maris, Mari-Yamm, Marri, Marta, Mary, Marzanna, Maya, Merjan, Meri, Meri-Ra, Mermaid, the Morerae, Morrigan, Myrrha, Myrrhine, Myrtea, and Wudu-Maer. Note that all of the above Goddess names derive from, or are cognates of, the Latin word *mare*, "sea." Thus all are various personifications of none other than 'Mother Sea,' the universal Mother-Goddess out of whose cosmic salty womb all life was born. She is known widely from the Paleolithic to the present, and in all countries and in all religions. Some of her primary titles are: "Stella Maris" ('Star of the Sea'), the "Queen of Heaven," and the "Great Mother and Creatress of All." Some of Mari's ancient Pagan titles, images, and symbols were later appended to the figure of the Virgin Mary, who, to this day, appears in the New Testament as the "woman clothed with the sun, and the moon under her feet, and upon her head a crown of twelve stars" (Revelation 12:1). For a more detailed discussion on the topic of Goddess worship, see my books, *Britannia Rules: The Goddess Worshipping Roots of Anglo-Celtic Society*, and also *The Goddess Dictionary of Words and Phrases*.

32. In 1542, the Portuguese-Spanish explorer, Juan Rodríguez Cabrillo (d. 1543), named the mineral-rich area of the central western coast of what is now the US "California," after the Spanish Goddess Califia, since she was said to rule over gold and silver. The word California literally means the 'the Land of [the Goddess] Califia'.

11

HUGO & THE EARLIEST BRITISH CAUDILLS

NOTHER REASON THE THEORY OF Spanish origins cannot
be considered legitimate is the obvious fact that centuries before
the alleged Cordillo families shipwrecked and entered Scotland
in 1588, the surname Caudill had already been thoroughly established,
not only in what we now know to be its country of origin, Normandy
(the first currently known *Norman* Caudill was *Roger Caudel*, in 1180),
but also throughout the entire British Isles as well.

Indeed, the earliest known Cadel/Caudill on British soil was a
man called *Hugo de Cadella*, whose name is recorded in the year 1048 in
Scotland. In England specifically, the first known Caudill was *John Cadel*,
in 1187, from Gloucestershire County, while the earliest known English
Caldwell was *Adam de Caldwella*, in 1195, from Derbyshire County
(certainly many English Caldwells derive their surname from the English
place-name, Caldwell, in Durham County). Other pre-16th-Century
examples could be given, such as *Walter Caudel*, whose name was
recorded in Norfolk County in 1198, and *William Kaldel*, chronicled in
London documents in 1277.

Those who embrace the Spanish origins theory must consider the
following: since all names are older (sometimes centuries older) than the
date they are first recorded, the surname Cadel/Caudill must have been
in Normandy even long before it first appears in Scotland in 1048.

This is precisely what our study of the evolution of the Caudill
name has shown. It first emerged as a nickname for a hot gruel or a
teetotaler, and then shortly after as a surname at some point between the
time of the first Danish Viking raids on France in 845, and 911, the year
this energetic people founded the Province of Normandy.

If we take the mean year between 845 and 911, which is 878, we
have a rough but respectable idea of when the nickname *caudel* may have
actually first come into being. Subtracting 878 from 1588, we arrive at
the following conclusion: the Caudill nickname and/or surname was

already in existence some 710 years *before* the Spanish armada—with its alleged crewmen named Cordillo—came ashore in Scotland!

Taken together, the above facts provide documented proof that the Caudill surname could not, and does not, have its roots in Spain.

Even if we discount my hypothetical Norman birth date of 878 for the Caudill nickname (*caudel*, which later became a surname), we still have both *Roger Caudel*—whose name appears in Normandy 408 years *before* 1588 (in 1180), and Hugo de Cadella—whose name appears in Scotland 540 years earlier (in 1048) before the Spaniards shipwrecked off Scotland.

The Italian-Spanish surname Caudillo cannot then be considered either the base-word for Caudill or a variation of Caudill. Instead it should be seen for exactly what it is: *caudillo* is the Spanish word for 'leader,' 'chief,' or 'commander,' a word that later became a surname in Spain (*Caudillo*), just as the Norman French word *caudel* later became a surname in Normandy (*de Caudella*).

Neither should Cordillo be considered the base-word for, or a variation of, Caudill. Rather it should be viewed for exactly what it is: *cordillo* is a diminutive of the Spanish word *cuerda*, meaning a 'cord,' and hence is a metonymic for 'a maker of cord.'

The etymology of these two Spanish-Italian words, Caudillo and Cordillo, alone sets them completely apart from the surname Caudel/Cadel/Caudill, which is purely Norman in origin, and means 'warm beverage.'

Indeed, it is far more likely that 16th-Century Spanish families living in France and the British Isles took their name from Norman, Celtic, and Anglo-Saxon Cadels/Caudills, and then hispanicized the name to Caudillo and Cordillo. And in fact, we have evidence that in some cases this may be exactly what occurred.

12

CONQUERING GIRONA

ECORDS SHOW THAT A NUMBER of Caudills once lived in what is now the Spanish province of *Gironés* (in Modern English, Girona; in Spanish, Gerona). An ancient town, early on known as *Gerunda*, it is today located just north of modern Barcelona, Spain.

The capital of the Girona Province is the city of Girona, Catalonia, Spain, whose location on the Onãr River *on the French border* betrays a revealing secret: the city of Girona, founded by the ancient Romans some 2,000 years ago, was named after the Gironde, a district near Bordeaux, France.[33] Indeed, Girona once belonged to France (though the Moors occupied the town from 795 to 1015) before it was finally taken from Emperor Napoleon Bonaparte (1769-1821) by Spain under the leadership of Mariano Álvarez de Castro (1749-1810) in 1809.

Because of its economically viable and politically strategic location, throughout the centuries countless wars and conflicts have been waged over the city. Yet, Girona remains a part of Spain to this day.[34]

If Norman Caudills actually lived in this area at one time as a number of chronicles state, then some of the Spaniards who took over the territory that included the city of Girona, France, may have adopted the surname Caudill from the Norman subjects who lived there. But why?

We will probably never know for sure, but if we consider this scenario a possibility, the most likely explanation is that female Spaniards married into Norman Caudill families that had chosen to remain in the town after its seizure by Spain. The Spanish wives of these Caudill men then would have taken the surname Caudill as their married name, after

---

33. Known for its fine wines, the Gironde also possesses the Gironde River and Estuary, created by the conflux of the Garonne and Dordogne Rivers, which opens into the Bay of Biscay. It is said that the French Girondists (in French, the *Girondins*), a moderate republican political party of Revolutionary France (1791-1793), borrowed their name from this body of water (just north of Bordeaux).

34. The county of Gerona, one of 14 making up the Kingdom of Catalonia, was founded by Charlemagne (my 34th great-grandfather) in 785.

which it was hispanicized to *Caudillo*. This is just a theory, and in truth, a barely plausible one.

In the end, we can be sure that the Spaniards neither adopted or hispanicized the Norman surname Caudill. As our study of the origins and history of European surnames has revealed, the Spaniards no doubt simply took the everyday Spanish word for 'leader,' *caudillo*, and began to use it as a surname: *Caudillo*.

This is precisely what occurred in England with similar English words such as "earl" (which became the surname, Earl), "knight" (which became the surname, Knight), and "king" (which became the surname, King). Indeed, the English word "leader" itself (in Old English, *lædere*) eventually became a surname in England: Leader, whose surviving variations include Leeder, Lader, and Ledder.

13

CLAN CAMPBELL & THE THANES OF CAWDOR

L ET US NOW EXAMINE A final theory of origins for the surname Caudill, one pertaining to Scotland. According to this hypothesis, because the earliest known Caudills are to be found in Scotland, Caudill then must be a purely Celtic name, and the Caudills must be of Celtic origins, and more specifically, of Scottish origins.

Here again numerous difficulties arise.

It is true that the Caudill surname is first recorded in Scotland (with Hugo de Cadella in 1048), and that the spellings Calder, Caddell, Caudill, and Caudle (in Scotland pronounced, and often written, *Cawdor*), are all associated with the Scottish clan and family, Campbell. Indeed, the *Thanes of Cawdor* gave rise to the third main Campbell line, still known today as the "Campbells of Cawdor," a branch possessing its own tartan.

This connection between the Calders and the Campbells, however, is not by way of genetic inheritance, it is by way of marriage. This occurred in the late 1400s when one of the sons (the seventh Thane) of Sir Duncan Campbell, Earl of Argyll, married Isabel, an infant daughter of the Calders, creating the Thanedom of Cawdor (i.e., the House of the Earls of Cawdor).

In 1398, the Thanes of Cawdor went on to build their own fortress castle—around a legendary holly tree it is said—near the foundation of an earlier fortification built in 1179 by William I "the Lion" (1143-1214), King of Scotland.[35]

The castle was purposefully and strategically built overlooking the River Nairn (not far from the famous Loch Ness), which runs into Moray Firth in the North Sea. The Cawdor Thanes, appointed Sheriffs of the royal castle, regulated the waterway between Elgin and Inverness.

---

35. William I "the Lion" is my 25th great-grandfather.

Cawdor Castle still stands in Nairn, Nairn County, Scotland, and is the residence of the present Lord and Lady Cawdor (see Appendix C).[36]

The question is, does this linkage with Clan Campbell make the Caudills Scottish?

While some today continue to maintain that the Caudills of Virginia and Kentucky "belonged to the Clan Campbell of Cawdor," there is actually no evidence at all for this. The earliest known ancestor of the Virginia and Kentucky Caudills is one William Caudle, possibly born about 1585, perhaps in Scotland (almost nothing is known of him). Still, he is not a proven ancestor yet, and even if he were, this would still leave almost two centuries unaccounted for between William and the Scottish Calders who intermarried with the Campbells in the late 15th Century.

Our earliest *proven* ancestor is Stephen James Caudill, born about 1685 in Argyllshire, Scotland. At the very least then we are still left with a mysterious 300 year gap between the Virginia and Kentucky Caudills and the Medieval Thanes of Cawdor. So large is this genealogical abyss that we may never be able to cross it.

---

36. Cawdor Castle is the geographical focus of Shakespeare's play *MacBeth* (written in 1605), which commemorates the historical murder of Duncan I "the Gracious" (1001-1040), King of Scotland (my 27th great-grandfather), at the hands of one of his enemies named Maelbaethe.

14

ENGLISH CAUDILLS, CLAN DISPUTES, & SCOTTISH KINGS

THREE OTHER PROBLEMS ESSENTIALLY PREVENT us from accepting purely Scottish origins for the Virginia and Kentucky Caudills.

To begin with, many Caudill researchers believe that James Caudill (1641-1684), Thomas Caudill (b. c. 1610), and William Caudill (b. c. 1585), the proposed father, grandfather, and great-grandfather of Stephen James Caudill (born c. 1685) respectively, were all born in England, *not* Scotland. Some even maintain that Stephen James Caudill (born c. 1685) himself was born in England, as there is record of a "Stephen Caudle" being christened in Withington, Gloucester County, England, in 1688, right around the time our Stephen was born (no corresponding record for a "Stephen Caudle" is to be found in Scotland at this time).

Perhaps, extrapolating from old chronicles then, we may theorize that Stephen was born in England, raised in Scotland, and then migrated from Scotland (aboard a ship under one "Captain Hawthorne") to the Virginia Colony with his parents in 1692, at around the age of seven. I believe this is a fair assessment of how our "Scottish" Caudills came to be.

Though no one yet knows for sure either way, it is my opinion that the idea that our Caudills began in England as Norman Caudles rather than in Scotland as Scottish Calders, has much to recommend it. Particularly since there is circumstantial evidence for a possible English origin, while almost none exists for a Scottish one. Let us look at this in more detail.

As our historical and etymological study has shown, the Caudills arose in Normandy between the years 845 and 911. Both before and after the Norman Conquest of England (in 1066), many Caudle (Caudill) families crossed the English Channel, settling permanently in England. Later, from here, some migrated north to Scotland. This alone tells us that the Caudills are not Scottish in origin.

Second, we must also consider the fact that the specific spelling *Caudill* is extremely rare, if not virtually nonexistent, in modern day Scotland. In fact, I could only find one listing in the telephone directory for this spelling in all of the United Kingdom, and it was not in Scotland. Revealingly, it was in *Manchester, England*!

We can often trace the actual origins of an Anglo-Celtic surname based on where it is currently most densely concentrated in the United Kingdom. Since we have no Caudills in Scotland today and at least one in England, we have here a possible indicator pointing to England as the British source of the so-called "Scottish" Caudills.[37]

Third, while many claim that the Virginia and Kentucky Caudills were members of the Medieval Calders (the Thanes of Cawdor), and, as such, belonged to the Clan Campbell, clan authorities contentiously disagree on which septs and families belong to which clans. Indeed, no definitive list has ever been constructed. This debate includes families named Calder, Cadel, Caddell, Cattell, Caudill, and Caudle, none of which are considered separate clans themselves, and none of whose association with Clan Campbell is accepted by all Scottish historical scholars.

Fourth, we must also consider that the existence of the Caudill family in Scotland does not in and of itself make the Caudills a Celtic family. While the specific spelling Caudill seems to be a modern English-Scottish spelling, etymology has shown us that the root-word of Caudill—that is, *caudel*—does not have Celtic roots, or even Celtic elements. What it does possess are distinct Scandinavian elements (*caud*) and French elements (the preposition *de* and *-ella*, thus giving *de*

---

37. As of Spring 2003, the most popular spelling variation of the Caudill surname throughout the United Kingdom is *Cadle* (115 listings). This is followed by *Caudle* (98 listings), then *Caddell* (74 listings), then *Cawdell* (54 listings), then *Caudell* (30 listings), then *Cadell* (21 listings, many in Scotland), then *Caudill* (1 listing), and finally *Caudel* (0 listings), *Cawdle* (0 listings), *Cadwal* (0 listings), and *Codill* (0 listings). In total, we have only 393 examples of the name Caudill and its variations in the entire United Kingdom (which comprises England, Scotland, Wales, and Northern Ireland), showing that the name itself, whatever the spelling, is still quite unique and uncommon in this region. While the name seems to be slowly going extinct in the UK, in contrast, it is positively flourishing in the USA, where thousands of Caudills and Caddells are listed in the telephone directory nationwide.

Caudella), both which surround the ancient Latin core-word *calere* (which gave rise to *caldellum,* which became, in Old Norse French, *caudel*) that was in usage in France in the Medieval period.

If more proof is needed that the Virginia and Kentucky Caudills are not Celtic in origin, we have only to examine the nationality of Hugo de Cadella himself, the first known person in the British Isles possessing this name.

As documents clearly show, Hugo de Cadella was neither French, English, Welsh, Scottish, or even Norman. He was a *Danish* knight who had emigrated to Scotland from Normandy, by the year 1048, to assist the King of Scotland, Malcolm III (d. in 1093).

Hugo had met Malcolm while the Scottish royal was being held hostage in Normandy during the ongoing 11th-Century conflict between Scotland, England, and France. During his stay in Normandy as a prisoner-of-war, Malcolm managed to win the support of his Norman captors (one of which may have been Hugo), whose help he sought (along with the English) in assisting him in subduing Donald Bane, the rival and brother of his father, King Duncan I of Scotland (d. in 1040).[38]

What we have here is overt proof that the earliest known and recorded Caudill was a Dane living in Normandy, one who later eventually migrated to Scotland. This fact, taken by itself, makes the theory of Scottish origins well nigh impossible.

We will also note here that even though Hugo de Cadella was the first *recorded* Caudill in all of the British Isles, this does not mean that he was the first Caudill to pass through or live on British soil. To the contrary, we can be quite certain that since the name already existed on continental Europe at least 100 to 200 years *before* the birth of Hugo de Cadella (probably sometime between the years 850 and 950), that individuals with this name were also in both England and Scotland long before Hugo as well.

While Scotland as the ancestral home of the Virginia and Kentucky Caudills cannot be completely ruled out, if my theory is correct, it is more likely that James, Thomas, and William Caudill (the

---

38. These were treacherous times: Malcolm III, a son of Duncan I, eventually died a perfidious death after being entrapped and violently killed by his uncle Bane's loyal followers. Malcolm III "Ceanmor" (i.e., 'Longneck') is my 26th great-grandfather.

probable ancestors of Stephen James Caudill, born c. 1685), if not Stephen himself, were all born in England rather than in Scotland. The fact that some early members of this very family used the *English* and *Norman* spellings, Caudle, Caudel, Coddill, and Cordell, rather than the more usual *Scottish* spellings, Cadle, Caddell, and Calder, suggest as much.

It is certainly true that the Caudill name and family have had a long history in Scotland, one stretching even into recent times. We have, for instance, *Robert Cadell* (1788-1849), the noted Scottish publisher who made his fortune printing the works of the Scottish poet and historian, Sir Walter Scott (1771-1832). And there was *Francis Cadell* (1822-1879), the famed Scottish explorer, who successfully surveyed parts of Australia, only to be later treacherously murdered by his crew.

There are those Scots with *Caldwell*-like surnames, as well, Caldwell being a name, as we have seen, that has close affinities with Caudill. And so this name too has an enduring tradition in Scotia, some of the earliest examples being records of a *Caulduell* in 1551; a *Caulduall* in 1661; and a *Calduall* in 1688. A noted gentleman, Bishop *James Caulduoll*, lived in Glasgow in 1548, where the spelling Caldwell is still to be found in higher concentrations than anywhere else in Scotland.[39]

Even here though we can be sure that most Scottish Caldwells did not inherit their surname from their ancestors, but rather adopted it from the Scottish place-name, Caldwell (pronounced "*Carwall*" in Renfrewshire County, Scotland).

As Scottish as such men and their ancestors are, this does not negate the fact that the Caudill name and family (this specific spelling) are Norman in origin, a region in northwestern France that was settled by Danish Vikings in 845.

For now then we must content ourselves with the fact that the American Caudills bear a distinctly Norman surname (taken from the name for a hot ale or gruel), while, as we will see momentarily, the Scottish Calders (Cawdors) bear an obviously Brittonic surname, taken

---

from one of the many British towns by this name: Calder. 'the place of hard or cold water.'

15

RAPID ENGLISH RIVERS & COLD IRISH WATERS

WHILE AT PRESENT THERE IS no conclusive proof of exactly when and where the specific spelling *Caudill* emerged, it is likely that it is a fairly recent Anglo-Celtic spelling variation of the English form *Cadel* or *Cadell*.

In fact, one of the earliest known Scottish spellings of Caudill is *Calder* (Cawdor) a celticized form meaning 'rapid river or stream' in England, and 'hard water'—deriving from the Brittonic words *caled*, 'hard,' and *dobhar*, 'water'—in Scotland.

From this Celtic word were named the River Calder (in Cumbria County, England), the town of Calder Bridge (Cumbria County, England), the town of Calder Vale (Lancashire County, England), and Loch Calder or Cawdor (Caithness County, Scotland), where the spelling *Caldell* was common into the 17th Century.[40]

Early English spellings of the surname Calder include *Hugh de Kaledouer* in 1178 (a name overtly revealing distant associations with the name of the ancient Indo-European Goddess Kale or Cale),[41] *Thomas de Calder* in 1246, and *Farchard de Caldor* in 1461, all from Cumberland (now Cumbria) County, England (though the name can also mean 'one who is from Calder/Cawdor, Caithness County, Scotland'). In more recent times, we have Baron Peter Ritchie-Calder of Balmashanner (1906-1982), a noted Scottish author and promoter of science.

In Ireland (Counties Dublin and Galway), the variation Caddell is known from the 13th Century, where it was eventually replaced by the Norman surname Blake. This was due to medieval confusion over the

---

40. Another Scottish spelling of Calder is Keillor or Keiller, named after a river in Angus, Scotland.

41. *Hugh de Kaledouer* was one of the witnesses of a charter instigated by the King of Scotland, William I "the Lion" (1143-1214), at Montrose. Among William's other accomplishments, he founded the Abbey of Arbroath (in 1178), received Scottish independence (in 1189), and established an autonomous Scottish Church that was subject only to the see of Rome.

Old English word *blác* (in Middle English, *blake*), whose original meaning was 'bleak,' or 'pale,' but which later came to mean 'black,' or 'dark.'

When English conquerors in Ireland insisted (often under threat of violence) that their subjects take on English names, the 'dark' connotations of blake were carried over to the 'dark' connotations of Caddell (from Cale / Kale, the Dark Goddess), and the "English" surname Blake was adopted in its place and spelled *le Bláca* ('the Black'). An Anglo-Gaelic form of Blake, spelled *Blacagh*, is still used in various parts of County Connacht, Ireland.

The Caldwell spelling form of Caudill also emerged in Ireland amid equally great confusion, where it has long been erroneously used as an anglicized version of the Gaelic names *Ó hUairisce* and *Ó hUarghuis* ('cold water'), which in English would actually be spelled O Houriskey and O Horish respectively. Caldwell also sometimes serves as an anglicized replacement for the Gaelic name *Mac Conluain* in Ireland (spelled Cullivan and Colavin in English).

It should be remembered, however, that possessing a surname spelled in Celtic form does not necessarily make the bearer of that name Celtic.

Indeed, male and female Caudills who trace their ancestry to Caudills in Scotland certainly have Scottish ancestry, but their Scottish "blood" would have *originated* on the maternal side of the family—that is, from among the native Scottish women who married the first male Norman Caudills who emigrated to Scotland (many by way of England). For as we have seen, male Caudills ultimately derive from Normandy (obviously so do the *original* female Caudills, but their surnames would have been dropped at marriage, and so would not have been passed on).

To prevent any misunderstanding, let me clarify this point: the so-called "Scottish" Caudills may have begun in Scotland with a Norman male (probably surnamed in the Danish-Norman way, *de Caudella* or *de Cadella*) who emigrated to Scotland in the late 10th or early 11th Century. His marriage to an indigenous Scottish female produced male and female Caudill descendants who, over the next 1,000 years, also married into the native Scottish population, essentially making both genders of the Scottish Caudills increasingly Scottish. From this viewpoint it could be said then that there *are* indeed Scottish Caudills. However, this does not mean, as many claim, that "the Caudills are Scottish in origin"; only that Norman Caudles (Caudills) eventually migrated to and settled in Scotland.

While we are on the topic of the so-called "Scottish" Caudills, we should remind ourselves that for many such families their surname is certainly not hereditary—that is, passed down genetically, family to family, from ancient Norman Caudill forebears. Instead it was simply adopted in earlier times by unrecorded and unnamed ancestors from the place-name, Calder or Cawdor, in Caithness County, Scotland, and in some instances from those Calder place-names located in what is now northern England, chiefly Yorkshire, Cumbria, and Lancashire Counties.

Interestingly, such Caudills would be more Scottish than those "Scottish" Caudle/Caudill families who descend from the Caudills of Normandy. Thus, in this one particular case we would actually have 100 percent true and pure Scottish Caudills. Unfortunately, most non-royal Scottish records do not go back far enough to ascertain where a particular family originally came from, so in most cases we can never know for sure.

In the end the fact remains that the nationality of the Caudill name itself is ultimately Norman—that is, Danish.

Caudill is not alone. Many surnames traditionally thought to be Scottish are actually of Norman origins. Among these are: *Ross* (from Rots, Calvados, Normandy); *Bruce* (from Le Bruce, Calvados, Normandy); *Fraser* (from Freseliere, Anjou, France); *Lyons* (from Lyon, Eure, Normandy);[42] *Sinclair* (from Saint-Clair-l'Evêque, Calvados, Normandy); *Delaney* (that is, *de la Aunay*; from Aunay, Calvados, Normandy); and *Agnew* (from Agneaux, Normandy).

---

42. The city of Lyons, France, has connections to Celtic culture and Goddess worship, both which are intimately associated with our early Norman Caudill ancestors. Lyons takes its name from the Celtic God of Light, *Lug* or *Lugus*, whose religious center there was called *Lugdunim* ('Fort of Lugus'). One of the most popular deities in the Celtic Pantheon, and also known as *Lugh, Lud, Lleu, Samildanach*, and *Find*, Lug also gave his name to the cities of London (originally known as *Lugdunum*), England; Loudun, France; Laon, France; León, Spain; Leiden, Netherlands; Leignitz, Prussia (now Poland); Carlisle, England; and Vienna, Austria. In ancient Rome, Lug's feast day, called *Lugnasad*, was held on August 1. Irish myth tells us that Lug was married to the great Celtic Earth-Goddess *Tailltiu* (the town of Taillten, Ireland, is named after her). Their marriage was celebrated at the English place that still bears Lug's name: Ludgate Hill (in London). Lug's "gate" was actually the Goddess' sacred stone, the *Crom Cruiach* ('Bloody Crescent'), which symbolized her magical reproductive powers and lunar associations. Lug was christianized in the Church to "Saint Lugad," "Saint Luan," "Saint Eluan," and "Saint Lugidus."

16

LINGUISTIC PARALLEL EVOLUTION: A FINAL THEORY

L ET US CONSIDER A FINAL theory of origins: is it possible that Caudill could be of Norman, Celtic, *and* Spanish origins?

A surname with the same spelling does occasionally arise spontaneously and simultaneously in more than one location, and even in two different time periods, in a process I have termed *linguistic parallel evolution*.[43] Many examples of this could be given.

There is some evidence, for instance, to suggest that this may have happened with the Norman surname Blakeney, which arose in two separate areas at roughly the same time: 1) in and around the English city of Blakeney, Norfolk County, and 2) in and around the city of Blakeney, Gloucestershire County.[44]

However, as we have clearly seen, this was not the case with the surname Caudill. For its emergence and evolution can be clearly traced from Danish Normandy in a direct line to Anglo-Saxon England during the Middle Ages. In essence, this eliminates any possibility of either Celtic or Spanish origins, nations where the variant spellings of Caudill show a much later development.

---

43. For more on this topic, see footnote 28.

44. For more information on this topic, see my book, *The Blakeneys: An Etymological and Ethnological Study*.

17

FROM ANCIENT INDIA TO MODERN AMERICA: IN SUMMARY

L ET US SUMMARIZE. THE SURNAME Caudill began life in Neolithic Asia, probably India, sometime before 3,500 years ago, in the etymon *kal* ('dark,' 'heat,' 'pot'). This base-word was used in the name of the Hindu Underworld-Goddess, Kali, whose great 'dark,' 'hot,' 'bubbling' womb was pictorially and ritually symbolized in the caldron (to this day still a sacred symbol in nearly all female-based religions, such as Wicce).[45]

During the Iron Age, Kali's name (meaning 'dark' and 'hot') spread west across Asia into the Near East and Europe, where she became *Calpe* to the Phoenicians, *Kalu* to the Palestinians, *Kale* to the Saxons, *Kalma* to the Fins, *Cailleach* (or *Carlin*) to the Scots, *Kelle* to the Irish, *Kalli* to the Greeks, and *Cale* to the Romans.

It was here, in the Latin of ancient Italy, that Kali's name gave birth to numerous 'hot' and 'warm liquid' words beginning with *cal*, all which slowly filtered out across the rest of Europe in the following centuries.

Among these were the Latin words: *calere*, 'to be warm'; *calidus*, 'a warm drink'; *calderia*, 'warm water'; and *caldellum*, meaning 'warm beverage,' and which became the name of a hot soup-like ale or gruel for the infirm and weak.

In Normandy, France, the Latin *caldellum* was normanized to *caudel*, after which it became a contemptuous nickname for someone who avoided (or could not take) hard liquor. Shortly thereafter, probably by 950, *caudel* became, in the Norman French of the day, a legitimate if slightly ignoble surname: *de Caudella*; that is, 'the

---

45. The scientific study of feminine religion is called *thealogy*. The scientific study of masculine religion is called *theology*.

teetotaler'—though sometimes the name was used ironically; that is for one who drank only the hardest alcoholic beverages.

Even before the Norman Conquest in 1066, the surname *de Caudella* was already spreading throughout the British Isles, as early Norman *de Caudella* families emigrated as far north as Scotland. What the Conquest did was to help rapidly disseminate the surname to all corners of England, Scotland, Wales, and Ireland, at which time we begin to see the Anglo-Celtic spelling form Cadel.

As the centuries passed, the British surname Cadel was modified by further anglicization and gaelicization, giving us the many current spelling forms and variations, including: Caddell, Cadell, Cadle, Cadwal (Welsh), Caldell, Caudell, Caudill, Caudle, Cawdell, Cawdle, Cawdor, Codill, Cordall, Cordell, Cordial, Cordill, Cordle, and Kaldel; as well as the closely related English surnames: Cadwall, Cadwel, Cadwell, Caldwell, Calwell, Cardwell, Caudwell, Cauldwell, Chadwell, Cholwell, Coddle, Coldwell, Cottle, Couldwell, and Kadewelle, Keiller, and Keillor.

Caudill also has linguistic affiliations, though more distant, with the following surnames: Calcott, Calcut, Calcutt, Caldecot, Caldecote, Caldecott, Caldecourt, Calder, Calderon, Caldicot, Calidcott, Callcott, Callicott, Caulcott, Caulcutt, Caulder, Cauldron, Caulkett, Cawcutt, Cawdron, Chalcot, Chaldecott, Colcott, Colcutt, Coldicott, Coldron, Colicot, Colkett, Collacot, Collacutt, Collcott, Collecott, Collicutt, Collkutt, Colocott, Corcut, Corkett, and Corkitt.

In the end, despite centuries of cross-cultural migration and a complex linguistic evolution, etymology clearly reveals that while the North Carolina, Virginia, and Kentucky Caudills have been tentatively traced to Scotland, their surname derives from the English surname Cadel, which derives from the Norman surname Caudle. Hence, Caudill is a Norman name and the Caudill family is ultimately of Danish blood.

APPENDICES

APPENDIX A
Resources & Items of Interest

- The Caudill Cabin: Website dedicated to an early Caudill homestead, located in Winston-Salem, North Carolina, on the Blue Ridge Parkway in Doughton Park (at milepost marker 241). It can only be reached on foot. Website: www.caudillcabin.org
- The Blue Ridge Parkway Foundation Website: www.nps.gov/blri/culture.htm Tel: 336-721-0260.
- The Caudill family crest, motto, etc. can be purchased through the "Coat of Arms Store." Website: http://www.4crests.com/. They also sell coffee mugs, T-shirts, key chains, etc. with the Caudill name and family crest. (I cannot vouch for the legitimacy of this company. Caveat emptor.)
- *Appalachian Crossroads*, a three-volume history on the Caudills, by Clayton R. Cox. Contact information: Clayton Cox, 2313 Glenview Road, Paris, KY 40361. Price: $116.00.
- *The Kentucky Explorer* ("a magazine for Kentuckians everywhere"): P.O. Box 227, 1248 Highway 15-N, Jackson, KY 41339. Tel: 606-666-5060. Website: www.kentuckyexplorer.com
- C. B. Caudill Store & History Center: Blackey, Letcher Co., KY. Website: www.appalshop.org/cbcaudill. Tel: 606-633-3281.
- Caudill family reunions: for information, please send email to: caudill@caudill.org
- Caudill book being assembled by Kay Caudill Riecke and the direct descendants of Col. Benjamin E. Caudill. Please send Kay your family stories, photos, newspaper articles, etc., anything related to the Caudills. She will include it in her book (unedited). Address: Kay Caudill Riecke, 1733 Hudson River Road, NE, Rio Rancho, NM, 87144. E-mail: LKCaud@aol.com
- Caudill Seed Company: green and organic products, out of Louisville, KY. Website: www.caudillseed.com

APPENDIX B
Some Useful Websites
Related to Caudill Research

- Caudill family forum: www.genforum.genealogy.com/caudill/
- Caudle family forum: www.genforum.genealogy.com/caudle/
- Caudell family forum: www.genforum.genealogy.com/caudell/
- Cordell family forum: www.genforum.genealogy.com/cordell/
- Coldwell family forum: www.genforum.genealogy.com/coldwell/
- Caldwell family forum: www.genforum.genealogy.com/caldwell/
- Cadwell family forum: www.genforum.genealogy.com/cadwell/
- Letcher County, KY Genealogy: www.rootsweb.com/~kyletch/letcher.htm
- Perry County, KY Genealogy: www.rootsweb.com/~kyperry/
- Harlan County, KY Genealogy: www.rootsweb.com/~kyharlan/
- Magoffin County, KY Genealogy: www.rootsweb.com/~kymagoff/
- Pike County, KY Genealogy: www.rootsweb.com/~kypike/
- Floyd County, KY Genealogy: www.rootsweb.com/~kyfloyd/floyd.htm
- Lawrence County, KY Genealogy:
      www.rootsweb.com/~kylawren/lawrence.html
- Breathitt County, KY Genealogy: www.breathittcounty.com/
- Johnson County, KY Genealogy: www.rootsweb.com/~kyjohnso/johnson.htm
- Rowan County, KY Genealogy:
      http://resources.rootsweb.ancestry.com/USA/KY/Rowan/
- Eastern KY Genealogy & History: www.rootsweb.ancestry.com/~kyekg/
- KY County Formation Maps: www.familyhistory101.com/maps/ky_cf.html
- Rootsweb Websites dedicated to KY research:
      www.rootsweb.com/~websites/usa/kentucky.html
- KY Military Research: www.rootsweb.com/~kymil/
- KY Veterans Tribute Memorial : www.rootsweb.com/~kyvets/
- USGenWeb Kentucky Research: www.kygenweb.net/index.html
- Rootsweb sites dedicated to NC research:
      www.rootsweb.com/~websites/usa/northcarolina.html
- Rootsweb sites dedicated to VA research:
      www.rootsweb.com/~websites/usa/virginia.html
- Caudill "Cousins" Exchange Website: www.caudill.org/
- Clan Campbell Society North America: http://www.ccsna.org/

APPENDIX C
Cawdor Castle, Nairn, Scotland

Contact information: Cawdor Castle (Tourism) Ltd, Cawdor Castle,
    Nairn, Scotland, IV12 5RD
Tel: (01667) 404615
Fax: (01667) 404674.
Official Website: www.cawdorcastle.com
Email: info@cawdorcastle.com

Location: Situated between Inverness and Nairn on the B9090 off the
A96.

Map Locator for Cawdor Castle

General location in Great Britain

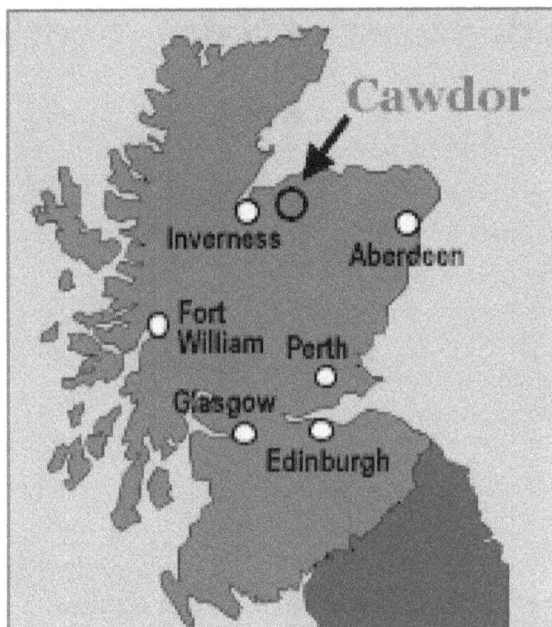

General location in Scotland (above)

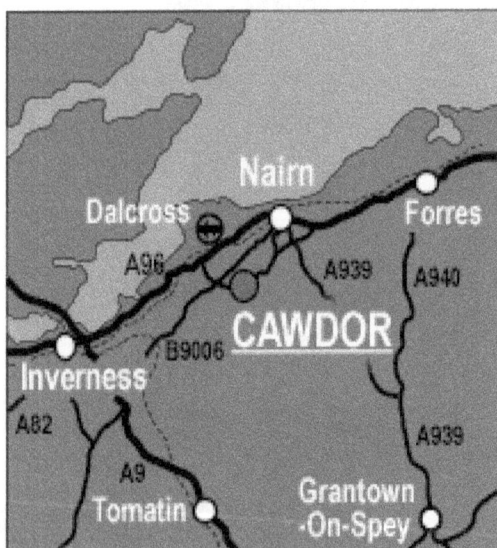

Specific location in Scotland (above; castle located at dark dot above the "C" in Cawdor)

APPENDIX D
A Caudill Family Tree

11 Generations

The Descendants of William Caudill (born c. 1585)

IMPORTANT NOTES

• I researched, compiled, and edited this family tree based on both my own research and the contributions of others (noted in bibliography whenever possible).

• Despite careful attention to detail, like all family trees, this one too is not only unfinished, but also contains errors, omissions, and some unproven data. Therefore consider this tree incomplete and at least partially inaccurate, and for use only as a foundation to begin from. Please seek your own authentic documentation and supporting evidence.

• Most of the individuals in this tree are not included in the Index.

THE DESCENDANTS OF WILLIAM CAUDILL

NOTES

1. The original, or sometimes alternate, surname spellings used by an individual and/or their family are listed after the modern spelling.
2. "Abt" (About) always indicates an estimate, or an educated guess.

1 William Caudill, Caudle (earliest probable Caudill ancestor; not yet proven) b: Abt. 1585 in Scotland or England? Number of children: ? Sex: Male (Note: Looking for his ancestors)
...+_____ _____? b: Abt. 1587 in Scotland or England? Number of children: ? Sex: Female (Note: Looking for her full name & ancestors)
..2 Thomas Caudill, (not proven) b: Abt. 1610 in Scotland (some say England) Number of children: ? Sex: Male
......+_____ _____? , b: Abt. 1615 in Scotland (or England?) m: Abt. 1635 in Scotland Number of children: ? Sex: Female (Note: Looking for her full name & ancestors)
.....3 James Caudill, (not proven) b: 1641 in Scotland (some say England) d: 1684 in Scotland Number of children: ? Sex: Male
.........+_____ _____? , b: Abt. 1645 in Scotland or England? m: Abt. 1665 in Scotland Number of children: ? Sex: Female
......4 Stephen James Caudill, Caudle, b: Bet. 1680 - 1690 in Argyllshire (Argyll Co.?), Scotland (Some say England) d: Bet. 1759 - 1763 in Lunenburg Co., VA Number of children: 10 Sex: Male Burial: 1759 Brunswick Co., VA
...........+Mary Elizabeth "Betsy" Fields, b: 1698 in Scotland m: Abt. 1720 in Scotland (some say in Lunenburg Co., VA) d: Aft. 1763 in Lunenburg Co., VA Number of children: 10 Father: Matchett Fields, Mother: Elizabeth "Betsy" Rhodes, Sex: Female
........5 James Caudill, Sr., Cordell, Coddill, Caudel b: Bet. 1718 - 1720 in Scotland , or Lunenburg, Surry Co., VA d: Abt. 1800 in Wilkes Co., NC Number of children: 12 Sex: Male
..............+Mary Yarborough, Yarbrough b: Bet. 1730 - 1731 in Lunenburg Co., VA m: 1748 in Lunenburg Co.,VA, or Wilkes Co., NC d: Abt. 1830 in Wilkes Co., NC Number of children: 12 Father: Ambrose Yarborough, Yarbrough, Sr. Mother: Mary Lee Mason Sex: Female
.........,6 Mary Caudill b: 1748 Sex: Female
..........6 [6] James "Jimmie" Caudill, Jr., Rev. War Soldier b: 1753 in Wilkes Co., NC d: May 30, 1840 in Blackey, Letcher Co., KY Number of children: 12 Sex: Male Burial: Rockhouse Creek, Perry Co., KY (Note: fought in Revolutionary War, Kings Mountain & Cowpens)
................+Mary (or Abigail) Adams b: 1760 in Letcher Co., KY m: Abt. 1770 in Wilkes Co., NC d: in Wilkes Co., NC Number of children: 12 Sex: Female (Note: Looking for her ancestors)
.............7 Abigail Caudill, Cordell, b: February 07, 1770 in Wilkes Co., NC d: Bet. 1860 - 1872

in Webb'ville, Lawrence Co., KY Number of children: 4 Sex: Female

................+William Pennington b: November 03, 1765 in Wilkes Co., NC m: February 09, 1785 in Webbville, Lawrence Co., KY, or Wilkes Co., NC d: Abt. 1842 in KY Number of children: 4 Father: Ephraim Pennington V Mother: _____ _____? Sex: Male

...............8 Thomas Pennington b: 1786 in Wilkes Co., NC Sex: Male

...................+Jane Caudill b: Abt. 1791 in Wilkes Co., NC Sex: Female (Note: Looking for ancestors)

...............8 Elizabeth "Betsy" Pennington b: February 07, 1792 in Lee Co., VA d: June 08, 1848 in Webbville, Lawrence Co., KY? Number of children: 11 Sex: Female

.....................+James F. Webb, Jr. b: May 15, 1787 in Lee Co., VA m: December 08, 1813 in in what is now Lawrence Co., KY d: June 1848 in Webbville ?, Lawrence Co., KY Number of children: 11 Father: James F. Webb, Sr., Soldier Mother: Elizabeth "Lettie" Jane Nelson (Nelson Note: Looking for Elizabeth's ancestors. I believe that she's part of the large Nelson clan from VA and NC, which spread out and migrated west into WV, TN, and KY in the 1830s. Like the author, the Judds [Naomi, Ashley, Wynonna], also descend from this family. The earliest known ancestor of this Nelson group is William "Old William" Nelson, born in 1747 in Prince Edward Co., VA, and died on August 9, 1834, in Hawkins Co., TN. Old William's wife was Rebecca Smith, born about 1757 in Stokes Co., NC. It's possible, in my opinion, that Elizabeth could be Old William's sister) Sex: Male (Webb Note: Like all of the other Webb individuals in this tree, this Webb family descends from the same line as the country singers Loretta (Webb) Lynn and her sister Brenda Gail "Crystal Gale" Webb. Loretta was born April 14, 1935, in Butcher Hollow, Pike Co., KY; Crystal Gale was born January 9, 1951, in Paintsville, Johnson Co., KY)

.................9 [1] William Riley Webb b: May 13, 1815 d: August 29, 1885 Number of children: 3 Sex: Male

........................+Rachel Harmon b: Abt. 1820 m: September 11, 1836 Sex: Female

.................2nd Wife of [1] William Riley Web b:

........................+Martha Patsy Jordan b: Abt. 1817 m: Abt. 1853 Number of children: 3 Sex: Female

....................10 [3] Lindsey D. Webb b: December 14, 1854 in East Fork, Lawrence Co., KY d: January 17, 1923 in Glenwood, Lawrence Co., KY Sex: Male

...........................+[2] Martha "Eliza" Louise Webb b: February 15, 1867 in Webbville, Lawrence Co., KY d: April 29, 1942 in Glenwood, Lawrence Co., KY Father: James Calvin Webb, (friend of Jesse James, bank robber) Mother: Rebecca Wright Sex: Female

....................10 Franklin Webb, Dr. b: March 15, 1856 in East Fork, Lawrence Co., KY Sex: Male

....................10 James Buchanon Webb b: March 04, 1857 in East Fork, Lawrence Co., KY d: September 21, 1926 in Lawrence Co., KY Sex: Male Burial: Webb Cemetery, Glenwood, Lawrence Co., KY

.......................3rd Wife of [1] William Riley Web b:

........................+Nancy Sturgill b: 1818 m: October 14, 1883 Father: John Sturgill Mother: Jemima Wells Sex: Female

.................9 James Calvin Webb, b: September 12, 1816 d: 1918 in Lawrence Co., KY Number of children: 9 Sex: Male Burial: James C. Webb Cemetery, RT-1, Caney Falls, near Webbville, Lawrence Co., KY, on the road to Louisa (Note: a friend of Jesse James, the bank robber)

.......................+Rebecca Wright b: Abt. 1841 in KY m: Abt. 1862 in Greenupsburg, Greenup Co., KY Number of children: 9 Father: James Wright Mother: Anna Hylton Sex: Female Burial: James C. Webb Cemetery, RT-1, Caney Falls, near Webbville, Lawrence Co., KY, on the road to Louisa (Note: Friend of Jesse James, the bank robber)

.....................10 Schrilda Webb b: Abt. 1863 Sex: Female Burial: James C. Webb Cemetery, RT-1, Caney Falls, near Webbville, Lawrence Co., KY, on the road to Louisa

...........................+John Black b: Abt. 1860 Sex: Male Burial: James C. Webb Cemetery, RT-1, Caney Falls, near Webbville, Lawrence Co., KY, on the road to Louisa

.....................10 Ben Jackson Webb b: Abt. 1865 d: Abt. 1934 Sex: Male

.....................10 [2] Martha "Eliza" Louise Webb b: February 15, 1867 in Webbville, Lawrence Co., KY d: April 29, 1942 in Glenwood, Lawrence Co., KY Sex: Female

...........................+[3] Lindsey D. Webb b: December 14, 1854 in East Fork, Lawrence Co., KY d: January 17, 1923 in Glenwood, Lawrence Co., KY Father: William Riley Webb Mother: Martha Patsy Jordan Sex: Male

.....................10 Julia Elizabeth Webb b: Abt. 1869 Sex: Female

...........................+Andrew Jackson Pennington b: Abt. 1865 Sex: Male

.....................10 James Monroe Webb b: February 06, 1872 d: November 23, 1943 Sex: Male

...........................+Luanna (or Lavanna) Caudill, Cordle b: Abt. 1875 Sex: Female

.....................10 Paris Webb b: February 14, 1873 in Webbville, Lawrence Co., KY d: August 18, 1955 in King's Daughter Hospital, Ashland, Boyd Co., KY Sex: Male

...........................+Anna Laura Radcliff b: Abt. 1875 m: 1896 Sex: Female

.....................10 Mary A. Webb b: Abt. 1876 in Webbville, Lawrence Co., KY Sex: Female

...........................+Christopher Columbus Green b: Abt. 1875 Sex: Male

.....................10 Levi Webb b: Abt. 1878 Sex: Male

...........................+Sarah Holmes b: Abt. 1880 Sex: Female

.....................10 [4] Florence Webb b: Abt. 1882 in KY Sex: Female

...........................+_____ Salyer, Salyers b: Abt. 1880 Sex: Male

.....................2nd Husband of [4] Florence Web b:

...........................+_____ Clevenger b: Abt. 1880 Sex: Male

.................9 John M. Webb b: October 19, 1817 in Harlan Co., KY d: June 12, 1911 in Lawrence Co., KY Number of children: 6 Sex: Male Burial: Queen Cemetery, Glenwood, Lawrence Co., KY (Webb Note: Like all of the other Webb individuals in this tree, this Webb family descends from the same line as the country singers Loretta (Webb) Lynn and her sister Brenda Gail "Crystal Gale" Webb. Loretta was born April 14, 1935, in Butcher Hollow, Pike Co., KY; Crystal Gale was born January 9, 1951, in Paintsville, Johnson Co., KY)

.....................+Elizabeth Sturgill b: 1820 m: August 13, 1839 in Harlan Co., KY Number of children: 6 Father: John Sturgill Mother: Jemima Wells Sex: Female Burial: Queen Cemetery, Glenwood, Lawrence Co., KY

.....................10 James F. Webb b: Abt. 1840 in Bell Trace, Lawrence Co., KY Sex: Male

...........................+Serena _____? b: Abt. 1842 m: Abt. 1859 Sex: Female

.....................10 [5] Andrew Jackson Webb b: March 1841 in Bell Trace, Lawrence Co., KY d: 1923 Sex: Male

...........................+Elizabeth Jane Thompson b: Abt. 1845 m: Abt. 1866 Sex: Female

.....................2nd Wife of [5] Andrew Jackson Web b:

...........................+Mary Elizabeth Childers b: Abt. 1850 m: September 17, 1876 in Lawrence Co., KY Sex: Female

.....................10 Rachel Webb b: April 01, 1844 in Bell Trace, Lawrence Co., KY d: October 20, 1886 Sex: Female Burial: Mt. Pleasant Cemetery near Guy, Faulkner Co., AR

...........................+Richard Francis Graham b: Abt. 1840 Sex: Male

.....................10 Jemima Webb b: March 1845 in Bell Trace, Lawrence Co., KY Sex: Female

...........................+John W. Pennington b: Abt. 1840 m: February 06, 1862 Sex: Male

.....................10 Elihu Webb b: Abt. 1848 in Bell Trace, Lawrence Co., KY d: Bef. 1922 Sex: Male Burial: Denton, Carter Co., KY

...........................+Samantha _____? b: Abt. 1850 Sex: Female

.....................10 Wesley J. Webb b: February 1850 in Bell Trace, Lawrence Co., KY Sex: Male

...........................+Mary J. Jordan b: Abt. 1855 m: Abt. 1871 Sex: Female

.................9 Benjamin R. Webb b: July 06, 1819 d: January 19, 1853 Sex: Male

.....................+Rhoda _____? b: Abt. 1820 Sex: Female

.................9 Levi J. Webb b: January 16, 1821 Sex: Male

.....................+Agnes Sturgill b: April 08, 1825 Father: John Sturgill Mother: Jemima Wells

Sex: Female

.................9 Wesley Webb b: February 06, 1823 in Harlan Co., KY d: April 27, 1907 Sex: Male Burial: Webbville Cemetery, Webbville, Lawrence Co., KY

.......................+Abigail Pennington b: Abt. 1825 m: April 09, 1859 in Webbville, Lawrence Co., KY Sex: Female Burial: Webbville Cemetery, Webbville, Lawrence Co., KY

.................9 Riley Webb b: August 25, 1824 Sex: Male

.................9 Rachel Webb b: March 10, 1826 Sex: Female

.......................+Fleming Kitchen b: Abt. 1825 m: April 03, 1845 in Lawrence Co., KY Sex: Male

.................9 Mary Webb b: July 05, 1829 in Lawrence Co., KY d: August 19, 1860 Sex: Female

.................9 George Washington Webb b: February 13, 1832 in Harlan Co., KY d: March 30, 1883 in Webbville, Lawrence Co., KY Sex: Male

.................9 Elizabeth Webb b: November 19, 1834 d: April 26, 1875 Sex: Female

.......................+Joseph Scisson b: Abt. 1830 m: July 15, 1850 Sex: Male

.................8 [168] Abigail Pennington, b: May 09, 1803 in Lee Co., VA d: 1887 in Salyersville, Magoffin Co., KY Number of children: 3 Sex: Female

.......................+[167] Benjamin E. Caudill, b: 1799 in Wilkes Co., NC d: February 27, 1851 in Salyersville, Magoffin Co., KY Number of children: 3 Father: Stephen A. Caudill, Rev. War Soldier, Mother: Sarah "Sally" Francis Adams, 2nd wife Sex: Male

.................9 [169] William Jackson "Jack" Caudill b: 1822 in Perry Co., KY Sex: Male Burial: Oil Springs, Johnson Co., KY

.......................+[170] Rebecca Harris b: Abt. 1826 in Floyd Co., KY Sex: Female Burial: Oil Springs, Johnson Co., KY

.................9 [171] Abel Caudill, b: January 16, 1827 in Morgan Co., KY Number of children: ? Sex: Male

.......................+[172] Phoebe Hitchcock b: November 28, 1827 in Floyd Co., KY m: October 28, 1846 in Johnson Co., KY Number of children: ? Sex: Female

.....................10 [173] Jesse E. Caudill, b: September 07, 1847 in Johnson Co., KY d: September 14, 1890 Number of children: ? Sex: Male

...........................+[174] Elizabeth "Lizzie" Elam b: November 28, 1847 in MaGoffin Co., KY m: February 18, 1869 in Magoffin Co., KY Number of children: ? Sex: Female

.......................11 [175] Abel Caudill, b: February 09, 1870 in MaGoffin Co., KY Sex: Male

...........................+[176] Elizabeth Bailey b: May 1876 in KY? Sex: Female

.................9 [177] Elizabeth Caudill b: 1833 in Perry Co., KY d: April 15, 1915 Number of children: ? Sex: Female

.......................+[178] Noah May b: Abt. 1831 in Magoffin Co., KY Number of children: ? Sex: Male

.....................10 [179] Campbell J. May b: 1851 Number of children: ? Sex: Male

.......................+[180] Rebecca E. Adams b: 1852 Number of children: ? Father: Gilbert A. Adams Mother: Perlina Prater Sex: Female

.......................11 [181] Augustus Noah May b: 1876 d: 1944 Number of children: ? Sex: Male

...........................+[182] Sarah Elizabeth Cornett b: 1876 d: 1966 Number of children: ? Father: Russell Cornett, Mother: Ailey Amburgey Sex: Female

.................8 [31] Elijah Pennington b: May 12, 1812 in Lawrence Co., KY d: December 18, 1878 in Lawrence Co., KY Number of children: ? Sex: Male

.......................+[29] Sarah Elizabeth Caudill b: 1790 in Wilkes Co., NC m: Abt. 1845 in Lawrence Co., KY d: April 30, 1881 in Lawrence Co., KY, or Ordinary, Elliott Co., KY Number of children: 12 Father: James "Jimmie" Caudill, Jr., Rev. War Soldier Mother: Mary A. Adams, Sex: Female (Note: she and James were 2nd cousins)

.................9 [32] Elijah Clarence Pennington b: January 01, 1849 in Lawrence Co., KY d: September 22, 1926 in Ordinary, Elliott Co., KY Number of children: ? Sex: Male

.......................+[33] Nancy Jane Barker b: April 15, 1859 in in what is now Elliott Co., KY m:

March 27, 1880 in Sandy Hook, Elliott Co. KY d: February 24, 1940 in Elliott Co., KY Number of children: ? Father: John Barker Mother: Evaline Virginia Bowling Sex: Female

..................10 [34] Bracton Jayson Pennington b: August 13, 1883 in in what is now Elliott Co., KY Sex: Male

..........................+[35] Mary Jane Forest b: Abt. 1885 in Fayette Co. KY d: December 13, 1964 Father: Louis Forest Mother: Jemima Evans Sex: Female

..........2nd Wife of [6] James "Jimmie" Caudill, Jr., Rev. War Soldier:

................+[1162] Mary A. Adams, b: 1760 in Letcher Co., KY m: February 09, 1785 in Wilkes Co., NC d: in Wilkes Co., NC Number of children: 11 Father: John Hobbs "Old John of KY" Adams, Sr., Mother: Ann Caudill, her parents are unknown, but they were probably Stephen James Caudill (d. 1759) and Mary Elizabeth "Betsy" Fields (b. 1698); Sex: Female

.............7 [7] William C. "Billy" Caudill, b: July 27, 1779 in Wilkes Co., NC d: July 27, 1880 in Letcher Co., KY Number of children: 14 Sex: Male

..................+[395] Nancy Adams b: 1785 Father: John Hobbs Adams, Jr., Mother: Nancy Ann "Ann" Caudill, Sex: Female

.............2nd Wife of [7] William C. "Billy" Caudill, :

..................+[237] Mary Nancy "Nancy" Craft b: 1784 in Harris Creek, Wilkes Co., NC m: Abt. 1804 d: July 27, 1877 in Letcher Co., KY Number of children: 14 Father: Archelous Craft, Sr., Rev. War Soldier Mother: Elizabeth "Betsy" Adams Sex: Female

...............8 [238] Ellender Caudill b: Abt. 1805 Sex: Female

...............8 [239] Betsy Caudill b: Abt. 1806 Sex: Female

...............8 [240] Delilah "Lila" Caudill b: May 08, 1807 Sex: Female

...............8 [241] Isabel Caudill b: Abt. 1809 Sex: Female

...............8 [242] Mary Caudill b: March 10, 1811 in KY d: September 13, 1880 Number of children: 10 Sex: Female

.....................+[243] Joshua Mullins b: November 18, 1809 in Knox Co., KY d: February 15, 1900 in Letcher Co., KY Number of children: 10 Father: Joshua Mullins, Mother: Anna Robinson Sex: Male

..................9 [244] John Mullins b: December 26, 1834 Sex: Male

..................9 [245] Joseph M. Mullins b: June 19, 1834 Sex: Male

..................9 [246] Solomon Mullins b: 1838 Sex: Male

..................9 [247] Caleb Mullins b: 1840 Sex: Male

..................9 [248] Joshua Mullins b: 1842 Sex: Male

..................9 [249] Anna Mullins b: September 18, 1842 Sex: Female

........................+[250] George Washington Adams b: September 02, 1839 in Letcher Co., KY d: 1943 in Washington Father: Moses "Smoot" Adams Mother: Rebecca (Roberts) Hall Sex: Male

..................9 [251] William Mullins b: 1846 Sex: Male

..................9 [252] Delilah Mullins b: Aft. 1846 Sex: Female

..................9 [253] Nancy Mullins b: Aft. 1847 Sex: Female

..................9 [254] James Henderson Mullins b: September 12, 1853 Sex: Male

...............8 [255] Rebecca "Becca" Caudill b: April 15, 1815 Sex: Female

...............8 [256] Elizabeth "Betsy" Caudill b: Abt. 1816 d: in Knox Co., KY Number of children: 12 Sex: Female

.....................+[257] Caleb Mullins b: 1810 in KY d: in KY Number of children: 12 Father: Joshua Mullins, Mother: Anna Robinson Sex: Male

..................9 [258] William Mullins b: 1834 Sex: Male

..................9 [259] Mary Mullins b: Abt. 1836 Sex: Female

..................9 [260] Ann Mullins b: Abt. 1838 Sex: Female

..................9 [261] Nancy Mullins b: Abt. 1838 Sex: Female

..................9 [262] Joab Mullins b: Abt. 1841 Sex: Male

..................9 [263] Sarah Mullins b: Abt. 1844 Sex: Female

..................9 [264] John Mullins b: Abt. 1847 Sex: Male

...................9 [265] Susan Mullins b: 1850 Sex: Female

...................9 [266] Hugh Mullins b: August 25, 1852 Sex: Male

...................9 [267] James K. Mullins b: September 03, 1856 Sex: Male

...................9 [268] Elizabeth Mullins b: 1860 Sex: Female

...................9 [269] Ann Mullins b: October 1868 Sex: Female

................8 [218] Nancy Caudill b: Abt. 1817 in KY d: 1894 Number of children: 2 Sex: Female

......................+[217] Wilburn E. Caudill b: Abt. 1812 in NC Number of children: 2 Father: William Caudill Mother: Rachel Joines Sex: Male

...................9 [186] William W. "Wild Bill" Caudill b: Abt. 1839 in NC d: June 22, 1920 in Wolfe Co., KY Number of children: 2 Sex: Male

........................+[185] Elizabeth "Betsy" Eldridge b: Abt. 1841 Number of children: 2 Father: Levi Eldridge Mother: Easter (or Esther) Caudill, Sex: Female

.....................10 [187] Martha Ann Caudill b: Abt. 1861 Number of children: ? Sex: Female

...........................+[188] Enoch Everidge b: Abt. 1860 Number of children: ? Sex: Male

........................11 [189] Susan "Susie" Everidge b: August 15, 1885 in KY d: December 29, 1962 in Perry Co., KY Number of children: 9 Sex: Female

...............................+[190] Hiram Combs b: May 07, 1882 d: April 29, 1962 Number of children: 9 Father: Benjamin Combs Mother: Matilda "Tilda" Combs Sex: Male

.....................10 [25] Sarah Caudill b: September 1872 in Campton, KY Number of children: ? Sex: Female

...........................+[24] John C. Caudill b: February 1868 in Harlan or Letcher Co., KY m: April 18, 1889 in Breathitt Co., KY Number of children: ? Father: Henry H. Caudill Mother: Susannah Back Sex: Male

........................11 [9] Cleveland Caudill b: June 1891 in Letcher Co., KY Sex: Male

..............................+[8] Peggy Caudill b: April 1890 in Letcher Co., KY m: July 14, 1909 in Letcher Co., KY d: January 14, 1916 Father: William B. Caudill Mother: Susannah "Sukie" Caudill Sex: Female

...................9 [18] Mary C. Caudill b: January 13, 1852 in Letcher Co., KY Number of children: ? Sex: Female

........................+[17] Lewis E. Caudill b: March 05, 1855 in Letcher Co., KY m: January 13, 1852 in Letcher Co., KY Number of children: ? Father: Henry H. Caudill Mother: Susannah Back Sex: Male

.....................10 [19] Phoebe Caudill b: May 02, 1878 in Letcher Co., KY Number of children: 2 Sex: Female

...........................+[20] Levi S. Caudill b: December 22, 1875 in KY m: September 30, 1895 in Letcher Co., KY d: March 20, 1955 Number of children: 2 Father: Samuel B. Caudill Mother: Mary Ann "Polly" Eldridge Sex: Male

........................11 [21] Benjamin "Bennie" Caudill b: Abt. 1902 Sex: Male

........................11 [22] Howard Caudill b: Abt. 1915 Number of children: 11 Sex: Male

...........................+[23] Gladys Madden b: Abt. 1915 m: Abt. 1935 Number of children: 11 Father: Charles Madden Sex: Female

................8 [270] James "Limber Jim" Caudill b: Abt. 1818 in Floyd Co., KY Number of children: 4 Sex: Male

.....................+[271] Elizabeth "Betsy" Mullins b: 1820 in KY d: 1899 Number of children: 4 Father: Joshua Mullins, Mother: Anna Robinson Sex: Female

...................9 [272] Mary "Polly" Caudill b: 1840 Sex: Female

........................+[273] Lewis Campbell b: 1830 Father: William C. Campbell Mother: Elizabeth Cornett, Sex: Male

...................9 [274] Nancy Ann Caudill b: Abt. 1841 Number of children: ? Sex: Female

........................+[275] Davis S. Fields b: Abt. 1840 Number of children: ? Sex: Male

.....................10 [276] William Fields b: December 22, 1861 in Letcher Co., KY d: 1938 in Whitley Co., KY Sex: Male

..........................+[277] Martha Brashear b: October 11, 1871 d: March 31, 1943 Father: James Nicholas Brashear, Jr. Mother: Elizabeth Pratt Sex: Female

..................9 [27] William B. Caudill b: April 23, 1845 in Letcher Co., KY d: January 18, 1929 Number of children: ? Sex: Male (Note: William & Susannah were cousins)

........................+[26] Susannah "Sukie" Caudill b: Abt. 1847 in KY m: February 28, 1867 in Letcher Co., KY d: August 14, 1925 Number of children: ? Father: Isom Caudill Mother: Elizabeth "Lizzie" Back, Bach Sex: Female (Note: Susannah & William were cousins)

.....................10 [8] Peggy Caudill b: April 1890 in Letcher Co., KY d: January 14, 1916 Sex: Female

...........................+[9] Cleveland Caudill b: June 1891 in Letcher Co., KY m: July 14, 1909 in Letcher Co., KY Father: John C. Caudill Mother: Sarah Caudill Sex: Male

..................9 [14] Joshua M. Caudill b: June 23, 1850 in Letcher Co., KY d: March 22, 1941 Sex: Male

........................+[13] Rhoda Caudill b: April 12, 1853 in Letcher Co., KY d: January 17, 1942 Father: Henry B. Caudill, twin, Mother: Margaret "Patsy" Campbell Sex: Female

................8 [278] Sarah "Sally" Caudill b: July 29, 1823 d: April 13, 1884 Sex: Female

................8 [279] Susannah Caudill b: April 18, 1825 in Perry Co., KY d: September 26, 1898 in Elk Creek, Letcher Co., KY Sex: Female Burial: Elder James Dixon Cemetery, Elk Creek, Letcher Co., KY

..............8 [280] William J. "Stiller Bill" Caudill b: July 05, 1827 in Letcher Co., KY d: November 26, 1908 Number of children: 16 Sex: Male

.....................+[281] Nancy Dixon, Dickson b: April 19, 1830 in Letcher Co., KY m: February 07, 1847 in Letcher Co., KY d: December 31, 1899 Number of children: 16 Father: Thomas Dixon Mother: Susannah Proffitt Sex: Female

..................9 [282] James William "Noah Jim" Caudill b: October 19, 1846 in Blackey, Letcher Co., KY d: August 14, 1911 Number of children: ? Sex: Male

........................+[283] Lucinda Sumner b: January 28, 1850 in KY m: December 24, 1868 in Letcher Co., KY d: June 16, 1911 in KY Number of children: ? Father: John Sumner Mother: Nancy Hampton Sex: Female

.....................10 [10] Henry H. Cleveland Caudill b: April 20, 1887 in KY d: May 06, 1971 in Whitesburg, Letcher Co., KY Number of children: 18 Sex: Male Burial: Cleveland Caudill Cemetery, Caudill's Branch, Blackey, Letcher Co., KY

...........................+[195] Rebecca Adams b: Abt. 1887 m: Abt. 1905 d: in Waynesburg, KY Number of children: 8 Father: Gideon Adams Mother: Sarah Blair Sex: Female

.....................11 [196] Sarah Caudill b: Abt. 1905 Sex: Female

............................+[197] _____ Neagle b: Abt. 1900 Sex: Male

.....................11 [198] Arthur Caudill b: Abt. 1907 Sex: Male

.....................11 [199] Mollie Caudill b: Abt. 1909 Sex: Female

............................+[200] _____ Sanders b: Abt. 1905 Sex: Male

.....................11 [201] Cormie Caudill b: Abt. 1911 Sex: Female

............................+[202] _____ Repass b: Abt. 1910 Sex: Male

.....................11 [203] Chester Caudill b: Abt. 1913 Sex: Male

.....................11 [204] Irene Caudill b: Abt. 1915 Sex: Female

.....................11 [205] Judy Caudill b: Abt. 1917 Sex: Female

.....................11 [194] Ida Caudill b: Abt. 1920 d: in Waynesburg, Lincoln Co., KY Sex: Female

............................+[193] Coy Adams b: Abt. 1911 d: in Waynesburg, Lincoln Co., KY Father: Hiram Adams Mother: _____ Caudill Sex: Male

.....................2nd Wife of [10] Henry H. Cleveland Caudill:

............................+[284] Lucinda "Cinda" Watts b: April 20, 1886 m: May 11, 1911 in Letcher Co., KY d: October 22, 1963 in Letcher Co., KY Number of children: 10 Father: Allen Watts Mother: Elizabeth Brashear Sex: Female

.....................11 [11] James W. Caudill b: February 21, 1912 in Blackey, Letcher Co., KY

Number of children: 3 Sex: Male

..............................+[1163] Geneva Cornett b: December 1929 in Cumberland, KY m: June 08, 1946 in Whitesburg, Letcher Co., KY Number of children: 3 Father: Kip Cornett Mother: Alice Jackson Sex: Female

.......................2nd Wife of [11] James W. Caudill:

..............................+[1164] Tessa Mae Caudill b: May 16, 1913 in Roxana, Letcher Co., KY m: April 21, 1967 Father: Silas Caudill Mother: Martha Fields Sex: Female

.......................11 [1165] Watson Caudill b: October 23, 1913 in Letcher Co., KY d: May 10, 1953 in Perry Co., KY Sex: Male Burial: Cleveland Caudill Cemetery, Caudill's Branch, Blackey, Letcher Co., KY

..............................+[1166] Florence Mullins b: Abt. 1932 in Noble, KY m: May 06, 1952 in Letcher Co., KY Sex: Female (Note: Looking for her ancestors)

.......................11 [1167] Wesley Allen Caudill b: April 15, 1915 in Letcher Co., KY d: March 12, 1979 in Harlan Co., KY Sex: Male Burial: Cleveland Caudill Cemetery, Caudill's Branch, Blackey, Letcher Co., KY

.......................11 [1168] Callie Jane Caudill b: March 27, 1917 in Blackey, Letcher Co., KY Number of children: 3 Sex: Female

..............................+[1169] Howard Ison b: May 08, 1912 in Whitesburg, Letcher Co., KY m: December 06, 1945 in Whitesburg, Letcher Co., KY d: May 01, 1970 in Lexington, KY Number of children: 3 Father: Arch Ison Mother: Phoebe Lewis Sex: Male

.......................11 [1170] Chester Caudill b: December 23, 1918 in Blackey, Letcher Co., KY d: November 11, 1988 in Whitesburg, Letcher Co., KY Number of children: 5 Sex: Male

..............................+[1171] Imogene Qualls b: January 13, 1924 in Centre, AL m: January 13, 1924 Number of children: 5 Father: William Qualls Mother: Bertha Hogue Sex: Female

.......................11 [1172] Verna Caudill b: March 01, 1921 in Blackey, Letcher Co., KY Number of children: 2 Sex: Female

..............................+[1173] Wallace R. Ison b: June 02, 1924 in Blackey, Letcher Co., KY m: May 28, 1945 Number of children: 2 Father: May Ison Mother: Betty Adams Sex: Male

.......................11 [1174] Herman Caudill b: April 23, 1923 Sex: Male

.......................11 [1175] Vaxie Caudill b: January 16, 1925 in Letcher Co., KY d: October 24, 1980 in Hazard, Perry Co., KY Number of children: ? Sex: Female

..............................+[1176] Wade Whitehead b: March 12, 1921 m: November 25, 1950 d: August 10, 1975 in Perry Co., KY Number of children: ? Sex: Male

.......................11 [1177] Rachel Caudill b: August 23, 1927 in Blackey, Letcher Co., KY Sex: Female

..............................+[1178] W. B. Watts b: February 09, 1937 in Hallie, KY Father: Pearl Watts Mother: Cinda Smith Sex: Male

.......................11 [1179] Louetta Caudill b: May 08, 1929 Sex: Female

..............................+[1180] William C. "Hawk" Dixon b: May 12, 1927 m: April 12, 1949 Sex: Male

..................9 [285] Thomas D. Caudill b: December 26, 1848 in Letcher Co., KY Sex: Male

.......................+[286] Elizabeth Ann "Betsy" Pratt b: Abt. 1852 in Letcher Co., KY m: February 29, 1872 Father: John M. "Knock" Pratt Mother: Elizabeth Campbell Sex: Female

..................9 [287] William J. "Miller Bill" Caudill b: May 27, 1850 in Letcher Co., KY d: December 11, 1924 Sex: Male Burial: Bill Caudill Cemetery, Blackey, Letcher Co., KY

..................9 [288] John Caudill b: Abt. 1851 d: Abt. 1851 Sex: Male (Note: died in infancy)

..................9 [289] Susannah Caudill b: February 20, 1853 in Letcher Co., KY d: November 23, 1941 in Perry Co., KY Sex: Female

..................9 [290] Hiram W. Caudill b: Abt. September 20, 1853 in Letcher Co., KY d: December 20, 1913 Sex: Male

.......................+[291] Ester Banks b: April 08, 1853 in Letcher Co., KY d: September 25, 1905 Father: Harrison Banks Mother: Sarah Emeline Pridemore Sex: Female

...................9 [292] Sarah Ann "Sally" Caudill b: January 22, 1855 d: March 02, 1930 Sex: Female

...................9 [293] Nancy Jane Caudill b: October 05, 1856 d: January 06, 1929 Sex: Female

...................9 [294] Isaac D. "Ike" Caudill b: February 17, 1859 in KY d: February 19, 1938 in Colson, or Roxanna, KY Sex: Male

...................9 [295] Elizabeth "Betsy" Caudill b: Abt. 1860 in Letcher Co., KY d: Abt. 1927 Sex: Female

...................9 [296] Jeremiah P. "Jerry" Caudill b: November 23, 1861 d: February 25, 1922 Sex: Male

...................9 [297] George W. Caudill b: October 05, 1863 d: February 02, 1945 Sex: Male

...................9 [298] Margaret Caudill b: August 25, 1865 d: September 21, 1939 Sex: Female

...................9 [299] Henry Clay Caudill b: December 08, 1866 in Caudill Branch, Blackey, Letcher Co., KY d: September 06, 1938 in Red Star, KY Number of children: 5 Sex: Male Burial: Elmer Dixon Cemetery, Blackey, Letcher Co., KY

.........................+[300] Margaret Elizabeth "Maggie" Collins b: November 08, 1870 in Letcher Co., KY m: December 22, 1887 in Letcher Co., KY d: September 19, 1965 in Cincinnati, OH Number of children: 5 Father: Henry Powell Collins, Civil War Soldier Mother: Clarissa Ann "Clara" Bowman Sex: Female Burial: Elmer Dixon Cemetery, Blackey, Letcher Co., KY

......................10 [301] Melissa Caudill b: 1890 d: August 10, 1964 in Nashville, TN Sex: Female Burial: Elmer Dixon Cemetery, Blackey, Letcher Co., KY

......................10 [302] William Henry "Bill" Caudill b: 1892 d: February 25, 1950 Sex: Male Burial: Elmer Dixon Cemetery, Blackey, Letcher Co., KY

......................10 [303] John Breckenridge "Johnny" Caudill b: January 21, 1894 in Camp Branch, Letcher Co., KY d: January 10, 1974 in Camp Branch, Letcher Co., KY Number of children: 9 Sex: Male Burial: George Caudill Cemetery, Blackey, Letcher Co., KY

.........................+[304] Thursa Ann Mason b: June 09, 1893 in Sandlick, Letcher Co., KY m: July 30, 1913 in McRoberts, Letcher Co., KY d: August 23, 1975 in Whitesburg, Letcher Co., KY Number of children: 9 Father: Tilghman (Tilton?) Howard Mason Mother: Cornelia "Kerneal" (Grant?) Kiser Sex: Female

......................11 [1181] Denver Caudill b: October 20, 1914 in Letcher Co., KY Sex: Male Burial: Mason Cemetery, Letcher Co., KY

......................11 [1182] Dalma Caudill b: September 05, 1915 in Letcher Co., KY d: April 02, 2000 in Phoenix, AZ Number of children: 2 Sex: Female

.............................+[1183] Carl Thomas b: June 01, 1909 in Knott Co., KY d: February 1970 Number of children: 2 Father: Robert "Big Pop" Thomas Mother: Rosa "Big Mom" Collins Sex: Male

......................11 [12] Delmer V. Caudill b: January 13, 1917 in Polly (Sandlick), Letcher Co., KY d: January 06, 1985 in Hazard, Perry Co., KY Number of children: 9 Sex: Male Burial: Green Acres Cemetery, Ermine, KY (Note: resided in Ulvah, Letcher Co., KY at time of death)

.............................+[1184] Mabel Breeding b: June 28, 1918 in Whitesburg, Letcher Co., KY m: December 17, 1934 in Letcher Co., KY Number of children: 8 Father: Brent Breeding Mother: Sarah Elizabeth "Lissie" Adams Sex: Female

......................Partner of [12] Delmer V. Caudill:

.............................+[800] Lava Collins b: March 04, 1913 in Bath, Knott Co., KY met: Abt. 1939 in (Note: they did not marry) Number of children: 3 Father: Watson Collins Mother: Maggie Banks Sex: Female

......................11 [1185] Dohina Caudill b: February 04, 1919 in Letcher Co., KY Sex: Female

......................11 [1186] Dale Caudill b: January 30, 1920 in Polly, Letcher Co., KY d: Abt. 1990 Sex: Male

......................11 [1187] Dana Caudill b: July 10, 1922 in WhitCo., Letcher Co., KY Sex: Female

......................11 [1188] Dorothy Caudill b: December 24, 1926 in Fleming, Letcher Co., KY Sex: Female

......................11 [1189] Della Mae Caudill b: June 09, 1928 in Campbranch, Letcher Co., KY Sex: Female

.......................11 [1190] Danola "Dainy" Caudill b: July 26, 1933 d: July 31, 1933 Sex: Female Burial: Mason Cemetery, Letcher Co., KY

....................10 [305] Louisa Caudill b: August 12, 1902 d: Abt. 1951 Sex: Female Burial: George Cemetery, Blackey, Letcher Co., KY

....................10 [306] Lavada Belle (Vada?) Caudill b: November 27, 1906 d: November 11, 1965 Sex: Female

.................9 [307] Martha Caudill b: May 10, 1868 in Lower Caudill Branch, Letcher Co., KY d: May 03, 1943 in Diablock, Perry Co., KY Sex: Female

.................9 [308] John Breckenridge Caudill b: March 11, 1870 in Letcher Co., KY d: February 24, 1947 in Stroud, Lincoln Co., OK Sex: Male (Note: resided in Chandler, OK, in 1938)

................8 [309] Henry B. Caudill, twin, b: February 08, 1829 in Perry, Letcher Co., KY d: Abt. 1913 Number of children: 10 Sex: Male Burial: Felix York Cemetery, Viper, KY

.......................+[310] Margaret "Patsy" Campbell b: May 21, 1826 in Linefork, Perry/Letcher Co., KY m: February 15, 1849 in Letcher Co., KY Number of children: 10 Father: William C. Campbell Mother: Elizabeth Cornett, Sex: Female Burial: Felix York Cemetery, Viper, KY

.................9 [311] Elizabeth "Betty" Caudill b: August 29, 1850 in Letcher Co., KY d: September 05, 1904 Sex: Female

.......................+[312] Audley A. Cornett b: 1848 m: 1869 in Letcher Co., KY d: June 08, 1932 Sex: Male (Note: Looking for ancestors)

.................9 [313] Robert B. Caudill b: February 14, 1852 in Letcher Co., KY Sex: Male

.......................+[314] Elizabeth "Betty" Brashear b: December 05, 1856 in Perry Co., KY m: January 15, 1876 in Hazard, Perry Co., KY Father: Robert Samuel Brashear Mother: Sarah "Sally" Hall Sex: Female

.................9 [13] Rhoda Caudill b: April 12, 1853 in Letcher Co., KY d: January 17, 1942 Sex: Female

.......................+[14] Joshua M. Caudill b: June 23, 1850 in Letcher Co., KY d: March 22, 1941 Father: James "Limber Jim" Caudill Mother: Elizabeth "Betsy" Mullins Sex: Male

.................9 [315] Sarah "Sally" Caudill b: June 17, 1854 in Letcher Co., KY Sex: Female

.......................+[316] William "Bill" Young b: 1851 in Letcher Co., KY Father: Reece Young, Sr. Mother: Oriah R. "Ora" or "Arry" Ritchie Sex: Male

.................9 [317] Juda (Judy or Judah?) Caudill, b: March 1855 in Perry Co., KY Number of children: ? Sex: Female

.......................+[318] Jeremiah H. "Jerry" Combs b: 1859 in Perry Co., KY? Number of children: ? Father: Hiram Combs Mother: Mary Williams Sex: Male

....................10 [319] Daniel Combs b: Abt. 1892 in KY Number of children: ? Sex: Male

.......................+[320] Juda _____? b: Abt. 1900 in KY Number of children: ? Sex: Female

.......................11 [1191] Georgia Combs b: Abt. 1919 in KY Sex: Female

.................9 [321] Harriett Caudill b: 1859 in Letcher Co., KY Sex: Female

.......................+[322] Robert Hamilton b: Abt. 1855 Sex: Male

.................9 [323] William Hartley "Fuzzy Bill" Caudill b: Bet. 1860 - 1861 in Letcher Co., KY d: April 05, 1942 Sex: Male

.......................+[324] Cynthia Brashear b: September 02, 1858 in Perry Co., KY d: December 04, 1943 Sex: Female

.................9 [15] Lucretia "Lucy" Caudill b: Abt. 1864 in Perry Co., KY Sex: Female

.......................+[325] Jeptha Hamilton b: Abt. 1862 Sex: Male

.................2nd Husband of [15] Lucretia "Lucy" Caudill:

.......................+[326] Henry "Bud" Fields b: Abt. 1865 d: April 30, 1947 Sex: Male

.................9 [327] Polly Ann Caudill b: 1866 Sex: Female

.................9 [328] John Caudill b: 1869 Sex: Male

................8 [329] Isom Jesse Caudill, Sr., twin b: February 08, 1829 d: Abt. 1917 Number of children: 12 Sex: Male

.......................+[330] Judah Sumner b: 1831 Number of children: 12 Father: James Sumner

Mother: Nancy Adams, Sex: Female
.................9 [331] Mary Caudill b: 1850 Sex: Female
.......................+[332] Enoch Campbell b: Abt. 1847 Sex: Male
.................9 [333] Nancy Caudill b: August 07, 1852 Sex: Female
.......................+[334] Alexander Singleton b: Abt. 1850 Sex: Male
.................9 [335] Isom Caudill, Jr. b: July 26, 1855 Sex: Male
.................9 [336] George Henry Caudill b: 1855 Sex: Male
.................9 [337] Elizabeth Caudill b: June 02, 1856 Sex: Female
.......................+[338] John Hall b: Abt. 1855 Sex: Male
.................9 [339] Lucinda Caudill b: Abt. 1857 Sex: Female
.................9 [340] Margaret E. Caudill b: 1861 Sex: Female
.......................+[341] William Young b: Abt. 1860 Sex: Male
.................9 [342] Sarah Sally Caudill b: 1864 Sex: Female
.................9 [343] Patty Caudill b: Abt. 1865 Sex: Female
.................9 [344] William Caudill b: 1867 Sex: Male
.......................+[345] Mary J. Adams b: Abt. 1870 Sex: Female
.................9 [346] Julia Ann Caudill b: 1870 d: Abt. 1934 Sex: Female
.......................+[347] Ezekial Brashear b: Abt. 1867 Sex: Male
.................9 [348] Ellen Caudill b: 1875 Sex: Female
.............7 [1192] Sarah Elizabeth Caudill b: Abt. 1781 Sex: Female
.................+[1193] Benjamin Adams b: Abt. 1780 Sex: Male (Note: Looking for his ancestors)
.............7 [1194] Sampson Caudill b: Abt. 1784 in Wilkes Co., NC Sex: Male
.............7 [1195] Henry Caudill b: 1785 in Wilkes Co., NC d: June 18, 1856 in Letcher Co., KY
Number of children: 5 Sex: Male
.................+[1196] Phoebe Jane Strailor b: 1794 in NC Number of children: 5 Sex: Female
(Note: looking for her ancestors)
..............8 [1197] Stephen Caudill b: Abt. 1810 in Wilkes Co., North Carolina Number of
children: ? Sex: Male
.................+[1198] Elizabeth "Betsy" Fields b: Abt. 1813 in KY m: November 21, 1833
Number of children: ? Sex: Female
.................9 [16] Henry R. Stephen Caudill b: February 22, 1837 d: March 02, 1910 Number of
children: 2 Sex: Male
.......................+[1199] Louisa Sumner b: Abt. 1833 in Perry Co., KY m: September 08, 1854
Sex: Female
.................2nd Wife of [16] Henry R. Stephen Caudill:
.......................+[1200] Mary Branson b: Abt. 1860 in Perry Co., KY m: Abt. 1888 Number of
children: 2 Sex: Female
.................10 [212] Martha Caudill b: February 14, 1882 in Perry Co., KY d: July 28, 1957 Sex:
Female
.........................+[211] General Adams b: January 29, 1874 in Letcher Co., KY m: January 29,
1902 d: 1959 Father: Benjamin Adams Mother: Lucinda "Cindy" Combs Sex: Male
.................10 [1201] Cro Carr Caudill b: December 09, 1891 in Middlesboro, Bell Co., KY d:
June 25, 1951 in Harlan, Harlan or Letcher Co., KY Number of children: 4 Sex: Male Burial: Dianah
Blair Cemetery, Letcher Co., KY
.........................+[1202] Martha Victoria Blair h: April 02, 1890 in Cowan, Letcher Co., KY
m: Abt. 1915 d: June 16, 1976 in Lexington, Fayette Co., KY Number of children: 4 Father: Franklin
"Dock" Blair, Doctor Mother: Dianah Day Sex: Female Burial: Dianah Blair Cemetery, Letcher Co.,
KY
.................11 [1203] Truman Caudill b: March 12, 1912 in Letcher Co., KY d: May 29, 1976
Sex: Male
.........................+[1204] Lovelle Frazier b: Abt. 1914 Sex: Female
.................11 [1205] Henrietta Caudill b: July 17, 1914 Sex: Female

.......................11 [1206] James Caudill b: 1917 Sex: Male

.......................11 [1207] Harry M. Caudill, author & statesman b: 1922 d: 1990 in Letcher Co., KY Sex: Male (Note: author of the book, *Slender is the Thread, Tales from a Country Law Office*)

...........................+[1208] Anne Frye b: March 06, 1924 in Harrison Co., KY m: December 15, 1946 Sex: Female

...............8 [105] Terry Caudill, b: Abt. 1812 in KY Number of children: 9 Sex: Female

.......................+[104] Matthew Caudill, Jr., b: Bet. 1801 - 1811 in Wilkes Co., NC m: April 16, 1829 in Perry/Letcher Co., KY Number of children: 9 Father: Matthew Caudill, Sr., Mother: Sarah H. Webb Sex: Male

.................9 [106] Henry M. "Dickie Henry" Caudill b: 1830 Sex: Male

.................9 [107] Phoebe Caudill b: 1832 Sex: Female

.......................+[108] Jeremiah Dixon b: 1827 Sex: Male

.................9 [109] Elizabeth "Betsy" Caudill b: December 25, 1835 Sex: Female

.................9 [110] Sarah Caudill b: 1844 Sex: Female

.......................+[111] Erasmus Bedwell b: Abt. 1840 Sex: Male

.................9 [112] Susan Caudill b: 1845 Sex: Female

.................9 [113] Rebecca Caudill b: 1846 Number of children: ? Sex: Female

.......................+[114] Benjamin Caudill b: 1842 in Letcher Co., KY m: October 28, 1867 in Letcher Co., KY Number of children: ? Sex: Male (Note: Looking for ancestors)

.................10 [115] Hiram Caudill b: Abt. 1870 in Letcher Co., KY Sex: Male

.................9 [116] William Caudill b: January 1848 Number of children: ? Sex: Male

.......................+[117] Sarah Sturgill b: Abt. 1845 Number of children: ? Sex: Female

.......................10 [118] George Washington Caudill, Sr. b: Abt. 1870 Number of children: ? Sex: Male

...........................+[119] Nannie Belle Stidham b: Abt. 1875 Number of children: ? Sex: Female

.......................11 [120] Emmett H. Caudill b: Abt. 1895 Number of children: ? Sex: Male

...........................+[121] Rena Vae Maggard b: Abt. 1900 Number of children: ? Sex: Female (Note: Looking for ancestors)

.................9 [122] Nancy Ann Caudill, b: August 06, 1850 d: 1904 Number of children: ? Sex: Female

.......................+[123] Andrew Jackson Crase, b: 1847 d: 1938 Number of children: ? Father: Peter Crase, Mother: Rebecca Christian Sex: Male

.................10 [124] Henry Peter Crase, b: 1886 d: 1981 Sex: Male

.................9 [125] Benjamin Caudill b: 1851 Sex: Male

...............8 [1209] Henry H. Caudill b: Abt. 1821 in Letcher Co., KY Number of children: 2 Sex: Male

.......................+[1210] Susannah Back b: Abt. 1830 in Harlan Co., KY m: October 03, 1846 Number of children: 2 Father: Henry Back, Bach Mother: Susannah Maggard Sex: Female

.................9 [17] Lewis E. Caudill b: March 05, 1855 in Letcher Co., KY Number of children: ? Sex: Male

.......................+[18] Mary C. Caudill b: January 13, 1852 in Letcher Co., KY m: January 13, 1852 in Letcher Co., KY Number of children: ? Father: Wilburn E. Caudill Mother: Nancy Caudill Sex: Female

.......................10 [19] Phoebe Caudill b: May 02, 1878 in Letcher Co., KY Number of children: 2 Sex: Female

...........................+[20] Levi S. Caudill b: December 22, 1875 in KY m: September 30, 1895 in Letcher Co., KY d: March 20, 1955 Number of children: 2 Father: Samuel B. Caudill Mother: Mary Ann "Polly" Eldridge Sex: Male

.......................11 [21] Benjamin "Bennie" Caudill b: Abt. 1902 Sex: Male

.......................11 [22] Howard Caudill b: Abt. 1915 Number of children: 11 Sex: Male

...........................+[23] Gladys Madden b: Abt. 1915 m: Abt. 1935 Number of children: 11 Father: Charles Madden Sex: Female

.................9 [24] John C. Caudill b: February 1868 in Harlan or Letcher Co., KY Number of children: ? Sex: Male

........................+[25] Sarah Caudill b: September 1872 in Campton, KY m: April 18, 1889 in Breathitt Co., KY Number of children: ? Father: William W. "Wild Bill" Caudill Mother: Elizabeth "Betsy" Eldridge Sex: Female

....................10 [9] Cleveland Caudill b: June 1891 in Letcher Co., KY Sex: Male

...........................+[8] Peggy Caudill b: April 1890 in Letcher Co., KY m: July 14, 1909 in Letcher Co., KY d: January 14, 1916 Father: William B. Caudill Mother: Susannah "Sukie" Caudill Sex: Female

...............8 [1211] Isom Caudill b: Abt. 1822 in Letcher Co., KY Number of children: 3 Sex: Male

.......................+[1212] Elizabeth "Lizzie" Back, Bach b: April 20, 1820 in KY Number of children: 3 Father: Henry Back, Bach Mother: Susannah Maggard Sex: Female

.................9 [1213] Samuel B. Caudill b: Abt. 1844 in KY Number of children: ? Sex: Male

........................+[1214] Mary Ann "Polly" Eldridge b: Abt. 1847 in KY Number of children: ? Sex: Female

....................10 [20] Levi S. Caudill b: December 22, 1875 in KY d: March 20, 1955 Number of children: 2 Sex: Male

...........................+[19] Phoebe Caudill b: May 02, 1878 in Letcher Co., KY m: September 30, 1895 in Letcher Co., KY Number of children: 2 Father: Lewis E. Caudill Mother: Mary C. Caudill Sex: Female

.......................11 [21] Benjamin "Bennie" Caudill b: Abt. 1902 Sex: Male

.......................11 [22] Howard Caudill b: Abt. 1915 Number of children: 11 Sex: Male

...........................+[23] Gladys Madden b: Abt. 1915 m: Abt. 1935 Number of children: 11 Father: Charles Madden Sex: Female

.................9 [26] Susannah "Sukie" Caudill b: Abt. 1847 in KY d: August 14, 1925 Number of children: ? Sex: Female (Note: Susannah & William were cousins)

........................+[27] William B. Caudill b: April 23, 1845 in Letcher Co., KY m: February 28, 1867 in Letcher Co., KY d: January 18, 1929 Number of children: ? Father: James "Limber Jim" Caudill Mother: Elizabeth "Betsy" Mullins Sex: Male (Note: William & Susannah were cousins)

....................10 [8] Peggy Caudill b: April 1890 in Letcher Co., KY d: January 14, 1916 Sex: Female

...........................+[9] Cleveland Caudill b: June 1891 in Letcher Co., KY m: July 14, 1909 in Letcher Co., KY Father: John C. Caudill Mother: Sarah Caudill Sex: Male

.................9 [1133] Lewis Jesse Caudill b: July 08, 1857 in Letcher Co., KY Number of children: 2 Sex: Male

........................+[1132] Sarah Banks b: February 18, 1859 in Letcher Co., KY m: March 18, 1875 in Letcher Co., KY d: August 1938 Number of children: 2 Father: Harrison Banks Mother: Sarah Emeline Pridemore Sex: Female

....................10 [1134] Wesley Caudill b: April 23, 1880 d: February 22, 1928 Number of children: ? Sex: Male

...........................+[1135] Hailey "Hade" Ison b: Abt. 1882 Number of children: ? Sex: Female

.......................11 [1136] Wendell Caudill b: Abt. 1898 Number of children: 3 Sex: Male Burial: Caudill Cemetery at Uz, Letcher Co., KY

...........................+[1137] Muriel J. Dixon b: December 30, 1900 d: June 09, 1937 Number of children: 3 Father: James C. Dixon Mother: Evelyn Back, Bach Sex: Female Burial: Caudill Cemetery at Uz, Letcher Co., KY

....................10 [1138] Walter Caudill b: April 13, 1886 in Jeremiah, KY d: January 01, 1911 Sex: Male

...........................+[1139] Hannah Ison b: 1886 in Letcher Co., KY m: November 01, 1907 in Letcher Co., KY Sex: Female

...............8 [28] Benjamin Caudill, b: 1824 in Harlan Co., KY d: October 20, 1876 in Letcher Co., KY Number of children: 5 Sex: Male

......................+[1215] Mary Roark b: Abt. 1828 Sex: Female

.................2nd Wife of [28] Benjamin Caudill, :

......................+[1216] Mary "Polly" Bowling, Bolling, b: Abt. 1826 in KY? m: January 04, 1849 in Letcher Co., KY Number of children: 5 Sex: Female (Note: Looking for her ancestors)

..................9 [1217] Rebecca Caudill b: 1850 d: 1935 Sex: Female

..................9 [1218] Sarah Caudill b: 1852 Sex: Female

..................9 [1219] Elizabeth Caudill b: 1853 Sex: Female

..................9 [1220] Dixon Caudill b: 1855 Sex: Male

..................9 [1221] Easter Caudill b: 1857 Sex: Female

.............7 [1222] Thomas Caudill b: 1786 in Wilkes Co., NC Sex: Male

....................+[1223] Jane Caudill b: Abt. 1788 Sex: Female

.............7 [161] Isom or Isham Caudill b: April 02, 1789 in Letcher Co., KY d: May 18, 1892 in Letcher Co., KY Number of children: ? Sex: Male

....................+[160] Elizabeth Caudill b: June 02, 1797 in GA m: October 02, 1814 in Franklin Co., Georgia d: May 18, 1892 Number of children: ? Father: Benjamin Caudill Mother: Sarah Humphries Sex: Female

.................8 [162] James Caudill b: January 20, 1830 in GA Sex: Male

......................+[163] Mary "Polly" Fields b: April 1825 in KY m: 1850 Sex: Female

.............7 [29] Sarah Elizabeth Caudill b: 1790 in Wilkes Co., NC d: April 30, 1881 in Lawrence Co., KY, or Ordinary, Elliott Co., KY Number of children: 12 Sex: Female (Note: she and James were 2nd cousins)

....................+[36] James "Jimmie" Caudill, Jr. b: Bet. 1790 - 1800 in Wilkes Co., NC or GA? m: Abt. 1811 in Elliott Co., KY d: July 18, 1865 in Ordinary, Elliott Co., KY Number of children: 11 Father: James "Jimmie" Caudill, Jr., Rev. War Soldier Mother: Mary A. Adams, Sex: Male

.................8 [37] Nancy Caudill b: Abt. 1812 in Letcher Co., KY? Sex: Female

......................+[38] James Roberts b: Abt. 1776 in SC m: Abt. 1841 in Letcher Co., KY d: Abt. 1867 in Perry Co., KY Sex: Male

.................8 [39] William Riley "Red Bill" Caudill b: Abt. 1814 Number of children: 10 Sex: Male

......................+[40] Cynthia Ann (or Cynthy?) Combs, or Stacy b: Abt. 1820 m: 1835 in Breathitt Co., KY Number of children: 10 Father: Shadrack Combs, Sr. Mother: Rebecca Stacy Sex: Female

..................9 [41] Sarah Caudill b: Abt. 1835 Sex: Female

......................+[42] William Mullins b: Abt. 1835 Sex: Male (Note: Looking for his ancestors)

..................9 [43] Margaret Lou "Peggy" Caudill b: 1836 Sex: Female

..................9 [44] James Patterson Caudill b: 1843 Sex: Male

......................+[45] Sarah Frances Clagg b: Abt. 1845 Sex: Female

..................9 [46] Shadrack Thompson Caudill b: 1845 Sex: Male

..................9 [30] Kendrick ("Kinick"?) Caudill b: 1848 Sex: Male

......................+[47] Nancy Sarles b: Abt. 1850 Sex: Female

.................2nd Wife of [30] Kendrick ("Kinick"?) Caudill:

......................+[48] Martilla Back b: Abt. 1855 Sex: Female

..................9 [49] Emmaline Caudill b: 1850 in KY Sex: Female

......................+[50] Hughie Combs b: Abt. 1845 in KY m: 1879 in Boyd, KY Sex: Male Burial: (Looking for ancestors)

..................9 [51] Mary Caudill b: August 13, 1853 Sex: Female

......................+[52] Asberry Back b: Abt. 1850 Sex: Male

..................9 [53] Louisa Jane Caudill b: 1854 Sex: Female

......................+[54] Talton Calhoun b: Abt. 1853 Sex: Male

..................9 [55] Manford May Caudill b: 1856 Sex: Male

......................+[56] Belle Elam b: Abt. 1858 Sex: Female

..................9 [57] William Breckenridge "Breck" Caudill b: 1859 Sex: Male

......................+[58] Elizabeth Taulbee b: Abt. 1860 Sex: Female

.................8 [59] Sarah Elizabeth Caudill b: Abt. 1815 d: Abt. 1851 Sex: Female

................8 [60] Miriam Caudill b: Abt. 1818 Sex: Female

................8 [61] Electious Thompson Caudill b: October 1822 Sex: Female

................8 [62] Mary Caudill b: Abt. 1824 Sex: Female

................8 [63] Rebecca Caudill b: August 06, 1829 d: July 06, 1911 in Wolfe Co., KY Sex: Female

......................+[64] Thomas Tolson b: Abt. 1825 m: November 20, 1849 in Letcher Co., KY Sex: Male

................8 [65] Benjamin Caudill b: Abt. 1830 Sex: Male

................8 [66] Emmaline Caudill b: 1831 d: September 06, 1894 Number of children: 8 Sex: Female

......................+[67] James Young b: 1837 d: December 24, 1886 Number of children: 8 Sex: Male

..................9 [68] Sallie Young b: 1851 Sex: Female

..................9 [69] Thomas Young b: 1853 Sex: Male

..................9 [70] James Young b: 1855 Sex: Male

..................9 [71] Elizabeth "Betty" Young b: 1858 Sex: Female

..................9 [72] Brackton "Uncle Brack" Young b: March 1861 Sex: Male

..................9 [73] Elisha Young b: 1864 Sex: Male

..................9 [74] Mary Young b: May 01, 1868 Sex: Female

..................9 [75] Horace Greeley Young b: March 18, 1874 d: April 03, 1942 Sex: Male

........................+[76] Louellen Fletcher b: March 03, 1877 d: December 16, 1911 Father: George Fletcher Mother: Jane Burkhart Sex: Female

................8 [77] Elijah Caudill b: October 15, 1837 d: February 22, 1915 Sex: Male

................8 [78] James Aaron Caudill b: March 21, 1841 d: August 24, 1930 Sex: Male

.............2nd Husband of [29] Sarah Elizabeth Caudill:

..................+[31] Elijah Pennington b: May 12, 1812 in Lawrence Co., KY m: Abt. 1845 in Lawrence Co., KY d: December 18, 1878 in Lawrence Co., KY Number of children: ? Father: William Pennington Mother: Abigail Caudill, Cordell, Sex: Male

................8 [32] Elijah Clarence Pennington b: January 01, 1849 in Lawrence Co., KY d: September 22, 1926 in Ordinary, Elliott Co., KY Number of children: ? Sex: Male

......................+[33] Nancy Jane Barker b: April 15, 1859 in in what is now Elliott Co., KY m: March 27, 1880 in Sandy Hook, Elliott Co. KY d: February 24, 1940 in Elliott Co., KY Number of children: ? Father: John Barker Mother: Evaline Virginia Bowling Sex: Female

..................9 [34] Bracton Jayson Pennington b: August 13, 1883 in in what is now Elliott Co., KY Sex: Male

........................+[35] Mary Jane Forest b: Abt. 1885 in Fayette Co. KY d: December 13, 1964 Father: Louis Forest Mother: Jemima Evans Sex: Female

.............7 [36] James "Jimmie" Caudill, Jr. b: Bet. 1790 - 1800 in Wilkes Co., NC or GA? d: July 18, 1865 in Ordinary, Elliott Co., KY Number of children: 11 Sex: Male

..................+[29] Sarah Elizabeth Caudill b: 1790 in Wilkes Co., NC m: Abt. 1811 in Elliott Co., KY d: April 30, 1881 in Lawrence Co., KY, or Ordinary, Elliott Co., KY Number of children: 12 Father: James "Jimmie" Caudill, Jr., Rev. War Soldier Mother: Mary A. Adams, Sex: Female (Note: she and James were 2nd cousins)

................8 [37] Nancy Caudill b: Abt. 1812 in Letcher Co., KY? Sex: Female

......................+[38] James Roberts b: Abt. 1776 in SC m: Abt. 1841 in Letcher Co., KY d: Abt. 1867 in Perry Co., KY Sex: Male

................8 [39] William Riley "Red Bill" Caudill b: Abt. 1814 Number of children: 10 Sex: Male

......................+[40] Cynthia Ann (or Cynthy?) Combs, or Stacy b: Abt. 1820 m: 1835 in Breathitt Co., KY Number of children: 10 Father: Shadrack Combs, Sr. Mother: Rebecca Stacy Sex: Female

..................9 [41] Sarah Caudill b: Abt. 1835 Sex: Female

......................+[42] William Mullins b: Abt. 1835 Sex: Male (Note: Looking for his ancestors)

..................9 [43] Margaret Lou "Peggy" Caudill b: 1836 Sex: Female

.................9 [44] James Patterson Caudill b: 1843 Sex: Male

.......................+[45] Sarah Frances Clagg b: Abt. 1845 Sex: Female

.................9 [46] Shadrack Thompson Caudill b: 1845 Sex: Male

.................9 [30] Kendrick ("Kinick"?) Caudill b: 1848 Sex: Male

.......................+[47] Nancy Sarles b: Abt. 1850 Sex: Female

.................2nd Wife of [30] Kendrick ("Kinick"?) Caudill:

.......................+[48] Martilla Back b: Abt. 1855 Sex: Female

.................9 [49] Emmaline Caudill b: 1850 in KY Sex: Female

.......................+[50] Hughie Combs b: Abt. 1845 in KY m: 1879 in Boyd, KY Sex: Male Burial:
(Looking for ancestors)

.................9 [51] Mary Caudill b: August 13, 1853 Sex: Female

.......................+[52] Asberry Back b: Abt. 1850 Sex: Male

.................9 [53] Louisa Jane Caudill b: 1854 Sex: Female

.......................+[54] Talton Calhoun b: Abt. 1853 Sex: Male

.................9 [55] Manford May Caudill b: 1856 Sex: Male

.......................+[56] Belle Elam b: Abt. 1858 Sex: Female

.................9 [57] William Breckenridge "Breck" Caudill b: 1859 Sex: Male

.......................+[58] Elizabeth Taulbee b: Abt. 1860 Sex: Female

.............8 [59] Sarah Elizabeth Caudill b: Abt. 1815 d: Abt. 1851 Sex: Female

.............8 [60] Miriam Caudill b: Abt. 1818 Sex: Female

.............8 [61] Electious Thompson Caudill b: October 1822 Sex: Female

.............8 [62] Mary Caudill b: Abt. 1824 Sex: Female

.............8 [63] Rebecca Caudill b: August 06, 1829 d: July 06, 1911 in Wolfe Co., KY Sex:
Female

.......................+[64] Thomas Tolson b: Abt. 1825 m: November 20, 1849 in Letcher Co., KY Sex:
Male

.............8 [65] Benjamin Caudill b: Abt. 1830 Sex: Male

.............8 [66] Emmaline Caudill b: 1831 d: September 06, 1894 Number of children: 8 Sex:
Female

.......................+[67] James Young b: 1837 d: December 24, 1886 Number of children: 8 Sex:
Male

.................9 [68] Sallie Young b: 1851 Sex: Female

.................9 [69] Thomas Young b: 1853 Sex: Male

.................9 [70] James Young b: 1855 Sex: Male

.................9 [71] Elizabeth "Betty" Young b: 1858 Sex: Female

.................9 [72] Brackton "Uncle Brack" Young b: March 1861 Sex: Male

.................9 [73] Elisha Young b: 1864 Sex: Male

.................9 [74] Mary Young b: May 01, 1868 Sex: Female

.................9 [75] Horace Greeley Young b: March 18, 1874 d: April 03, 1942 Sex: Male

.......................+[76] Louellen Fletcher b: March 03, 1877 d: December 16, 1911 Father: George
Fletcher Mother: Jane Burkhart Sex: Female

.............8 [77] Elijah Caudill b: October 15, 1837 d: February 22, 1915 Sex: Male

.............8 [78] James Aaron Caudill b: March 21, 1841 d: August 24, 1930 Sex: Male

...........7 [1224] Stephen Caudill b: Abt. 1792 Sex: Male

...........7 [1225] John Caudill b: 1793 in NC d: July 15, 1859 in Breathitt Co., KY Number of
children: 2 Sex: Male

.................+[1226] Nancy Roberts b: 1805 in VA Number of children: 2 Father: Moses Roberts
Mother: Polly King Sex: Female

.............8 [1227] Mary Polly "Maggie" Caudill, Caudle b: 1824 in Perry Co., KY Number of
children: ? Sex: Female

.......................+[1228] Cyrus Syra Combs, Sr., b: December 1821 in Perry Co., KY m: 1848 d:
Aft. 1900 Number of children: 2 Father: Preston Combs, Sr., Mother: Nancy B. Stacy Sex: Male

...................9 [1229] _____ Combs b: Abt. 1860 Number of children: ? Sex: Male

.........................+[1230] _____ _____? b: Abt. 1865 Number of children: ? Sex: Female

.....................10 [1231] Judy Combs Sex: Female

................8 [79] Tabitha Caudill, Caudle b: May 31, 1830 in Shoulder Blade, Clay Co., KY d: July 19, 1908 Number of children: ? Sex: Female

.........................+[1232] Samuel Spicer b: Abt. 1830 in Clay Co., KY or Ashe Co., NC m: January 1852 in Breathitt Co., KY Number of children: ? Sex: Male

...................9 [1233] _____ Spicer b: Abt. 1860 Number of children: ? Sex: Unknown

.....................10 [1234] _____ Spicer Number of children: ? Sex: Unknown

........................11 [1235] Lois Vincent Sex: Female

................2nd Husband of [79] Tabitha Caudill, Caudle:

.........................+[1236] Isham Arrowood b: 1826 in KY m: Abt. 1860 in Clay Co., KY Sex: Male

.............7 [81] Jesse P. Caudill, Cordell b: April 24, 1795 in Wilkes or Alleghany Co., NC, some say Pocahantas, WV d: April 23, 1891 in Ashe or Alleghany Co., NC Number of children: 25 Sex: Male Burial: Family Cemetery on the Lonnie Edwards farm, two miles southeast of Whitehead, NC

...................+[1237] Sarah "Sary" Roberts, Roberds b: 1799 in Wilkes or Alleghany Co., NC m: October 11, 1817 in Wilkes or Alleghany Co., NC Number of children: 11 Father: Melachi Roberts Mother: Frances Simmons Sex: Female

................8 [1238] Hugh Caudill b: 1817 in Alleghany Co., NC Number of children: 5 Sex: Male

.........................+[1239] Elizabeth Blevins b: Abt. 1820 m: Abt. 1837 Number of children: 5 Sex: Female

...................9 [1240] Sarah Caudill b: Abt. 1838 Sex: Female

...................9 [1241] Nancy J. Caudill b: Abt. 1840 Sex: Female

................9 [1242] Thomas Jefferson Caudill b: Abt. 1842 Number of children: ? Sex: Male

.........................+[1243] Adeline Bowling, Bolling b: Abt. 1844 in Titusville, PA Number of children: ? Sex: Female

.....................10 [1244] Edward F. Caudill b: Abt. 1865 Number of children: ? Sex: Male

.............................+[1245] Virginia Rhoades b: Abt. 1867 Number of children: ? Sex: Female

........................11 [1246] Edward Thomas Lee Caudill b: Abt. 1888 Sex: Male

...................9 [1247] James Caudill b: Abt. 1844 Sex: Male

...................9 [1248] Enoch R. Caudill b: Abt. 1846 Number of children: ? Sex: Male

.........................+[1249] Rebecca _____? b: Abt. 1848 Number of children: ? Sex: Female

.....................10 [1250] Hugh L. Caudill b: Abt. 1870 Sex: Male

................8 [1251] James Robert Caudill b: November 10, 1818 in Ashe Co., NC d: November 07, 1887 in Alleghany Co., NC Number of children: 2 Sex: Male (Notes: owned slaves)

.........................+[1252] Phoebe Louise Holloway b: April 10, 1818 d: December 31, 1879 Number of children: 2 Father: Daniel Holloway Mother: Mary Woodruff Sex: Female

...................9 [80] James Franklin Caudill, Civil War Soldier b: May 10, 1845 in Alleghany Co., NC d: June 08, 1921 Number of children: 13 Sex: Male (Note: His home is off of the Blue Ridge Parkway, near Sparta, NC. At age 16, he joined the Confederate Army, served in Co. G, 45th NC Calvary. He was wounded in the hip at Gatlinburg, TN)

.........................+[1253] Catherine "Katie" Crouse b: Abt. 1847 m: Abt. 1860 Number of children: 2 Sex: Female

.....................10 [1254] James Reeves Caudill b: September 26, 1861 Sex: Male

.....................10 [1255] David Rufus Caudill b: June 05, 1865 Sex: Male

...................2nd Wife of [80] James Franklin Caudill, Civil War Soldier:

.........................+[1256] Elvira Koontz b: January 09, 1850 m: July 10, 1869 Number of children: 11 Sex: Female

.....................10 [1257] Edwin E. Caudill b: February 06, 1871 Sex: Male

.....................10 [1258] Frances Dona Caudill b: January 28, 1872 Sex: Female

.....................10 [1259] Hillery Cleve Caudill b: April 22, 1874 Number of children: 12 Sex: Male

.............................+[1260] Celia Catherine Edwards b: Abt. 1875 Number of children: 12 Sex:

Female

......................11 [1261] Kyle Andrew Caudill b: Abt. 1895 Sex: Male

......................11 [1262] Charlie Caudill b: Abt. 1897 Sex: Male

......................11 [1263] Sherman Caudill b: Abt. 1899 Sex: Male

......................11 [1264] Kemp Caudill b: Abt. 1901 Sex: Male

......................11 [1265] Dean Caudill b: Abt. 1903 Sex: Male

......................11 [1266] Bertha Caudill b: Abt. 1905 Sex: Female

......................11 [1267] Ella Caudill b: Abt. 1907 Sex: Female

......................11 [1268] Zelma Caudill b: Abt. 1909 Sex: Female

......................11 [1269] Merle Caudill b: Abt. 1911 Sex: Male

......................11 [1270] Alma Caudill b: Abt. 1913 Sex: Female

......................11 [1271] Faye Caudill b: Abt. 1915 Sex: Female

......................11 [1272] Clay Caudill b: Abt. 1917 Sex: Male

....................10 [1273] James Benjamin Caudill b: November 23, 1875 Sex: Male

....................10 [1274] Robert C. Caudill b: July 27, 1877 Sex: Male

....................10 [1275] Phoebe L. Caudill b: July 08, 1879 Sex: Female

....................10 [1276] W. Vance Caudill b: April 03, 1881 Sex: Male

....................10 [1277] Nora Mae Caudill b: December 17, 1882 Sex: Female

....................10 [1278] Lula Elvira Caudill b: July 09, 1884 Sex: Female

....................10 [1279] Maude E. Caudill b: October 17, 1886 Sex: Female

....................10 [1280] Effie Geneva Caudill b: April 15, 1894 Sex: Female

..................9 [1281] Martha Elizabeth Caudill b: Abt. 1850 d: October 28, 1938 Number of children: ? Sex: Female Burial: The Joines Family Cem. Pine Swamp, NC

......................+[1282] Richard Hayward Joines b: August 29, 1851 m: April 06, 1873 d: April 06, 1923 Number of children: ? Father: Ezekiel Joines Mother: Jane Crouse Sex: Male

....................10 [1283] Henry Clay Joines b: 1897 d: 1975 Sex: Male

..........................+[1284] Frona Caudill b: Abt. 1899 Sex: Female

................8 [1285] Malachi Caudill, Caudle b: 1822 Number of children: ? Sex: Male

......................+[1286] Martha French b: Abt. 1824 Number of children: ? Sex: Female

..................9 [1287] Amanda Biddie Caudill b: August 17, 1866 in Wise Co., VA Sex: Female

................8 [1288] Biddy Caudill b: 1825 Sex: Female

................8 [1289] Pherby (Ferba) Caudill b: 1828 in Ashe Co., NC d: 1916 in Alleghany Co., NC Number of children: 4 Sex: Female

......................+[1290] Leander "Lee" Andrews, Anders b: Abt. 1826 m: Abt. 1846 Number of children: 4 Father: William Andrews Mother: Sarah Cheek Sex: Male

..................9 [1291] William Andrews b: 1849 Sex: Male

..................9 [1292] Sarah Jane Andrews b: March 08, 1852 in Ashe Co., NC d: December 26, 1921 in Alleghany Co., NC Sex: Female

..................9 [1293] Francis "Frankie" Andrews b: 1855 in Ashe Co., NC d: March 17, 1931 Sex: Female

......................+[1294] James W. Crouse b: Abt. 1853 m: March 03, 1872 Sex: Male

..................9 [1295] Jessie F. Andrews b: 1847 in Ashe Co., NC d: 1924 in Alleghany Co., NC Sex: Male Burial: Antioch PBCC, Stratford Area

......................+[1296] Elizabeth "Bettie" Sanders b: Abt. 1849 m: December 29, 1866 in Alleghany Co., NC d: in Alleghany Co., NC Sex: Female Burial: Antioch PBCC, Stratford Area

................8 [1297] Frankie Caudill b: 1832 in Ashe Co., NC d: November 1919 Number of children: ? Sex: Female

......................+[1298] Calvin Osborne b: Abt. 1830 Number of children: ? Sex: Male

..................9 [1299] Jesse Osborne b: 1847 Sex: Female

................8 [1300] Jessie M. Caudill b: 1836 in Ashe Co., NC d: May 31, 1870 in Scott Co., VA Sex: Male

......................+[1301] Ferelda Hensley b: 1841 m: 1855 Sex: Female (Note: Looking for ancestors)

................8 [1302] Andrew Jackson Caudill, Civil War Soldier b: 1837 in Ashe Co., NC d: 1862 Number of children: 2 Sex: Male (Note: he was in the 12th Reg. NC. Vol. in the Civil War. His Captain was Jesse F. Reeves)

.....................+[1303] Rosanna "Rowsey" Phipps b: Abt. 1839 m: January 03, 1856 Number of children: 2 Sex: Female

................9 [1304] Mary J. Caudill b: 1857 Sex: Female

................9 [1305] Candis Caudill b: 1859 Sex: Female

................8 [1306] Nancy Caudill b: May 22, 1839 in Ashe Co., NC d: December 06, 1895 Sex: Female

.....................+[1307] Adam J. Waggoner, Wagoner, Wagner b: November 09, 1833 m: March 08, 1855 d: December 27, 1920 Father: Jacob Waggoner Mother: Annie Roberts Sex: Male Burial: New Hope Church Cemetery Strafford, NC (Note: He was an Elder and a Primitive Baptist Minister)

................8 [1308] Jeremiah "Jerry" Caudill b: 1841 in Ashe Co., NC Sex: Male

.....................+[1309] Mary Koontz b: Abt. 1843 Sex: Female

................8 [1310] Jane Caudill b: 1841 in Ashe Co., NC Sex: Female

.............2nd Wife of [81] Jesse P. Caudill, Cordell:

...................+[1311] Lubidda "Biddy" Bledsoe b: April 10, 1828 in Letcher Co., KY m: June 25, 1842 in Ashe or Alleghany Co., NC d: August 08, 1904 Number of children: 14 Father: Tyrell Bledsoe Mother: Nancy Reeves Sex: Female Burial: Family Cemetery on the Lonnie Edwards farm, two miles southeast of Whitehead, NC

................8 [1312] Jane Caudill b: 1842 in NC Sex: Female

................8 [1313] Isaac G. "Shade" Caudill b: October 08, 1843 in Whitehead, Ashe Co., NC Sex: Male

................8 [1314] Shadrack Caudill b: 1844 in NC Sex: Male

................8 [1315] Sarah E. Caudill b: December 20, 1845 in Ashe Co., NC d: March 28, 1910 in Alleghany Co., NC Number of children: ? Sex: Female Burial: Union Primitive Baptist Church Cemetery, Whitehead, NC

.....................+[1316] John Whitehead b: December 17, 1848 in Ashe Co., NC m: February 10, 1867 d: September 27, 1938 Number of children: ? Sex: Male Burial: Pine Grove Cem. in Willow Springs, MO

...................9 [1317] James Pierce Whitehead b: August 08, 1884 in Alleghany Co., NC Sex: Male

.........................+[1318] Christina Caudill b: Abt. 1886 m: June 02, 1909 in Alleghany Co., NC Sex: Female (Note: Looking for her ancestors)

................8 [1319] Matthew (or Mathis) Franklin Caudill b: April 28, 1848 in Ashe Co., NC Sex: Male

.....................+[1320] Margaret Gentry b: Abt. 1850 m: September 25, 1867 Sex: Female

................8 [1321] Tyrell Robert Caudill b: November 20, 1850 in Ashe Co., NC d: October 24, 1918 in Whitehead Township, Alleghany Co. NC Number of children: 11 Sex: Male

.....................+[1322] Nancy Caroline Fender b: April 02, 1853 in Ashe Co., NC m: March 07, 1869 in Alleghany Co. NC d: January 12, 1942 in Whitehead Township, Alleghany Co. NC Number of children: 11 Father: Allen Fender Mother: Nancy Edwards Sex: Female

...................9 [1323] Shade George Caudill b: January 02, 1870 in Whitehead, NC d: September 17, 1957 Number of children: 10 Sex: Male (Note: he was a Primitive Baptist Minister)

.........................+[1324] Susan Martha Long b: April 14, 1866 in Alleghany Co., NC m: August 09, 1890 d: October 03, 1934 in Statesville, Iredell Co., NC Number of children: 10 Sex: Female

...................10 [1325] Jesse Reid Caudill b: 1900 d: 1985 Sex: Male

.........................+[1326] Esther Ruth Lackey b: 1910 d: March 19, 201/02 Sex: Female

...................10 [1327] Helen Caudill b: Abt. 1891 Sex: Female

...................10 [1328] Robert Caudill b: Abt. 1893 Sex: Male

...................10 [1329] Mamie Caudill b: Abt. 1895 Sex: Female

...................10 [1330] George Caudill b: Abt. 1897 Sex: Male

..................10 [1331] Bayne Caudill b: Abt. 1902 Sex: Male

..................10 [1332] Edna Caudill b: Abt. 1904 Sex: Female

..................10 [1333] Stella Caudill b: Abt. 1906 Sex: Female

..................10 [1334] Eura Caudill b: Abt. 1908 Sex: Female

..................10 [1335] Emory Lipe Caudill b: Abt. 1910 Sex: Male

................9 [1336] Nancy Catherine "Nannie" Caudill b: March 18, 1872 in Scotsville, NC d: March 04, 1956 Sex: Female

...................+[1337] Muncey H. Waddle b: Abt. 870 m: 1894 d: February 20, 1967 Sex: Male

................9 [1338] Robert Franklin Caudill b: October 01, 1874 d: January 12, 1892 Sex: Male

................9 [1339] Martha (Mattie) Ellen Caudill b: January 20, 1877 in Alleghany Co., NC d: April 02, 1946 in Fountain Green Hospital, Harford Co., MD Number of children: ? Sex: Female

...................+[1340] William Amadeus Greene b: December 31, 1877 in NC m: February 01, 1900 d: March 29, 1960 in Mt. Carmel, MD Number of children: ? Father: Solomon Green, Greene Mother: Sarah Green Sex: Male

..................10 [1341] James Hoyt Greene b: July 11, 1918 in Statesville, Falston Township, Iredel County, NC d: November 08, 1975 in Towson, Baltimore, Co.,MD Number of children: 2 Sex: Male

........................+[1342] Louise Christina Hausner b: July 27, 1919 d: October 09, 1994 Number of children: 2 Sex: Female

................9 [1347] Candace Jane Caudill b: May 23, 1879 d: October 29, 1965 Number of children: ? Sex: Female

...................+[1348] Hiram Edwards b: Abt. 1877 m: June 15, 1898 in Alleghany Co., NC Number of children: ? Sex: Male

..................10 [1349] Breece L. Caudill, (adopted) b: December 08, 1911 Sex: Unknown

................9 [1350] Florence Alzenia Caudill b: January 07, 1882 d: March 10, 1959 Sex: Female Burial: Union Primitive Baptist Ch. Cem. Whitehead, NC

...................+[1351] Center Joshua Edwards b: 1873 d: 1951 Sex: Male Burial: Union Primitive Baptist Ch. Cem. Whitehead, NC

................9 [82] Tyrell Oscar Caudill b: August 08, 1884 d: May 01, 1937 in Whitehead Township, Alleghany Co., NC Number of children: 7 Sex: Male

...................+[1352] Lou Choate b: Abt. 1886 m: December 21, 1910 Sex: Female

................2nd Wife of [82] Tyrell Oscar Caudill:

...................+[1353] Hattie Maud Edwards b: August 10, 1893 m: March 1913 d: February 03, 1930 in Whitehead Township, Alleghany Co., NC Number of children: 7 Sex: Female

..................10 [1354] Evelyn Caudill b: Abt. 1914 Sex: Female

..................10 [1355] Louise Caudill b: Abt. 1916 Sex: Female

..................10 [1356] Earl Caudill b: Abt. 1918 Sex: Male

..................10 [1357] Bayne Caudill b: Abt. 1920 Sex: Male

..................10 [1358] Edward Caudill b: Abt. 1922 Sex: Male

..................10 [1359] Hubert Caudill b: Abt. 1924 Sex: Male

..................10 [1360] Caery Caudill b: Abt. 1926 Sex: Female

................9 [1361] Walter Cleveland Caudill, Senator & Dr. b: June 09, 1888 d: January 18, 1963 Number of children: ? Sex: Male Burial: (Notes: Was a member of the Virginia State Legislature 1936-1956 as a State Senator and also was Ltg. Govenor of the State of VA. Along with his brother Estell and Dr. J. O. Woods, built St. Elizabeth Hospital, in Elizabeathion, TN.)

...................+[1362] Mary Ring Cornett b: Abt. 1890 m: June 30, 1920 d: September 29, 1964 Number of children: ? Sex: Female

..................10 [1363] Carol Caudill b: Abt. 1921 Sex: Female

................9 [1364] Estill Leftrage Caudill, Sr., Dr. b: October 23, 1890 d: September 03, 1977 in Giles Co., VA Number of children: 3 Sex: Male Burial: Memorial Presbyterian Church Cemetery

...................+[1365] Flora Weatherly b: Abt. 1892 in VA m: Abt. 1912 d: February 27, 1966 in Giles Co., VA Number of children: 3 Sex: Female Burial: Memorial Presbyterian Church Cem.

......................10 [1366] Mary Burns Caudill b: Abt. 1913 Sex: Female

......................10 [1367] Estill Leftrage Caudill, Jr. b: Abt. 1915 Sex: Male

......................10 [1368] Julian Tyrell Caudill b: Abt. 1917 Sex: Female

..................9 [1369] Munsey Edwin Caudill b: August 14, 1894 d: September 02, 1984 in Dallastown, PA Number of children: 2 Sex: Male

........................+[1370] Kate Tedder, Tudor b: Abt. 1895 Number of children: 2 Sex: Female

......................10 [1371] Kyle Caudill b: Abt. 1915 Sex: Male

......................10 [1372] Irene Caudill b: Abt. 1917 Sex: Female

..................9 [1373] Alta Blanche Caudill b: August 23, 1898 d: 1996 Sex: Female (Note: Lived at the Caudill Home Place, and still owns it.)

........................+[1374] Lonnie Edwards b: February 28, 1894 d: May 11, 1968 Sex: Male Burial: (Notes: Farmer in Alleghany Co. and was County Commissoner, 1952 and 1953)

................8 [1375] Bledsoe E. "Bleth" Caudill b: May 17, 1853 in Ashe Co., NC d: December 23, 1921 Sex: Male

......................+[1376] Margaret "Maggie" Douglas b: Abt. 1855 m: December 08, 1875 Sex: Female

................8 [1377] Biddy Louisa Caudill b: 1856 in NC Sex: Female

................8 [1378] Cynthia Jane Caudill b: September 11, 1858 in Ashe Co., NC d: May 06, 1922 Sex: Female

......................+[1379] Richard J. Fender b: Abt. 1856 m: November 24, 1886 Sex: Male

................8 [1380] Candace S. Caudill b: December 19, 1861 in Alleghany Co., NC d: February 16, 1950 Sex: Female

......................+[1381] Thomas J. Shepherd b: Abt. 1859 m: July 13, 1889 Sex: Male

................8 [1382] Virginia Ellen Caudill b: December 19, 1861 in Alleghany Co., NC d: February 16, 1950 Sex: Female

......................+[1383] Emery Floyd Poole b: Abt. 1860 m: February 04, 1892 in Alleghany Co., NC Sex: Male

................8 [1384] Louisa B. Caudill b: Abt. 1863 in Ashe Co., NC d: October 29, 1907 Sex: Female

......................+[1385] Thomas Jefferson Mitchell b: Abt. 1860 m: September 24, 1876 Sex: Male

................8 [1386] T. A. Caudill b: June 05, 1866 in Alleghany Co., NC d: June 05, 1866 in Alleghany Co., NC Sex: Male

................8 [1387] George Thomas Caudill b: February 02, 1868 in Alleghany Co., NC d: July 19, 1937 Sex: Male

......................+[1388] Cornelia J. Choate b: Abt. 1870 m: February 14, 1887 Sex: Female

..........6 Matthew Caudill, Sr., b: 1755 in Lunenburg Co., VA d: 1837 in Millstone Creek, Letcher Co., KY Number of children: 13 Sex: Male

................+Sarah H. Webb b: November 08, 1778 in Wilkes Co., NC m: Abt. 1793 in Wilkes Co., NC d: 1873 in Letcher Co., KY Number of children: 13 Father: James F. Webb, Sr., Soldier Mother: Elizabeth "Lettie" Jane Nelson (Nelson Note: Looking for Elizabeth's ancestors. I believe that she's part of the large Nelson clan from VA and NC, which spread out and migrated west into WV, TN, and KY in the 1830s. Like the author, the Judds [Naomi, Ashley, Wynonna], also descend from this family. The earliest known ancestor of this Nelson group is William "Old William" Nelson, born in 1747 in Prince Edward Co., VA, and died on August 9, 1834, in Hawkins Co., TN. Old William's wife was Rebecca Smith, born about 1757 in Stokes Co., NC. It's possible, in my opinion, that Elizabeth could be Old William's sister) Sex: Female (Webb Note: Like all of the other Webb individuals in this tree, this Webb family descends from the same line as the country singers Loretta (Webb) Lynn and her sister Brenda Gail "Crystal Gale" Webb. Loretta was born April 14, 1935, in Butcher Hollow, Pike Co., KY; Crystal Gale was born January 9, 1951, in Paintsville, Johnson Co., KY)

.............7 [92] Stephen Caudill, b: February 07, 1794 in Wilkes, NC (or SC) d: January 07, 1857 in Letcher or Lawrence Co., KY Number of children: 11 Sex: Male

...................+Sarah Yonts, Younts, Jans; b: March 18, 1796 in Lunenburg Co., VA (or NC or Floyd Co., KY) m: June 25, 1814 in Floyd Co., KY d: 1850 in Letcher Co., KY Number of children: 6 Father: William Yonts, Sr., Mother: Margaret Bentley, Sex: Female (Yonts Note: like the author and all of the other Yonts individuals in this tree, this family descends from Wilhelm Jans, born in 1714 in the town of Oberalben, Rheineland-Pfalz, Germany; Wilhelm died in 1778 in Rowan Co., NC)

................8 John Caudill, b: April 25, 1815 in SC or Floyd Co., KY d: April 15, 1891 in Johnson Co., KY Number of children: ? Sex: Male Burial: April 1891 John Caudill Cemetery, Sitka, Johnson Co., KY

....................+Phoebe Fitzpatrick b: June 15, 1821 in Johnson Co., KY m: January 27, 1844 in Johnson Co., KY d: February 05, 1870 in Johnson Co., KY Number of children: ? Father: John Fitzpatrick Mother: Fanny Rice Sex: Female Burial: February 1870 Caudill Fork Cemetery, Sitka, Johnson Co., KY

..................9 [83] Benjamin F. Caudill, b: September 15, 1860 in Johnson Co., KY d: September 1915 Number of children: ? Sex: Male

........................+[95] Margaret E. Caudill, b: January 10, 1859 in Johnson Co., KY m: May 03, 1878 in Johnson Co., KY Father: C. Abner Caudill, Mother: Mary Emily Justice Sex: Female

..................2nd Wife of [83] Benjamin F. Caudill, :

........................+Cynthia Ann Ward b: April 12, 1871 in Johnson Co., KY m: Abt. 1886 d: November 17, 1931 in Ashland, Boyd Co., KY Number of children: ? Sex: Female

....................10 William Henry Caudill, b: Abt. 1895 Sex: Male

..........................+Minerva Dixon b: Abt. 1897 Sex: Female

................8 Jesse "Jess" Franklin Caudill, Jr., Cordell b: January 18, 1818 in Floyd Co., KY d: October 27, 1874 in Left Fork of Beaver Creek, Floyd Co., KY Number of children: 8 Sex: Male

......................+Eleanor (Ellinder/Ellender) "Nellie" Estep b: 1815 in Floyd Co., KY m: August 06, 1834 in Pike Co., KY Number of children: 8 Father: Joel Estep, Sr. Mother: Nancy Nelson - parentage unknown; Sex: Female

..................9 [136] Matthew Caudill b: Abt. 1836 in Floyd Co., KY Number of children: 2 Sex: Male Burial: Amil Little Cemetery, Pike Co., KY

........................+[135] Elizabeth Tackett, Tackitt b: October 03, 1835 in Pike Co., KY m: April 05, 1855 in Pike Co., KY d: November 07, 1918 in Tackett, Pike Co., KY Number of children: 2 Father: William "Bucky" Tackett, Tackitt, Jr. Mother: Sarah "Sally" Caudill Sex: Female (Tackett Note: The Tacketts also married into both the author's Yonts family relations and also into the family of Elvis Presley. Elvis' great-grandmother, for example, was Martha Tackett, born 1856 in AL or MS)

....................10 [84] Abel Caudill b: 1858 in KY? Number of children: 7 Sex: Male

..........................+[137] Rosaline (Rosalyn) Hall b: Abt. 1860 in KY? m: December 26, 1877 Number of children: 4 Sex: Female (Note: Looking for ancestors)

......................11 [138] Walter Caudill b: Abt. 1878 Sex: Male

......................11 [139] Bessie Caudill b: Abt. 1882 Sex: Female

......................11 [140] Ethel Caudill b: Abt. 1887 Sex: Female

......................11 [141] Dell Caudill b: 1890 Sex: Female

....................2nd Wife of [84] Abel Caudill:

..........................+[142] Mary Francis Keel b: Abt. 1880 m: December 27, 1898 Number of children: 3 Sex: Female

......................11 [143] Martha Caudill b: December 16, 1899 Sex: Female

......................11 [144] Mendia (Mindy) Caudill b: 1901 Sex: Female

......................11 [145] Edward Doutin Caudill b: January 04, 1903 Sex: Male

....................10 [146] William Caudill b: March 1863 d: October 16, 1941 Number of children: ? Sex: Male

..........................+[147] Elizabeth Caudill b: July 1863 m: 1880 d: 1942 Number of children: ? Sex: Female

......................11 [148] Marion Caudill b: June 03, 1884 in Hartly or Jonancy, KY d: February 02,

1959 in Hartly, KY Number of children: ? Sex: Male

.............................+[149] Rhilda (Rilda) Mae Tackett b: September 28, 1888 in Jonancy, KY d: January 20, 1960 in Jonancy, KY Number of children: ? Sex: Female (Tackett Note: The Tacketts also married into both the author's Yonts family relations and also into the family of Elvis Presley. Elvis' great-grandmother, for example, was Martha Tackett, born 1856 in AL or MS)

..................9 [134] Rebecca Elizabeth Caudill b: August 19, 1837 in Boone Co., WV (or Boone Co., VA) d: January 13, 1913 in Pike Co., KY Sex: Female

........................+[133] Abel Tackett, Tackitt b: July 22, 1833 in Long Fork Creek, Pike Co., KY m: February 22, 1855 in Pike Co., KY Father: William "Bucky" Tackett, Tackitt, Jr. Mother: Sarah "Sally" Caudill Sex: Male (Tackett Note: The Tacketts also married into both the author's Yonts family relations and also into the family of Elvis Presley. Elvis' great-grandmother, for example, was Martha Tackett, born 1856 in AL or MS)

..................9 [151] Rachel Caudill b: Abt. 1839 in Floyd Co., KY d: May 28, 1910 Number of children: ? Sex: Female

........................+[150] George W. Tackett, Tackitt b: October 27, 1837 in Pike Co., KY m: September 09, 1855 in Pike Co., KY d: December 13, 1906 in Pike Co., KY Number of children: ? Father: William "Bucky" Tackett, Tackitt, Jr. Mother: Sarah "Sally" Caudill Sex: Male

.....................10 [152] Abner Tackett, Tackitt b: August 01, 1860 in Pike Co., KY Sex: Male

...........................+[153] Nancy Jane Bryant b: Abt. 1843 in Pike Co., KY Sex: Female

..................9 William Caudill b: 1841 in Republican, Floyd Co., KY d: July 1904 in Dry Creek, Floyd Co., KY Number of children: ? Sex: Male

........................+Nancy Martin b: 1842 in Floyd Co., KY m: September 16, 1859 in Floyd Co., KY d: Abt. 1906 Number of children: ? Father: Alexander (Alamander) Martin Mother: Malinda Martin Sex: Female

.....................10 Johnny Caudill b: Abt. 1860 in Floyd Co., KY? Number of children: ? Sex: Male

...........................+Hulda Isaacs b: Abt. 1860 in Floyd Co., KY? Number of children: ? Sex: Female

........................11 Hiram Caudill b: Abt. 1885 in Floyd Co., KY? Number of children: ? Sex: Male

..............................+Julia Slone b: Abt. 1885 in Floyd Co., KY? Number of children: ? Sex: Female

..................9 Matilda Caudill b: Abt. 1844 in Floyd Co., KY Sex: Female

........................+Riley Roberts b: Abt. 1838 in Floyd Co., KY m: September 18, 1859 Sex: Male

..................9 [155] Elizabeth Caudill b: 1846 Number of children: ? Sex: Female

........................+[154] Abner Tackett, Tackitt b: February 08, 1845 in Pike Co., KY m: September 30, 1860 d: May 31, 1920 Number of children: ? Father: William "Bucky" Tackett, Tackitt, Jr. Mother: Sarah "Sally" Caudill Sex: Male Burial: Caudill Cemetery, Rowan Co., KY (Tackett Note: The Tacketts also married into both the author's Yonts family relations and also into the family of Elvis Presley. Elvis' great-grandmother, for example, was Martha Tackett, born 1856 in AL or MS)

.....................10 [156] Abel Tackett b: Abt. 1875 Number of children: ? Sex: Male

...........................+[157] Roseann Caudill b: Abt. 1880 Number of children: ? Sex: Female

........................11 [158] Elijah Tackett b: Abt. 1900 Sex: Male

..................9 John Wesley Caudill b: March 15, 1847 in Floyd Co., KY d: November 23, 1923 Number of children: ? Sex: Male

........................+Celia Ann McBrayer b: April 14, 1846 in Ohio Number of children: ? Sex: Female

.....................10 George Caudill b: Abt. 1865 Number of children: ? Sex: Male

...........................+Mattie Tiller b: Abt. 1870 Number of children: ? Sex: Female

........................11 Lafe Richard Caudill b: Abt. 1900 Number of children: ? Sex: Male

..............................+Loretta Wilson b: Abt. 1905 Number of children: ? Sex: Female

..................9 Martha Caudill b: Abt. 1853 in Floyd Co., KY Number of children: ? Sex: Female

........................+William ("Bill") Johnson b: 1849 in Floyd Co., KY Number of children: ? Sex:

Male

....................10 Elisha Johnson b: 1876 Number of children: ? Sex: Male

..........................+Cindi Cook b: 1880 Number of children: ? Sex: Female

....................11 Martha Johnson b: 1898 Sex: Female

..........................+Isaac Caudill b: 1884 Sex: Male

...............8 [85] Matthew James Caudill b: March 16, 1820 in Perry/Letcher Co., KY Sex: Male

....................+Temperance Hitchcock b: 1824 in KY? m: March 1845 Sex: Female

...............2nd Wife of [85] Matthew James Caudill:

....................+Nancy Jane Williams b: 1827 in Floyd Co., KY m: April 15, 1854 in Floyd Co., KY Sex: Female

...............3rd Wife of [85] Matthew James Caudill:

....................+Elizabeth Keaton Lemaster b: Abt. 1850 m: June 04, 1887 Sex: Female

...............8 William Caudill b: November 20, 1821 in Perry Co., KY d: June 1909 in Johnson Co., KY Number of children: 12 Sex: Male Burial: June 1909 John Caudill Cemetery, Sitka, Johnson Co., KY

....................+Martha Hitchcock b: February 26, 1825 in Floyd or Johnson Co., KY m: 1842 d: April 27, 1916 in Johnson Co., KY Number of children: 12 Father: John Hitchcock Mother: Mahala Fitzpatrick Sex: Female Burial: April 1916 John Caudill Cemetery, Sitka, Johnson Co., KY

..................9 [86] Samuel Caudill b: 1842 in Letcher Co., KY d: 1911 Number of children: 12 Sex: Male

........................+Tina Quintena Christian b: January 14, 1846 in Lexington, Fayette Co. , KY m: 1864 d: Abt. 1918 in Great Bend, KS Number of children: 2 Father: Thomas S. "Tom" Christian, Jr. Mother: Mary "Polly" Amburgey Sex: Female

....................10 James Wilson Caudill b: June 15, 1865 in Johnson Co., KY. d: March 22, 1924 Sex: Male

...........................+Dulcena Hammonds b: Abt. 1870 d: in Long Beach, CA. Father: William Hammonds, Hammons Mother: Isabella Combs Sex: Female

....................10 Mary Caudill b: Abt. 1878 Sex: Female

..................2nd Wife of [86] Samuel Caudill:

........................+Lydia Margaret Picklesimmer b: 1851 in Letcher Co., KY m: 1872 d: 1916 Number of children: 10 Sex: Female

....................10 Benjamin F. Caudill b: Abt. 1872 in Johnson Co., KY. Sex: Male

...........................+Effie _____? b: Abt. 1870 in KY? Sex: Female

....................10 Addie Caudill b: September 14, 1873 in Johnson Co., KY. Sex: Female

...........................+Alfred (Cap) Stanley b: Abt. 1870 in KY? m: October 08, 1896 in Johnson Co., KY Sex: Male

....................10 [87] Winfield Caudill b: 1876 in Johnson Co., KY. Sex: Male

...........................+Dora Pennington b: Abt. 1880 in KY? Sex: Female

....................2nd Wife of [87] Winfield Caudill:

...........................+Pearl Dean b: Abt. 1876 in KY? Sex: Female

....................3rd Wife of [87] Winfield Caudill:

...........................+Savannah Clark b: Abt. 1880 Sex: Female

....................10 Minneapolis Caudill b: December 1879 in Johnson Co., KY. Sex: Female

...........................+Manford Stambaugh b: Abt. 1875 in KY? m: October 30, 1898 Sex: Male

....................10 Millard Caudill b: 1881 in Johnson Co., KY. Sex: Female

...........................+Osie Hays b: Abt. 1880 m: March 1906 Sex: Male

....................10 William Bristo Caudill b: March 21, 1882 in Magoffin Co., KY d: March 26, 1937 in Denver, CO. (train accident) Sex: Male

...........................+Ada May Stevens b: August 10, 1882 in Exline Co., IA m: March 08, 1908 in Rosevale, KS Father: Ira Stevens Mother: Mary Jane Hayes Sex: Female

....................10 Martha Caudill b: 1883 in Magoffin Co., KY Sex: Female

....................10 Mary Belle Caudill b: 1884 in Magoffin Co., KY d: 1970 Sex: Female

...................+William Thompson b: Abt. 1880 in KY? m: 1915 Sex: Male

...................10 Ethel Caudill b: 1900 in Magoffin Co., KY Sex: Female

...................10 Grace Caudill b: 1904 in Magoffin Co., KY Sex: Female

...................+Henry Bennett b: Abt. 1900 in KY? Sex: Male

...................9 Mahalah Caudill b: 1846 in Johnson Co., KY Sex: Female

...................+Thomas Salyer, Salyers b: Abt. 1846 in Johnson Co., KY Sex: Male

...................9 James Caudill, twin b: November 1847 d: in Died young Sex: Male

...................9 John Caudill, twin b: November 1847 Sex: Male

...................9 Lewis F. Caudill b: September 26, 1852 in Johnson Co., KY Sex: Male

...................+Cynthia Conley b: Abt. 1852 in Johnson Co., KY Sex: Female

...................9 Zephaniah M. Caudill b: January 28, 1856 in Rowan Co., KY Number of children: 11 Sex: Male

...................+Mary J. Bays b: May 29, 1857 in Morgan, KY Number of children: 11 Sex: Female

...................10 Leonard B. Caudill b: August 03, 1876 in Barnetts Creek, Johnson Co., KY Sex: Male

...................+Della Trimble b: Abt. 1876 in Barnetts Creek, Johnson Co., KY Sex: Female

...................10 William Alford Caudill b: November 04, 1877 in Barnetts Creek, Johnson Co., KY Sex: Male

...................10 Martha Della Caudill b: July 08, 1879 in Barnetts Creek, Johnson Co., KY Sex: Female

...................+Isaac Rice b: Abt. 1879 in Barnetts Creek, Johnson Co., KY Sex: Male

...................10 Oscar D. Caudill b: April 05, 1881 in Barnetts Creek, Johnson Co., KY Sex: Male

...................10 Zora M. Caudill b: September 14, 1882 in Barnetts Creek, Johnson Co., KY Sex: Female

...................10 Lee Roy Caudill b: October 21, 1884 in Barnetts Creek, Johnson Co., KY Sex: Male

...................+Aurora Picklesimmer b: 1888 in Barnetts Creek, Johnson Co., KY Sex: Female

...................10 Lou Verna Caudill b: February 21, 1886 in Barnetts Creek, Johnson Co., KY Sex: Female

...................10 Denny D. Caudill b: June 21, 1887 in Barnetts Creek, Johnson Co., KY Sex: Male

...................10 Virgie Marie Caudill b: August 24, 1888 in Barnetts Creek, Johnson Co., KY Sex: Female

...................+Bruce Sullivan b: Abt. 1888 in Barnetts Creek, Johnson Co., KY Sex: Male

...................10 Hattie Mabel Caudill b: July 08, 1891 in Barnetts Creek, Johnson Co., KY Sex: Female

...................+Asa Samuel Poole b: December 12, 1899 in Coshocton, Coshocton Co., OH Sex: Male

...................10 Sarah Mildred Caudill b: May 29, 1894 in Barnetts Creek, Johnson Co., KY Sex: Female

...................9 Elizabeth Jane Caudill b: October 10, 1858 in KY Sex: Female

...................+Thomas Jefferson Rice b: Abt. 1859 in KY Sex: Male

...................9 [88] Jesse W. (Wilburn?) Caudill b: February 03, 1861 in Johnson Co., KY d: July 14, 1953 in Lucasville, Scioto Co., OH Number of children: 6 Sex: Male Burial: Lucasville Cem

...................+Vergie Jenkins b: Abt. 1870 Sex: Female

...................2nd Wife of [88] Jesse W. (Wilburn?) Caudill:

...................+Hattie Zornes b: Abt. 1872 Sex: Female

...................3rd Wife of [88] Jesse W. (Wilburn?) Caudill:

...................+Martha Holsinger b: Abt. 1880 Sex: Female

...................4th Wife of [88] Jesse W. (Wilburn?) Caudill:

...................+Randi Blaire, same as Miranda Blair? ? ? b: Abt. 1890 Sex: Female

.................5th Wife of [88] Jesse W. (Wilburn?) Caudill:

......................+Miranda Blair b: August 01, 1865 in Johnson Co., KY m: Abt. 1891 d: July 05, 1930 in Lucasville, Scioto Co., OH Number of children: 6 Father: George Blair Mother: Sarah Spradlin Sex: Female Burial: Lucasville Cemetery

....................10 Nora Delphia Caudill b: March 28, 1885 in Johnson Co., KY d: November 03, 1949 in Lucasville, Ohio Sex: Female

..........................+Walter Hamilton Conley b: April 20, 1884 in Magoffin Co., KY m: July 30, 1906 in Johnson Co., KY d: November 03, 1959 in Lucasville, Ohio Sex: Male

....................10 Dora Etta Caudill b: March 28, 1887 in Johnson Co., KY d: June 24, 1975 in Lucasville, Scioto Co., OH Sex: Female

..........................+Edward Harwood b: November 12, 1893 m: April 18, 1914 in Scioto Co., OH d: April 03, 1937 in Scioto Co., OH Sex: Male

....................10 Flora Lee Caudill b: December 06, 1888 in Johnson Co., KY d: 1953 in Scioto Co., OH Sex: Female

..........................+Leonard Bradshaw b: December 03, 1891 d: August 1984 Sex: Male

....................10 Verlie Green Caudill b: May 01, 1890 in Johnson Co., KY d: December 11, 1918 in Rush Twp. Scioto Co., Ohio Sex: Male

..........................+Mabel Harwood b: April 04, 1890 d: December 01, 1958 Sex: Female

....................10 Lonnie Zelphinire Caudill b: January 06, 1892 in Johnson Co., KY d: August 24, 1972 in Circleville, OH Number of children: 2 Sex: Male Burial: Muhlenberg Twp. Cem. near Pherson, OH

..........................+Emma Faye Harwood b: February 08, 1896 in Rush Twp., Scioto Co., OH d: November 22, 1974 in Martins Ferry, OH Number of children: 2 Father: Daniel Lincoln Harwood Mother: Lucy Jane Double Sex: Female Burial: Muhlenberg Twp. Cem. near Pherson, OH

....................11 Norma J. Caudill b: 1923 Sex: Female

..........................+Dr. Charles V. Lee b: 1918 d: 2001 Sex: Male

....................11 Donald H. Caudill b: 1929 Sex: Male

..........................+Patricia A. Imbody b: 1931 Sex: Female

....................10 Cora Francis Caudill b: March 31, 1893 in Johnson Co., KY d: 1991 Sex: Female

..........................+Walter Willis Dunlap b: August 20, 1880 in Scioto Co., OH m: May 20, 1912 in Scioto Co., OH d: October 22, 1950 in Lucasville, Ohio Sex: Male

.................9 John Milton Caudill b: 1867 in Johnson Co., KY Sex: Male

.................9 [89] Albert M. Caudill b: February 12, 1867 in KY Sex: Male

......................+Mary LeMaster b: Abt. 1870 in KY? Sex: Female

.................2nd Wife of [89] Albert M. Caudill:

......................+Merridith Caudill b: October 1869 in Johnson Co., KY. Sex: Female

.................3rd Wife of [89] Albert M. Caudill:

......................+Luncia Salyer, Salyers b: 1875 in KY m: February 04, 1887 Sex: Female

.................9 Sylvester Caudill b: 1869 in Johnson Co., KY Sex: Male

.................9 [90] Merridith M. Caudill b: Abt. 1873 in KY Sex: Male

......................+Ellen Hitchcock b: Abt. 1873 in KY Sex: Female

.................2nd Wife of [90] Merridith M. Caudill:

......................+Verna _____? b: Abt. 1873 in KY Sex: Female

.................8 [91] James Calvin Caudill b: April 26, 1823 in Letcher Co., KY d: October 27, 1874 in Johnson Co., KY? Sex: Male

......................+Mary or Nancy ("Polly") Fitzpatrick b: 1826 in KY? m: June 13, 1846 in Johnson Co., KY Father: John Fitzpatrick Mother: Fanny Rice Sex: Female

.................2nd Wife of [91] James Calvin Caudill:

......................+Emeritta Castle b: Abt. 1850 m: March 05, 1878 in Johnson Co., KY Sex: Female

.................8 Reuben G. Caudill, b: May 07, 1825 in Perry/Letcher Co., KY d: 1896 in Johnson Co., KY Number of children: 13 Sex: Male

......................+Levisa (Levista) or Lousia Jane Barnett b: 1829 in Floyd Co., KY m: September

01, 1845 in Johnson Co., KY d: in Johnson Co., KY Number of children: 13 Sex: Female
...................9 Arminta Caudill b: October 14, 1846 in Johnson Co., KY Number of children: 3 Sex: Female
.........................+Daniel Boone LeMaster b: August 05, 1848 in Big Paint Creek, near Manila (AR or UT?) Number of children: 3 Sex: Male
.....................10 Cynthia E. LeMaster b: October 1872 in Johnson Co., KY Sex: Female
.............................+Proctor Lasalle LeMaster b: Abt. 1876 in Morgan Co., KY Sex: Male
.....................10 Dora Maggie LeMaster b: May 1878 in Johnson Co., KY Sex: Female
.............................+Hansford Clark LeMaster b: April 1874 in Morgan Co., KY Sex: Male
.....................10 Galen LeMaster b: November 01, 1888 in Johnson Co., KY Sex: Male
.............................+Recie Castle b: January 25, 1890 in Lawrence Co., KY Sex: Female
..................9 William T. Caudill b: Abt. 1848 Sex: Male
..................9 John W. Caudill b: Abt. 1851 Sex: Male
..................9 Lydia (Liddia) M. Caudill b: November 30, 1853 in Johnson Co., KY Number of children: 2 Sex: Female
.........................+Rufus McKenzie b: January 10, 1859 in Johnson Co., KY Number of children: 2 Sex: Male
.....................10 Callie McKenzie b: 1876 in Johnson Co., KY Sex: Female
.....................10 Elsie P. "Fred" McKenzie b: Abt. 1878 in Johnson Co., KY Sex: Male
..................9 Harrison Caudill b: November 11, 1855 Sex: Male
..................9 Martha J. Caudill b: Abt. 1857 Sex: Female
..................9 Srythia Francis Caudill b: April 26, 1860 d: August 20, 1897 Sex: Female
..................9 Matthew Caudill, b: Abt. 1862 d: May 14, 1941 in Barrnett's Creek, KY Number of children: 2 Sex: Male Burial: Hurricane Fork Cemetery, Barrnett's Creek, KY
.........................+Millie Lewis b: 1862 in Perry Co., KY d: July 13, 1945 in Volga, Johnson Co., KY Number of children: 2 Father: Samuel Lewis Mother: Mary _____? Sex: Female
.....................10 Cordia "Cordie" Caudill, b: January 02, 1886 d: March 18, 1971 in Oil Springs, KY Sex: Female Burial: Rice Cemetery, Oil Springs, KY
.............................+Harry Conley b: Abt. 1884 m: November 10, 1905 Sex: Male
.....................10 Nola Caudill, b: May 17, 1896 in Lesley Co., KY d: February 28, 1921 in Johnson Co., KY Number of children: ? Sex: Female Burial: Auxier Cemetery, Big Paint, Johnson Co., KY
.............................+Roy Salyer b: January 09, 1892 in Johnson Co., KY d: March 15, 1976 in Columbus, OH Number of children: ? Father: Abraham Lincoln Salyer Mother: Elizabeth Salyer Sex: Male Burial: New Holland Cemetery, New Holland, OH
.........................11 Willie "Bill" Salyer, b: June 05, 1912 in Cane Branch, Big Paint, Johnson Co., KY d: December 23, 1996 in Mt. Carmel Hospital, Columbus, OH Number of children: 7 Sex: Male Burial: Sunset Cemetery, West Broad Street, Galloway, OH
.............................+Christina "Christine" Blair b: March 23, 1918 in Johnson Co., KY d: June 16, 1994 in Mt. Carmel Hospital, Columbus, OH Number of children: 7 Father: Bosier Ellis Blair Mother: Myrtie Salyer Sex: Female Burial: Sunset Cemetery, West Broad Street, Galloway, OH
..................9 Rosalane Caudill b: Abt. 1864 Sex: Female
..................9 Elisa Caudill b: Abt. 1866 Sex: Female
..................9 Manerva Caudill b: 1868 Sex: Female
..................9 Benjamin F. Caudill b: 1870 d: January 20, 1937 in Columbus, OH Sex: Male
..................9 Mary R. Caudill b: Abt. 1873 Sex: Female
.............2nd Wife of [92] Stephen Caudill, :
.....................+Elizabeth Casebolt b: Abt. 1811 in KY? m: May 01, 1828 in Pike Co., KY d: Bef. 1850 in Lawrence Co., KY Number of children: 5 Father: John Casebolt Mother: Sabrina "Sabra" Estep Sex: Female
..................8 Jane Caudill b: 1834 in Letcher Co., KY Sex: Female
..................8 Rachel Caudill b: 1838 in Letcher Co., KY Sex: Female
.........................+Robert Hiram Fields b: Abt. 1840 in KY? Sex: Male

................8 Mary Caudill b: 1840 in Letcher Co., KY Sex: Female

................8 Anne "Anny" Caudill b: 1845 Sex: Female

.............7 Rachel Caudill, b: Abt. 1795 in NC? Sex: Female

...................+[363] Peter Crase, b: 1792 in Austusta Co., VA d: 1867 in Roxana, Letcher Co., KY Number of children: 13 Father: George Crase, Jr., Crace, Cress, Kress, Mother: Charity Morgan, Sex: Male

.............7 Abner Caudill, Sr., b: 1797 in SC d: Bet. 1860 - 1870 in AL Number of children: 9 Sex: Male

...................+Elender or Eleanor "Nellie" Johnson b: December 03, 1796 in KY (or NC?) m: December 03, 1814 in SC, or Floyd Co., KY d: Bet. 1879 - 1880 in KY Number of children: 9 Father: Patrick Johnson Mother: Delila Jacobs Sex: Female

................8 Abijah Caudill b: Abt. 1817 d: Bef. 1860 in Floyd Co., KY Number of children: 3 Sex: Male

......................+Elizabeth A. Sloan b: June 1822 m: April 29, 1835 in Floyd Co., KY d: Aft. 1900 in Knott Co., KY Number of children: 3 Father: Shadrack "Hall" Sloan Mother: Katherine "Katie" Reynolds Sex: Female

...................9 Preston Caudill b: Abt. 1836 Number of children: ? Sex: Male

.......................+Martha Osborne b: Abt. 1838 Number of children: ? Sex: Female

.....................10 John Wesley "Dunk" Caudill b: Abt. 1865 Number of children: ? Sex: Male

...........................+Celia Gibson b: Abt. 1867 m: September 17, 1898 in Pike Co., KY Number of children: ? Father: Burdine Gibson Mother: Melissa Collins Sex: Female

.......................11 [93] Ellen Caudill b: Abt. 1900 Sex: Female

.............................+Miles Thornsberry b: Abt. 1898 Sex: Male

.......................2nd Husband of [93] Ellen Caudill:

.............................+Elbert Slone b: Abt. 1898 Father: Jake Slone Mother: Sally Ann _____? Sex: Male

...................9 William Harvey "Harvey" Caudill b: Bet. 1839 - 1843 in Floyd Co., KY Number of children: 2 Sex: Male

.........................+Sarah "Sally" Mullins b: 1843 in KY m: Abt. 1864 in Floyd Co., KY Number of children: 2 Father: William Varner Mullins, Jr., Rev. Mother: Sarah "Sallie" Waltrip, or Walstrip Sex: Female

......................10 Eliott Caudill b: May 1865 in KY d: in KY Number of children: ? Sex: Male

...........................+Mazy (or Maisy) Cook b: November 20, 1869 in KY d: December 23, 1927 in KY Number of children: ? Father: Solomon C. Cook Mother: Ceatta or Seatta Hall Sex: Female

.......................11 Cordellia Caudill b: January 1889 in Lane Fork, Letcher Co., KY? Number of children: ? Sex: Female

............................+Mack Mullins b: October 31, 1882 in Floyd or Letcher Co., KY? d: July 1968 in Knott Co., KY? Number of children: ? Father: Alexander Mullins Mother: Polly Osborne Sex: Male

......................10 Isaac Caudill b: 1884 Sex: Male

...........................+Mary Jane Johnson b: Abt. 1885 Sex: Female

...................9 Isaac Caudill b: 1847 Number of children: ? Sex: Male

.......................+Judah (Judith) _____? b: Abt. 1850 Number of children: ? Sex: Female

.....................10 Harvey Caudill b: 1863 in Floyd Co., KY Sex: Male

................8 Sarah Caudill b: 1820 in Melvin, Floyd Co., KY d: 1925 in KY (105 years old!) Sex: Female

......................+William Harvey "Harvey" Johnson b: Abt. 1817 m: November 18, 1836 in Perry Co., KY Father: Eli Johnson Mother: Susanah Martin Sex: Male

................8 Alford (or Alfred) Caudill b: March 10, 1824 in Floyd Co., KY d: September 06, 1905 in Rowan Co., KY Sex: Male

......................+Drucella (or Druscilla) Hammonds b: Abt. 1815 m: March 05, 1840 Sex: Female

................8 Delilah Caudill b: 1827 Number of children: ? Sex: Female

......................+Owen Roberts b: Abt. 1825 Number of children: ? Father: Cornelius Roberts Mother: Nancy Stanley Sex: Male

.................9 Jacob Roberts b: April 13, 1861 Sex: Male

................8 Lucinda Caudill b: Abt. 1828 Sex: Female

......................+Isaac Little b: Abt. 1825 m: August 26, 1841 in Pike Co., KY Sex: Male

................8 Elizabeth Caudill b: Abt. 1829 Sex: Female

......................+Stephen Hammonds b: Abt. 1825 m: November 20, 1844 Sex: Male

................8 Mary Caudill b: 1832 Sex: Female

......................+James Little b: Abt. 1830 Sex: Male

................8 [94] Abner Caudill, Jr., b: 1835 d: May 21, 1886 Number of children: ? Sex: Male

......................+Naomi Johnson b: Abt. 1840 Sex: Female

................2nd Wife of [94] Abner Caudill, Jr., :

......................+Jemima Hammonds b: February 15, 1839 in Pulaski, KY? d: May 06, 1878 Number of children: ? Sex: Female

.................9 Marion Caudill, b: Abt. 1860 Number of children: ? Sex: Male

.........................+Mary Johnson b: Abt. 1865 in Wheelwright, KY Number of children: ? Sex: Female

......................10 Dowell Caudill, b: Abt. 1895 d: in Cincinnati, OH Number of children: ? Sex: Male

............................+Carrie Conn b: Abt. 1897 d: in Cincinnati, OH Number of children: ? Sex: Female

........................11 James Caudill, b: Abt. 1920 in Rowan Co., KY Number of children: ? Sex: Male

...............................+Amanda Carty b: Abt. 1920 in MaGoffin Co., KY Number of children: ? Sex: Female (Note: she descends from George "Golden Hawk" Sizemore)

................8 Jackson Caudill b: 1845 in Floyd Co., KY Sex: Male

......................+Jane Hall b: 1848 in Floyd Co., KY m: Abt. 1865 in Floyd Co., KY Father: Alfred Hall Mother: Temperance Justice Sex: Female

.............7 [220] Jane "Jenny" Caudill, b: 1799 in NC d: Abt. 1870 Number of children: 8 Sex: Female

...................+[219] Thomas Caudill, Jr., b: Abt. 1797 in SC m: December 12, 1816 in Floyd Co., KY d: 1870 Number of children: 8 Father: Thomas Aaron Caudill, Sr. Mother: Mary "Polly" Everest Sex: Male

................8 [221] Sarah Caudill b: Abt. 1816 in KY d: April 24, 1861 in Johnson Co., KY Sex: Female

......................+[222] James Fitzpatrick b: Abt. 1815 m: February 11, 1836 in Floyd Co., KY Sex: Male

...............8 [223] Isom Caudill b: 1822 in Brushy Fork, Lawrence Co., KY d: June 01, 1857 in Brushy Fork, Lawrence Co., KY Number of children: ? Sex: Male

......................+[224] Nancy Bailey b: Abt. 1825 m: April 15, 1843 in Morgan Co., KY Number of children: ? Sex: Female

.................9 [225] Mahala Caudill b: 1844 d: 1905 Sex: Female

...............8 [226] Matthew Jackson Caudill b: Abt. 1823 in Scott Co., VA Sex: Male

......................+[227] Temperance Fitzpatrick b: Abt. 1825 m: August 1842 Sex: Female

...............8 [228] James Caudill b: March 10, 1824 in Scott Co., VA d: August 25, 1895 Sex: Male

......................+[229] Angeline Bailey b: Abt. 1827 m: November 08, 1846 Sex: Female

...............8 [230] Nancy Jane Caudill b: Abt. 1826 in Scott Co., VA Sex: Female

......................+[231] John L. Blair b: Abt. 1825 m: May 04, 1854 Sex: Male

...............8 [232] C. Abner Caudill, b: Abt. 1829 in KY d: Aft. 1880 Number of children: ? Sex: Male

......................+[233] Mary Emily Justice b: Abt. 1830 in Johnson Co., KY? m: July 24, 1849 in Johnson Co., KY Number of children: ? Sex: Female

.................9 [95] Margaret E. Caudill, b: January 10, 1859 in Johnson Co., KY Sex: Female

..........................+[83] Benjamin F. Caudill, b: September 15, 1860 in Johnson Co., KY m: May 03, 1878 in Johnson Co., KY d: September 1915 Number of children: ? Father: John Caudill, Mother: Phoebe Fitzpatrick Sex: Male

................8 [234] Thomas Caudill b: Abt. 1833 Sex: Male

................8 [235] Mary J. Caudill b: Abt. 1843 Sex: Female

........................+[236] _____ Smith b: Abt. 1840 Sex: Male

............7 Mary Caudill b: July 27, 1801 in Wilkes Co., NC Number of children: 4 Sex: Female

....................+Richard Collier b: January 11, 1798 in VA or Pike Co., KY m: August 30, 1832 in Pike Co., KY d: August 30, 1871 in Millstone, Letcher Co., KY Number of children: 4 Father: Daniel Collier Mother: _____ Prather Sex: Male

................8 William D. Collier b: Abt. 1833 Number of children: 2 Sex: Male

........................+Mary Rebecca Meade b: Abt. 1840 Number of children: 2 Father: Thomas Meade Mother: Mary Polly Hall Sex: Female

....................9 [99] Mary Jane Collier b: April 29, 1855 in Letcher Co., KY d: March 17, 1939 Number of children: 11 Sex: Female Burial: March 19, 1939 Quillen Cem, Greenup Co., KY

..........................+Andrew Wright b: January 18, 1853 in Letcher Co., KY m: April 27, 1873 in Letcher Co., KY d: January 14, 1886 Murdered, Letcher Co., KY Number of children: 6 Father: Andrew Steele Mother: Susan Wright Sex: Male Burial: McRoberts Cem, Letcher Co., KY

....................10 [96] Anna Hannon Wright b: October 29, 1877 in KY? d: October 01, 1953 in Troy, OH Number of children: 9 Sex: Female Burial: October 03, 1953 Quillen Cem, Greenup Co., KY

............................+Simon Bentley Number of children: ? Sex: Male

........................11 Mary Jane Bentley b: June 18, 1906 Sex: Female

..............................+Wilder Quillen b: Abt. 1905 m: July 03, 1923 Sex: Male

....................2nd Husband of [96] Anna Hannon Wright:

............................+Albert Evans b: Abt. 1875 Number of children: 3 Sex: Male

........................11 Julius Everette Evans b: Abt. 1914 Sex: Male

............................+Cathleen _____? b: Abt. 1915 Sex: Female

........................11 William Douglas Evans b: Abt. 1916 in Letcher Co., KY d: June 09, 1970 in Kose, MI Sex: Male

..............................+Thelma Ball (Baugh?) b: Abt. 1920 Sex: Female

........................11 Elijah Denver Evans b: April 14, 1920 Sex: Male

............................+Anna B. Stevens b: Abt. 1920 Sex: Female

....................3rd Husband of [96] Anna Hannon Wright:

............................+George Washington Cook b: 1874 in KY? m: February 11, 1892 in Letcher Co., KY d: July 01, 1902 Murdered, Greenup Co., KY Number of children: 5 Father: William Cook Mother: Jane "Jennie" Adams Sex: Male Burial: July 02, 1902 Quillen Cemetery, Greenup Co., KY

........................11 Charles Cook b: 1893 Sex: Male

........................11 Andrew Thomas Cook b: June 1894 in Letcher Co., KY d: September 07, 1934 Number of children: ? Sex: Male

..............................+Elizabeth Thacker b: Abt. 1895 Number of children: ? Sex: Female

........................11 Belle Dora Cook b: February 08, 1897 in Letcher Co., KY d: November 08, 1969 in Troy Ohio Sex: Female

..............................+Everette Johnson b: Abt. 1895 Sex: Male

........................11 James "Jimmy" Lewis Cook b: March 1899 in Letcher Co., KY d: June 19, 1919 in Greenup Co., KY Sex: Male

........................11 Sherman Kirk Cook b: October 14, 1901 Sex: Male

....................10 Susan Wright b: September 18, 1878 in Letcher Co., KY d: March 15, 1903 Sex: Female Burial: Letcher Co., Ky

............................+James "Jim" Wright b: Abt. 1875 Sex: Male

....................10 [97] William Ervin Wright b: February 16, 1880 in Letcher Co., KY d: March 31, 1961 in Letcher Co., KY Number of children: 12 Sex: Male Burial: April 03, 1961 Tolliver

Cemetery, Millstone, KY

..........................+Mary M. Tolliver b: October 20, 1883 in Letcher Co., KY m: December 15, 1900 d: March 12, 1922 in Letcher Co., KY Number of children: 7 Sex: Female Burial: Tolliver Cem, Millstone Ky

......................11 William Howard Wright b: November 12, 1901 in Letcher Co., KY Sex: Male

......................11 Emma Alice Wright b: January 10, 1904 in Letcher Co., KY d: January 03, 1906 Sex: Female

......................11 Thelma Wright b: October 03, 1906 in Letcher Co., KY d: November 30, 1936 Sex: Female

..........................+Wilson Riley m: July 01, 1923 Sex: Male

......................11 Julia A. Wright b: March 21, 1908 in Letcher Co., KY Sex: Female

..........................+Mike P Elliott m: October 04, 1925 Sex: Male

......................11 Arlemia Wright b: June 15, 1911 in Letcher Co., KY d: September 22, 1911 in Letcher Co., KY Sex: Female

......................11 Lawrence Wright b: August 08, 1918 in Letcher Co., KY d: March 07, 1939 Sex: Male

......................11 Juanita Wright b: June 17, 1921 in Letcher Co., KY d: April 17, 1922 Sex: Female

....................2nd Wife of [97] William Ervin Wright:

..........................+Nannie B Johnson b: Abt. 1902 m: May 06, 1922 Number of children: 5 Father: Timothy Paul Johnson Mother: Cosby Jane Quillen Sex: Female

......................11 Warren G. Wright b: April 02, 1923 in Letcher Co., KY Sex: Male

..........................+Rachel _____? b: Abt. 1925 m: February 25, 1944 Sex: Female

......................11 Norma Lee Wright b: April 17, 1926 in Letcher Co., KY Sex: Female

......................11 Walter Ervin Wright b: August 14, 1929 in Letcher Co., KY Sex: Male

......................11 Cosby Anita Wright b: August 25, 1931 in Letcher Co., KY Sex: Female

..........................+Franklin P Stanley m: May 19, 1952 Sex: Male

......................11 [98] Paul Nelson Wright b: December 01, 1938 in Letcher Co., KY Sex: Male

..........................+Barbara Robinson Sex: Female

....................2nd Wife of [98] Paul Nelson Wright:

..........................+Helen Yates Sex: Female

..................2nd Husband of [99] Mary Jane Collier:

......................+Wilburn Ready b: March 1870 m: August 20, 1887 in Letcher Co., KY d: 1939 Number of children: 5 Father: Hezekiah Ready Sex: Male

....................10 Sarah Elizabeth Ready b: July 1888 Sex: Female

....................10 Martha A. Ready b: August 1891 Sex: Female

....................10 Christopher C. Ready b: April 1892 Sex: Male

....................10 James Monroe Ready b: May 1895 Sex: Male

....................10 Vina M. Ready b: May 1897 Sex: Female

..................9 Robert Collier b: May 15, 1856 d: May 16, 1938 in Neon, Letcher Co., KY Number of children: 4 Sex: Male Burial: Letcher Co., KY

......................+Martha Yonts b: 1862 in Letcher Co., KY m: April 30, 1878 in Letcher Co., KY d: August 08, 1928 in Leslie, AR Number of children: 4 Father: Solomon Yonts Mother: Frances "Frankie" Whitaker Sex: Female Burial: Leslie (near Little Rock) , AR (Yonts Note: like the author and all of the other Yonts individuals in this tree, this family descends from Wilhelm Jans, born in 1714 in the town of Oberalben, Rheineland-Pfalz, Germany; Wilhelm died in 1778 in Rowan Co., NC)

....................10 Sarah Frances Collier b: 1885 in Letcher Co., KY Number of children: 9 Sex: Female

..........................+John Quiller Yonts b: April 26, 1881 in Letcher Co., KY m: 1902 in Letcher Co., KY Number of children: 9 Father: Solomon "Sollie" "Saul" "Judge" Yonts Mother: Virginia "Jenny" or "Jane" Quillen Sex: Male (Yonts Note: like the author and all of the other Yonts individuals in this tree, this family descends from Wilhelm Jans, born in 1714 in the town of Oberalben, Rheineland-Pfalz, Germany; Wilhelm died in 1778 in Rowan Co., NC)

...................11 Marcus Yonts b: Abt. 1903 Sex: Male

...................11 Martha Yonts b: Abt. 1905 Sex: Female

...........................+Johnny Pass, ? b: Abt. 1900 Sex: Male

...................11 [802] William "Luther" Yonts b: March 19, 1906 in Neon, Letcher Co., KY d: July 22, 1962 in Jeffersonville, Clark Co., IN Number of children: 4 Sex: Male Burial: Walnut Ridge Cemetery, Jeffersonville, IN

...........................+[801] Lilly Collins b: February 27, 1919 in SeCo., Letcher Co., KY m: April 27, 1940 in Camp Branch, Colson, Letcher Co., KY d: March 24, 2003 in Hospital in New Albany, IN (lived in Clarksville, Clark Co., IN at time of death) Number of children: 4 Father: Watson Collins Mother: Maggie Banks Sex: Female

...................11 Quilva Yonts b: Abt. 1908 Sex: Unknown

...................11 [100] Elijah "Buster" Yonts b: November 16, 1910 d: July 17, 1957 Number of children: 5 Sex: Male Burial: 1957 Quillen or Meade Family Cemetery, Rockcastle, KY

...........................+Kathleen Williams b: Abt. 1910 d: Abt. November 16, 1985 Number of children: ? Sex: Female

...................2nd Wife of [100] Elijah "Buster" Yonts:

...........................+Ollie (Olive?) Meade b: Abt. 1910 Number of children: 4 Sex: Female

...................11 Gladys Yonts b: Abt. 1911 Sex: Female

...................11 Jenny Ellen Yonts b: Abt. 1917 Sex: Female

...................11 Vernon Yonts b: Abt. 1919 Sex: Male

...................11 Renavae Yonts b: Abt. 1921 d: Abt. 1923 Sex: Female

................10 Solomon Daniel "Sod" Collier b: Abt. 1887 Sex: Male

................10 Amanda "Mandy" Elizabeth Collier b: September 08, 1888 in Baker, KY d: June 20, 1953 in Fleming Hospital, Jenkins, KY Number of children: 3 Sex: Female

........................+Holly Powers Nickols Yonts, Yontz b: August 15, 1878 in Baker, KY m: November 14, 1904 in Letcher Co., KY d: December 21, 1948 in Johnson City, TN Number of children: 3 Father: Solomon "Sollie" "Saul" "Judge" Yonts Mother: Virginia "Jenny" or "Jane" Quillen Sex: Male Burial: Wright and Collier Cemetery, Little Creek, KY (Yonts Note: like the author and all of the other Yonts individuals in this tree, this family descends from Wilhelm Jans, born in 1714 in the town of Oberalben, Rheineland-Pfalz, Germany; Wilhelm died in 1778 in Rowan Co., NC)

...................11 [101] Leutillis "Ted" Franklin Yonts b: November 19, 1905 in Hemphill, KY d: December 22, 1977 in Whitesburg, KY Number of children: 3 Sex: Male

...........................+Gladys _____? b: Abt. 1905 m: Abt. 1929 Number of children: ? Sex: Female

...................2nd Wife of [101] Leutillis "Ted" Franklin Yonts:

...........................+Hazel Adams b: Abt. 1905 m: November 27, 1935 Number of children: 2 Sex: Female

...................11 Leona Yonts, Yontz b: December 13, 1924 in McRoberts, KY d: September 11, 1986 in Norton, VA Number of children: ? Sex: Female Burial: September 14, 1986 Tempel Hill Cemetery, Castlewood, VA

...........................+Chester Smallwood b: June 02, 1920 in Pike Co., KY m: October 17, 1942 in Letcher Co., KY Number of children: ? Father: James Smallwood Mother: Margie Elkins Sex: Male

...................11 Willie Opal Yonts b: April 16, 1927 d: November 19, 1957 Number of children: ? Sex: Female

...........................+Clifford Bush b: Abt. 1925 Number of children: ? Sex: Male

................10 Henderson Nicholl Collier b: Abt. 1900 Number of children: ? Sex: Male

...........................+Ella Alafair Bentley b: Abt. 1900 Number of children: ? Father: Moses "Mosie" Bentley Mother: Margaret White Sex: Female

...................11 Gladys Collier b: Abt. 1925 Number of children: ? Sex: Female

...........................+_____ Skeens b: Abt. 1925 Number of children: ? Sex: Male

.................8 [103] Stephen Collier b: September 01, 1834 d: February 27, 1907 Number of children: ? Sex: Male

......................+_____ Roarke b: Abt. 1835 Number of children: ? Sex: Female

..................9 [102] Richard Collier b: 1857 Number of children: ? Sex: Male

.........................+Vicey Yonts b: Abt. 1865 Sex: Female (Note: Looking for her ancestors; is she the same as Vicey E. (Louvicy Emeline?) Yonts, born 1879?)

..................2nd Wife of [102] Richard Collier:

.........................+Mary Bell Cook b: September 02, 1853 m: April 12, 1878 d: February 01, 1935 Number of children: ? Father: Anderson Cook Mother: Drucilla Huffman Sex: Female

......................10 Arminda Collier b: August 16, 1905 d: May 24, 1973 Number of children: ? Sex: Female

...........................+Elijah Honeycutt b: February 01, 1902 m: November 29, 1923 d: April 05, 1945 Number of children: ? Father: Robert Honeycutt Mother: _____ Reynolds Sex: Male

.........................11 Bertha Gene Honeycutt b: February 08, 1935 d: April 10, 1998 Number of children: ? Sex: Female

..............................+James Oscar Proffitt, Profit b: November 20, 1919 d: March 30, 1965 Number of children: ? Father: George Washington Proffitt, Profit Mother: _____ Ritchie Sex: Male

.................2nd Wife of [103] Stephen Collier:

......................+_____ Meade b: Abt. 1840 Sex: Female

................8 Samuel Collier b: Abt. 1838 Sex: Male

................8 Sally Collier b: Abt. 1839 Sex: Female

.............7 [104] Matthew Caudill, Jr., b: Bet. 1801 - 1811 in Wilkes Co., NC Number of children: 9 Sex: Male

..................+[105] Terry Caudill, b: Abt. 1812 in KY m: April 16, 1829 in Perry/Letcher Co., KY Number of children: 9 Father: Henry Caudill Mother: Phoebe Jane Strailor Sex: Female

................8 [106] Henry M. "Dickie Henry" Caudill b: 1830 Sex: Male

................8 [107] Phoebe Caudill b: 1832 Sex: Female

......................+[108] Jeremiah Dixon b: 1827 Sex: Male

................8 [109] Elizabeth "Betsy" Caudill b: December 25, 1835 Sex: Female

................8 [110] Sarah Caudill b: 1844 Sex: Female

......................+[111] Erasmus Bedwell b: Abt. 1840 Sex: Male

................8 [112] Susan Caudill b: 1845 Sex: Female

................8 [113] Rebecca Caudill b: 1846 Number of children: ? Sex: Female

......................+[114] Benjamin Caudill b: 1842 in Letcher Co., KY m: October 28, 1867 in Letcher Co., KY Number of children: ? Sex: Male (Note: Looking for his ancestors)

..................9 [115] Hiram Caudill b: Abt. 1870 in Letcher Co., KY Sex: Male

................8 [116] William Caudill b: January 1848 Number of children: ? Sex: Male

......................+[117] Sarah Sturgill b: Abt. 1845 Number of children: ? Sex: Female

..................9 [118] George Washington Caudill, Sr. b: Abt. 1870 Number of children: ? Sex: Male

.........................+[119] Nannie Belle Stidham b: Abt. 1875 Number of children: ? Sex: Female

......................10 [120] Emmett H. Caudill b: Abt. 1895 Number of children: ? Sex: Male

...........................+[121] Rena Vae Maggard b: Abt. 1900 Number of children: ? Sex: Female (Note: Looking for her ancestors)

......................11 Ned Caudill b: Abt. 1925 Number of children: ? Sex: Male

.............................+Patricia Elizabeth Pritchard b: Abt. 1927 Number of children: ? Sex: Female

................8 [122] Nancy Ann Caudill, b: August 06, 1850 d: 1904 Number of children: ? Sex: Female

......................+[123] Andrew Jackson Crase, b: 1847 d: 1938 Number of children: ? Father: Peter Crase, Mother: Rebecca Christian Sex: Male

..................9 [124] Henry Peter Crase, b: 1886 d: 1981 Sex: Male

................8 [125] Benjamin Caudill b: 1851 Sex: Male

.............7 Samuel Caudill, b: September 24, 1804 in Wilkes Co., NC d: August 13, 1883 in Rowan

Co., KY Number of children: 11 Sex: Male Burial: Family farm, or Blair's Mill Cemetery, in Rowan Co., KY

.................+Sarah Maggard b: November 08, 1809 in KY m: March 30, 1825 in Pike Co., KY d: June 18, 1898 Number of children: 11 Father: Samuel Maggard, Sr. Mother: Rebecca Robertson Sex: Female Burial: Family farm, or Blair's Mill Cemetery, in Rowan Co., KY

...............8 Rebecca Caudill b: August 14, 1827 in Letcher Co., KY Sex: Female

...............8 Henry Clay Caudill b: December 09, 1828 in Letcher Co., KY d: January 07, 1882 in Rowan Co., KY Sex: Male

.....................+Elizabeth Short b: October 17, 1830 in Wise Co., VA m: November 09, 1848 in Letcher Co., KY d: March 22, 1910 Sex: Female

...............8 David Jesse Caudill, Sr. b: February 15, 1831 in Perry Co., KY d: February 02, 1872 in Dry Creek, Rowan Co., KY Number of children: 12 Sex: Male

.....................+Roseanna Christian b: June 30, 1837 in Scott Co., VA m: January 12, 1854 in Letcher Co., KY d: March 27, 1894 in Dry Creek, Rowan Co., KY Number of children: 12 Father: Thomas S. "Tom" Christian, Jr. Mother: Mary "Polly" Amburgey Sex: Female

.................9 Henry Clay Caudill b: November 21, 1854 in Rowan Co., KY? d: April 20, 1928 in Rowan Co., KY Number of children: 6 Sex: Male Burial: Caudill Cemetery, Morehead, KY

.......................+Elizabeth Deboard b: June 30, 1854 in Morgan Co., KY m: February 24, 1881 in Morgan Co., KY d: December 03, 1926 in Rowan Co., KY Number of children: 6 Father: Sampson Deboard Mother: Nancy Davis Sex: Female Burial: Caudill Cemetery, Morehead, KY

....................10 [126] Stephen Wilson "Steve" Caudill b: July 25, 1882 in Rowan Co., KY d: February 02, 1942 in Rowan Co., KY Number of children: 11 Sex: Male Burial: Stewart Cemetery, Rowan Co., KY

..........................+Sylvania Campbell b: June 16, 1882 d: March 11, 1913 in Rowan Co., KY Number of children: 5 Sex: Female Burial: Stewart Cemetery, Rowan Co., KY

.....................11 Sanford Caudill b: 1901 d: 1903 Sex: Male

.....................11 Jordan Caudill b: November 11, 1903 Sex: Male

.....................11 Sheridan Caudill b: January 17, 1906 in Rowan Co., KY? d: November 12, 1992 in Redding , Shasta Co., CA Number of children: 2 Sex: Male

...........................+Nellie Blanche Evans b: November 19, 1908 in Tollesboro, Lewis Co., KY m: April 16, 1927 in Rowan Co., KY d: June 15, 1994 in Redding , Shasta Co., CA Number of children: 2 Father: Claude/Cloid Evans Mother: Bertha Lyons Sex: Female

.....................11 Elda Caudill b: February 12, 1908 Sex: Female

.....................11 Dosha Caudill b: March 11, 1911 Sex: Female

....................2nd Wife of [126] Stephen Wilson "Steve" Caudill:

..........................+Birchie Patton b: Abt. 1885 m: Abt. 1915 Number of children: 6 Sex: Female

.....................11 Winfield Chester Caudill, Rev. b: October 24, 1916 in Rowan Co., KY d: June 03, 1974 in Durham, NC Sex: Male

..........................+Nola Stamper b: Abt. 1915 in Rowan Co., KY m: January 30, 1937 in Morehead, Rowan Co., KY Sex: Female

.....................11 James Caudill b: October 24, 1916 Sex: Male

.....................11 Stephen Elmo Caudill b: January 12, 1920 in Rowan Co., KY d: July 18, 1927 in Rowan Co., KY Sex: Male

.....................11 Clay Patrick Caudill b: June 20, 1929 in Rowan Co., KY d: July 01, 1989 in Rowan Co., KY Sex: Male

.....................11 Elizabeth Louise Caudill b: April 24, 1935 Sex: Female

.....................11 Charles Dixon Caudill b: January 26, 1938 Sex: Male

....................10 David Simpson Caudill b: October 26, 1883 in Morgan Co., KY d: January 27, 1976 in Worthington, Greenup Co., KY Sex: Male

..........................+Polly Ann King b: August 14, 1883 d: March 10, 1950 Sex: Female

....................10 John Beauford Caudill b: August 06, 1887 in Morgan Co., KY d: December 22, 1957 Sex: Male

..........................+Ida McBrayer b: July 13, 1895 in Rowan Co., KY m: March 19, 1913 in Wagoner, Rowan Co., KY Sex: Female

....................10 [127] Maude Prudence "Prudie" Caudill b: May 11, 1890 Sex: Female

..........................+Harlan Nickels b: Abt. 1888 m: January 20, 1915 in Rowan Co., KY Sex: Male

....................2nd Husband of [127] Maude Prudence "Prudie" Caudill:

..........................+William "Bill" Geary b: Abt. 1888 m: Abt. 1920 Sex: Male (Note: he owned the General Store in Morehead, Rowan Co., KY)

....................10 Rosa "Rosie" Kathryn Caudill b: June 22, 1892 d: March 27, 1971 Sex: Female

..........................+John Messer b: January 28, 1894 in Rowan Co., KY m: September 23, 1916 in Rowan Co., KY d: February 19, 1973 Sex: Male

....................10 Nancy Ann "Nannie" Caudill b: June 30, 1895 Sex: Female

..........................+John Hargis b: Abt. 1893 Sex: Male

.................9 Mary "Polly" Caudill b: February 23, 1856 in Dry Creek, Rowan Co., KY Sex: Female

.......................+James Franklin b: Abt. 1855 Sex: Male

.................9 Sarah Caudill b: August 08, 1857 in Elliott Co., KY d: June 10, 1930 Sex: Female

.......................+Charles Mabry b: April 11, 1858 in Elliott Co., KY d: August 10, 1926 in Rowan Co., KY Sex: Male

.................9 John D. Caudill b: January 18, 1860 Sex: Male

........................+Elizabeth "Lizzie" Deboard b: Abt. 1862 m: December 20, 1883 Sex: Female

.................9 Robert Caudill b: July 18, 1861 Sex: Male

.................9 Anna Caudill b: January 10, 1863 Sex: Female

.......................+William Royce b: Abt. 1860 Sex: Male

.................9 Elizabeth Caudill b: September 08, 1864 Sex: Female

.......................+Alvin Royce b: Abt. 1862 Sex: Male

.................9 Thomas H. Caudill b: June 05, 1866 Sex: Male

.................9 Lydia Margaret Caudill b: August 31, 1868 d: April 20, 1924 in White Lake, WI Sex: Female

.......................+James Anderson Mabry b: December 26, 1865 in Ordinary, Elliott Co., KY m: October 22, 1885 in Dry Creek, Rowan Co., KY d: April 20, 1924 Sex: Male

.................9 Nancy Caudill b: April 14, 1870 d: November 26, 1936 Sex: Female

.......................+James Wesley Williams b: Abt. 1868 m: November 25, 1886 in Rowan Co., KY Sex: Male

.................9 [128] Nancy Elizabeth "Bettie" Caudill b: April 14, 1870 Number of children: ? Sex: Female

.......................+James Wesley Williams b: Abt. 1860 m: Abt. 1885 Number of children: ? Sex: Male

....................10 Nora Williams b: April 27, 1891 in Stacy Fork, Morgan Co. KY d: January 29, 1967 in OH Number of children: ? Sex: Female

..........................+George Washington Bentley b: April 08, 1882 in Stacy Fork, Morgan Co. KY d: January 29, 1967 in Jeffersonville, OH Number of children: ? Father: John T. Bentley Mother: Sarah Turner Sex: Male

.......................11 William S. Bentley b: January 21, 1915 in Stacy Fork, Morgan Co. KY d: August 08, 1995 in Howell, MI Number of children: ? Sex: Male

..........................+Mary Ellen Wood b: Abt. 1925 Number of children: ? Sex: Female

.................2nd Husband of [128] Nancy Elizabeth "Bettie" Caudill:

.......................+Will Bentley b: Abt. 1862 m: Abt. 1895 Father: John T. Bentley Mother: Sarah Turner Sex: Male

.................9 David Caudill, Jr. b: January 17, 1872 Sex: Male

...............8 [129] John M. Caudill b: March 23, 1833 in Louisa, Lawrence Co., VA d: April 03, 1895 in Rowan Co., KY Number of children: ? Sex: Male

......................+Jane Boggs b: June 10, 1833 in Letcher Co., KY m: July 10, 1851 Number of children: ? Sex: Female

..................9 [131] Abel E. Caudill, b: November 04, 1857 in Letcher Co., KY d: July 17, 1937 Sex: Male

........................+[130] Lydia J. Caudill, b: November 12, 1874 in Rowan Co., KY d: 1936 Father: Abel Caudill, Mother: Mary Ann Hall Sex: Female Burial: Caudill Cemetery, Morehead, Rowan Co., KY

................2nd Wife of [129] John M. Caudill:

......................+Fannie Pennington b: September 13, 1841 in Lawrence Co., KY m: January 18, 1866 d: February 14, 1930 Sex: Female

................8 Mary A. "Polly" Caudill b: Abt. 1835 Sex: Female

......................+Benjamin Caudill b: January 20, 1830 in Perry Co., KY m: January 02, 1851 in Letcher Co., KY Sex: Male (Note: Looking for ancestors)

................8 Margaret Caudill b: Abt. 1837 Sex: Female

......................+Daniel P. Short b: Abt. 1835 in Russell Co., KY m: September 23, 1854 in Letcher Co., KY Sex: Male

................8 Abner Caudill b: Abt. 1839 d: Abt. 1860 Sex: Male

......................+Leah Short b: Abt. 1840 in Russell Co., KY Sex: Female

................8 Susannah Caudill b: March 07, 1841 d: December 04, 1899 in Big Branch, Troublesome Creek, Knott Co., KY Sex: Female

......................+Joseph E. (Enoch?) Cornett b: March 03, 1836 m: August 1858 in Perry Co., KY d: August 01, 1917 in Big Branch, Troublesome Creek, Knott Co., KY Sex: Male (Note: Looking for his ancestors)

................8 Abel Caudill, b: February 04, 1843 in Letcher Co., KY d: July 01, 1925 Number of children: 15 Sex: Male Burial: Caudill Cemetery, Morehead, Rowan Co., KY

......................+Mary Ann Hall b: March 30, 1849 in Rowan Co., KY m: November 15, 1866 d: November 28, 1927 Number of children: 15 Father: George M. Hall Mother: Susan Downing Sex: Female Burial: Caudill Cemetery, Morehead, Rowan Co., KY

..................9 Robert E. Caudill, twin b: November 14, 1867 d: 1930 Sex: Male Burial: Caudill Cemetery, Morehead, Rowan Co., KY

........................+Mahala Wells b: Abt. 1870 Sex: Female

..................9 John T. Caudill, twin b: November 14, 1867 d: 1920 Sex: Male Burial: Caudill Cemetery, Morehead, Rowan Co., KY

........................+Kalah Wells b: Abt. 1872 Sex: Female

..................9 Amanda Caudill b: April 02, 1869 d: 1929 Sex: Female Burial: Caudill Cemetery, Morehead, Rowan Co., KY

........................+Sanford Debord b: Abt. 1867 Sex: Male

..................9 Samuel M. Caudill, twin b: December 29, 1870 d: 1949 Sex: Male Burial: Caudill Cemetery, Morehead, Rowan Co., KY

........................+Lucinda Blair b: Abt. 1872 Sex: Female

..................9 Sarah Caudill, twin b: December 29, 1870 d: 1949 Sex: Female Burial: Caudill Cemetery, Morehead, Rowan Co., KY

........................+Alexander "Alex" Skaggs, Scaggs b: Abt. 1868 Sex: Male (Note: looking for his ancestors; Alex must certainly be from the huge Skaggs family out of eastern KY, to which the country singer Ricky Skaggs belongs. Ricky was born July 18, 1954, in Brushy Creek, near Cordell, in Lawrence Co., KY)

..................9 Emma Caudill b: August 16, 1873 d: 1922 Sex: Female Burial: Caudill Cemetery, Morehead, Rowan Co., KY

......................+J. Nelson Caudill b: Abt. 1870 Sex: Male (Note: looking for ancestors)

..................9 [130] Lydia J. Caudill, b: November 12, 1874 in Rowan Co., KY d: 1936 Sex: Female Burial: Caudill Cemetery, Morehead, Rowan Co., KY

......................+[131] Abel E. Caudill, b: November 04, 1857 in Letcher Co., KY d: July 17,

1937 Father: John M. Caudill Mother: Jane Boggs Sex: Male

.................9 George W. Caudill b: November 12, 1876 d: 1959 Sex: Male Burial: Caudill Cemetery, Morehead, Rowan Co., KY (Note: he never married)

.................9 William C. Caudill b: June 15, 1878 d: 1941 Sex: Male Burial: Caudill Cemetery, Morehead, Rowan Co., KY

........................+Mary Arnold b: Abt. 1880 Sex: Female

.................9 Daniel B. Caudill b: October 02, 1879 d: 1967 Sex: Male Burial: Caudill Cemetery, Morehead, Rowan Co., KY

........................+Etta Proctor b: Abt. 1881 Sex: Female

.................9 Joseph Caudill b: April 29, 1881 d: 1967 Sex: Male Burial: Caudill Cemetery, Morehead, Rowan Co., KY

........................+Lillie Williams b: Abt. 1883 Sex: Female

.................9 David C. Caudill b: April 28, 1883 d: 1961 Sex: Male Burial: Caudill Cemetery, Morehead, Rowan Co., KY

........................+Eva Cooper b: Abt. 1885 Sex: Female

.................9 [132] Cornelius P. Caudill b: January 14, 1885 d: 1968 Sex: Male Burial: Caudill Cemetery, Morehead, Rowan Co., KY

........................+Myrtle Whitaker b: Abt. 1887 m: Abt. 1907 Sex: Female

.................2nd Wife of [132] Cornelius P. Caudill:

........................+Rebecca Thompson b: Abt. 1895 m: Abt. 1920 Sex: Female

.................9 Hannah Mae Caudill b: July 05, 1886 d: 1981 Sex: Female Burial: Caudill Cemetery, Morehead, Rowan Co., KY

........................+Isaac Blair b: Abt. 1884 Sex: Male

.................9 Watson H. Caudill b: April 07, 1889 d: 1961 Sex: Male Burial: Caudill Cemetery, Morehead, Rowan Co., KY

........................+Esther White b: Abt. 1891 Sex: Female

..............8 Samuel Caudill b: September 18, 1844 in Letcher Co., KY d: June 17, 1927 Sex: Male

.....................+Cynthia Hall b: Abt. 1850 in Rowan Co., KY d: October 11, 1911 Sex: Female

...............8 James M. Caudill b: January 01, 1850 in Letcher Co., KY d: September 19, 1895 Sex: Male

.....................+Rebecca McClain b: October 24, 1852 in Rowan Co., KY m: Abt. 1869 d: January 30, 1904 Father: _____ McClain Mother: _____ _____? Sex: Female

.............7 Richard Isom Caudill b: 1810 in Wilkes Co., NC Sex: Male

.................+Nancy Phillips b: Abt. 1810 in North Carolina? m: February 13, 1843 Sex: Female

.............7 Nancy Caudill b: Abt. 1811 in Georgia Number of children: 4 Sex: Female

.................+James Roberts b: 1776 in SC d: in Letcher/Perry Co., KY? Number of children: 4 Sex: Male (Note: Looking for his ancestors)

...............8 William Roberts b: 1842 Sex: Male

...............8 Obediah Roberts b: 1848 Sex: Male

...............8 Betty Roberts b: 1860 Sex: Female

...............8 Elijah Roberts b: 1862 Sex: Male

.............7 Sarah "Sally" Caudill b: July 05, 1813 in Perry Co., KY d: February 11, 1898 in Tackett, Pike Co., KY Number of children: 14 Sex: Female

.................+William "Bucky" Tackett, Tackitt, Jr. b: March 04, 1809 in Cumberland River, Knox Co., KY, or Harlan, KY m: March 02, 1828 in Pike Co., KY d: May 27, 1894 in Virgie (Pike Co.,), KY Number of children: 14 Father: William "Preacher Billy" Tackett, Tackitt, Sr. Mother: Amy Anna Johnson Sex: Male Burial: Emil Little Cm, Pike Co., KY (Tackett Note: The Tacketts also married into both the author's Yonts family relations and also into the family of Elvis Presley. Elvis' great-grandmother, for example, was Martha Tackett, born 1856 in AL or MS)

...............8 James Tackett b: Abt. 1820 Number of children: 11 Sex: Male

.....................+Delilah Osborne b: Abt. 1823 Number of children: 11 Father: Sherwood Osborne Mother: Louisa (Levisa) Collier Sex: Female

.................9 Sarah (Sally) Tackett b: Abt. 1842 Sex: Female

.......................+Kindrick Johnson b: Abt. 1840 Sex: Male

.................9 Sherwood Tackett b: Abt. 1844 Number of children: 2 Sex: Male

.......................+Sally Tackett b: Abt. 1845 Number of children: 2 Sex: Female

....................10 Alma Tackett Sex: Female

....................10 John Tackett Sex: Male

.................9 Hulda Tackett b: Abt. 1846 Sex: Female

.......................+David Johnson Sex: Male

.................9 Rhoda Tackett b: Abt. 1848 Number of children: 5 Sex: Female

.......................+King Tackett Number of children: 5 Sex: Male

....................10 Anderson Tackett Sex: Male

....................10 Ulysses Tackett Sex: Male

....................10 Ellison Tackett Sex: Male

....................10 Cordelia Tackett Sex: Female

....................10 Virgie Tackett Sex: Female

.................9 Rebecca Tackett b: Abt. 1850 Sex: Female

.......................+George W. Tackett b: Abt. 1845 Father: Solomon Tackett Mother: Merba Hall Sex: Male

.................9 Hiram Tackett b: Abt. 1852 Sex: Male

.......................+Martha Jane Johnson Sex: Female

.................9 William Henry ("Will") Tackett b: Abt. 1855 Sex: Male

.......................+Mahala Tackett Sex: Female

.................9 Abel "Scape" Tackett b: Abt. 1858 Sex: Male

.......................+Jane Worrix b: Abt. 1860 Sex: Female

.................9 A. H. "Hawk" Tackett b: Abt. 1860 Sex: Male

.......................+Sarah Ann "Pud" Johnson Sex: Female

.................9 Siltany Tackett b: Abt. 1862 Sex: Female

.......................+Martin Johnson Sex: Male

.................9 Greenville Tackett b: Abt. 1864 Sex: Male

.......................+Nancy Akers b: Abt. 1865 Sex: Female

...............8 [133] Abel Tackett, Tackitt b: July 22, 1833 in Long Fork Creek, Pike Co., KY Sex: Male

.......................+[134] Rebecca Elizabeth Caudill b: August 19, 1837 in Boone Co., WV (or Boone Co., VA) m: February 22, 1855 in Pike Co., KY d: January 13, 1913 in Pike Co., KY Father: Jesse "Jess" Franklin Caudill, Jr., Cordell Mother: Eleanor (Ellinder/Ellender) "Nellie" Estep Sex: Female

...............8 [135] Elizabeth Tackett, Tackitt b: October 03, 1835 in Pike Co., KY d: November 07, 1918 in Tackett, Pike Co., KY Number of children: 2 Sex: Female

.......................+[136] Matthew Caudill b: Abt. 1836 in Floyd Co., KY m: April 05, 1855 in Pike Co., KY Number of children: 2 Father: Jesse "Jess" Franklin Caudill, Jr., Cordell Mother: Eleanor (Ellinder/Ellender) "Nellie" Estep Sex: Male Burial: Amil Little Cemetery, Pike Co., KY

.................9 [84] Abel Caudill b: 1858 in KY? Number of children: 7 Sex: Male

.......................+[137] Rosaline (Rosalyn) Hall b: Abt. 1860 in KY? m: December 26, 1877 Number of children: 4 Sex: Female (Note: Looking for ancestors)

....................10 [138] Walter Caudill b: Abt. 1878 Sex: Male

....................10 [139] Bessie Caudill b: Abt. 1882 Sex: Female

....................10 [140] Ethel Caudill b: Abt. 1887 Sex: Female

....................10 [141] Dell Caudill b: 1890 Sex: Female

.................2nd Wife of [84] Abel Caudill:

.......................+[142] Mary Francis Keel b: Abt. 1880 m: December 27, 1898 Number of children: 3 Sex: Female

....................10 [143] Martha Caudill b: December 16, 1899 Sex: Female

....................10 [144] Mendia (Mindy) Caudill b: 1901 Sex: Female

......................10 [145] Edward Doutin Caudill b: January 04, 1903 Sex: Male

...................9 [146] William Caudill b: March 1863 d: October 16, 1941 Number of children: ? Sex: Male

.........................+[147] Elizabeth Caudill b: July 1863 m: 1880 d: 1942 Number of children: ? Sex: Female

......................10 [148] Marion Caudill b: June 03, 1884 in Hartly or Jonancy, KY d: February 02, 1959 in Hartly, KY Number of children: ? Sex: Male

............................+[149] Rhilda (Rilda) Mae Tackett b: September 28, 1888 in Jonancy, KY d: January 20, 1960 in Jonancy, KY Number of children: ? Sex: Female

........................11 Melissa Dearl Caudill b: October 14, 1930 in Jonancy, KY d: December 30, 1998 in Pikeville, KY Number of children: 2 Sex: Female

.............................+John Smith Anderson b: August 06, 1929 m: July 21, 1951 d: December 17, 1998 Number of children: 2 Father: Ervin Anderson Mother: Hattie Mae Mullins Sex: Male

.................8 [150] George W. Tackett, Tackitt b: October 27, 1837 in Pike Co., KY d: December 13, 1906 in Pike Co., KY Number of children: ? Sex: Male

......................+[151] Rachel Caudill b: Abt. 1839 in Floyd Co., KY m: September 09, 1855 in Pike Co., KY d: May 28, 1910 Number of children: ? Father: Jesse "Jess" Franklin Caudill, Jr., Cordell Mother: Eleanor (Ellinder/Ellender) "Nellie" Estep Sex: Female

...................9 [152] Abner Tackett, Tackitt b: August 01, 1860 in Pike Co., KY Sex: Male

.........................+[153] Nancy Jane Bryant b: Abt. 1843 in Pike Co., KY Sex: Female

.................8 Matthew Tackett, Tackitt b: March 14, 1840 in Pike Co., KY d: 1939 in Pike Co., KY Number of children: ? Sex: Male

......................+Lucinda Newsome, or Johnson b: Abt. 1840 Number of children: ? Father: Henry Newsome, Newsom Mother: Unisiah "Unis" Hall Sex: Female

...................9 Eveline Tackett b: 1882 in Floyd, KY Number of children: 9 Sex: Female

.........................+William Newsome b: June 22, 1882 d: November 04, 1969 Number of children: 11 Father: Elias Newsome, ? ? Sex: Male

......................10 Cora Lee Newsome b: May 07, 1907 d: June 10, 1992 Number of children: ? Sex: Female

............................+Archie Ray b: Abt. 1900 Number of children: ? Father: John Farmer Mother: Nancy Ray, Rhea Sex: Male

........................11 Emogene Ray, Rhea b: January 29, 1926 in Island Creek, Pikeville Co., KY Number of children: ? Sex: Female

.............................+Lestin Fields b: November 29, 1924 in Island Creek, Pikeville Co., KY Number of children: ? Father: Candy Fields Mother: Lydia Akers Sex: Male

......................10 Evan Newsome b: Abt. 1910 Sex: Male

......................10 Elizabeth "Lizzie" Newsome b: Abt. 1912 Sex: Female

......................10 Jane Newsome b: Abt. 1914 Sex: Female

......................10 Cindy Newsome b: Abt. 1916 Sex: Female

......................10 Matthew Newsome b: Abt. 1918 Sex: Male

......................10 Ida Newsome b: Abt. 1920 Sex: Female

......................10 Cordelia Newsome b: Abt. 1922 Sex: Female

......................10 Barbara Newsome b: Abt. 1925 Sex: Female

.................8 [154] Abner Tackett, Tackitt b: February 08, 1845 in Pike Co., KY d: May 31, 1920 Number of children: ? Sex: Male Burial: Caudill Cemetery, Rowan Co., KY

......................+[155] Elizabeth Caudill b: 1846 m: September 30, 1860 Number of children: ? Father: Jesse "Jess" Franklin Caudill, Jr., Cordell Mother: Eleanor (Ellinder/Ellender) "Nellie" Estep Sex: Female

...................9 [156] Abel Tackett b: Abt. 1875 Number of children: ? Sex: Male

.........................+[157] Roseann Caudill b: Abt. 1880 Number of children: ? Sex: Female

......................10 [158] Elijah Tackett b: Abt. 1900 Sex: Male

.................8 Rebecca Tackett b: Abt. 1847 Sex: Female

................8 Enoch Tackett b: Abt. 1850 Sex: Male

................8 Amy Tackett b: Abt. 1852 Sex: Female

................8 Zilphia Tackett b: Abt. 1854 Sex: Female

................8 Mary Tackett b: Abt. 1856 Sex: Female

................8 Enon Tackett b: Abt. 1857 Sex: Female

................8 Patty Tackett b: Abt. 1859 Number of children: ? Sex: Female

....................+Bradley Elswick Number of children: ? Sex: Male

..................9 Will Elswick Sex: Male

................8 Enos Tackett b: Abt. 1860 Number of children: ? Sex: Male

....................+Mary Jane Johnson Number of children: ? Sex: Female

..................9 Maryland Tackett Sex: Female

............7 Elizabeth Caudill b: 1816 in Wilkes Co., NC, or Lunenburg Co., VA Sex: Female

..................+Sylvester Hampton, Hampston b: December 20, 1819 in Camp Branch, Floyd Co., KY m: November 28, 1844 in Letcher Co., KY d: January 27, 1903 in Letcher Co., KY Sex: Male

............7 Abel Caudill b: 1817 in Wilkes Co., NC d: 1898 Number of children: 4 Sex: Male

..................+Mary Ann Polly Crase, Crace b: Abt. 1826 m: 1842 in Letcher Co., KY Number of children: 4 Sex: Female (Note: Looking for her ancestors)

................8 Pleasant Caudill b: Abt. 1844 Sex: Male

....................+Kate Ellen Wiley b: Abt. 1850 m: Abt. 1868 in Johnson Co., KY Father: William Wiley Mother: Nancy Alalena Tackett Sex: Female

................8 Samuel Caudill b: February 09, 1848 Number of children: ? Sex: Male

....................+Mary Jane Whitt b: March 08, 1847 m: in Johns Creek, Pike Co., KY Number of children: ? Sex: Female

..................9 Walter Clay Caudill b: April 12, 1887 in McGoffin Co., KY d: September 1977 in Ashland, Boyd Co., KY Number of children: ? Sex: Male Burial: Social Security Number: 402-05-1077

........................+Grace Reffitt b: March 16, 1889 in Boyd Co., KY? d: August 31, 1966 in Boyd Co., KY? Number of children: ? Sex: Female

....................10 Dora Jane Caudill b: July 08, 1911 in Boyd Co., KY d: June 22, 1973 Number of children: ? Sex: Female Burial: Bellefonte Memorial Gardens, Flatwoods, KY

..........................+William Buford McAllister b: Abt. 1910 Number of children: ? Sex: Male

........................11 Barbara McAllister b: Abt. 1935 Sex: Female

................8 Maryan Caudill b: Abt. 1850 Sex: Female

................8 Sarah Jane Caudill b: 1852 in Wilkes Co., NC Sex: Female

....................+Linvel (Linville?) Dehler/Eller b: Abt. 1850 Sex: Male

............7 Susannah Caudill b: 1820 in Lunenburg Co., VA Number of children: 7 Sex: Female

..................+Joseph Hampton, Hampston b: Abt. 1815 m: Abt. 1837 in Perry Co., KY Number of children: 7 Father: Turner Hampton Mother: Mary Profit Sex: Male

................8 Abel Hampton b: Abt. 1838 Sex: Male

................8 Mary Hampton b: Abt. 1840 Sex: Female

................8 Sarah Hampton b: Abt. 1842 Sex: Female

................8 Nancy Hampton b: Abt. 1843 Sex: Female

................8 Matthew Hampton b: Abt. 1845 Sex: Male

................8 Soloman M. Hampton b: Abt. 1847 Number of children: ? Sex: Male

....................+Athalyle "Atha" Caudill b: Abt. 1850 Number of children: ? Sex: Female (Note: Looking for ancestors)

..................9 John Hampton b: February 03, 1868 in KY d: June 13, 1944 Sex: Male

........................+Lourania "Ranie" Whitaker b: April 30, 1874 d: April 19, 1955 Father: Alamander Whitaker Mother: Catherine Campbell Sex: Female

................8 [159] Samuel Hampton b: May 22, 1850 in Letcher Co., KY Sex: Male

....................+Sylvania Tackett b: Abt. 1855 Sex: Female

................2nd Wife of [159] Samuel Hampton:

......................+Nancy Caudill b: Abt. 1860 m: October 26, 1879 in Pike Co., KY Sex: Female
..........6 Abner Caudill b: 1758 in Lunenburg Co., VA d: 1855 in Wilkes Co., NC Number of children: 4 Sex: Male
................+Jane Adams b: 1787 in Wilkes Co., NC m: Abt. 1807 Number of children: 4 Father: Spencer Adams Mother: Mary Towson, (or Townson?) Sex: Female (Note: looking for her ancestors)
..............7 Mary Caudill b: 1808 Sex: Female
..............7 Thomas Caudill b: 1810 Sex: Male
..............7 Jesse Caudill b: 1822 Sex: Male
..............7 Martha Caudill b: 1825 Sex: Female
..........6 Benjamin Caudill b: 1759 in Lunenburg Co., VA Number of children: 3 Sex: Male
................+Sarah Humphries b: Abt. 1760 d: Aft. 1850 Number of children: 3 Sex: Female
..............7 Stephen Caudill b: Abt. 1790 Sex: Male
..............7 David Caudill b: Abt. 1793 Sex: Male
..............7 [160] Elizabeth Caudill b: June 02, 1797 in GA d: May 18, 1892 Number of children: ? Sex: Female
...................+[161] Isom or Isham Caudill b: April 02, 1789 in Letcher Co., KY m: October 02, 1814 in Franklin Co., Georgia d: May 18, 1892 in Letcher Co., KY Number of children: ? Father: James "Jimmie" Caudill, Jr., Rev. War Soldier Mother: Mary A. Adams, Sex: Male
................8 [162] James Caudill b: January 20, 1830 in GA Sex: Male
....................+[163] Mary "Polly" Fields b: April 1825 in KY m: 1850 Sex: Female
..........6 Henrietta Caudill b: 1760 Sex: Female
..........6 David Caudill b: 1761 Sex: Male
..........6 [164] Stephen A. Caudill, Rev. War Soldier, b: 1763 in Lunenburg Co., VA (or NC?) d: July 26, 1839 in Sandlick, Letcher Co., KY Number of children: 16 Sex: Male Burial: Watty Caudill Cemetery, Dry Fork, Letcher Co., KY (Note: fought in Revolutionary War, Kings Mountain & Cowpens)
................+Jane DeHart b: Abt. 1765 m: April 03, 1784 in Wilkes Co., North Carolina Number of children: 3 Sex: Female
..............7 Mary Caudill b: June 01, 1785 in Wilkes Co., NC d: August 14, 1862 in MO Sex: Female
...................+Abraham Adams b: September 05, 1780 in Wilkes Co., NC d: May 01, 1851 in Johnson Co., MO Sex: Male
..............7 David Caudill b: January 26, 1788 in Wilkes Co., NC Sex: Male
...................+Sina Walker b: Abt. 1790 Sex: Female
..............7 Fannie Caudill b: Abt. 1790 in NC Sex: Female
..........2nd Wife of [164] Stephen A. Caudill, Rev. War Soldier, :
...............+[451] Sarah "Sally" Francis Adams, 2nd wife b: 1776 in Lunenburg Co., VA m: 1790 in Wilkesboro, Wilkes Co., NC d: October 1842 in Letcher Co., KY Number of children: 13 Father: Benjamin "Ben" Adams, Jr., Mother: Henrietta "Henny" Caudill, Sex: Female
..............7 [452] Henrietta Caudill, b: 1792 in NC d: 1829 in Pert Creek, Letcher Co., KY Number of children: 6 Sex: Female
...................+[453] George M. Adams, b: September 16, 1800 in Elizabethton, Carter Co., TN m: February 25, 1820 in Prestonsburg, Floyd Co., KY d: October 25, 1869 in Taney Co., MO Number of children: 14 Father: Moses Adams, Mother: Mary Garland Sex: Male
................8 [454] Sarah "Sallie" Adams b: 1821 Sex: Female
................8 [455] Mary Adams b: 1825 Sex: Female
................8 [456] John Adams b: Abt. 1826 Sex: Male
................8 [457] Lydia Adams b: December 31, 1829 Sex: Female
....................+[458] Edward Combs b: August 21, 1824 in Smoot Creek, Perry Co., KY d: May 17, 1911 Father: Shadrach "Old Shade" Combs, Jr., Mother: Martha Patsy Casebolt Sex: Male
................8 [459] Nancy Adams b: Abt. 1830 Sex: Female
....................+[460] Stephen Polly b: 1826 in Perry Co., KY m: August 25, 1848 in Letcher Co., KY Father: Edward Oliver "Ned" Polly Mother: Jane Bunton "Jennie" Adams Sex: Male

................8 [461] Dianah Adams b: May 15, 1831 in Perry Co., KY d: June 06, 1873 Sex: Female

.............7 [462] John Adams Caudill, b: January 01, 1798 in Wilkes or Ashe Co., NC d: May 10, 1873 in Letcher Co., KY Number of children: 14 Sex: Male

..................+[463] Rachel Cornett, b: February 10, 1807 in Bull Creek, Perry Co., KY m: March 20, 1824 in Perry Co., KY d: April 15, 1887 in Perry (Knott/Letcher) Co., KY Number of children: 14 Father: William Jesse Cornett, Mother: Mary Ann Everage Sex: Female

................8 [464] William J. Caudill b: February 11, 1825 in Wilkes Co., NC d: January 11, 1899 in Rowan Co., KY Sex: Male

................8 [465] Stephen Jacob Caudill b: November 18, 1826 in Perry Co., KY d: July 26, 1906 in Letcher Co., KY Sex: Male

................8 [466] Mary A. Caudill b: August 04, 1828 d: December 31, 1839 Sex: Female

................8 [467] Benjamin Everage Caudill, Civil War Col. b: January 11, 1830 in Whitesburg, Perry/Letcher Co., KY d: February 11, 1889 in Claybourne Co., TN Number of children: 11 Sex: Male Burial: Slate Hill Baptist Cemetery, London, Laurel Co., KY (Note: he led the famous 13th KY Cavalry known as "Caudill's Army")

......................+[468] Martha Lucinda Asbury b: July 11, 1828 in Tazewell Co., VA m: February 16, 1848 in Whitesburg, Letcher Co., KY d: September 20, 1900 in Scott Co., VA Number of children: 11 Father: William Asbury Mother: Elizabeth Chaffins Sex: Female

..................9 [469] John Asbury Caudill b: March 26, 1849 in Letcher Co., KY d: May 30, 1912 in Ivan, Stephens Co., TX Sex: Male Burial: Veale's Creek Cemetery

......................+[470] Alice Reeves b: 1854 in Ashe Co., NC. Sex: Female

......................10 Frederic "Fred" Caudill b: Feb. 12, 1868 in KY. d: NM? Sept. 17. 1941. Sex: Male. Burial: Mountain View Cemetery, Albuquerque, NM.

......................+Lizzie S. Caudill (2nd wife), b: abt. 1870? in TX.

......................11 Coney Claud Caudill b: 1897 in TX (?).

......................11 Faro Caudill b: June 18, 1908 in TX. d: June 13, 1976; burial: Mount Calvary Cemetery, Albuquerque, NM. Faro and his wife Doris were homesteaders in New Mexico, where they were photographed in 1940 by Russell W. Lee, a photographer for the U.S. Farm Security Administration. (Note: Faro is pictured on the title page and also the back cover of this work, Lochlainn Seabrook's book, *The Caudills*)

.............................+Doris Altizer b: abt. 1910 in Sweetwater, TX. (Note: Doris is pictured on the title page and also the front cover of this work, Lochlainn Seabrook's book, *The Caudills*)

.............................12 Josie Lerlene Caudill b: July 31, 1934 in TX (?). d: March 18, 2000 in TX (?). Female. Burial: Holly Hills Memorial Park, Granbury, TX.

.....................................+Jesse L. "Buddy" Endsley. m: Dec. 20, 1952, Albuquerque, NM.

..................9 [471] William Jesse Caudill b: December 28, 1850 in Whitesburg, Letcher Co., KY d: April 14, 1914 in Hobart, Kiowa Co., OK Sex: Male

..................9 [472] Samuel Houston Caudill b: March 29, 1853 in Whitesburg, Letcher Co., KY d: 1928 in OK? Sex: Male

..................9 [473] Stephen B. Caudill b: March 29, 1855 in Whitesburg, Letcher Co., KY d: in KY Sex: Male

..................9 [474] Margaret Caudill b: 1857 in Whitesburg, Letcher Co., KY d: May 1937 in Lovington, NM Sex: Female

..................9 [475] Rachel Caudill b: 1860 Sex: Female

..................9 [476] James Watson Caudill b: 1862 in Whitesburg, Letcher Co., KY d: December 24, 1945 in Hatch, Dona Ana Co., NM Sex: Male

..................9 [477] Evelyn Caudill b: 1865 Sex: Female

..................9 [165] Benjamin Franklin Caudill b: May 03, 1867 in Sparta, Alleghanney Co., NC d: 1952 in Clay Co., KY Number of children: 10 Sex: Male Burial: Clay Co., KY

......................+[478] Lucy Benge House b: September 30, 1867 in Manchester, Clay Co., KY m: December 26, 1885 in Manchester, Clay Co., KY d: April 01, 1938 in OK Number of children: 10 Father: James House Mother: Elizabeth Benge Sex: Female Burial: Erick Cemetery, Oklahoma

City, OK
....................10 [479] Lilly "Lizzie" Belle Caudill b: August 04, 1886 in Clay Co., KY d: August 22, 1945 Sex: Female
....................10 [480] Victor Cleveland Caudill b: October 28, 1889 in Clay Co., KY d: December 12, 1948 in Hot Springs, Sierra, NM Number of children: 4 Sex: Male Burial: Hot Springs, Sierra, NM
...........................+[481] Mae D. Baker b: December 29, 1893 in Sewal, Wayne Co., IA m: Abt. 1911 d: February 20, 1976 in Clovis, NM Number of children: 4 Father: B. F. Baker Mother: Minnie Ensminger Sex: Female Burial: Clovis, NM
.......................11 Juanita C. Caudill b: August 12, 1912 in Erick, OK d: March 09, 1976 in Clovis, Curry Co., NM Sex: Female
...........................+Casey Jones b: Abt. 1910 Sex: Male
.......................11 Frank B. Caudill b: Abt. 1914 d: September 02, 1994 Sex: Male
.......................11 Thurman Caudill b: April 03, 1916 d: June 24, 1995 in Pleasanton, CA Sex: Male
.......................11 Sanford Caudill b: December 10, 1917 in Beckham Co., OK d: July 02, 1993 in Tucumcari, or Clayton, or Albuquerque, NM Number of children: 3 Sex: Male Burial: National Cemetery, Santa Fe, NM
...........................+Mildred Milnes b: March 21, 1921 in OK m: February 23, 1940 in OK d: July 02, 1996 in Tucumcari, NM Number of children: 3 Father: Floyd Milnes Sex: Female
...........................12 Kay Caudill, b: 1941 in Clovis, Curry Co., NM
...........................12 Marshall Sanford Caudill, b: about 1943
...........................12 Robert A. Caudill, b: abt 1945
....................10 [482] Grover Garrett Garrard Caudill b: March 02, 1891 in Pigeon Roost, Clay Co., KY d: October 30, 1948 in Washington Co., OR Sex: Male
....................10 [483] Minnie Dora Caudill b: April 25, 1893 in Clay Co., KY d: May 1976 in Oklahoma City, OK Sex: Female
....................10 [484] Henry Clay Caudill b: June 01, 1896 in Clay Co., KY d: August 04, 1931 in Erick, Beckham Co., OK Sex: Male
....................10 [485] Margaret Luinda Caudill b: September 1897 in Clay Co., KY Sex: Female
....................10 [486] Mayme Ellen Caudill b: June 11, 1899 in Clay Co., KY d: June 17, 1977 in Whittier, Los Angeles Co., CA Sex: Female
....................10 [487] Lucy Mae Caudill b: May 07, 1901 in KY d: August 1986 in Dalhart, TX Sex: Female
....................10 [488] Elizabeth Beatrice Caudill b: June 10, 1904 in Sayre, Beckham Co., OK d: April 18, 1995 in Minneapolis, MN Sex: Female
....................10 [489] Benjamin Kathleen Caudill b: October 07, 1907 in Sayre, Beckham Co., OK d: October 10, 1997 in Albuquerque, NM Sex: Female
.................2nd Wife of [165] Benjamin Franklin Caudill:
.......................+[490] Stella Louise Lovelace b: February 25, 1898 in KY m: Bet. 1917 - 1923 in NC d: December 1976 in Marana, AZ Father: Frank Lovelace Sex: Female
.................9 [491] Emery M. Caudill, Sr. b: April 07, 1869 in Sparta, Alleghanney Co., NC d: January 09, 1953 in Albuquerque, NM Sex: Male
.................9 [492] Elizabeth Caudill b: Abt. 1871 Sex: Female
...............8 [166] Samuel Patton Caudill b: December 29, 1831 in Perry/Letcher Co., KY d: October 29, 1907 in Letcher Co., KY? Sex: Male Burial: Caudill Cemetery, Letcher Co., KY
....................+[493] Letitia Meade b: 1835 in Russell Co., VA m: Abt. 1852 d: 1884 Sex: Female
................2nd Wife of [166] Samuel Patton Caudill:
....................+[494] Mary Ann Greer b: Abt. 1837 in Scott Co., VA m: November 14, 1854 d: Abt. 1862 Sex: Female
...............3rd Wife of [166] Samuel Patton Caudill:
....................+[495] Sarah J. Hart b: Abt. 1875 m: Aft. 1854 in Letcher Co., KY Father: Hugh

Hart Mother: Jane Adams Sex: Female

................8 [496] Sarah L. Caudill b: October 23, 1834 in Whitesburg, Letcher Co., KY d: May 17, 1914 in Letcher Co., KY Sex: Female

................8 [497] John Dixon Caudill b: October 06, 1836 in Sandlick or Whitesburg, Letcher Co., KY d: June 17, 1917 in Sandlick, Letcher Co., KY Sex: Male

.....................+[498] Mary Ann Green b: November 25, 1838 in VA m: January 12, 1859 in Letcher Co., KY? d: June 23, 1920 in Sandlick, Letcher Co., KY Sex: Female (Note: Looking for her ancestors)

................8 [499] David Jesse Caudill b: March 09, 1839 in Letcher Co., KY d: April 09, 1907 in Olive Hill, Carter Co., KY Sex: Male

................8 [353] Nancy "Jane" Caudill, Caudell, b: November 05, 1840 in Whitesburg, Letcher Co., KY d: November 12, 1922 in London, Laurel Co., KY Number of children: 2 Sex: Female Burial: Lincks Cemetery

.....................+[352] John Henderson Craft b: December 20, 1834 in Millstone, KY m: October 11, 1855 in Letcher Co., KY d: September 13, 1920 in Larue, Laurel Co., KY Number of children: 2 Father: Joseph Craft Mother: Martha Irby Bates Sex: Male Burial: Lincks Cemetery

..................9 [354] John Dixon Craft b: April 12, 1856 in Craftsville, Letcher Co., KY d: December 20, 1945 in KY Number of children: ? Sex: Male

........................+[355] Mary Elizabeth Webb b: July 11, 1861 in Letcher Co., KY m: September 13, 1879 in KY d: November 25, 1956 Number of children: ? Father: Henry T. "Chunk" Webb Mother: Francis Elizabeth "Franky" Adams Sex: Female (Webb Note: Like all of the other Webb individuals in this tree, this Webb family descends from the same line as the country singers Loretta (Webb) Lynn and her sister Brenda Gail "Crystal Gale" Webb. Loretta was born April 14, 1935, in Butcher Hollow, Pike Co., KY; Crystal Gale was born January 9, 1951, in Paintsville, Johnson Co., KY)

.....................10 [500] Nancy Catherine "Nannie" Craft b: February 08, 1882 in Letcher Co., KY d: August 06, 1913 in KY? Sex: Female

...........................+[501] William Wash Webb b: October 1883 in KY Father: Nelson Robinette Webb Mother: Frances Catherine Spangler Sex: Male

..................9 [356] Martha A. Craft b: September 12, 1860 in Craftsville, KY d: September 16, 1951 in TN Number of children: 3 Sex: Female

........................+[357] Noah Milburn Reynolds, Jr. b: December 15, 1855 in KY m: November 15, 1879 in Blountsville, TN d: April 30, 1923 in Mayo Clinic in TN Number of children: 3 Father: Noah Milburn Reynolds, Sr. Mother: Mary Chaney Stone Sex: Male

.....................10 [502] John Henderson Reynolds b: Abt. 1880 Number of children: ? Sex: Male

...........................+[503] Nancy Jane Caudill Craft b: Abt. 1882 Number of children: ? Sex: Female

........................11 Martha Reynolds Sex: Female

.....................10 [504] Christopher Columbus Reynolds b: Abt. 1883 Sex: Male

.....................10 [505] Mary C. Reynolds b: November 06, 1885 in Letcher Co., KY d: September 14, 1955 in Whitley Co., KY Sex: Female

...........................+[506] Woodson Hodge Brown b: October 24, 1881 in Clay Co., KY m: December 06, 1906 in Clay Co., KY Sex: Male

................8 [507] Elizabeth "Betty" Caudill b: August 22, 1842 in Letcher Co., KY Sex: Female Burial: Buffalo Cemetery, Sayre, OK

................8 [508] Joseph Caudill, twin b: 1844 d: 1848 Sex: Male

................8 [509] Nathaniel Caudill, twin b: 1844 d: 1848 Sex: Male

................8 [350] Polly Ann Caudill b: April 15, 1847 in Letcher Co., KY d: February 11, 1937 in Millstone, Letcher Co., KY Number of children: ? Sex: Female

.....................+[349] Enoch "Chunk" A. Craft b: December 29, 1842 m: May 02, 1867 in Letcher Co., KY d: February 16, 1937 in Millstone, Letcher Co., KY Number of children: ? Father: Archelous Craft Mother: Letty Webb Sex: Male

..................9 [351] Nancy Craft b: January 1872 in Letcher Co., KY d: August 1872 in Letcher

Co., KY Sex: Female

................8 [510] Watson Garrard Caudill b: June 17, 1849 in Whitesburg, Letcher Co., KY d: August 05, 1930 in Perry Co., KY Sex: Male

.............7 [167] Benjamin E. Caudill, b: 1799 in Wilkes Co., NC d: February 27, 1851 in Salyersville, Magoffin Co., KY Number of children: 3 Sex: Male

..................+[168] Abigail Pennington, b: May 09, 1803 in Lee Co., VA d: 1887 in Salyersville, Magoffin Co., KY Number of children: 3 Father: William Pennington Mother: Abigail Caudill, Cordell, Sex: Female

................8 [169] William Jackson "Jack" Caudill b: 1822 in Perry Co., KY Sex: Male Burial: Oil Springs, Johnson Co., KY

......................+[170] Rebecca Harris b: Abt. 1826 in Floyd Co., KY Sex: Female Burial: Oil Springs, Johnson Co., KY

................8 [171] Abel Caudill, b: January 16, 1827 in Morgan Co., KY Number of children: ? Sex: Male

......................+[172] Phoebe Hitchcock b: November 28, 1827 in Floyd Co., KY m: October 28, 1846 in Johnson Co., KY Number of children: ? Sex: Female

..................9 [173] Jesse E. Caudill, b: September 07, 1847 in Johnson Co., KY d: September 14, 1890 Number of children: ? Sex: Male

........................+[174] Elizabeth "Lizzie" Elam b: November 28, 1847 in MaGoffin Co., KY m: February 18, 1869 in Magoffin Co., KY Number of children: ? Sex: Female

.....................10 [175] Abel Caudill, b: February 09, 1870 in MaGoffin Co., KY Sex: Male

...........................+[176] Elizabeth Bailey b: May 1876 in KY? Sex: Female

................8 [177] Elizabeth Caudill b: 1833 in Perry Co., KY d: April 15, 1915 Number of children: ? Sex: Female

......................+[178] Noah May b: Abt. 1831 in Magoffin Co., KY Number of children: ? Sex: Male

..................9 [179] Campbell J. May b: 1851 Number of children: ? Sex: Male

........................+[180] Rebecca E. Adams b: 1852 Number of children: ? Father: Gilbert A. Adams Mother: Perlina Prater Sex: Female

.....................10 [181] Augustus Noah May b: 1876 d: 1944 Number of children: ? Sex: Male

...........................+[182] Sarah Elizabeth Cornett b: 1876 d: 1966 Number of children: ? Father: Russell Cornett, Mother: Ailey Amburgey Sex: Female

.......................11 Edith Rebecca May b: 1914 d: 1892 Sex: Female

.............................+James Sutherd Carroll b: 1913 d: 1989 Sex: Male

.............7 [511] Elizabeth "Betsy" C. Caudill, b: June 18, 1800 in Wilkes Co., NC d: October 11, 1881 in Letcher Co., KY Number of children: ? Sex: Female Burial: Watty Caudill Cemetery, at the mouth of Dry Fork, Letcher Co., KY

..................+[512] John Quincy Brown b: 1788 in Ireland m: 1814 d: November 19, 1872 in Letcher Co., KY Number of children: ? Sex: Male

................8 [513] Sarah "Sallie" Brown b: April 12, 1815 in KY d: April 19, 1892 in Letcher Co., KY Number of children: 3 Sex: Female

......................+[514] Joseph Enoch Cornett, Judge b: April 28, 1814 in KY m: Abt. 1837 d: May 30, 1881 in Crown, Letcher Co., KY Number of children: 3 Father: William Jesse Cornett, Mother: Mary Ann Everage Sex: Male

..................9 [515] Samuel A. Cornett b: April 18, 1840 d: Abt. 1931 Number of children: 6 Sex: Male

........................+[516] Alcyann Couch, 4th wife b: Abt. 1870 in Perry Co., KY? m: Abt. 1888 Number of children: 6 Father: Samuel Couch, ? Mother: Emaline Wooten, ? Sex: Female

.....................10 [517] Granville Cornett b: Abt. 1889 Sex: Male

.....................10 [518] Lucy Cornett b: Abt. 1891 Sex: Female

.....................10 [519] Susan Cornett b: Abt. 1893 Sex: Female

.....................10 [520] James Cornett b: Abt. 1895 Sex: Male

..................10 [521] Stephen Cornett b: Abt. 1897 Sex: Male

..................10 [522] Armine Cornett b: Abt. 1900 Sex: Female

................9 [523] Elizabeth Ann 'Betty' Cornett b: Abt. 1842 Number of children: 4 Sex: Female

....................+[524] Ira Stamper b: October 11, 1829 in Perry Co., KY m: April 26, 1876 in Letcher Co., KY d: February 05, 1910 in Rome, Douglas Co., MO Number of children: 4 Father: Isom Stamper Mother: Sarah Creech Sex: Male

..................10 [525] Mary Ann 'Polly' Stamper Sex: Female

..................10 [526] Neale Stamper Sex: Male

..................10 [527] Nancy Elizabeth Stamper Sex: Female

..................10 [528] Joseph Stamper Sex: Male

................9 [529] Rachel Cornett b: 1846 in Dry Fork, Pike Co. (or Letcher Co.) , KY Sex: Female

............7 [530] Nancy Caudill, b: June 18, 1804 Number of children: 2 Sex: Female

..................+[531] Randolph "Randall" Adams b: 1802 in Roaring River, Wilkes Co., NC d: December 23, 1872 in Cowan, Perry/Letcher Co., KY Number of children: 2 Father: John Hobbs Adams, Jr., Mother: Lydia "Letty" or "Lettie" Simpson Sex: Male

................8 [532] Lydia Adams b: Abt. 1825 Number of children: 10 Sex: Female

....................+[533] Robert Collins b: October 21, 1823 in Rockhouse Creek, Perry Co., KY m: Abt. 1850 d: November 27, 1883 Number of children: 10 Father: James Shepherd Collins Mother: Elizabeth Lewis Sex: Male

................9 [534] Randolph Collins b: October 12, 1852 in Hazard, Perry Co., KY d: December 14, 1947 in Red Bluff, CA Sex: Male

......................+[535] Eliza Jane Turner b: Abt. 1854 in Letcher Co., KY m: January 18, 1872 Father: James Turner Mother: Sarah Bailey Sex: Female

................9 [536] Nancy Collins b: December 15, 1855 in Colson, Letcher Co., KY d: February 06, 1918 in Colson, Letcher Co., KY Sex: Female

......................+[537] James Jasper "Babe" Collins b: December 25, 1852 in Letcher Co., KY m: July 31, 1873 in Letcher Co., KY d: September 06, 1876 in Letcher Co., KY Father: Eli Collins Mother: Mary Barrett Sex: Male

................9 [538] James H. Collins b: July 18, 1857 in Rockhouse Creek, Letcher Co., KY d: September 01, 1942 Sex: Male

......................+[539] Nancy Sarah Breeding b: Abt. 1859 in Letcher Co., KY m: September 18, 1879 Father: John Breeding Mother: Elizabeth "Betty" Combs Sex: Female

................9 [540] Sarah Collins b: May 04, 1859 in Rockhouse Creek, Letcher Co., KY d: May 15, 1859 in Letcher Co., KY Sex: Female

................9 [541] Elijah Collins b: Abt. 1860 Sex: Male

................9 [183] William Silas Collins b: April 21, 1865 d: December 15, 1937 in Letcher Co., KY Sex: Male

......................+[542] Nancy Hale b: 1862 Father: William Rowlette Hale Mother: Elizabeth Collins Sex: Female

................2nd Wife of [183] William Silas Collins:

......................+[358] Martha E. Crase b: Abt. 1868 m: March 03, 1888 in Letcher Co., KY Father: James Crase Mother: Elizabeth Stallard Sex: Female

................9 [360] Greenbury Collins b: February 26, 1868 d: May 03, 1924 Sex: Male

......................+[359] Christina Adams b: June 10, 1858 d: January 07, 1951 Father: Jesse "Colly Jesse" Adams Mother: Mary "Polly" Craft Sex: Female

................9 [543] Lucinda Collins b: Abt. 1872 Sex: Female

................9 [544] Lorenzo Dow Collins b: January 20, 1875 in Rockhouse Creek, Letcher Co., KY d: December 13, 1949 Sex: Male

......................+[545] Nancy Ann Caudill b: Abt. 1877 in Letcher Co., KY m: February 04, 1897 Father: Watson Caudill Mother: Elizabeth Combs Sex: Female

................9 [546] Eliza Collins b: 1879 Sex: Female

................8 [184] Watson E. "Watty" Adams b: April 1837 d: 1919 Number of children: 9 Sex: Male

...................+[547] Rosa "Rausey" Hogg b: 1842 m: 1860 Number of children: ? Father: Hiram "Courthouse Hiram" Hogg Mother: Melvina "Viney" Polly Sex: Female

.................9 [548] Henry C. Adams b: 1863 Sex: Male

.........................+[549] Catherine Campbell b: September 1884 d: 1966 Father: John Henry Campbell Mother: Elizabeth Maggard Sex: Female

...............2nd Wife of [184] Watson E. "Watty" Adams:

.........................+[550] Minerva Collins b: January 13, 1846 m: October 16, 1881 in Letcher Co., KY Number of children: 8 Father: Nathaniel "Nat" Collins Mother: Nancy Branham-Smith Sex: Female

.................9 [551] Floyd Adams b: Abt. 1882 Sex: Male

.................9 [552] Boyd Adams b: Abt. 1883 Sex: Male

.................9 [553] Randall Adams b: March 19, 1884 Sex: Male

.................9 [554] Francis Adams b: September 28, 1885 Sex: Female

.................9 [555] Patton Adams b: Abt. 1886 Sex: Male

.................9 [556] Green Ison Adams b: March 10, 1887 d: September 19, 1951 Sex: Male

.................9 [557] Hattie Adams b: August 21, 1889 Sex: Female

.................9 [558] Elizabeth Adams b: Abt. 1891 Sex: Female

............7 [559] Easter (or Esther) Caudill, b: 1806 in Wilkes Co., NC d: Abt. 1887 in Letcher Co., KY Number of children: ? Sex: Female

.................+[560] Levi Eldridge b: August 1810 in Scott Co., VA d: 1877 in Rowan Co., KY Number of children: ? Sex: Male

...............8 [185] Elizabeth "Betsy" Eldridge b: Abt. 1841 Number of children: 2 Sex: Female

.........................+[186] William W. "Wild Bill" Caudill b: Abt. 1839 in NC d: June 22, 1920 in Wolfe Co., KY Number of children: 2 Father: Wilburn E. Caudill Mother: Nancy Caudill Sex: Male

.................9 [187] Martha Ann Caudill b: Abt. 1861 Number of children: ? Sex: Female

.......................+[188] Enoch Everidge b: Abt. 1860 Number of children: ? Sex: Male

....................10 [189] Susan "Susie" Everidge b: August 15, 1885 in KY d: December 29, 1962 in Perry Co., KY Number of children: 9 Sex: Female

...........................+[190] Hiram Combs b: May 07, 1882 d: April 29, 1962 Number of children: 9 Father: Benjamin Combs Mother: Matilda "Tilda" Combs Sex: Male

.......................11 Dicie Combs b: 1903 Sex: Female

.......................11 [191] Tilda Combs b: December 22, 1906 d: 1998 Number of children: ? Sex: Female

............................+Isaac Jacob Johnson b: Abt. 1905 Sex: Male

.......................2nd Husband of [191] Tilda Combs:

...........................+William "Bill" Banks b: Abt. 1898 m: Abt. 1939 Number of children: 7 Sex: Male

.......................11 Enoch Combs b: Abt. 1908 Sex: Male

.......................11 Willie Combs b: Abt. 1910 Sex: Male (Note: He changed his name fo "Bill Caudill")

.......................11 Betty Combs b: Abt. 1912 Sex: Female

.......................11 Monroe Combs b: Abt. 1914 Sex: Male

.......................11 Martha Combs b: Abt. 1916 Sex: Female

.......................11 Ann Combs b: Abt. 1918 Sex: Female

.......................11 Benjamin ("Bennie") Combs b: Abt. 1920 Sex: Male

.................9 [25] Sarah Caudill b: September 1872 in Campton, KY Number of children: ? Sex: Female

.......................+[24] John C. Caudill b: February 1868 in Harlan or Letcher Co., KY m: April 18, 1889 in Breathitt Co., KY Number of children: ? Father: Henry H. Caudill Mother: Susannah Back Sex: Male

..................10 [9] Cleveland Caudill b: June 1891 in Letcher Co., KY Sex: Male

..........................+[8] Peggy Caudill b: April 1890 in Letcher Co., KY m: July 14, 1909 in Letcher Co., KY d: January 14, 1916 Father: William B. Caudill Mother: Susannah "Sukie" Caudill Sex: Female

.............7 [561] Sarah "Sally" Caudill, b: 1810 in Wilkes Co., NC d: 1863 in Hazard, Letcher Co., KY Number of children: 9 Sex: Female

...................+[361] Moses "Rockhouse Moses" Adams b: July 18, 1808 in Letcher Co., KY m: July 20, 1825 in Hazard, Perry/Letcher Co., KY d: 1885 in Hazard, Letcher Co., KY Number of children: 12 Father: Stephen "Rockhouse Steve" Adams Mother: Ellendar "Nellie" Buntin, or Benton Sex: Male

.................8 [562] Sarah Adams b: Abt. 1826 Sex: Female

.................8 [563] Mary Adams b: Abt. 1827 in Rockhouse Creek, Floyd Co., KY d: in Letcher Co., KY Sex: Female

.................8 [564] Green Adams b: Abt. 1828 in Hazard, Letcher Co., KY d: in Hazard, Letcher Co., KY Number of children: 4 Sex: Male

.....................+[565] Nancy Maggard b: Abt. 1830 m: Abt. 1850 d: in Hazard, Letcher Co., KY Number of children: 4 Sex: Female

..................9 [566] Esther Adams b: March 1850 Sex: Female

........................+[567] S. S. Banks b: Abt. 1850 m: September 24, 1897 Sex: Male

..................9 [568] Martha Adams b: Abt. 1855 d: October 15, 1939 in Letcher Co., KY Sex: Female

........................+[569] Daugherty Adams b: Abt. 1850 Sex: Male

..................9 [570] Mary Ann "Polly" Adams b: Abt. 1860 Sex: Female

........................+[571] George M. Gilley b: Abt. 1850 m: January 20, 1896 in Letcher Co., KY Sex: Male

..................9 [209] Sarah Adams b: 1874 in Rockhouse Creek, Letcher Co., KY d: November 11, 1940 in Rockhouse Creek, Letcher Co., KY Sex: Female

........................+[208] Elijah Adams b: May 31, 1866 in Rockhouse Creek, Letcher Co., KY m: March 25, 1890 in Letcher Co., KY d: September 02, 1932 in Rockhouse Creek, Letcher Co., KY Father: Stephen Adams Mother: Ursula Ison Sex: Male

.................8 [572] Stephen Adams b: 1827 in Hazard, Perry/Letcher Co., KY d: April 11, 1902 in Hazard, Perry/Letcher Co., KY Number of children: 10 Sex: Male

.....................+[573] Ursula Ison b: January 10, 1825 in Hazard, Perry/Letcher Co., KY m: 1848 in Hazard, Perry/Letcher Co., KY d: April 11, 1904 in Letcher Co., KY Number of children: 10 Father: Gideon Ison Mother: Rachel Stamper Sex: Female

..................9 [574] Sarah Adams b: Abt. 1848 Sex: Female

..................9 [575] Rachel Adams b: 1849 in Letcher Co., KY d: December 09, 1929 in Knott Co., KY Sex: Female

........................+[576] Frazier Adams b: March 01, 1841 in Perry Co., KY m: in Whitesburg, KY d: July 04, 1917 in Knott Co., KY Sex: Male

..................9 [577] Moses Adams b: Abt. 1850 Sex: Male

..................9 [578] Gideon Adams b: June 26, 1851 in Jeremiah, Letcher Co., KY d: April 17, 1927 in Jeremiah, Letcher Co., KY Number of children: 13 Sex: Male

........................+[579] Sarah Blair b: 1849 in Whitesburg, Letcher Co., KY m: Bet. 1877 - 1878 in Jeremiah, Letcher Co., KY d: August 11, 1924 in Jeremiah, Letcher Co., KY Number of children: 13 Father: Hiram "Humpy" Blair Mother: Drusilla "Raillie" Craft Sex: Female

....................10 [192] Celia Ann Adams b: June 23, 1877 d: November 14, 1969 in Letcher Co., KY Number of children: 9 Sex: Female

..........................+[580] Solomon Banks b: September 07, 1856 in Letcher Co., KY m: December 16, 1896 d: September 05, 1936 in Colson, Letcher Co., KY Number of children: 7 Father: Samuel G. Banks Mother: Mary Frazier Sex: Male

........................11 [1141] Hettie Banks b: November 27, 1899 in Letcher Co., KY Sex: Female

..............................+[1142] Clinton Sexton b: Abt. 1887 Sex: Male

.....................11 [1143] Juda Banks b: 1905 Sex: Male

.....................11 [1144] L. C. "Lucky" Banks b: December 13, 1908 in Letcher Co., KY Sex: Male

...........................+[1145] Kathryn Sexton b: Abt. 1910 m: February 27, 1928 Sex: Female

.....................11 [1146] Martha Banks b: March 26, 1914 Sex: Female

...........................+[1147] Wallace Sturgill b: Abt. 1912 m: June 04, 1935 Sex: Male

.....................11 [1148] Robert "Bobby" Banks b: April 04, 1915 Sex: Male

...........................+[1149] Hoffa Sturgill b: Abt. 1917 m: April 07, 1932 Sex: Female

...................2nd Husband of [192] Celia Ann Adams:

.........................+[581] Preston Blair b: Abt. 1880 m: Abt. 1900 Number of children: 4 Sex: Male

.....................11 Sara Blair b: Abt. 1900 Sex: Female

.....................11 Bennie Blair b: Abt. 1902 Sex: Male

.....................11 Mollie Blair b: Abt. 1904 Sex: Female

.....................11 Millie Blair b: Abt. 1906 Sex: Female

...........................+_____ Sloane b: Abt. 1905 Sex: Male

...................10 [582] Ursula "Usley" Adams b: Abt. 1878 Sex: Female Burial: Waynesburg, KY

...................10 [583] Annie Adams b: Abt. 1879 d: in Jeremiah, KY Number of children: 7 Sex: Female

.........................+[584] Jim Adams b: Abt. 1875 m: Abt. 1905 d: in Jeremiah, Letcher Co., KY Number of children: 7 Sex: Male

.....................11 Moses Adams b: Abt. 1905 Sex: Male

.....................11 John Quincy Adams b: Abt. 1907 Sex: Male

.....................11 Watson Adams b: Abt. 1909 Sex: Male

.....................11 Tishia Adams b: Abt. 1911 Sex: Female

.....................11 Lissa Adams b: Abt. 1913 Sex: Female

.....................11 Betty Jane Adams, twin b: Abt. 1915 Sex: Female

.....................11 David Adams, twin b: Abt. 1915 Sex: Male

...................10 [585] Hiram Adams b: Abt. 1881 d: in Waynesburg, Lincoln Co., KY Number of children: 6 Sex: Male

.........................+[586] _____ Caudill b: Abt. 1885 m: Abt. 1905 d: in Waynesburg, Lincoln Co., KY Number of children: 6 Sex: Female (Note: looking for her ancestors)

.....................11 Milvin Adams b: Abt. 1905 Sex: Female

.....................11 Lina Adams b: Abt. 1907 Sex: Female

.....................11 Fred Adams b: Abt. 1909 Sex: Male

.....................11 [193] Coy Adams b: Abt. 1911 d: in Waynesburg, Lincoln Co., KY Sex: Male

.........................+[194] Ida Caudill b: Abt. 1920 d: in Waynesburg, Lincoln Co., KY Father: Henry H. Cleveland Caudill Mother: Rebecca Adams Sex: Female

.....................11 Ellis Adams b: Abt. 1913 Sex: Male

.....................11 Bertha Adams b: Abt. 1915 Sex: Female

...................10 [587] Fannie Adams b: Abt. 1885 d: in Jeremiah, KY Number of children: 7 Sex: Female Burial: Blair Branch, Letcher Co., KY

.........................+[588] William Adams b: Abt. 1885 m: Abt. 1905 in Jeremiah, Letcher Co., KY d: in Jeremiah, Letcher Co., KY Number of children: 7 Sex: Male

.....................11 Minnie (Arminta?) Adams b: Abt. 1905 Sex: Female

.....................11 Susan Adams b: Abt. 1907 Sex: Female

.....................11 Alpha Adams b: Abt. 1909 Sex: Male

.....................11 Lettie Adams b: Abt. 1911 Sex: Female

.....................11 Corbin Adams b: Abt. 1913 Sex: Male

.....................11 Hettie Adams b: 1914 d: 1915 Sex: Female

.....................11 Gezhia Adams b: Abt. 1915 Sex: Female

...................10 [195] Rebecca Adams b: Abt. 1887 d: in Waynesburg, KY Number of children:

8 Sex: Female

.............................+[10] Henry H. Cleveland Caudill b: April 20, 1887 in KY m: Abt. 1905 d: May 06, 1971 in Whitesburg, Letcher Co., KY Number of children: 18 Father: James William "Noah Jim" Caudill Mother: Lucinda Sumner Sex: Male Burial: Cleveland Caudill Cemetery, Caudill's Branch, Blackey, Letcher Co., KY

........................11 [196] Sarah Caudill b: Abt. 1905 Sex: Female

.............................+[197] _____ Neagle b: Abt. 1900 Sex: Male

........................11 [198] Arthur Caudill b: Abt. 1907 Sex: Male

........................11 [199] Mollie Caudill b: Abt. 1909 Sex: Female

.............................+[200] _____ Sanders b: Abt. 1905 Sex: Male

........................11 [201] Cormie Caudill b: Abt. 1911 Sex: Female

.............................+[202] _____ Repass b: Abt. 1910 Sex: Male

........................11 [203] Chester Caudill b: Abt. 1913 Sex: Male

........................11 [204] Irene Caudill b: Abt. 1915 Sex: Female

........................11 [205] Judy Caudill b: Abt. 1917 Sex: Female

........................11 [194] Ida Caudill b: Abt. 1920 d: in Waynesburg, Lincoln Co., KY Sex: Female

.............................+[193] Coy Adams b: Abt. 1911 d: in Waynesburg, Lincoln Co., KY Father: Hiram Adams Mother: _____ Caudill Sex: Male

......................10 [206] Stephen B. Adams b: July 15, 1888 in Letcher Co., KY d: July 02, 1963 in Waynesburg, KY Number of children: ? Sex: Male

.............................+[589] Flora Banks b: Abt. 1890 m: Abt. 1910 d: February 17, 1963 Number of children: ? Sex: Female

........................11 Alma Adams b: December 27, 1915 d: in IN Sex: Female

.............................+Anthony J. Alder b: Abt. 1915 m: 1937 d: November 21, 1991 in IN Sex: Male

......................2nd Wife of [206] Stephen B. Adams:

.............................+[590] Minnie Blair b: November 20, 1892 in Letcher Co., KY m: 1924 d: May 13, 1982 in Waynesburg, Lincoln Co., KY Sex: Female

......................10 [591] Judy Adams b: Abt. 1889 in Jeremiah, KY d: Abt. 1890 in Jeremiah, KY Sex: Female

......................10 [592] Dan Adams b: 1897 in Jeremiah, Letcher Co., KY d: 1937 in Horsemill Point, KY Number of children: 6 Sex: Male

.............................+[593] Virgie Smith b: Abt. 1900 m: Abt. 1920 d: in Jeremiah, Letcher Co., KY Number of children: 6 Sex: Female

........................11 Mamie Adams b: Abt. 1920 Sex: Female

.............................+_____ Engle b: Abt. 1920 Sex: Male

........................11 Dock Adams b: Abt. 1922 Sex: Male

........................11 Ivan Adams b: Abt. 1924 Sex: Male

........................11 Margaret Adams b: Abt. 1926 Sex: Female

.............................+_____ Caudill b: Abt. 1925 Sex: Male

........................11 Coreen Adams b: Abt. 1928 Sex: Female

.............................+_____ Pridemore b: Abt. 1925 Sex: Male

........................11 Mary Adams b: Abt. 1930 Sex: Female

.............................+_____ Denny b: Abt. 1925 Sex: Male

......................10 [594] Frazier C. Adams, Sr. b: January 23, 1899 in Jeremiah, KY d: in Waynesburg, Lincoln Co., KY Number of children: 11 Sex: Male

.............................+[595] Melvina "Viney" Jent b: February 11, 1903 in Smithbough, Knott Co., KY m: October 03, 1920 in Smithbough, Knott Co., KY d: October 13, 2000 in Somerset, KY Number of children: 11 Father: Sylvester Jent, Gent, Mother: Lucinda "Cinda" Smith, Sex: Female Burial: Double Springs Cemetery, Cemetery Road, Waynesburg, KY

........................11 Keith Adams b: Abt. 1920 d: in Hebron, WV? Sex: Male

........................11 Cindy Adams b: Abt. 1921 d: in Eubank, WV? Sex: Female

..............................+_____ Pumphrey b: Abt. 1920 Sex: Male

.........................11 Kermit Adams b: January 22, 1921 in Jeremiah, KY d: November 30, 1984 in Camden, TN Number of children: 4 Sex: Male

..............................+Jeannette Grace Miller b: December 11, 1930 in Stevens Point, WI m: June 17, 1952 in Lincoln Co., KY Number of children: 4 Father: Marvin Miller Mother: Grace Doty Sex: Female

.........................11 [207] Beryl Adams b: Abt. 1923 Number of children: 3 Sex: Male

..............................+Barbara ____? b: Abt. 1925 m: Abt. 1948 Number of children: 3 Sex: Female

.........................2nd Wife of [207] Beryl Adams:

..............................+Hilda ____? b: Abt. 1930 m: Abt. 1955 in Somerset, KY Sex: Female

.........................11 Rudell Adams b: Abt. 1925 Sex: Female

.........................11 Evylee Adams b: Abt. 1927 d: in Waynesburg, WV? Number of children: 5 Sex: Female

..............................+Paul Lanigan b: Abt. 1925 m: Abt. 1955 d: in Waynesburg, Lincoln Co., KY Number of children: 5 Sex: Male

.........................11 Dennis Adams b: March 20, 1929 d: in Waynesburg, WV? Sex: Male

..............................+Mavis Stacy b: Abt. 1930 m: March 31, 1956 Sex: Female

.........................11 Billie Jean Adams b: Abt. 1930 d: in Waynesburg, WV? Number of children: 6 Sex: Female

..............................+Patrick Lanigan, Sr b: Abt. 1925 m: Abt. 1955 Number of children: 6 Sex: Male

.........................11 Frazier C. Adams, Jr. b: Abt. 1932 Sex: Male

..............................+Kay ____? b: Abt. 1935 Sex: Female

.........................11 Kenneth Adams b: Abt. 1934 d: in Waynesburg, WV? Sex: Male

.........................11 Ora Sue Adams b: Abt. 1935 d: in New Carlisle, OH? Sex: Female

..............................+Homer Todd b: Abt. 1935 Sex: Male

.....................10 [596] Ritter Adams b: December 02, 1902 d: 1967 in Waynesburg, KY Number of children: 11 Sex: Female Burial: Double Creek, KY

...........................+[597] George Calfee b: Abt. 1900 m: Abt. 1920 d: in Waynesburg, Lincoln Co., KY Number of children: 11 Sex: Male

.........................11 Wendell Calfee b: Abt. 1920 Sex: Male

.........................11 Weldon Calfee b: Abt. 1922 Sex: Male

.........................11 Bennie Calfee b: Abt. 1924 Sex: Male

.........................11 Dana Calfee b: Abt. 1926 Sex: Male

.........................11 Broma Calfee b: Abt. 1928 Sex: Female

..............................+_____ Gross b: Abt. 1925 Sex: Male

.........................11 Ruby Calfee b: Abt. 1930 Sex: Female

..............................+_____ Shelton b: Abt. 1930 Sex: Male

.........................11 Velma Calfee b: Abt. 1932 Sex: Female

.........................11 Vina Calfee b: Abt. 1934 Sex: Female

.........................11 Mack Calfee b: Abt. 1936 Sex: Male

.........................11 Jack Calfee b: Abt. 1938 Sex: Male

.........................11 Lorraine Calfee b: Abt. 1940 Sex: Female

.....................10 [598] Nancy Adams b: January 17, 1904 d: May 1928 Number of children: 6 Sex: Female

...........................+[599] Curtis Stamper b: October 17, 1898 m: 1923 d: January 1932 Number of children: 6 Sex: Male

.........................11 Cecil Stamper b: Abt. 1923 Sex: Male

.........................11 Gertrude Stamper b: April 09, 1924 d: in Pequot Lakes, MN Sex: Female

..............................+Ross Gish b: Abt. 1925 m: 1945 in Pequot Lakes, MN d: in Pequot Lakes, MN Sex: Male

.......................11 Lettie Joyce Stamper b: Abt. 1925 Sex: Female

.......................11 Marjorie Stamper b: April 19, 1925 Sex: Female

............................+Shade Adams b: Abt. 1925 Sex: Male

.......................11 Mildred Stamper b: June 09, 1926 Sex: Female

.......................11 Laura Stamper b: February 06, 1928 Sex: Female

..................10 [600] John Adams b: 1919 in Jeremiah, KY d: in died in WW I in Germany Sex: Male Burial: Horsemill Point, KY

.................9 [601] Anna "Annie" Adams b: October 04, 1853 in Letcher Co., KY d: in Letcher Co., KY Sex: Female

.......................+[602] Stephen C. Hampton b: 1851 Sex: Male

.................9 [603] Ester Adams b: January 18, 1855 in Letcher Co., KY d: January 26, 1929 Sex: Female

.................9 [604] Ison Moses Adams b: July 28, 1859 in Letcher Co., KY d: in Martin Co., KY Sex: Male

.......................+[605] Mary A. "Polly" Elkins b: 1860 in VA m: 1878 in Whitesburg, KY d: in Martin Co., KY Sex: Female

.................9 [606] Nancy Adams b: April 1860 in Letcher Co., KY d: 1901 Sex: Female

.......................+[607] Daniel E. Adams b: June 05, 1849 in Letcher Co., KY m: 1874 in Whitesburg, KY Sex: Male

.................9 [608] John Adams b: October 06, 1864 in Letcher Co., KY d: April 26, 1933 Sex: Male

.......................+[609] Laurena Roark b: November 24, 1874 d: May 20, 1965 Sex: Female

.................9 [208] Elijah Adams b: May 31, 1866 in Rockhouse Creek, Letcher Co., KY d: September 02, 1932 in Rockhouse Creek, Letcher Co., KY Sex: Male

.......................+[209] Sarah Adams b: 1874 in Rockhouse Creek, Letcher Co., KY m: March 25, 1890 in Letcher Co., KY d: November 11, 1940 in Rockhouse Creek, Letcher Co., KY Father: Green Adams Mother: Nancy Maggard Sex: Female

...............8 [610] Ellender Adams b: January 20, 1829 in Rockhouse Creek, Floyd Co., KY d: March 07, 1886 in Letcher Co., KY Sex: Female

.......................+[611] Preston Blair b: 1827 in Perry/Letcher Co., KY m: March 04, 1849 in Letcher Co., KY d: 1878 in Letcher Co., KY Sex: Male

...............8 [612] Nancy Adams b: 1834 in Letcher Co., KY d: April 23, 1900 in Magoffin Co., KY Sex: Female

.......................+[613] George Adams b: 1832 in Pert Creek, Floyd Co., KY m: December 08, 1852 in Prestonburg, Floyd Co., KY d: 1876 in Magoffin Co., KY Sex: Male

...............8 [614] Esther Adams b: November 03, 1837 in Rockhouse Creek, Floyd Co., KY d: December 11, 1911 in Eolina, Perry/Letcher Co., KY Sex: Female

.......................+[615] Martin D. Collier b: March 27, 1834 in Eolina, Perry/Letcher Co., KY m: 1856 in Whitesburg, KY d: March 12, 1901 in Eolina, Perry/Letcher Co., KY Sex: Male

...............8 [616] John C. Adams b: July 02, 1841 in Rockhouse Creek, Floyd Co., KY d: February 27, 1930 in Letcher Co., KY Number of children: 8 Sex: Male

.......................+[617] Susanna Back b: December 18, 1845 in Letcher Co., KY m: July 02, 1867 in Letcher Co., KY d: September 13, 1926 in Letcher Co., KY Number of children: 8 Father: John Back Mother: Sarah _____? Sex: Female

.................9 [618] Susan Adams b: Abt. 1868 Sex: Female

.................9 [619] Henry Adams b: November 05, 1868 in Letcher Co., KY d: July 21, 1939 in Letcher Co., KY Sex: Male

.......................+[620] Amanda Combs b: Abt. 1870 m: January 03, 1892 in Whitesburg, KY d: 1910 in Letcher Co., KY Sex: Female

.................9 [621] Stephen Adams b: October 16, 1871 in Letcher Co., KY d: July 21, 1954 in Letcher Co., KY Sex: Male

.......................+[622] Ardelia Craft b: 1874 in Letcher Co., KY m: November 17, 1893 in

Whitesburg, KY d: 1921 in Letcher Co., KY Sex: Female

................9 [623] Moses Adams b: 1874 in Letcher Co., KY Sex: Male

......................+[624] Elizabeth Jane Caudill b: Abt. 1875 m: 1895 Sex: Female

................9 [625] Joseph Adams b: 1877 in Letcher Co., KY d: September 01, 1954 in Letcher Co., KY Sex: Male

......................+[626] Rachel Craft b: Abt. 1880 m: 1910 in Whitesburg, KY Sex: Female

................9 [627] Frances "Fanny" Adams b: November 1879 Sex: Female

......................+[628] Creed Craft b: Abt. 1875 Sex: Male

................9 [629] James M. Adams b: 1882 in Letcher Co., KY d: in Jeremiah, Letcher Co., KY Sex: Male

......................+[630] Anna _____? b: Abt. 1885 m: in Whitesburg, KY Sex: Female

................9 [631] William Adams b: June 27, 1885 in Letcher Co., KY d: June 06, 1970 in Letcher Co., KY Sex: Male

......................+[632] Frances _____? b: Abt. 1890 m: in Whitesburg, KY d: in Letcher Co., KY Sex: Female

................8 [210] Benjamin Adams b: 1843 in Rockhouse Creek, Letcher Co., KY Number of children: 8 Sex: Male

......................+[633] Sarah Sally Maggard b: Abt. 1845 m: Abt. 1861 Father: Henry Maggard Mother: Mary "Polly" Stamper Sex: Female

................2nd Wife of [210] Benjamin Adams:

......................+[634] Lucinda "Cindy" Combs b: June 06, 1847 in Letcher Co., KY m: 1862 in Whitesburg, KY d: February 07, 1874 in Jeremiah, KY Number of children: 8 Father: John Wesley Combs, Mother: Polly (Mary) Hogg Sex: Female

................9 [635] Isaac Adams b: Abt. 1863 in Letcher Co., KY Sex: Male

................9 [636] Millie Adams b: Abt. 1865 Sex: Female

......................+[637] Leonard Crocker b: Abt. 1865 m: 1896 in Whitesburg, KY Sex: Male

................9 [638] Elizabeth Adams b: 1863 in Letcher Co., KY Sex: Female

......................+[639] John Cook b: Abt. 1860 m: August 26, 1882 in Whitesburg, KY Sex: Male

................9 [640] Shadrack Adams b: March 03, 1865 in Letcher Co., KY d: December 24, 1937 Sex: Male

......................+[641] Susan Brown b: March 24, 1876 m: July 03, 1898 in Whitesburg, KY d: December 27, 1965 Sex: Female

................9 [642] Marianne Adams b: October 10, 1867 in Letcher Co., KY d: August 20, 1947 Sex: Female

......................+[643] Shade Combs b: December 22, 1859 m: January 29, 1885 in Whitesburg, KY d: January 27, 1940 Sex: Male

................9 [644] James M. Adams b: 1868 Sex: Male

................9 [645] William Adams b: 1870 Sex: Male

................9 [211] General Adams b: January 29, 1874 in Letcher Co., KY d: 1959 Sex: Male

......................+[212] Martha Caudill b: February 14, 1882 in Perry Co., KY m: January 29, 1902 d: July 28, 1957 Father: Henry R. Stephen Caudill Mother: Mary Branson Sex: Female

............7 [646] Lydia Caudill, b: July 19, 1816 Number of children: ? Sex: Female

................+[647] Nathaniel Woolery Cornett, b: 1811 d: 1899 Number of children: ? Father: William Jesse Cornett, Mother: Mary Ann Everage Sex: Male

..............8 [648] Pollyann Cornett, b: 1842 in Knott Co., KY Sex: Female

............7 [649] Jesse B. Caudill, b: November 10, 1818 in Perry Co., KY d: 1904 in Letcher Co., KY Number of children: 8 Sex: Male Burial: Watty Caudill Cemetery, at the mouth of Dry Fork, Letcher Co., KY

................+[650] Mary "Polly" Back, Bach b: February 03, 1827 in Letcher Co.,? KY m: April 04, 1844 in Letcher Co., KY d: July 29, 1888 Number of children: 8 Father: Henry Back, Bach Mother: Susannah Maggard Sex: Female Burial: Watty Caudill Cemetery, at the mouth of Dry Fork, Letcher Co., KY

...............8 [213] Benjamin "Paw Paw" Caudill, b: 1846 in Letcher Co., KY d: Abt. 1927 Number of children: 2 Sex: Male

.....................+[651] Sarah "Sallie" Brashear b: Abt. 1856 in Perry Co., KY Sex: Female (Note: Looking for ancestors)

...............2nd Wife of [213] Benjamin "Paw Paw" Caudill, :

.....................+[652] Terry Hampton b: 1847 in Letcher Co., KY m: 1868 in KY d: March 06, 1877 in Letcher Co., KY Number of children: 2 Father: Wilburn Hampton Mother: Phoebe Caudill Sex: Female Burial: Watty Caudill Cemetery, at the mouth of Dry Fork, Letcher Co., KY

..................9 [653] Polly Ann Caudill, b: May 1872 in KY Number of children: 4 Sex: Female

........................+[654] Elhannon Jent, b: September 12, 1873 in Indian Bottom, Perry Co., KY m: Abt. 1895 in Perry or Letcher Co., KY d: May 05, 1947 in Scuddy, Perry Co., KY Number of children: 4 Father: John Jent, Ghent; Mother: Nellie or Nella or "Nell" Sumner, Sex: Male Burial: May 06, 1947 Sumner Cem., Perry Co., KY

.....................10 [655] Sally Jent b: March 1896 Sex: Female

.....................10 [656] John D. Jent b: June 1898 Sex: Male

.....................10 [657] Phoebe Jent b: 1909 in KY Sex: Female

...........................+[658] Ira Combs b: 1901 in KY? Father: Richard Nicholas "Dick" Combs Mother: Nancy Martin Sex: Male

.....................10 [659] Chester Jent, b: Abt. 1911 in VicCo., KY? Number of children: ? Sex: Male

...........................+[660] Oma Smith b: Abt. 1913 in VicCo., KY? Number of children: ? Father: Thomas "Tom" Smith, Mother: Vinabelle Smith, Sex: Female

..................9 [661] John D. Caudill b: July 29, 1875 in KY d: October 17, 1955 in Perry Co., KY Number of children: ? Sex: Male

........................+[662] Martha (or Patsy) Polly b: August 10, 1878 in KY m: Abt. 1897 in KY d: October 31, 1949 Number of children: ? Sex: Female (Note: Looking for her ancestors)

.....................10 [663] Enoch Caudill b: Abt. 1910 Number of children: ? Sex: Male

...........................+[664] Hazel McIntry b: Abt. 1912 m: February 11, 1933 Number of children: ? Sex: Female

........................11 _____ Caudill b: Abt. 1940 Number of children: ? Sex: Male

...........................+_____ _____? b: Abt. 1942 Number of children: ? Sex: Female

...............8 [665] Susanna Caudill b: January 1850 d: February 27, 1920 Sex: Female Burial: Watty Caudill Cemetery, at the mouth of Dry Fork, Letcher Co., KY

.....................+[666] Stephen Roberts b: Abt. 1848 Father: Preston Roberts Mother: Rebecca Caudill Sex: Male

...............8 [214] John Maggard Caudill b: June 25, 1852 in Letcher Co., KY d: August 31, 1939 Number of children: ? Sex: Male

.....................+[667] Susanna Hampton b: Abt. 1861 d: June 30, 1877 Father: Wilburn Hampton Mother: Phoebe Caudill Sex: Female Burial: Watty Caudill Cemetery, at the mouth of Dry Fork, Letcher Co., KY

...............2nd Wife of [214] John Maggard Caudill:

.....................+[668] Polly Ann Morgan b: 1861 in Letcher Co., KY m: May 31, 1882 in Letcher Co., KY Number of children: ? Sex: Female (Note: Looking for her ancestors)

..................9 [669] William H. Caudill b: January 02, 1893 in Letcher Co., KY d: September 25, 1963 in Elkhorn City, Pike Co., KY Number of children: ? Sex: Male

........................+[670] Ollie Mae Sumner b: September 02, 1897 in Fusonia, Perry Co., KY m: March 23, 1917 in Perry Co., KY d: July 11, 1953 in Grundy, VA Number of children: ? Sex: Female

.....................10 [671] Edith Caudill b: January 31, 1919 in Cornettsville, Perry Co., KY d: 1999 in Perry Co., KY Number of children: ? Sex: Female

...........................+[672] Marcellus Combs b: September 05, 1916 in Allais, Perry Co., KY m: November 03, 1939 in Perry Co., KY d: March 10, 1988 in Hazard, Perry Co., KY Number of children: ? Father: Owen Combs Mother: Mahala Campbell Sex: Male

.....................11 Norma Leigh Combs b: Abt. 1943 in Perry Co., KY Sex: Female

................8 [673] Nancy C. Caudill b: December 09, 1853 d: January 06, 1915 Number of children: 5 Sex: Female Burial: Watty Caudill Cemetery, at the mouth of Dry Fork, Letcher Co., KY
......................+[674] James Dixon Caudill b: December 13, 1854 d: May 04, 1938 Number of children: 5 Sex: Male Burial: Watty Caudill Cemetery, at the mouth of Dry Fork, Letcher Co., KY
.................9 [675] Watson Caudill b: February 08, 1878 d: December 1878 Sex: Male Burial: Watty Caudill Cemetery, at the mouth of Dry Fork, Letcher Co., KY
.................9 [215] Mary Caudill b: December 05, 1881 d: November 29, 1930 Sex: Female Burial: Watty Caudill Cemetery, at the mouth of Dry Fork, Letcher Co., KY
........................+[676] Jeremiah P. Dixon b: Abt. 1880 Sex: Male
.................2nd Husband of [215] Mary Caudill:
........................+[677] Joe Hawkins b: Abt. 1879 Sex: Male
.................9 [678] James Caudill b: February 10, 1890 d: September 19, 1899 Sex: Male Burial: Watty Caudill Cemetery, at the mouth of Dry Fork, Letcher Co., KY
.................9 [679] Rachel Caudill b: July 13, 1898 d: October 02, 1900 Sex: Female Burial: Watty Caudill Cemetery, at the mouth of Dry Fork, Letcher Co., KY
.................9 [680] Boyd Caudill b: November 22, 1898 d: December 22, 1919 Sex: Male Burial: Watty Caudill Cemetery, at the mouth of Dry Fork, Letcher Co., KY
...............8 [681] Watson "Watty" Caudill b: Abt. 1854 Number of children: ? Sex: Male
......................+[682] Rachel Hampton b: March 23, 1852 d: December 25, 1881 Number of children: ? Father: Wilburn Hampton Mother: Phoebe Caudill Sex: Female Burial: Watty Caudill Cemetery, at the mouth of Dry Fork, Letcher Co., KY
.................9 [216] Jesse Wilburn Caudill b: Abt. 1876 Number of children: ? Sex: Male
........................+[683] Rosanna Tyree b: Abt. 1878 d: July 14, 1899 Sex: Female Burial: Watty Caudill Cemetery, at the mouth of Dry Fork, Letcher Co., KY
.................2nd Wife of [216] Jesse Wilburn Caudill:
........................+[684] Mary Miller b: Abt. 1879 Number of children: ? Sex: Female
....................10 [685] unnamed Caudill b: June 14, 1901 d: June 14, 1901 Sex: Male Burial: Watty Caudill Cemetery, at the mouth of Dry Fork, Letcher Co., KY
...............8 [686] Henry Caudill, b: November 15, 1856 in Letcher Co., KY? d: March 07, 1899 Number of children: 2 Sex: Male
......................+[687] Barilla Jones b: May 22, 1877 d: January 29, 1899 Number of children: 2 Sex: Female
.................9 [688] William M. Caudill, World War I Soldier b: April 27, 1896 d: July 12, 1966 Number of children: 2 Sex: Male Burial: Caudill Cemetery at Uz, Letcher Co., KY
......................+[689] Etta B. Dixon b: September 10, 1899 d: September 08, 1938 Number of children: 2 Father: James C. Dixon Mother: Evelyn Back, Bach Sex: Female
....................10 [690] Harold K. Caudill, b: Abt. 1910 Number of children: ? Sex: Male
..........................+[691] Dociphene Frazier b: Abt. 1915 Number of children: ? Father: Enoch Flanery Frazier Mother: Sarah "Elizabeth" Boatright Sex: Female
....................10 [692] Helen M. Caudill b: August 23, 1935 d: September 09, 1935 Sex: Female Burial: Caudill Cemetery at Uz, Letcher Co., KY
.................9 [693] Jesse Caudill b: July 21, 1898 d: November 25, 1935 Killed by his wife with an axe Sex: Male
......................+[694] Artie Cornett, b: Abt. 1900 Sex: Female (Note: Looking her for ancestors)
...............8 [695] Easter Caudill, Johnny's 7th wife b: December 17, 1859 d: November 08, 1882 Sex: Female Burial: Watty Caudill Cemetery, at the mouth of Dry Fork, Letcher Co., KY
......................+[696] Johnny C. Brown b: Abt. 1820 Father: George W. Brown Mother: Susanna Wells Sex: Male
...............8 [697] David J. Caudill b: December 21, 1860 d: September 15, 1882 Sex: Male Burial: Watty Caudill Cemetery, at the mouth of Dry Fork, Letcher Co., KY
.............7 [698] Henry Caudill, b: Abt. 1820 Sex: Male
.............7 [699] Watson E. "Old Watty" Caudill, b: March 14, 1822 in Perry Co., KY d: December

05, 1898 in Letcher Co., KY Number of children: 4 Sex: Male

.....................+[700] Elizabeth "Betty" Branham-Smith, b: March 19, 1827 in Perry Co., KY m: Abt. 1846 in Perry Co., KY? Number of children: 4 Father: William "Billy" Branham-Smith Mother: Elizabeth (Betty) Childers Sex: Female

.................8 [701] Polly Ann Caudill b: Abt. 1847 Sex: Female

.................8 [702] Rachel Caudill b: December 24, 1855 d: October 09, 1876 Sex: Female Burial: Watty Caudill Cemetery, at the mouth of Dry Fork, Letcher Co., KY

.................8 [703] Martha Salina Caudill b: Abt. 1860 Number of children: ? Sex: Female

.........................+[704] Rudolphus "Dolph" A. Lafayette Draughn b: Abt. 1855 m: Abt. 1882 Number of children: ? Sex: Male (Note: looking for ancestors)

.....................9 [705] _____ Draughn, ? b: Abt. 1895 Number of children: ? Sex: Male

..........................+[706] _____ _____? b: Abt. 1900 Number of children: ? Sex: Female

.................8 [709] Lucinda Caudill b: April 10, 1862 d: October 13, 1906 Number of children: ? Sex: Female Burial: Watty Caudill Cemetery, at the mouth of Dry Fork, Letcher Co., KY

.........................+[710] Steve Hall b: Abt. 1860 Number of children: ? Sex: Male

.....................9 [711] Beckham Hall b: June 04, 1904 d: June 04, 1904 Sex: Male Burial: Watty Caudill Cemetery, at the mouth of Dry Fork, Letcher Co., KY

.............7 [712] Walter E. Caudill, b: Abt. 1824 Sex: Male

.............7 [713] Fanny Caudill, b: Abt. 1826 Sex: Female

..........6 Thomas Aaron Caudill, Sr. b: June 04, 1764 in Logan Co., KY d: May 05, 1848 in Simpson Co., KY Number of children: 12 Sex: Male

.................+Mary "Polly" Everest b: Abt. 1752 d: August 23, 1846 Number of children: 12 Sex: Female

.............7 Polly Caudill b: Abt. 1775 Sex: Female

.............7 Sarah Caudill b: Bet. 1775 - 1794 Sex: Female

.................+Richard Rafferty b: Abt. 1775 m: December 21, 1807 in Logan Co., WV Sex: Male

.............7 William Caudill b: Abt. 1790 in Wilkes Co., NC Number of children: ? Sex: Male

.................+Rachel Joines b: Abt. 1788 in Wilkes Co., NC m: October 28, 1811 in Wilkes Co., NC Number of children: ? Father: Thomas Joines Mother: Sarah Caudill Sex: Female

.................8 [217] Wilburn E. Caudill b: Abt. 1812 in NC Number of children: 2 Sex: Male

.........................+[218] Nancy Caudill b: Abt. 1817 in KY d: 1894 Number of children: 2 Father: William C. "Billy" Caudill, Mother: Mary Nancy "Nancy" Craft Sex: Female

.....................9 [186] William W. "Wild Bill" Caudill b: Abt. 1839 in NC d: June 22, 1920 in Wolfe Co., KY Number of children: 2 Sex: Male

.........................+[185] Elizabeth "Betsy" Eldridge b: Abt. 1841 Number of children: 2 Father: Levi Eldridge Mother: Easter (or Esther) Caudill, Sex: Female

.....................10 [187] Martha Ann Caudill b: Abt. 1861 Number of children: ? Sex: Female

..............................+[188] Enoch Everidge b: Abt. 1860 Number of children: ? Sex: Male

..............................11 [189] Susan "Susie" Everidge b: August 15, 1885 in KY d: December 29, 1962 in Perry Co., KY Number of children: 9 Sex: Female

..................................+[190] Hiram Combs b: May 07, 1882 d: April 29, 1962 Number of children: 9 Father: Benjamin Combs Mother: Matilda "Tilda" Combs Sex: Male

.....................10 [25] Sarah Caudill b: September 1872 in Campton, KY Number of children: ? Sex: Female

..............................+[24] John C. Caudill b: February 1868 in Harlan or Letcher Co., KY m: April 18, 1889 in Breathitt Co., KY Number of children: ? Father: Henry H. Caudill Mother: Susannah Back Sex: Male

..........................11 [9] Cleveland Caudill b: June 1891 in Letcher Co., KY Sex: Male

..............................+[8] Peggy Caudill b: April 1890 in Letcher Co., KY m: July 14, 1909 in Letcher Co., KY d: January 14, 1916 Father: William B. Caudill Mother: Susannah "Sukie" Caudill Sex: Female

.....................9 [18] Mary C. Caudill b: January 13, 1852 in Letcher Co., KY Number of children:

? Sex: Female

...................+[17] Lewis E. Caudill b: March 05, 1855 in Letcher Co., KY m: January 13, 1852 in Letcher Co., KY Number of children: ? Father: Henry H. Caudill Mother: Susannah Back Sex: Male

...................10 [19] Phoebe Caudill b: May 02, 1878 in Letcher Co., KY Number of children: 2 Sex: Female

.......................+[20] Levi S. Caudill b: December 22, 1875 in KY m: September 30, 1895 in Letcher Co., KY d: March 20, 1955 Number of children: 2 Father: Samuel B. Caudill Mother: Mary Ann "Polly" Eldridge Sex: Male

...................11 [21] Benjamin "Bennie" Caudill b: Abt. 1902 Sex: Male

...................11 [22] Howard Caudill b: Abt. 1915 Number of children: 11 Sex: Male

.............................+[23] Gladys Madden b: Abt. 1915 m: Abt. 1935 Number of children: 11 Father: Charles Madden Sex: Female

.............7 Elizabeth Caudill b: Bet. 1790 - 1800 Sex: Female

.............7 Aaron Caudill b: April 30, 1794 Sex: Male

.............7 Catherine Caudill b: Bet. 1795 - 1804 Sex: Female

.............7 Moses Caudill b: November 16, 1796 Sex: Male

.............7 [219] Thomas Caudill, Jr., b: Abt. 1797 in SC d: 1870 Number of children: 8 Sex: Male

..................+[220] Jane "Jenny" Caudill, b: 1799 in NC m: December 12, 1816 in Floyd Co., KY d: Abt. 1870 Number of children: 8 Father: Matthew Caudill, Sr., Mother: Sarah H. Webb Sex: Female

...............8 [221] Sarah Caudill b: Abt. 1816 in KY d: April 24, 1861 in Johnson Co., KY Sex: Female

.....................+[222] James Fitzpatrick b: Abt. 1815 m: February 11, 1836 in Floyd Co., KY Sex: Male

...............8 [223] Isom Caudill b: 1822 in Brushy Fork, Lawrence Co., KY d: June 01, 1857 in Brushy Fork, Lawrence Co., KY Number of children: ? Sex: Male

.....................+[224] Nancy Bailey b: Abt. 1825 m: April 15, 1843 in Morgan Co., KY Number of children: ? Sex: Female

.................9 [225] Mahala Caudill b: 1844 d: 1905 Sex: Female

...............8 [226] Matthew Jackson Caudill b: Abt. 1823 in Scott Co., VA Sex: Male

.....................+[227] Temperance Fitzpatrick b: Abt. 1825 m: August 1842 Sex: Female

...............8 [228] James Caudill b: March 10, 1824 in Scott Co., VA d: August 25, 1895 Sex: Male

.....................+[229] Angeline Bailey b: Abt. 1827 m: November 08, 1846 Sex: Female

...............8 [230] Nancy Jane Caudill b: Abt. 1826 in Scott Co., VA Sex: Female

.....................+[231] John L. Blair b: Abt. 1825 m: May 04, 1854 Sex: Male

...............8 [232] C. Abner Caudill, b: Abt. 1829 in KY d: Aft. 1880 Number of children: ? Sex: Male

.....................+[233] Mary Emily Justice b: Abt. 1830 in Johnson Co., KY? m: July 24, 1849 in Johnson Co., KY Number of children: ? Sex: Female

.................9 [95] Margaret E. Caudill, b: January 10, 1859 in Johnson Co., KY Sex: Female

.....................+[83] Benjamin F. Caudill, b: September 15, 1860 in Johnson Co., KY m: May 03, 1878 in Johnson Co., KY d: September 1915 Number of children: ? Father: John Caudill, Mother: Phoebe Fitzpatrick Sex: Male

...............8 [234] Thomas Caudill b: Abt. 1833 Sex: Male

...............8 [235] Mary J. Caudill b: Abt. 1843 Sex: Female

.....................+[236] _____ Smith b: Abt. 1840 Sex: Male

.............7 James Caudill b: September 16, 1800 Sex: Male

.............7 Jane Caudill b: October 13, 1802 Sex: Female

.............7 Agnes Caudill b: August 31, 1804 Sex: Female

.............7 Polly Caudill b: Bef. November 06, 1848 Sex: Female

..........6 William Caudill b: 1765 Sex: Male

..........6 John Caudill b: Abt. 1768 Sex: Male

..........6 Jesse Caudill b: Abt. 1770 Sex: Male

........5 Sampson Caudill b: 1722 in Lunenburg Co., VA Sex: Male

........5 William Caudill b: Abt. 1724 in VA Sex: Male

........5 Benjamin "Ben of Sussex" Caudill, Sr., b: 1730 in Brunswick or Sussex Co., VA d: Bet. 1776 - 1777 in Anson Co., NC Number of children: 15 Sex: Male

..............+Elizabeth Buckner, b: 1728 in VA? m: Abt. 1751 d: 1800 Number of children: 15 Sex: Female (Note: looking for her ancestors; it is not known if all the children listed below are hers & Ben's)

..........6 [804] Nancy Ann "Ann" Caudill, b: 1752 in Sussex Co., VA d: 1787 in Roaring River, Wilkes Co., NC Number of children: 3 Sex: Female

................+[803] John Hobbs Adams, Jr., b: 1747 in NC m: August 10, 1768 in Loudoun Co., Virginia d: July 15, 1815 in Pine Creek, Floyd Co., KY Number of children: 12 Father: John Hobbs "Old John of KY" Adams, Sr., Mother: Ann Caudill, her parents are unknown, but they were probably Stephen James Caudill (d. 1759) and Mary Elizabeth "Betsy" Fields (b. 1698); Sex: Male Burial: Webb Cemetery, Mayking, Letcher Co., KY

..............7 [805] Elizabeth "Betsy" Adams b: Abt. 1770 in Loudon Co.,(or Lunenburg Co.) VA Number of children: 11 Sex: Female (Note: looking for her ancestors; she is connected to Governor Owsley)

...................+[806] Archelous Craft, Sr., Rev. War Soldier b: December 25, 1749 in England (born on a ship en route from England to America) m: December 11, 1785 in Wilkes Co., NC d: November 08, 1853 in North Fork (of the KY River, 5 miles from the VA line) , Letcher Co., KY Number of children: 11 Father: _____ Craft Mother: _____ _____? Sex: Male (Note: he fought in the Rev. War)

................8 [237] Mary Nancy "Nancy" Craft b: 1784 in Harris Creek, Wilkes Co., NC d: July 27, 1877 in Letcher Co., KY Number of children: 14 Sex: Female

......................+[7] William C. "Billy" Caudill, b: July 27, 1779 in Wilkes Co., NC m: Abt. 1804 d: July 27, 1880 in Letcher Co., KY Number of children: 14 Father: James "Jimmie" Caudill, Jr., Rev. War Soldier Mother: Mary A. Adams, Sex: Male

..................9 [238] Ellender Caudill b: Abt. 1805 Sex: Female

..................9 [239] Betsy Caudill b: Abt. 1806 Sex: Female

..................9 [240] Delilah "Lila" Caudill b: May 08, 1807 Sex: Female

..................9 [241] Isabel Caudill b: Abt. 1809 Sex: Female

..................9 [242] Mary Caudill b: March 10, 1811 in KY d: September 13, 1880 Number of children: 10 Sex: Female

.......................+[243] Joshua Mullins b: November 18, 1809 in Knox Co., KY d: February 15, 1900 in Letcher Co., KY Number of children: 10 Father: Joshua Mullins, Mother: Anna Robinson Sex: Male

....................10 [244] John Mullins b: December 26, 1834 Sex: Male

....................10 [245] Joseph M. Mullins b: June 19, 1834 Sex: Male

....................10 [246] Solomon Mullins b: 1838 Sex: Male

....................10 [247] Caleb Mullins b: 1840 Sex: Male

....................10 [248] Joshua Mullins b: 1842 Sex: Male

....................10 [249] Anna Mullins b: September 18, 1842 Sex: Female

...........................+[250] George Washington Adams b: September 02, 1839 in Letcher Co., KY d: 1943 in Washington Father: Moses "Smoot" Adams Mother: Rebecca (Roberts) Hall Sex: Male

....................10 [251] William Mullins b: 1846 Sex: Male

....................10 [252] Delilah Mullins b: Aft. 1846 Sex: Female

....................10 [253] Nancy Mullins b: Aft. 1847 Sex: Female

....................10 [254] James Henderson Mullins b: September 12, 1853 Sex: Male

..................9 [255] Rebecca "Becca" Caudill b: April 15, 1815 Sex: Female

..................9 [256] Elizabeth "Betsy" Caudill b: Abt. 1816 d: in Knox Co., KY Number of children:

12 Sex: Female
.......................+[257] Caleb Mullins b: 1810 in KY d: in KY Number of children: 12 Father: Joshua Mullins, Mother: Anna Robinson Sex: Male
.....................10 [258] William Mullins b: 1834 Sex: Male
.....................10 [259] Mary Mullins b: Abt. 1836 Sex: Female
.....................10 [260] Ann Mullins b: Abt. 1838 Sex: Female
.....................10 [261] Nancy Mullins b: Abt. 1838 Sex: Female
.....................10 [262] Joab Mullins b: Abt. 1841 Sex: Male
.....................10 [263] Sarah Mullins b: Abt. 1844 Sex: Female
.....................10 [264] John Mullins b: Abt. 1847 Sex: Male
.....................10 [265] Susan Mullins b: 1850 Sex: Female
.....................10 [266] Hugh Mullins b: August 25, 1852 Sex: Male
.....................10 [267] James K. Mullins b: September 03, 1856 Sex: Male
.....................10 [268] Elizabeth Mullins b: 1860 Sex: Female
.....................10 [269] Ann Mullins b: October 1868 Sex: Female
..................9 [218] Nancy Caudill b: Abt. 1817 in KY d: 1894 Number of children: 2 Sex: Female
.......................+[217] Wilburn E. Caudill b: Abt. 1812 in NC Number of children: 2 Father: William Caudill Mother: Rachel Joines Sex: Male
.....................10 [186] William W. "Wild Bill" Caudill b: Abt. 1839 in NC d: June 22, 1920 in Wolfe Co., KY Number of children: 2 Sex: Male
...........................+[185] Elizabeth "Betsy" Eldridge b: Abt. 1841 Number of children: 2 Father: Levi Eldridge Mother: Easter (or Esther) Caudill, Sex: Female
.......................11 [187] Martha Ann Caudill b: Abt. 1861 Number of children: ? Sex: Female
...........................+[188] Enoch Everidge b: Abt. 1860 Number of children: ? Sex: Male
.......................11 [25] Sarah Caudill b: September 1872 in Campton, KY Number of children: ? Sex: Female
...........................+[24] John C. Caudill b: February 1868 in Harlan or Letcher Co., KY m: April 18, 1889 in Breathitt Co., KY Number of children: ? Father: Henry H. Caudill Mother: Susannah Back Sex: Male
.....................10 [18] Mary C. Caudill b: January 13, 1852 in Letcher Co., KY Number of children: ? Sex: Female
...........................+[17] Lewis E. Caudill b: March 05, 1855 in Letcher Co., KY m: January 13, 1852 in Letcher Co., KY Number of children: ? Father: Henry H. Caudill Mother: Susannah Back Sex: Male
.......................11 [19] Phoebe Caudill b: May 02, 1878 in Letcher Co., KY Number of children: 2 Sex: Female
...........................+[20] Levi S. Caudill b: December 22, 1875 in KY m: September 30, 1895 in Letcher Co., KY d: March 20, 1955 Number of children: 2 Father: Samuel B. Caudill Mother: Mary Ann "Polly" Eldridge Sex: Male
..................9 [270] James "Limber Jim" Caudill b: Abt. 1818 in Floyd Co., KY Number of children: 4 Sex: Male
.......................+[271] Elizabeth "Betsy" Mullins b: 1820 in KY d: 1899 Number of children: 4 Father: Joshua Mullins, Mother: Anna Robinson Sex: Female
.....................10 [272] Mary "Polly" Caudill b: 1840 Sex: Female
...........................+[273] Lewis Campbell b: 1830 Father: William C. Campbell Mother: Elizabeth Cornett, Sex: Male
.....................10 [274] Nancy Ann Caudill b: Abt. 1841 Number of children: ? Sex: Female
...........................+[275] Davis S. Fields b: Abt. 1840 Number of children: ? Sex: Male
.......................11 [276] William Fields b: December 22, 1861 in Letcher Co., KY d: 1938 in Whitley Co., KY Sex: Male
...........................+[277] Martha Brashear b: October 11, 1871 d: March 31, 1943 Father: James Nicholas Brashear, Jr. Mother: Elizabeth Pratt Sex: Female

.....................10 [27] William B. Caudill b: April 23, 1845 in Letcher Co., KY d: January 18, 1929 Number of children: ? Sex: Male (Note: William & Susannah were cousins)

..........................+[26] Susannah "Sukie" Caudill b: Abt. 1847 in KY m: February 28, 1867 in Letcher Co., KY d: August 14, 1925 Number of children: ? Father: Isom Caudill Mother: Elizabeth "Lizzie" Back, Bach Sex: Female (Note: Susannah & William were cousins)

.....................11 [8] Peggy Caudill b: April 1890 in Letcher Co., KY d: January 14, 1916 Sex: Female

...........................+[9] Cleveland Caudill b: June 1891 in Letcher Co., KY m: July 14, 1909 in Letcher Co., KY Father: John C. Caudill Mother: Sarah Caudill Sex: Male

.....................10 [14] Joshua M. Caudill b: June 23, 1850 in Letcher Co., KY d: March 22, 1941 Sex: Male

..........................+[13] Rhoda Caudill b: April 12, 1853 in Letcher Co., KY d: January 17, 1942 Father: Henry B. Caudill, twin, Mother: Margaret "Patsy" Campbell Sex: Female

..................9 [278] Sarah "Sally" Caudill b: July 29, 1823 d: April 13, 1884 Sex: Female

..................9 [279] Susannah Caudill b: April 18, 1825 in Perry Co., KY d: September 26, 1898 in Elk Creek, Letcher Co., KY Sex: Female Burial: Elder James Dixon Cemetery, Elk Creek, Letcher Co., KY

..................9 [280] William J. "Stiller Bill" Caudill b: July 05, 1827 in Letcher Co., KY d: November 26, 1908 Number of children: 16 Sex: Male

........................+[281] Nancy Dixon, Dickson b: April 19, 1830 in Letcher Co., KY m: February 07, 1847 in Letcher Co., KY d: December 31, 1899 Number of children: 16 Father: Thomas Dixon Mother: Susannah Proffitt Sex: Female

.....................10 [282] James William "Noah Jim" Caudill b: October 19, 1846 in Blackey, Letcher Co., KY d: August 14, 1911 Number of children: ? Sex: Male

...........................+[283] Lucinda Sumner b: January 28, 1850 in KY m: December 24, 1868 in Letcher Co., KY d: June 16, 1911 in KY Number of children: ? Father: John Sumner Mother: Nancy Hampton Sex: Female

.......................11 [10] Henry H. Cleveland Caudill b: April 20, 1887 in KY d: May 06, 1971 in Whitesburg, Letcher Co., KY Number of children: 18 Sex: Male Burial: Cleveland Caudill Cemetery, Caudill's Branch, Blackey, Letcher Co., KY

.............................+[195] Rebecca Adams b: Abt. 1887 m: Abt. 1905 d: in Waynesburg, KY Number of children: 8 Father: Gideon Adams Mother: Sarah Blair Sex: Female

.......................2nd Wife of [10] Henry H. Cleveland Caudill:

.............................+[284] Lucinda "Cinda" Watts b: April 20, 1886 m: May 11, 1911 in Letcher Co., KY d: October 22, 1963 in Letcher Co., KY Number of children: 10 Father: Allen Watts Mother: Elizabeth Brashear Sex: Female

.....................10 [285] Thomas D. Caudill b: December 26, 1848 in Letcher Co., KY Sex: Male

..........................+[286] Elizabeth Ann "Betsy" Pratt b: Abt. 1852 in Letcher Co., KY m: February 29, 1872 Father: John M. "Knock" Pratt Mother: Elizabeth Campbell Sex: Female

.....................10 [287] William J. "Miller Bill" Caudill b: May 27, 1850 in Letcher Co., KY d: December 11, 1924 Sex: Male Burial: Bill Caudill Cemetery, Blackey, Letcher Co., KY

.....................10 [288] John Caudill b: Abt. 1851 d: Abt. 1851 Sex: Male (Note: died in infancy)

.....................10 [289] Susannah Caudill b: February 20, 1853 in Letcher Co., KY d: November 23, 1941 in Perry Co., KY Sex: Female

.....................10 [290] Hiram W. Caudill b: Abt. September 20, 1853 in Letcher Co., KY d: December 20, 1913 Sex: Male

..........................+[291] Ester Banks b: April 08, 1853 in Letcher Co., KY d: September 25, 1905 Father: Harrison Banks Mother: Sarah Emeline Pridemore Sex: Female

.....................10 [292] Sarah Ann "Sally" Caudill b: January 22, 1855 d: March 02, 1930 Sex: Female

.....................10 [293] Nancy Jane Caudill b: October 05, 1856 d: January 06, 1929 Sex: Female

.....................10 [294] Isaac D. "Ike" Caudill b: February 17, 1859 in KY d: February 19, 1938 in

Colson, or Roxanna, KY Sex: Male

.....................10 [295] Elizabeth "Betsy" Caudill b: Abt. 1860 in Letcher Co., KY d: Abt. 1927 Sex: Female

.....................10 [296] Jeremiah P. "Jerry" Caudill b: November 23, 1861 d: February 25, 1922 Sex: Male

.....................10 [297] George W. Caudill b: October 05, 1863 d: February 02, 1945 Sex: Male

.....................10 [298] Margaret Caudill b: August 25, 1865 d: September 21, 1939 Sex: Female

.....................10 [299] Henry Clay Caudill b: December 08, 1866 in Caudill Branch, Blackey, Letcher Co., KY d: September 06, 1938 in Red Star, KY Number of children: 5 Sex: Male Burial: Elmer Dixon Cemetery, Blackey, Letcher Co., KY

...........................+[300] Margaret Elizabeth "Maggie" Collins b: November 08, 1870 in Letcher Co., KY m: December 22, 1887 in Letcher Co., KY d: September 19, 1965 in Cincinnati, OH Number of children: 5 Father: Henry Powell Collins, Civil War Soldier Mother: Clarissa Ann "Clara" Bowman Sex: Female Burial: Elmer Dixon Cemetery, Blackey, Letcher Co., KY

.......................11 [301] Melissa Caudill b: 1890 d: August 10, 1964 in Nashville, TN Sex: Female Burial: Elmer Dixon Cemetery, Blackey, Letcher Co., KY

.......................11 [302] William Henry "Bill" Caudill b: 1892 d: February 25, 1950 Sex: Male Burial: Elmer Dixon Cemetery, Blackey, Letcher Co., KY

.......................11 [303] John Breckenridge "Johnny" Caudill b: January 21, 1894 in Camp Branch, Letcher Co., KY d: January 10, 1974 in Camp Branch, Letcher Co., KY Number of children: 9 Sex: Male Burial: George Caudill Cemetery, Blackey, Letcher Co., KY

...........................+[304] Thursa Ann Mason b: June 09, 1893 in Sandlick, Letcher Co., KY m: July 30, 1913 in McRoberts, Letcher Co., KY d: August 23, 1975 in Whitesburg, Letcher Co., KY Number of children: 9 Father: Tilghman (Tilton?) Howard Mason Mother: Cornelia "Kerneal" (Grant?) Kiser Sex: Female

.......................11 [305] Louisa Caudill b: August 12, 1902 d: Abt. 1951 Sex: Female Burial: George Cemetery, Blackey, Letcher Co., KY

.......................11 [306] Lavada Belle (Vada?) Caudill b: November 27, 1906 d: November 11, 1965 Sex: Female

.....................10 [307] Martha Caudill b: May 10, 1868 in Lower Caudill Branch, Letcher Co., KY d: May 03, 1943 in Diablock, Perry Co., KY Sex: Female

.....................10 [308] John Breckenridge Caudill b: March 11, 1870 in Letcher Co., KY d: February 24, 1947 in Stroud, Lincoln Co., OK Sex: Male (Note: resided in Chandler, OK, in 1938)

..................9 [309] Henry B. Caudill, twin, b: February 08, 1829 in Perry, Letcher Co., KY d: Abt. 1913 Number of children: 10 Sex: Male Burial: Felix York Cemetery, Viper, KY

.......................+[310] Margaret "Patsy" Campbell b: May 21, 1826 in Linefork, Perry/Letcher Co., KY m: February 15, 1849 in Letcher Co., KY Number of children: 10 Father: William C. Campbell Mother: Elizabeth Cornett, Sex: Female Burial: Felix York Cemetery, Viper, KY

.....................10 [311] Elizabeth "Betty" Caudill b: August 29, 1850 in Letcher Co., KY d: September 05, 1904 Sex: Female

...........................+[312] Audley A. Cornett b: 1848 m: 1869 in Letcher Co., KY d: June 08, 1932 Sex: Male (Note: Looking for ancestors)

.....................10 [313] Robert B. Caudill b: February 14, 1852 in Letcher Co., KY Sex: Male

...........................+[314] Elizabeth "Betty" Brashear b: December 05, 1856 in Perry Co., KY m: January 15, 1876 in Hazard, Perry Co., KY Father: Robert Samuel Brashear Mother: Sarah "Sally" Hall Sex: Female

.....................10 [13] Rhoda Caudill b: April 12, 1853 in Letcher Co., KY d: January 17, 1942 Sex: Female

...........................+[14] Joshua M. Caudill b: June 23, 1850 in Letcher Co., KY d: March 22, 1941 Father: James "Limber Jim" Caudill Mother: Elizabeth "Betsy" Mullins Sex: Male

.....................10 [315] Sarah "Sally" Caudill b: June 17, 1854 in Letcher Co., KY Sex: Female

...........................+[316] William "Bill" Young b: 1851 in Letcher Co., KY Father: Reece Young,

Sr. Mother: Oriah R. "Ora" or "Arry" Ritchie Sex: Male

.....................10 [317] Juda (Judy or Judah?) Caudill, b: March 1855 in Perry Co., KY Number of children: ? Sex: Female

............................+[318] Jeremiah H. "Jerry" Combs b: 1859 in Perry Co., KY? Number of children: ? Father: Hiram Combs Mother: Mary Williams Sex: Male

..........................11 [319] Daniel Combs b: Abt. 1892 in KY Number of children: ? Sex: Male

...............................+[320] Juda _____? b: Abt. 1900 in KY Number of children: ? Sex: Female

.....................10 [321] Harriett Caudill b: 1859 in Letcher Co., KY Sex: Female

............................+[322] Robert Hamilton b: Abt. 1855 Sex: Male

.....................10 [323] William Hartley "Fuzzy Bill" Caudill b: Bet. 1860 - 1861 in Letcher Co., KY d: April 05, 1942 Sex: Male

.............................+[324] Cynthia Brashear b: September 02, 1858 in Perry Co., KY d: December 04, 1943 Sex: Female

.....................10 [15] Lucretia "Lucy" Caudill b: Abt. 1864 in Perry Co., KY Sex: Female

............................+[325] Jeptha Hamilton b: Abt. 1862 Sex: Male

.....................2nd Husband of [15] Lucretia "Lucy" Caudill:

............................+[326] Henry "Bud" Fields b: Abt. 1865 d: April 30, 1947 Sex: Male

.....................10 [327] Polly Ann Caudill b: 1866 Sex: Female

.....................10 [328] John Caudill b: 1869 Sex: Male

..................9 [329] Isom Jesse Caudill, Sr., twin b: February 08, 1829 d: Abt. 1917 Number of children: 12 Sex: Male

...........................+[330] Judah Sumner b: 1831 Number of children: 12 Father: James Sumner Mother: Nancy Adams, Sex: Female

.....................10 [331] Mary Caudill b: 1850 Sex: Female

............................+[332] Enoch Campbell b: Abt. 1847 Sex: Male

.....................10 [333] Nancy Caudill b: August 07, 1852 Sex: Female

............................+[334] Alexander Singleton b: Abt. 1850 Sex: Male

.....................10 [335] Isom Caudill, Jr. b: July 26, 1855 Sex: Male

.....................10 [336] George Henry Caudill b: 1855 Sex: Male

.....................10 [337] Elizabeth Caudill b: June 02, 1856 Sex: Female

............................+[338] John Hall b: Abt. 1855 Sex: Male

.....................10 [339] Lucinda Caudill b: Abt. 1857 Sex: Female

.....................10 [340] Margaret E. Caudill b: 1861 Sex: Female

............................+[341] William Young b: Abt. 1860 Sex: Male

.....................10 [342] Sarah Sally Caudill b: 1864 Sex: Female

.....................10 [343] Patty Caudill b: Abt. 1865 Sex: Female

.....................10 [344] William Caudill b: 1867 Sex: Male

............................+[345] Mary J. Adams b: Abt. 1870 Sex: Female

.....................10 [346] Julia Ann Caudill b: 1870 d: Abt. 1934 Sex: Female

............................+[347] Ezekial Brashear b: Abt. 1867 Sex: Male

.....................10 [348] Ellen Caudill b: 1875 Sex: Female

................8 [807] Sarah "Sally" Craft b: Abt. 1786 in Letcher Co., KY? d: Abt. 1862 in Letcher Co., KY Sex: Female

.....................+[808] William Hammonds b: Abt. 1792 in NC m: April 12, 1812 in Floyd Co., KY d: Abt. 1862 in Letcher Co., KY Father: Joseph Hammonds Mother: Sarah _____? Sex: Male

................8 [809] Ezekiel Craft b: Abt. 1788 Sex: Male

................8 [810] James Craft b: Abt. 1790 in Wilkes Co., NC d: December 1879 in Wayne Co., KY Number of children: 10 Sex: Male

.....................+[811] Druscilla Hammonds b: Abt. 1790 in NC m: February 13, 1812 in Floyd Co., KY d: January 12, 1867 Number of children: 10 Father: Joseph Hammonds Mother: Sarah _____? Sex: Female

..................9 [812] Archibald Craft b: Abt. 1820 Sex: Male

........................+[813] Lettishia "Lettie" Webb b: Abt. 1813 Father: Benjamin Webb Mother: Jane "Jennie" "Jincy" Adams, Sex: Female (Webb Note: Like all of the other Webb individuals in this tree, this Webb family descends from the same line as the country singers Loretta (Webb) Lynn and her sister Brenda Gail "Crystal Gale" Webb. Loretta was born April 14, 1935, in Butcher Hollow, Pike Co., KY; Crystal Gale was born January 9, 1951, in Paintsville, Johnson Co., KY)

..................9 [814] Archelous Craft b: Abt. 1814 in KY Number of children: 5 Sex: Male

.........................+[815] Letty Webb b: Abt. 1816 Number of children: 5 Sex: Female

....................10 [349] Enoch "Chunk" A. Craft b: December 29, 1842 d: February 16, 1937 in Millstone, Letcher Co., KY Number of children: ? Sex: Male

...........................+[350] Polly Ann Caudill b: April 15, 1847 in Letcher Co., KY m: May 02, 1867 in Letcher Co., KY d: February 11, 1937 in Millstone, Letcher Co., KY Number of children: ? Father: John Adams Caudill, Mother: Rachel Cornett, Sex: Female

......................11 [351] Nancy Craft b: January 1872 in Letcher Co., KY d: August 1872 in Letcher Co., KY Sex: Female

....................10 [816] Jane Craft b: Abt. 1846 Sex: Female

....................10 [817] Joseph Craft b: Abt. 1848 Sex: Male

....................10 [818] Benjamin Craft b: Abt. 1852 Sex: Male

....................10 [819] Wiley Craft b: Abt. 1855 Sex: Male

..................9 [820] Joseph Craft b: December 07, 1816 d: December 05, 1886 Number of children: 12 Sex: Male

.....................+[821] Martha Irby Bates b: December 11, 1816 m: March 20, 1834 d: April 18, 1895 Number of children: 12 Father: John Wallis Bates, Sr., Sheriff Mother: Sarah Walthrop, or Waltrop Sex: Female

....................10 [352] John Henderson Craft b: December 20, 1834 in Millstone, KY d: September 13, 1920 in Larue, Laurel Co., KY Number of children: 2 Sex: Male Burial: Lincks Cemetery

...........................+[353] Nancy "Jane" Caudill, Caudell, b: November 05, 1840 in Whitesburg, Letcher Co., KY m: October 11, 1855 in Letcher Co., KY d: November 12, 1922 in London, Laurel Co., KY Number of children: 2 Father: John Adams Caudill, Mother: Rachel Cornett, Sex: Female Burial: Lincks Cemetery

......................11 [354] John Dixon Craft b: April 12, 1856 in Craftsville, Letcher Co., KY d: December 20, 1945 in KY Number of children: ? Sex: Male

............................+[355] Mary Elizabeth Webb b: July 11, 1861 in Letcher Co., KY m: September 13, 1879 d: November 25, 1956 Number of children: ? Father: Henry T. "Chunk" Webb Mother: Francis Elizabeth "Franky" Adams Sex: Female (Webb Note: Like all of the other Webb individuals in this tree, this Webb family descends from the same line as the country singers Loretta (Webb) Lynn and her sister Brenda Gail "Crystal Gale" Webb. Loretta was born April 14, 1935, in Butcher Hollow, Pike Co., KY; Crystal Gale was born January 9, 1951, in Paintsville, Johnson Co., KY)

......................11 [356] Martha A. Craft b: September 12, 1860 in Craftsville, KY d: September 16, 1951 in TN Number of children: 3 Sex: Female

...........................+[357] Noah Milburn Reynolds, Jr. b: December 15, 1855 in KY m: November 15, 1879 in Blountsville, TN d: April 30, 1923 in Mayo Clinic in TN Number of children: 3 Father: Noah Milburn Reynolds, Sr. Mother: Mary Chaney Stone Sex: Male

....................10 [822] Sarah Craft b: Abt. 1836 Sex: Female

...........................+[823] Smith Mullins b: Abt. 1835 Sex: Male

....................10 [824] James W. Craft b: Abt. 1841 Sex: Male

....................10 [825] Martha Manerva Craft b: Abt. 1846 Sex: Female

...........................+[826] _____ Fouts, or Foote b: Abt. 1845 Sex: Male

....................10 [827] Mary Craft b: Abt. 1848 d: Aft. 1898 Sex: Female

...........................+[828] James Mullins b: Abt. 1845 d: Bef. 1898 Sex: Male

....................10 [829] Joseph Craft b: Abt. 1850 Number of children: ? Sex: Male

..........................+[830] Rasuea Bagwell b: March 29, 1850 in Grayson Co., VA m: September 02, 1869 in Letcher Co., KY Number of children: ? Sex: Female

.........................11 [415] Archie C. Craft, Jr. b: May 09, 1884 d: July 06, 1959 Number of children: 7 Sex: Male

.............................+[414] Lettie Dallas Wright b: January 08, 1894 in SeCo., KY m: November 05, 1919 in Letcher Co., KY d: April 04, 1974 Number of children: 7 Father: William S. Wright Mother: Letitia "Lettie/Moody" Bates Sex: Female Burial: Thorton, KY

.....................10 [831] William Craft b: Abt. 1852 d: in Letcher Co., KY? Sex: Male

...........................+[832] _____ Sergeant b: Abt. 1855 m: in Letcher Co., KY d: in Letcher Co., KY? Sex: Female

.....................10 [833] Eliza Craft b: Abt. 1854 in Letcher Co., KY Sex: Female

...........................+[834] John Christopher Reynolds b: Abt. 1851 in Scott Co., VA m: January 04, 1871 d: in SeCo., Letcher Co., KY Father: Noah Milburn Reynolds, Sr. Mother: Mary Chaney Stone Sex: Male

.....................10 [835] Nancy Craft b: Abt. 1856 Sex: Female

...........................+[836] William Greer b: Abt. 1850 Sex: Male

.....................10 [837] Morgan Craft b: Abt. 1868 Sex: Male

...........................+[838] Sallie _____? b: Abt. 1870 Sex: Female

.....................10 [839] Robert Craft b: Abt. 1870 Sex: Male

.....................10 [840] Drusilla Craft b: April 07, 1839 in Letcher Co., KY d: August 27, 1876 in Letcher Co., KY Number of children: 5 Sex: Female

...........................+[841] Stephen Nathaniel Reynolds b: Bet. 1838 - 1839 in Scott Co., VA d: Abt. June 1877 in Letcher Co., KY Number of children: 5 Father: Noah Milburn Reynolds, Sr. Mother: Mary Chaney Stone Sex: Male

.....................11 [842] Joseph Reynolds b: 1861 Sex: Male

.....................11 [843] Noah Christopher Reynolds b: February 08, 1864 Sex: Male

.....................11 [844] John C. Reynolds b: 1866 Sex: Male

.....................11 [845] Stephen Nathaniel Reynolds b: January 05, 1872 Sex: Male

.....................11 [846] Mary Chaney Reynolds b: May 1873 in Letcher Co., KY d: December 21, 1874 in Letcher Co., KY Sex: Female

.................9 [365] Mahala Craft b: Abt. 1818 Number of children: 13 Sex: Female

.......................+[364] Campbell C. Crase b: Abt. 1814 Number of children: 13 Father: Peter Crase, Mother: Annie Adams, Sex: Male

.....................10 [366] James Crase b: Abt. 1835 Number of children: 2 Sex: Male (Note: Not sure if James is the son of Campbell Crase & Mahala Craft)

...........................+[367] Elizabeth Stallard b: Bet. 1837 - 1841 m: December 04, 1856 in Letcher Co., KY Number of children: 2 Sex: Female

.....................11 [368] Hiram Monroe Crase b: March 16, 1866 Sex: Male

...........................+[369] Dicy Collins b: July 13, 1859 in Rockhouse Creek, Letcher Co., KY m: March 04, 1877 in Letcher Co., KY d: November 27, 1900 Father: William Sherman Collins Mother: Eliza Breeding Sex: Female

.....................11 [358] Martha E. Crase b: Abt. 1868 Sex: Female

...........................+[183] William Silas Collins b: April 21, 1865 m: March 03, 1888 in Letcher Co., KY d: December 15, 1937 in Letcher Co., KY Father: Robert Collins Mother: Lydia Adams Sex: Male

.....................10 [370] Peter C. Crase b: Abt. 1837 Sex: Male

.....................10 [371] Elizabeth Crase b: Abt. 1839 Sex: Female

.....................10 [372] Nehemiah Crase b: 1841 Number of children: 9 Sex: Male

...........................+[373] Mary Franklin b: February 1843 Number of children: 9 Sex: Female

.....................11 [374] Campbell M. Crase b: September 1861 Sex: Male

.....................11 [375] Elizabeth Crase b: Abt. 1866 Sex: Female

.....................11 [376] Lousia Crase b: Abt. 1868 Sex: Female

.....................11 [377] Frances Crase b: Abt. 1871 Sex: Male

.....................11 [378] Mantford L. Crase b: Abt. 1873 Sex: Male

.....................11 [379] Dora I. Crase b: Abt. 1875 Sex: Female

.....................11 [380] Cornelia Crase b: Abt. 1879 Sex: Male

.....................11 [381] Loly J. Crase b: Abt. 1883 Sex: Female

.....................11 [382] Malcolm Crase b: 1886 in Magoffin Co., KY d: 1932 in Magoffin Co., KY Number of children: 10 Sex: Male

..........................+[383] Lula LeMaster b: July 31, 1887 in Magoffin Co., KY d: June 1977 in Pike Co., OH Number of children: 10 Sex: Female

...................10 [384] Pricilla Crase b: Abt. 1843 Sex: Female

...................10 [385] Ciney M. Crase b: Abt. 1845 Sex: Unknown

...................10 [386] Noah Crase b: August 1849 Sex: Male

...................10 [387] Alfred W. Crase b: January 06, 1852 Sex: Male

...................10 [388] Morgan Crase b: Abt. 1854 Sex: Male

...................10 [389] Sarah Crase b: November 04, 1856 Sex: Female

...................10 [390] Martha M. Crase b: Abt. 1860 Sex: Female

...................10 [391] Frankie J. Crase b: May 06, 1861 Sex: Female

...................10 [392] Benjamin H. Crase b: June 1863 Sex: Male

................9 [847] Elizabeth Craft b: Abt. 1820 Number of children: 8 Sex: Female

.....................+[848] Jason L. Webb b: Abt. 1820 m: Abt. 1840 Number of children: 9 Father: Benjamin Webb Mother: Jane "Jennie" "Jincy" Adams, Sex: Male (Webb Note: Like all of the other Webb individuals in this tree, this Webb family descends from the same line as the country singers Loretta (Webb) Lynn and her sister Brenda Gail "Crystal Gale" Webb. Loretta was born April 14, 1935, in Butcher Hollow, Pike Co., KY; Crystal Gale was born January 9, 1951, in Paintsville, Johnson Co., KY)

...................10 [849] Nelson Webb b: Abt. 1840 Sex: Male

...................10 [850] Mahala Webb b: Abt. 1843 Sex: Female

...................10 [851] Archibald Webb b: Abt. 1845 Sex: Male

...................10 [852] Wiley W. Webb b: 1847 in Letcher Co., KY Sex: Male

..........................+[853] Nancy Adams b: March 07, 1847 in Smoot Creek, Letcher Co., KY d: September 25, 1925 Father: Isaac B. Adams Mother: Nancy Hayes Sex: Female

...................10 [854] Mary Webb b: Abt. 1849 Sex: Female

...................10 [855] Anna Webb b: Abt. 1851 Sex: Female

...................10 [856] Benjamin Webb b: Abt. 1855 Sex: Male

...................10 [857] Drusilla Webb b: Abt. 1857 Sex: Female

................9 [397] Sarah "Sallie" Craft b: April 02, 1821 d: March 26, 1863 in Letcher Co., KY Number of children: 7 Sex: Female

.....................+[396] John Isom Adams b: 1818 m: August 16, 1838 d: 1863 in (Note: Died trying to open an unexploded bomb to get at the gun powder inside) Number of children: 7 Father: Benjamin Adams, Mother: Nancy Holbrook, Sex: Male

...................10 [398] Benjamin Burford Adams b: 1840 Sex: Male

...................10 [399] James W. Adams b: 1842 Sex: Male

...................10 [400] Nancy Jane Adams b: 1845 Sex: Female

...................10 [401] Jesse Adams b: 1847 Sex: Male

...................10 [402] Joseph Simpson Adams b: 1851 Sex: Male

...................10 [403] Randolph N. Adams b: 1854 Sex: Male

...................10 [404] Archelous Adams b: 1858 Sex: Male

................9 [858] Benjamin Craft b: Abt. 1824 Sex: Male

.....................+[859] Jennifer "Jennie" Adams b: Abt. 1825 Sex: Female

................9 [860] Nehemiah Craft b: Abt. 1826 Sex: Male

.....................+[861] Artie Thornburg b: Abt. 1830 in Letcher Co., KY? Sex: Female

................9 [862] Archelous Craft b: Abt. 1828 in Letcher Co., KY? d: 1897 in Letcher Co., KY

Sex: Male

.........................+[863] Nancy Polly b: Abt. 1830 in Letcher Co., KY? d: 1897 in Letcher Co., KY
Sex: Female

....................9 [864] Stephen Craft b: Abt. 1830 Sex: Male

.................8 [865] John William Craft b: Abt. 1792 Sex: Male

.................8 [866] Stephen Craft b: Abt. 1794 Sex: Male

.................8 [867] Simon Craft b: Abt. 1796 Sex: Male

.................8 [868] Malinda Craft b: Abt. 1798 Sex: Female

.................8 [869] Archaelous "Cheed" Craft, Jr. b: 1802 in Harris Creek, Wilkes Co., NC Number
of children: 14 Sex: Male

........................+[870] Nancy Jane Polly b: 1805 in Carter Co., TN m: August 23, 1822 in Perry
Co., KY d: Aft. 1880 in Letcher Co., KY Number of children: 14 Father: Edward Polly, Mother:
Mary Agnes Mullins, Sex: Female

....................9 [871] Henry Craft b: 1825 Sex: Male

....................9 [872] Wiley Craft b: 1825 Sex: Male

....................9 [873] Elizabeth ("Betsy") Craft b: 1831 Sex: Female

....................9 [874] Susanna Craft b: 1832 Sex: Female

....................9 [875] David K. Craft b: February 22, 1837 Sex: Male

....................9 [876] Henrietta Craft b: 1838 Sex: Female

....................9 [877] Serena Craft b: 1840 Sex: Female

....................9 [878] Melvina Jane ("Viny") Craft b: 1842 Sex: Female

....................9 [879] Margaret Craft b: 1844 Sex: Female

....................9 [880] John P. Craft b: 1845 Sex: Male

....................9 [881] Martha Craft b: 1846 Sex: Female

....................9 [882] Joseph Wiley Craft b: May 1848 Sex: Male

....................9 [883] Edward Craft b: July 29, 1852 Sex: Male

....................9 [884] Mary "Polly" Craft b: 1828 in Perry Co., KY Number of children: 2 Sex:
Female

........................+[885] Jesse "Colly Jesse" Adams b: December 08, 1827 in Perry Co., KY m: July
24, 1845 in Letcher Co., KY d: January 18, 1912 in Letcher Co., KY Number of children: 2 Father:
Stephen "Shank Steve" Adams, Mother: Elizabeth "Betsy" Whitaker Sex: Male

....................10 [886] Cecilia "Celia" Adams b: May 20, 1852 in Letcher Co., KY Number of
children: 2 Sex: Female

........................+[887] James Taylor Addington b: October 19, 1850 in Russell Co., VA m:
March 13, 1870 in Letcher Co., KY d: May 30, 1917 in Letcher Co., KY Number of children: 2
Father: John Addington Mother: Cora Lucinda Roberts Sex: Male

....................11 [888] Mary Elizabeth "Polly Ann" Addington b: September 15, 1869 in Crafts
Colly (Ermine) , Letcher Co., KY Number of children: ? Sex: Female

...........................+[889] William Basil Adkins, b: April 16, 1871 m: 1897 d: September 06,
1962 in Letcher Co., KY Number of children: ? Father: Peter Adkins, Mother: Louisa Ann Belcher
Sex: Male Burial: Isom, Letcher Co., KY (Adkins Note: like the author and all of the other Adkins
individuals in this tree and their descendants, this family descends from European royalty through
Elizabeth Parker, born about 1697 in Charles City or Richmond, Henrico Co., VA. Elizabeth's
husband was William Adkins/Atkinson, born March 28, 1689, in Charles City, Henrico Co. VA.
Elizabeth is the proven 12th great-granddaughter of the King of England, Henry III, born October 1,
1206, in Winchester Castle, Hampshire Co., England)

....................11 [890] Harvey Addington b: Abt. 1871 Number of children: 2 Sex: Male

...........................+[891] Floria Collins b: November 24, 1883 in Lee Co., VA d: May 11, 1952
Number of children: 2 Father: James M. "Big Jimmer" Collins Mother: America Ann Bentley Sex:
Female

....................10 [359] Christina Adams b: June 10, 1858 d: January 07, 1951 Sex: Female

...........................+[360] Greenbury Collins b: February 26, 1868 d: May 03, 1924 Father:

Robert Collins Mother: Lydia Adams Sex: Male
................8 [892] William Craft b: Abt. 1807 d: 1898 in Letcher Co., KY Number of children: ?
Sex: Male
......................+[893] Rachel Parker b: Abt. 1800 Number of children: ? Sex: Female
..................9 [784] Martha Ann ("Patsy") Craft b: Abt. 1835 d: in Letcher Co., KY Number of
children: 3 Sex: Female
........................+[361] Moses "Rockhouse Moses" Adams b: July 18, 1808 in Letcher Co., KY m:
October 03, 1867 in Letcher Co., KY d: 1885 in Hazard, Letcher Co., KY Number of children: 12
Father: Stephen "Rockhouse Steve" Adams Mother: Ellendar "Nellie" Buntin, or Benton Sex: Male
......................10 [785] Mary Adams b: 1867 in Letcher Co., KY Sex: Female
............................+[786] Creed Craft b: 1873 in Letcher Co., KY m: November 20, 1900 in
Whitesburg, KY Sex: Male
......................10 [787] Joseph Adams b: 1870 in Rockhouse Creek, Floyd Co., KY Sex: Male
............................+[788] Flora Tyree b: 1878 m: September 10, 1894 in Letcher Co., KY Sex:
Female
......................10 [789] Lucinda Adams b: 1878 in Letcher Co., KY Sex: Female
............................+[790] Robert E. Banks b: Abt. 1875 m: August 10, 1897 in Letcher Co., KY
Sex: Male
................8 [894] Charity Craft b: Abt. 1810 Sex: Female
............7 [362] Stephen Adams, b: 1778 in NC d: 1858 in Morgan Co., KY Number of children:
10 Sex: Male
..................+[895] Mary "Polly" Holbrook b: Abt. 1785 in Rockhouse, Floyd Co., KY Father:
Randolph Holbrook Mother: Elizabeth _____? Sex: Female
............2nd Wife of [362] Stephen Adams, :
..................+[896] Mary "Mollie" Webb b: 1774 in NC m: Abt. 1798 in Wilkesboro, Wilkes Co.,
NC d: 1851 in Morgan Co., KY Number of children: 9 Father: James F. Webb, Sr., Soldier Mother:
Elizabeth "Lettie" Jane Nelson (Nelson Note: Looking for Elizabeth's ancestors. I believe that she's
part of the large Nelson clan from VA and NC, which spread out and migrated west into WV, TN,
and KY in the 1830s. Like the author, the Judds [Naomi, Ashley, Wynonna], also descend from this
family. The earliest known ancestor of this Nelson group is William "Old William" Nelson, born in
1747 in Prince Edward Co., VA, and died on August 9, 1834, in Hawkins Co., TN. Old William's
wife was Rebecca Smith, born about 1757 in Stokes Co., NC. It's possible, in my opinion, that
Elizabeth could be Old William's sister) Sex: Female (Webb Note: Like all of the other Webb
individuals in this tree, this Webb family descends from the same line as the country singers Loretta
(Webb) Lynn and her sister Brenda Gail "Crystal Gale" Webb. Loretta was born April 14, 1935, in
Butcher Hollow, Pike Co., KY; Crystal Gale was born January 9, 1951, in Paintsville, Johnson Co.,
KY)
................8 [897] Annie Adams, b: 1798 d: Abt. 1844 Number of children: 4 Sex: Female
......................+[363] Peter Crase, b: 1792 in Austusta Co., VA m: March 16, 1816 in Floyd (now
Pike) Co., KY d: 1867 in Roxana, Letcher Co., KY Number of children: 13 Father: George Crase,
Jr., Crace, Cress, Kress, Mother: Charity Morgan, Sex: Male
..................9 [364] Campbell C. Crase b: Abt. 1814 Number of children: 13 Sex: Male
......................+[365] Mahala Craft b: Abt. 1818 Number of children: 13 Father: James Craft
Mother: Druscilla Hammonds Sex: Female
......................10 [366] James Crase b: Abt. 1835 Number of children: 2 Sex: Male (Note: Not sure
if James is the son of Campbell Crase & Mahala Craft)
............................+[367] Elizabeth Stallard b: Bet. 1837 - 1841 m: December 04, 1856 in Letcher
Co., KY Number of children: 2 Sex: Female
........................11 [368] Hiram Monroe Crase b: March 16, 1866 Sex: Male
............................+[369] Dicy Collins b: July 13, 1859 in Rockhouse Creek, Letcher Co., KY
m: March 04, 1877 in Letcher Co., KY d: November 27, 1900 Father: William Sherman Collins
Mother: Eliza Breeding Sex: Female

......................11 [358] Martha E. Crase b: Abt. 1868 Sex: Female

.............................+[183] William Silas Collins b: April 21, 1865 m: March 03, 1888 in Letcher Co., KY d: December 15, 1937 in Letcher Co., KY Father: Robert Collins Mother: Lydia Adams Sex: Male

......................10 [370] Peter C. Crase b: Abt. 1837 Sex: Male

......................10 [371] Elizabeth Crase b: Abt. 1839 Sex: Female

......................10 [372] Nehemiah Crase b: 1841 Number of children: 9 Sex: Male

.............................+[373] Mary Franklin b: February 1843 Number of children: 9 Sex: Female

......................11 [374] Campbell M. Crase b: September 1861 Sex: Male

......................11 [375] Elizabeth Crase b: Abt. 1866 Sex: Female

......................11 [376] Lousia Crase b: Abt. 1868 Sex: Female

......................11 [377] Frances Crase b: Abt. 1871 Sex: Male

......................11 [378] Mantford L. Crase b: Abt. 1873 Sex: Male

......................11 [379] Dora I. Crase b: Abt. 1875 Sex: Female

......................11 [380] Cornelia Crase b: Abt. 1879 Sex: Male

......................11 [381] Loly J. Crase b: Abt. 1883 Sex: Female

......................11 [382] Malcolm Crase b: 1886 in Magoffin Co., KY d: 1932 in Magoffin Co., KY Number of children: 10 Sex: Male

.............................+[383] Lula LeMaster b: July 31, 1887 in Magoffin Co., KY d: June 1977 in Pike Co., OH Number of children: 10 Sex: Female

......................10 [384] Pricilla Crase b: Abt. 1843 Sex: Female

......................10 [385] Ciney M. Crase b: Abt. 1845 Sex: Unknown

......................10 [386] Noah Crase b: August 1849 Sex: Male

......................10 [387] Alfred W. Crase b: January 06, 1852 Sex: Male

......................10 [388] Morgan Crase b: Abt. 1854 Sex: Male

......................10 [389] Sarah Crase b: November 04, 1856 Sex: Female

......................10 [390] Martha M. Crase b: Abt. 1860 Sex: Female

......................10 [391] Frankie J. Crase b: May 06, 1861 Sex: Female

......................10 [392] Benjamin H. Crase b: June 1863 Sex: Male

..................9 [898] Henry Crase b: July 1816 Sex: Male

..................9 [899] Alfred Crase b: 1818 d: 1880 Sex: Male

..................9 [900] Stephen M. Crase b: 1824 Sex: Male

..............8 [901] Daniel Adams b: July 16, 1799 in NC d: 1885 in Brainard, KY Sex: Male

......................+[902] Jane Stone b: Abt. 1800 m: 1818 in Floyd Co., KY Sex: Female

..............8 [903] Elizabeth "Betsy" Adams b: 1801 in NC Sex: Female

......................+[904] John Caudill b: Abt. 1798 m: 1819 in Prestonsburg, KY Sex: Male

..............8 [905] William "Uncle Billy" Adams b: Abt. 1802 d: 1881 Number of children: ? Sex: Male

......................+[906] Elizabeth Mullins b: Abt. 1805 Number of children: ? Sex: Female

..............9 [907] Minerva Adams Number of children: ? Sex: Female

......................+[908] Thomas Reid Number of children: ? Sex: Male

......................10 [909] William Marion Reid Number of children: ? Sex: Male

.............................+[910] Susan Prater Number of children: ? Sex: Female

......................11 [911] Ida Belle Reid Number of children: ? Sex: Female

.............................+[912] Charles T. Hammond Number of children: ? Sex: Male

..............8 [913] Gilbert Adams b: 1804 Sex: Male

......................+[914] Nancy Adams b: Abt. 1805 m: 1823 in Perry Co., KY Sex: Female

..............8 [915] Francis Adams b: Abt. 1810 Number of children: ? Sex: Female

......................+[916] William Tolson Adams b: 1806 Number of children: ? Sex: Male

..............9 [917] Gilbert A. Adams b: 1826 Number of children: ? Sex: Male

......................+[918] Perlina Prater b: Abt. 1830 Number of children: ? Sex: Female

......................10 [180] Rebecca E. Adams b: 1852 Number of children: ? Sex: Female

..........................+[179] Campbell J. May b: 1851 Number of children: ? Father: Noah May Mother: Elizabeth Caudill Sex: Male

.......................11 [181] Augustus Noah May b: 1876 d: 1944 Number of children: ? Sex: Male

.............................+[182] Sarah Elizabeth Cornett b: 1876 d: 1966 Number of children: ? Father: Russell Cornett, Mother: Ailey Amburgey Sex: Female

...............8 [393] Sarah "Sally" Adams b: March 21, 1813 in Rockhouse, Floyd Co., KY d: November 26, 1876 in Wolfe, KY Sex: Female

......................+[919] Blair May b: Abt. 1808 m: May 17, 1829 in Floyd, KY Sex: Male

...............2nd Husband of [393] Sarah "Sally" Adams:

......................+[920] Daniel Conley b: Abt. 1809 in Rockhouse, Floyd Co., KY m: March 12, 1860 in KY? Sex: Male

...............8 [420] Zilpha (Zelphia) Adams b: August 01, 1811 in Rockhouse Creek, Letcher Co., KY d: 1893 Number of children: 5 Sex: Female

......................+[419] Randolph Holbrook b: March 15, 1811 in Floyd Co., KY m: 1827 in Perry Co., KY Number of children: 5 Father: Randolph (or Randel) "Buck" Holbrook, Mother: Elizabeth Nancy Rebecca Adams, Sex: Male

.................9 [421] Kelsey Holbrook b: April 05, 1829 Sex: Male

.......................+[422] Rutha Mullins b: Abt. 1830 Sex: Female

.................9 [423] Nancy A. Holbrook b: 1830 in Floyd Co., KY Number of children: ? Sex: Female

.........................+[424] Richard Lee Spradling b: June 22, 1822 in Floyd Co., KY Number of children: ? Sex: Male

.....................10 [425] Sarah Jane Spradling b: May 26, 1851 in Harrison Co., KY Number of children: ? Sex: Female

.............................+[426] Reuben Porter Dennis b: June 04, 1848 in West Liberty, Morgan Co., KY Number of children: ? Sex: Male

.......................11 [427] Nancy Katherine Dennis b: July 05, 1870 in Hazel Green, KY Number of children: ? Sex: Female

.............................+[428] Jasper Bond Suiter b: September 06, 1872 in Wise Co., VA Number of children: ? Sex: Male

.................9 [429] Benjamin May Holbrook b: March 26, 1832 Number of children: 2 Sex: Male

.......................+[430] Rhoda Bays Spradlin b: 1834 Number of children: 2 Sex: Female

.....................10 [394] Randolph Holbrook b: May 21, 1853 Number of children: 9 Sex: Male

...........................+[431] Virgie Bays b: Abt. 1851 Number of children: 9 Sex: Female

.....................11 [432] Adam Gus Holbrook b: Abt. 1877 Number of children: ? Sex: Male

...........................+[433] Kate Miller b: 1876 Number of children: ? Sex: Female

.....................11 [434] Eva Jane Holbrook b: January 1880 Sex: Female

...........................+[435] Harrison Puckett b: Abt. 1875 Sex: Male

.....................11 [436] Jacob Holbrook b: March 07, 1882 Sex: Male

...........................+[437] Lisa Puckett b: Abt. 1886 Sex: Female

.....................11 [438] John A. Holbrook b: April 1885 Sex: Male

...........................+[439] Cynthia Prater b: Abt. 1889 Sex: Female

.....................11 [440] Samuel Holbrook b: Abt. 1887 Sex: Male

.....................11 [441] Jim Holbrook b: December 1887 Sex: Male

...........................+[442] Lethia Stone b: Abt. 1889 Sex: Female

.....................11 [443] Campbell May Holbrook b: June 16, 1890 Sex: Male

.....................11 [444] Virginia Maxine Holbrook b: Abt. 1891 Sex: Female

.....................11 [445] Elizabeth "Addie" Holbrook b: Abt. 1892 Sex: Female

.....................2nd Wife of [394] Randolph Holbrook:

...........................+[446] Sarah Shepherd b: 1852 Sex: Female

.....................10 [447] Harvey Trimble Holbrook b: June 21, 1879 Sex: Male

...........................+[448] Molly B. Hall b: Abt. 1880 Sex: Female

...............9 [449] Mary B. Holbrook b: 1837 Sex: Female

...............9 [450] Elizabeth Holbrook b: 1838 Sex: Female

...............8 [921] Lucy Adams b: February 16, 1818 in Floyd Co., KY Sex: Female

...................+[922] Lewis Patrick b: Abt. 1810 m: 1837 in Morgan Co., KY Sex: Male

...........3rd Wife of [362] Stephen Adams, :

...................+[923] Katherine T. Reid b: Abt. 1792 in VA m: March 11, 1853 in Morgan, KY Number of children: ? Sex: Female

...............8 [924] Annie Adams b: Abt. 1855 Sex: Female

...........7 [395] Nancy Adams b: 1785 Sex: Female

...................+[7] William C. "Billy" Caudill, b: July 27, 1779 in Wilkes Co., NC d: July 27, 1880 in Letcher Co., KY Number of children: 14 Father: James "Jimmie" Caudill, Jr., Rev. War Soldier Mother: Mary A. Adams, Sex: Male

..........6 [1151] Henrietta "Henny" Caudill, b: 1753 in Sussex (Stafford) Co., VA. d: November 1836 in Mayking, Letcher Co., KY. Number of children: 5 Sex: Female Burial: 1836 Letcher Co., KY. NOTE: Henny is the author's 6th great-grandmother.

...............+[1150] Benjamin "Ben" Adams, Jr., b: 1749 in Fairfax Co., VA m: 1774 in Leesburg, Loudon Co., VA d: 1824 in Mayking, Perry (now Letcher) Co., KY Number of children: 5 Father: John Hobbs "Old John of KY" Adams, Sr., Mother: Ann Caudill, her parents are unknown, but they were probably Stephen James Caudill (d. 1759) and Mary Elizabeth "Betsy" Fields (b. 1698); Sex: Male. NOTE: Ben is the author's 6th great-grandfather.

...........7 [1152] Elizabeth Nancy Rebecca Adams, b: 1775 in Loudon Co., VA d: 1861 in Letcher Co., KY Number of children: 3 Sex: Female

...................+[1153] Randolph (or Randel) "Buck" Holbrook, b: Bet. 1770 - 1778 in Wilkes Co., NC m: 1795 in Wilkesboro, Wilkes Co. N.C. d: April 1847 in Mayking, Letcher Co., KY Number of children: 3 Father: John Henry Holbrook, Mother: Mary Elizabeth Hargis, Sex: Male

...............8 [1003] Nancy Holbrook, b: 1799 in Roaring Rv., Wilkes, N.C. d: Aft. 1870 in Letcher Co. KY Number of children: 4 Sex: Female

...................+[1002] Benjamin Adams, b: 1794 in Roaring Rv., Wilkes, N.C. m: February 10, 1816 in Prestonburg, Floyd, KY d: November 11, 1855 in Letcher Co. KY Number of children: 4 Father: John Hobbs Adams, Jr., Mother: Lydia "Letty" or "Lettie" Simpson Sex: Male

...................9 [396] John Isom Adams b: 1818 d: 1863 in (Note: Died trying to open an unexploded bomb to get at the gun powder inside) Number of children: 7 Sex: Male

...................+[397] Sarah "Sallie" Craft b: April 02, 1821 m: August 16, 1838 d: March 26, 1863 in Letcher Co., KY Number of children: 7 Father: James Craft Mother: Druscilla Hammonds Sex: Female

...................10 [398] Benjamin Burford Adams b: 1840 Sex: Male

...................10 [399] James W. Adams b: 1842 Sex: Male

...................10 [400] Nancy Jane Adams b: 1845 Sex: Female

...................10 [401] Jesse Adams b: 1847 Sex: Male

...................10 [402] Joseph Simpson Adams b: 1851 Sex: Male

...................10 [403] Randolph N. Adams b: 1854 Sex: Male

...................10 [404] Archelous Adams b: 1858 Sex: Male

...............9 [1004] Jesse Adams, b: 1821 in Perry Co., KY d: in Letcher Co., KY Number of children: ? Sex: Male

...................+[1005] Margaret Jenkins b: 1826 in Perry Co., KY m: August 20, 1846 in Letcher Co., KY d: October 09, 1882 in Letcher Co., KY Number of children: ? Father: William Jenkins Sex: Female

...................10 [1006] Elizabeth Adams, b: Bet. November 1844 - 1845 in Letcher Co., KY Sex: Female

...................+[1007] Jesse S. Holbrook, b: February 06, 1837 in Perry Co., KY m: Abt. 1861 in Harlan, KY or Letcher Co., KY Father: Benjamin Holbrook, Mother: Nancy Jenkins Sex: Male Burial: Craft Cemetery, Millstone, KY?

.................9 [1008] Elizabeth Adams b: Abt. 1824 d: July 1880 Number of children: 9 Sex: Female
.....................+[1009] James Bates, Sr. b: Abt. 1823 in Perry or Letcher Co., KY, m: February 26, 1843 in Letcher Co., KY d: April 11, 1864 Murdered in Letcher Co., KY during the Civil War Number of children: 9 Father: John Wallis Bates, Sr., Sheriff Mother: Sarah Walthrop, or Waltrop Sex: Male Burial: Kona KY, Bates Cemetery
....................10 [1010] Henry C. Bates b: Abt. 1844 in Letcher Co., KY Sex: Male
.........................+[1011] Rachel Lee b: Abt. 1840 in Russell Co., VA m: March 13, 1868 in Letcher Co., KY Sex: Female
....................10 [1012] Sarah Bates b: Abt. 1846 Sex: Female
....................10 [1013] Nancy Bates b: October 28, 1848 in Millstone, Letcher Co., KY d: September 10, 1927 in Beefhide, Letcher Co., KY Number of children: 12 Sex: Female Burial: Nancy Wright Cemetery, Beefhide, KY
.........................+[1014] Andrew J. Wright, b: November 14, 1847 in Beefhide, Letcher Co., KY m: December 09, 1870 in Joel Wright's home? , Letcher Co., KY d: January 28, 1919 in Beefhide, Letcher Co., KY Number of children: 12 Father: Samuel W. Wright, Mother: Elizabeth "Betsy" Adams, Sex: Male Burial: Samuel W. Wright Cemetery, Beefhide, KY
.......................11 [405] Joel M. "Big Joel" Wright b: December 08, 1871 in Beefhide Creek, Beefhide, KY d: December 20, 1921 in Jenkins, Letcher Co., KY Number of children: 6 Sex: Male Burial: Nancy Wright Cemetery, Beefhide, KY
.........................+[1015] Cordelia Mullins b: Abt. 1871 in KY? m: February 24, 1892 Sex: Female
.......................2nd Wife of [405] Joel M. "Big Joel" Wright:
.........................+[1016] Susan Wright b: Abt. 1875 in KY? m: August 20, 1895 Sex: Female
.......................3rd Wife of [405] Joel M. "Big Joel" Wright:
.........................+[1017] Mahala Sowards b: Abt. 1875 in KY? m: February 27, 1896 Number of children: 6 Sex: Female
.......................11 [1018] Elizabeth Wright b: March 30, 1874 in Beefhide Creek, Beefhide, KY d: October 16, 1957 Number of children: 5 Sex: Female
.........................+[1019] Henry Blevins b: Abt. 1875 in KY? m: November 21, 1901 Number of children: 5 Sex: Male
.......................11 [406] Eliza J. Wright b: December 13, 1875 in Beefhide Creek, Beefhide, KY d: January 10, 1946 in Norton, VA Sex: Female
.........................+[1020] Joe Willis b: Abt. 1875 in KY? Sex: Male
.......................2nd Husband of [406] Eliza J. Wright:
.........................+[1021] Isaac "Ike" Mills b: Abt. 1875 in KY? m: October 04, 1900 Sex: Male
.......................11 [1022] Sarah J. Wright b: November 16, 1877 in Beefhide KY d: May 02, 1920 in Burdine, Letcher Co., KY Number of children: 5 Sex: Female Burial: Burdine, Letcher Co., KY
.........................+[1023] William "Willie" Blevins b: Abt. 1875 in KY? m: March 01, 1900 Number of children: 5 Sex: Male
.......................11 [1024] Victoria Wright b: October 26, 1878 in Beefhide, KY d: December 11, 1940 in Letcher Co., KY Sex: Female Burial: Beefhide Creek, Beefhide, KY
.........................+[1025] Rathburn Burke b: November 12, 1859 m: April 18, 1922 d: May 13, 1942 Sex: Male
.......................11 [1026] Margaret "Maggie" Wright b: August 06, 1880 in Beefhide, KY d: September 01, 1923 in Letcher Co., KY Number of children: 12 Sex: Female Burial: Nancy Wright Cemetery, Beefhide, KY
.........................+[1027] John Brown b: Abt. 1880 in KY? m: June 22, 1899 Number of children: 12 Sex: Male
.......................11 [1028] William James Wright b: December 28, 1882 in Beefhide, KY d: April 15, 1940 in VA Number of children: 10 Sex: Male Burial: Nancy Wright Cemetery, Beefhide, KY
.........................+[1029] Elizabeth Mullins b: Abt. 1885 in KY? m: 1913 Number of children: 10 Sex: Female

......................11 [1030] Martha Josephine Wright b: November 18, 1884 in Beefhide, KY d: March 26, 1960 in VA Number of children: 8 Sex: Female Burial: Nancy Wright Cemetery, Beefhide, KY

.............................+[1031] John Wesley Ellison b: Abt. 1885 in KY? m: November 23, 1905 Number of children: 8 Sex: Male

......................11 [1032] John Wallis Wright b: February 06, 1887 in Beefhide, KY d: June 26, 1965 in Virginia Beach, VA Number of children: 10 Sex: Male Burial: Nancy Wright Cemetery, Beefhide, KY

.............................+[1033] Alka Mae Wright b: April 23, 1903 in Beefhide, KY m: November 05, 1919 d: October 19, 1986 in Virginia Beach, VA Number of children: 10 Father: Austin McJesse Wright Mother: Elizabeth Mullins Sex: Female Burial: Colonial Grove, Cemetery VA Beach, VA

......................11 [407] Etta Wright b: November 16, 1888 in Beefhide, Letcher Co., KY d: October 09, 1977 in Jenkins, Letcher Co., KY Sex: Female Burial: Nancy Wright Cemetery, Beefhide, Letcher Co., KY

.............................+[1034] T. O. Webb b: Abt. 1885 in KY? m: August 20, 1913 Sex: Male

......................2nd Husband of [407] Etta Wright:

.............................+[1035] Lemuel Haynes b: Abt. 1890 in KY? m: September 21, 1915 Sex: Male

......................11 [1036] Samuel Wright b: April 03, 1891 in Beefhide, KY d: May 18, 1936 in Beefhide, KY Number of children: 10 Sex: Male Burial: Nancy Wright Cemetery, Beefhide, KY

.............................+[1037] Ollie Bentley b: Abt. 1890 in KY? m: 1917 Number of children: 10 Sex: Female

......................11 [1038] Ritter Wright, b: July 06, 1893 in Beefhide, KY d: September 15, 1953 in Fleming, KY Number of children: 5 Sex: Female Burial: Thornton Cem, Thornton, Letcher Co., KY

.............................+[1039] Jacob "Jake" Martin Adkins, b: March 24, 1893 in Greasy Creek, KY m: June 07, 1916 in Letcher Co., KY d: October 05, 1959 in Fleming, KY Number of children: 5 Father: Nelson Adkins, Mother: Malinda Robinson Sex: Male Burial: Thornton Cem, Thornton, Letcher Co., KY (Adkins Note: like the author and all of the other Adkins individuals in this tree and their descendants, this family descends from European royalty through Elizabeth Parker, born about 1697 in Charles City or Richmond, Henrico Co., VA. Elizabeth's husband was William Adkins/Atkinson, born March 28, 1689, in Charles City, Henrico Co. VA. Elizabeth is the proven 12th great-granddaughter of the King of England, Henry III, born October 1, 1206, in Winchester Castle, Hampshire Co., England)

....................10 [408] John W. 'Ringer' Bates b: November 23, 1852 in Letcher Co., KY d: November 24, 1932 Number of children: 7 Sex: Male

.............................+[1041] Mary Pigmon m: Abt. 1882 Number of children: 7 Sex: Female

......................11 [1042] Wlliam Bates b: Abt. 1883 d: August 16, 1959 Sex: Male

......................11 [1043] George Washington Bates b: 1884 in KY Sex: Male

......................11 [1044] James Bates b: 1886 in KY d: 1910 in Lexington, KY Sex: Male

......................11 [1045] Martin Van Bates b: 1888 d: 1904 in KY Sex: Male

......................11 [1046] Landis Dewey Bates b: December 25, 1890 in Knox Co., KY d: March 21, 1973 Sex: Male

.............................+[1047] Mary L. Hayes m: August 14, 1915 in Jenkins, KY Sex: Female

......................11 [1048] T. Monroe Bates b: 1892 in Pine Top, KY d: 1956 in Wise, VA Sex: Male

.............................+[1049] Edna Dale b: Abt. 1895 Sex: Female

......................11 [1050] Maggie Bates b: 1894 in Pine Top, KY Sex: Female

.............................+[1051] Christopher Columbus Tackett b: Abt. 1890 Sex: Male

......................2nd Wife of [408] John W. 'Ringer' Bates:

.............................+[1052] Elizabeth Gibson b: Abt. 1855 m: July 26, 1901 in Letcher Co., KY Sex: Female

....................10 [1053] Martha Bates b: January 19, 1855 in Letcher Co., KY Sex: Female
....................10 [1054] Letha Jane 'Jenny' Bates b: Abt. 1858 in Letcher Co., KY d: October 21,
1919 in Letcher Co., KY Sex: Female
....................10 [1055] Margaret Bates b: Abt. 1860 in Letcher Co., KY d: 1874 in Letcher Co.,
KY Sex: Female
....................10 [1056] James Bates, Jr. b: Abt. 1863 in Letcher Co., KY Sex: Male
....................10 [1057] Letitia "Lettie/Moody" Bates b: November 15, 1851 in Letcher Co., KY?
d: May 12, 1934 in Letcher Co., KY ? Number of children: 12 Sex: Female Burial: Thornton
Cemetery, Letcher Co., KY
..........................+[1058] William S. Wright b: Bet. July 07 - 09, 1855 in Letcher Co., KY or
Scott Co., VA m: April 12, 1872 in Letcher Co., KY d: January 30, 1900 in Boone Creek (Letcher
Co.,?) , KY Number of children: 12 Father: Wilhelm "Bill" Luntz Mother: Sidney Wright Sex: Male
Burial: Thornton Cem, Letcher Co., Ky
....................11 [1059] Nancy Wright b: April 25, 1873 in Baker, KY d: February 04, 1927 in
Pikeville, KY Sex: Female
..........................+[412] James Johnson, Sr. b: Abt. 1870 m: April 26, 1888 in Letcher Co.,
KY Number of children: 4 Sex: Male
....................11 [409] Martha E. Wright b: December 12, 1874 in Seco or Baker, KY d: Bet.
November 22, 1925 - 1926 in Seco or Baker, KY Number of children: 4 Sex: Female Burial: Thornton
Cemetery, Letcher Co., KY
..........................+[1060] _____ Pigman b: Abt. 1870 Sex: Male
....................2nd Husband of [409] Martha E. Wright:
..........................+[1061] _____ Bullard b: Abt. 1870 Sex: Male (Notes: not sure if he was her
husband or not) .
....................3rd Husband of [409] Martha E. Wright:
..........................+[1062] William "Willie" Venters b: April 09, 1874 in Jenkins, Letcher Co.,
KY m: July 31, 1893 in SeCo., Letcher Co., KY d: August 31, 1901 in Dunham, Jenkins, Letcher
Co., KY Number of children: 4 Father: John Venters Mother: Mary Juliette Mullins Sex: Male Burial:
Thornton Cemetery, Letcher Co., KY
....................11 [1064] Samuel Tilden Wright b: March 31, 1878 in Seco or McRoberts, KY d:
April 27, 1974 in Letcher Co., KY Sex: Male Burial: Thornton Cemetery, Letcher Co., KY
..........................+[1065] Lydia Margaret Craft b: 1880 m: June 29, 1899 in Letcher Co., KY
d: 1964 Sex: Female
....................11 [1066] Mary Wright b: April 04, 1880 in Letcher Co., KY d: March 1969 in
Lexington, KY Sex: Female
..........................+[1067] William Wiley Craft b: Abt. 1880 in Letcher Co., KY? m: 1897 in
Letcher Co., KY Sex: Male
....................11 [1068] William Wright b: June 30, 1882 in Letcher Co., KY d: April 10, 1901
in SeCo., KY Sex: Male
....................11 [410] Theophalis Garret Wright b: Bet. May 15, 1884 - 1885 in Letcher Co.,
KY d: April 13, 1953 Sex: Male
..........................+[1069] Mandy _____? b: Abt. 1890 Sex: Female
....................2nd Wife of [410] Theophalis Garret Wright:
..........................+[1070] Carrie Blair b: Abt. 1885 in Letcher Co., KY? m: August 30, 1907
in Letcher Co., KY Sex: Female
....................3rd Wife of [410] Theophalis Garret Wright:
..........................+[1071] Sylvia Hicks b: Abt. 1885 m: June 21, 1935 Sex: Female
....................11 [411] Joseph F. Wright b: July 01, 1886 in Baker, KY d: January 1975 in
Russell, KY Number of children: 3 Sex: Male
..........................+[1072] Lillie Smallwood b: Abt. 1890 Number of children: 2 Sex: Female
....................2nd Wife of [411] Joseph F. Wright:
..........................+[1073] Lilly Isom b: Abt. 1890 Number of children: ? Sex: Female

........................11 [1074] John W. Wright b: April 09, 1888 d: December 30, 1945 Sex: Male

.............................+[1075] Arlena Mason b: Abt. 1890 Sex: Female

........................11 [1076] Nancy "Nan" Wright b: April 25, 1873 in Baker, KY d: February 04, 1927 in Pikeville, KY Number of children: 4 Sex: Female

.............................+[412] James Johnson, Sr. b: Abt. 1870 m: April 26, 1888 in Letcher Co., KY Number of children: 4 Sex: Male

........................11 [1077] Henrietta "Ritter" Wright b: September 21, 1876 in Letcher Co., KY d: October 16, 1961 Number of children: 11 Sex: Female

.............................+[1078] L. Bert Tolliver b: Abt. 1870 in Letcher Co., KY? m: July 12, 1894 in Letcher Co., KY d: Abt. 1934 Number of children: 11 Sex: Male

........................11 [413] Benjamin Franklin Wright, Dr. b: March 12, 1891 in Whitaker, KY d: August 11, 1969 in Whitaker, KY Number of children: 3 Sex: Male Burial: SeCo., Ky

.............................+[1079] Scottie McClure b: Abt. 1895 Sex: Female

........................2nd Wife of [413] Benjamin Franklin Wright, Dr.:

.............................+[1080] Hazel Iris Adams b: Abt. 1895 Sex: Female

........................3rd Wife of [413] Benjamin Franklin Wright, Dr.:

.............................+[1081] Fanny Hall b: May 15, 1894 in Wise Co., VA d: April 03, 1940 in Letcher Co., KY ? Number of children: 3 Father: L. M. Hall Sex: Female Burial: Thornton Cemetery, Letcher Co., KY

........................11 [414] Lettie Dallas Wright b: January 08, 1894 in SeCo., KY d: April 04, 1974 Number of children: 7 Sex: Female Burial: Thorton, KY

.............................+[415] Archie C. Craft, Jr. b: May 09, 1884 m: November 05, 1919 in Letcher Co., KY d: July 06, 1959 Number of children: 7 Father: Joseph Craft Mother: Rasuea Bagwell Sex: Male

...................9 [416] Randolph "Randall" Adams b: November 30, 1834 in Perry Co., KY d: 1909 in Letcher Co., KY Number of children: ? Sex: Male Burial: Webb Cemetery, Mayking, Letcher, KY

........................+[1084] Martha Hale b: 1841 in VA d: Bef. 1900 in Letcher Co., KY Number of children: ? Father: James Dickerson Hale Mother: Jane Grizzle Sex: Female

.....................10 [1085] Martha "Mattie" Adams b: March 27, 1880 d: December 03, 1945 Sex: Female

.............................+[1086] Stephen Gilley b: Abt. 1875 Sex: Male

...................2nd Wife of [416] Randolph "Randall" Adams:

........................+[1087] Louise Jenkins b: 1840 Sex: Female

...................3rd Wife of [416] Randolph "Randall" Adams:

........................+[1088] Sarah Fields b: Abt. 1875 m: 1901 Sex: Female

................8 [715] William B. "Buckie" Holbrook, Sr., b: 1809 in Floyd Co., KY Number of children: 9 Sex: Male

........................+[714] Sarah "Sally" Adams, parents unknown b: 1807 in NC m: Abt. 1826 in Floyd Co., KY Number of children: 9 Father: John Washington "Wash" Adams, Mother: _____ _____? , Sex: Female (Note: Looking for her ancestors; I think her Father MAY be John Washington "Wash" Adams. b. 1785 in NC)

...................9 [716] Mary "Polly" Holbrook, b: 1827 in Perry Co., KY d: April 11, 1854 in Letcher Co., KY Number of children: 2 Sex: Female

........................+[717] Esquire "Squire" Bentley, b: 1821 in Letcher Co., KY m: October 24, 1850 in Letcher Co., KY Number of children: 2 Father: John Queller Bentley, Sr., Mother: Margaret "Peggy" Hamilton, Sex: Male

.....................10 [718] William Barlow "Barlow" Bentley b: March 1849 in KY Number of children: 13 Sex: Male

.............................+[719] Susannah Quillen b: September 20, 1857 in Letcher Co., KY m: September 19, 1872 in Letcher Co., KY d: February 14, 1926 Number of children: 13 Father: Richard Teague Quillen Mother: Catherine Yonts Sex: Female (Note: some say she was born 9 22 1859) .

........................11 [720] William D. Bentley b: 1874 in KY Sex: Male
........................11 [721] Mary Bentley b: 1876 in KY Sex: Female
........................11 [722] Polly Bentley b: November 1876 Sex: Female
........................11 [723] Arminda "Armindy" Bentley b: December 1878 in KY Sex: Female
........................11 [724] Squire Richard Bentley b: December 12, 1879 d: May 06, 1933 Number of children: 16 Sex: Male
..............................+[725] Rosemond Fidel Hall b: Abt. 1880 Number of children: 16 Sex: Female
........................11 [726] Benjamin Franklin Bentley b: June 1882 Number of children: ? Sex: Male
........................11 [727] James M. Bentley b: May 1888 Sex: Male
........................11 [728] Wiley A. Bentley b: July 1889 Sex: Male
........................11 [729] Nancy J. Bentley b: March 1894 Sex: Female
........................11 [730] Samantha Bentley b: Abt. August 1895 Sex: Female
........................11 [731] Robert S. Bentley b: March 1896 Sex: Male
........................11 [732] Sarah E. Bentley b: April 1898 Sex: Female
........................11 [733] Ira J. Bentley b: 1902 Sex: Male
.....................10 [734] Sarah "Sally" Bentley, b: July 1852 in Letcher Co., KY d: Aft. 1920 in Pulaski Co., KY? Number of children: 3 Sex: Female
.............................+[735] William James Yonts, b: December 1845 in Letcher Co., KY m: March 18, 1870 in Letcher Co., KY d: Aft. 1920 in Pulaski Co., KY? Number of children: 3 Father: William Yonts, Jr., Yants, Mother: Nancy F. Ray, Sex: Male (Yonts Note: like the author and all of the other Yonts individuals in this tree, this family descends from Wilhelm Jans, born in 1714 in the town of Oberalben, Rheineland-Pfalz, Germany; Wilhelm died in 1778 in Rowan Co., NC)
........................11 [417] Esquire "Squire" Lincoln Yonts, Yantz, b: April 30, 1874 in Letcher Co., KY d: December 10, 1942 in Knoxville, TN Number of children: 9 Sex: Male Burial: Abt. December 13, 1942 Sharp Cemetery (Note: Letcher Co. Birth Records state that his middle initial was "F"). NOTE: Squire is the author's great-grandfather.
.............................+[736] Mary Frances Wright, b: January 27, 1872 in Upper Elkhorn Creek, Pike Co., KY ? m: April 23, 1890 in Letcher Co., KY d: April 12, 1950 in Neon, Hogg Hollow, Letcher Co., KY Number of children: 9 Father: William A. Wright, Mother: Arty (Artie or Arta) M. Potter, Sex: Female Burial: Abt. April 15, 1950 Yonts Cemetery, Craft Funeral Home, Neon, Letcher Co., KY. NOTE: Mary is the author's great-grandmother.
........................2nd Wife of [417] Squire Lincoln Yonts, Yantz, :
.............................+[737] Louise _____? b: Abt. 1880 m: December 1907 Sex: Female
........................3rd Wife of [417] Squire Lincoln Yonts, Yantz, :
.............................+[738] Alice _____? b: Abt. 1900 m: Aft. 1920 Sex: Female Burial: Sharp Cemetery
........................11 [739] Nancy Chaney Yonts b: April 15, 1878 in Letcher Co., KY d: November 20, 1927 in at her daughter's home in Wise, VA or Waynesburg, Lincoln Co., KY Number of children: 9 Sex: Female
.............................+[740] Archibald "Archie" Lincoln Meade b: 1874 in Letcher Co., KY m: August 06, 1895 in Neon, Letcher Co., KY Number of children: 9 Sex: Male
........................11 [418] Robert Grant Yonts b: May 04, 1883 in Letcher Co., KY d: September 13, 1964 Number of children: 15 Sex: Male
.............................+[741] Henrietta "Hennie" Ritter Holbrook b: December 05, 1881 in Letcher Co., KY? m: 1901 in Letcher Co., KY d: April 02, 1965 Number of children: 9 Father: Enoch A. Holbrook Mother: Nancy Evelyn Webb Sex: Female
........................2nd Wife of [418] Robert Grant Yonts:
.............................+[742] Dorothy Pence b: Abt. 1890 in KY? m: Aft. 1922 Number of children: 6 Sex: Female
...................9 [743] Nancy Ann Holbrook b: 1831 Sex: Female
...................9 [744] Susannah Holbrook b: 1834 Sex: Female

................9 [745] James E. Holbrook b: November 18, 1836 Number of children: 7 Sex: Male

.....................+[746] Tabitha Bentley b: 1843 Number of children: 7 Father: Daniel Bentley, Sr., Mother: Marinda (Brinkley?) Ramey (Note: Marinda descends from the same family line as country singer Patty (Ramey) Loveless, born January 4, 1957 in Pikeville, Pike Co., KY) Sex: Female

.................10 [747] Mary E. "Polly" Holbrook b: 1867 Number of children: ? Sex: Female

.........................+[748] Noah "Paw" Bentley b: Abt. 1865 Number of children: ? Father: Benjamin Bentley Mother: Elizabeth E. "Patsy" Reynolds Sex: Male

....................11 [749] Lincoln Bentley b: Abt. 1890 Number of children: ? Sex: Male

.............................+[750] Etta Bentley b: Abt. 1895 Number of children: ? Sex: Female

...................10 [751] William B. Holbrook b: May 1869 Sex: Male

.........................+[752] Sarah Clark b: Abt. 1870 Sex: Female

...................10 [753] John A. Holbrook b: April 1871 Sex: Male

.........................+[754] Lucinda Huff b: 1874 Sex: Female

...................10 [755] Sarah M. Holbrook b: 1872 Sex: Female

...................10 [756] Didamey Holbrook b: Abt. 1876 Sex: Female

...................10 [757] Zilpha P. Holbrook b: 1879 Sex: Female

...................10 [758] Gracie Holbrook b: 1889 Sex: Female

................9 [759] William B. Holbrook, Jr. b: 1839 Sex: Male

................9 [760] Randolph E. Holbrook b: 1841 Sex: Male

................9 [761] Benjamin W. Holbrook b: 1845 Sex: Male

................9 [762] Ransom T. Holbrook b: March 21, 1846 d: March 01, 1894 Number of children: 5 Sex: Male Burial: Bottom Fork, Letcher Co., KY

.....................+[763] Elizabeth Ann Hughes b: March 10, 1850 in Letcher Co., KY m: July 10, 1866 d: October 22, 1917 Number of children: 5 Father: John Hughes Mother: Matilda Bentley, (Note: Looking for her ancestors) Sex: Female Burial: Bottom Fork, Letcher Co., KY

...................10 [764] John A. Holbrook b: Abt. 1865 Number of children: ? Sex: Male (Note: Looking for his ancestors)

.........................+[765] Mary Ann Stewart b: Abt. 1860 Number of children: ? Father: Thomas "Tom" Stewart Mother: Susannah Fleming Sex: Female

....................11 [766] Gabriel Holbrook b: Abt. 1880 Number of children: ? Sex: Male

.............................+[767] Norma Sturgill b: Abt. 1880 in Pound, VA Number of children: ? Father: Gordon Sturgill Sex: Female

...................10 [768] Sarah "Sally" Holbrook b: November 05, 1867 in Letcher Co., KY d: February 16, 1929 Sex: Female

.........................+[769] Wiley W. Quillen b: September 1861 in Letcher Co., KY m: November 30, 1882 in Letcher Co., KY d: 1938 Father: Richard Teague Quillen Mother: Catherine Yonts Sex: Male

...................10 [770] Nancy "Nannie" Holbrook b: 1868 Sex: Female

...................10 [771] Francis Holbrook b: 1880 Sex: Female

...................10 [772] John A. Holbrook b: Abt. 1880 Sex: Male

................9 [773] Doctor "Dock" Holbrook b: 1850 Sex: Male

...............8 [419] Randolph Holbrook b: March 15, 1811 in Floyd Co., KY Number of children: 5 Sex: Male

.....................+[420] Zilpha (Zelphia) Adams b: August 01, 1811 in Rockhouse Creek, Letcher Co., KY m: 1827 in Perry Co., KY d: 1893 Number of children: 5 Father: Stephen Adams, Mother: Mary "Mollie" Webb Sex: Female

................9 [421] Kelsey Holbrook b: April 05, 1829 Sex: Male

.....................+[422] Rutha Mullins b: Abt. 1830 Sex: Female

................9 [423] Nancy A. Holbrook b: 1830 in Floyd Co., KY Number of children: ? Sex: Female

.....................+[424] Richard Lee Spradling b: June 22, 1822 in Floyd Co., KY Number of children: ? Sex: Male

.....................10 [425] Sarah Jane Spradling b: May 26, 1851 in Harrison Co., KY Number of children: ? Sex: Female

...........................+[426] Reuben Porter Dennis b: June 04, 1848 in West Liberty, Morgan Co., KY Number of children: ? Sex: Male

.....................11 [427] Nancy Katherine Dennis b: July 05, 1870 in Hazel Green, KY Number of children: ? Sex: Female

...........................+[428] Jasper Bond Suiter b: September 06, 1872 in Wise Co., VA Number of children: ? Sex: Male

.....................9 [429] Benjamin May Holbrook b: March 26, 1832 Number of children: 2 Sex: Male

........................+[430] Rhoda Bays Spradlin b: 1834 Number of children: 2 Sex: Female

.....................10 [394] Randolph Holbrook b: May 21, 1853 Number of children: 9 Sex: Male

...........................+[431] Virgie Bays b: Abt. 1851 Number of children: 9 Sex: Female

.....................11 [432] Adam Gus Holbrook b: Abt. 1877 Number of children: ? Sex: Male

...........................+[433] Kate Miller b: 1876 Number of children: ? Sex: Female

.....................11 [434] Eva Jane Holbrook b: January 1880 Sex: Female

...........................+[435] Harrison Puckett b: Abt. 1875 Sex: Male

.....................11 [436] Jacob Holbrook b: March 07, 1882 Sex: Male

...........................+[437] Lisa Puckett b: Abt. 1886 Sex: Female

.....................11 [438] John A. Holbrook b: April 1885 Sex: Male

...........................+[439] Cynthia Prater b: Abt. 1889 Sex: Female

.....................11 [440] Samuel Holbrook b: Abt. 1887 Sex: Male

.....................11 [441] Jim Holbrook b: December 1887 Sex: Male

...........................+[442] Lethia Stone b: Abt. 1889 Sex: Female

.....................11 [443] Campbell May Holbrook b: June 16, 1890 Sex: Male

.....................11 [444] Virginia Maxine Holbrook b: Abt. 1891 Sex: Female

.....................11 [445] Elizabeth "Addie" Holbrook b: Abt. 1892 Sex: Female

.....................2nd Wife of [394] Randolph Holbrook:

...........................+[446] Sarah Shepherd b: 1852 Sex: Female

.....................10 [447] Harvey Trimble Holbrook b: June 21, 1879 Sex: Male

...........................+[448] Molly B. Hall b: Abt. 1880 Sex: Female

.................9 [449] Mary B. Holbrook b: 1837 Sex: Female

.................9 [450] Elizabeth Holbrook b: 1838 Sex: Female

.............7 [451] Sarah "Sally" Francis Adams, 2nd wife b: 1776 in Lunenburg Co., VA d: October 1842 in Letcher Co., KY Number of children: 13 Sex: Female

...................+[164] Stephen A. Caudill, Rev. War Soldier, b: 1763 in Lunenburg Co., VA (or NC?) m: 1790 in Wilkesboro, Wilkes Co., NC d: July 26, 1839 in Sandlick, Letcher Co., KY Number of children: 16 Father: James Caudill, Sr., Cordell, Coddill, Caudel Mother: Mary Yarborough, Yarbrough Sex: Male Burial: Watty Caudill Cemetery, Dry Fork, Letcher Co., KY (Note: fought in Revolutionary War, Kings Mountain & Cowpens)

.................8 [452] Henrietta Caudill, b: 1792 in NC d: 1829 in Pert Creek, Letcher Co., KY Number of children: 6 Sex: Female

.....................+[453] George M. Adams, b: September 16, 1800 in Elizabethton, Carter Co., TN m: February 25, 1820 in Prestonsburg, Floyd Co., KY d: October 25, 1869 in Taney Co., MO Number of children: 14 Father: Moses Adams, Mother: Mary Garland Sex: Male

.................9 [454] Sarah "Sallie" Adams b: 1821 Sex: Female

.................9 [455] Mary Adams b: 1825 Sex: Female

.................9 [456] John Adams b: Abt. 1826 Sex: Male

.................9 [457] Lydia Adams b: December 31, 1829 Sex: Female

.....................+[458] Edward Combs b: August 21, 1824 in Smoot Creek, Perry Co., KY d: May 17, 1911 Father: Shadrach "Old Shade" Combs, Jr., Mother: Martha Patsy Casebolt Sex: Male

.................9 [459] Nancy Adams b: Abt. 1830 Sex: Female

.....................+[460] Stephen Polly b: 1826 in Perry Co., KY m: August 25, 1848 in Letcher

Co., KY Father: Edward Oliver "Ned" Polly Mother: Jane Bunton "Jennie" Adams Sex: Male

.................9 [461] Dianah Adams b: May 15, 1831 in Perry Co., KY d: June 06, 1873 Sex: Female

.............8 [462] John Adams Caudill, b: January 01, 1798 in Wilkes or Ashe Co., NC d: May 10, 1873 in Letcher Co., KY Number of children: 14 Sex: Male

.................+[463] Rachel Cornett, b: February 10, 1807 in Bull Creek, Perry Co., KY m: March 20, 1824 in Perry Co., KY d: April 15, 1887 in Perry (Knott/Letcher) Co., KY Number of children: 14 Father: William Jesse Cornett, Mother: Mary Ann Everage Sex: Female

.................9 [464] William J. Caudill b: February 11, 1825 in Wilkes Co., NC d: January 11, 1899 in Rowan Co., KY Sex: Male

.................9 [465] Stephen Jacob Caudill b: November 18, 1826 in Perry Co., KY d: July 26, 1906 in Letcher Co., KY Sex: Male

.................9 [466] Mary A. Caudill b: August 04, 1828 d: December 31, 1839 Sex: Female

.................9 [467] Benjamin Everage Caudill, Civil War Col. b: January 11, 1830 in Whitesburg, Perry/Letcher Co., KY d: February 11, 1889 in Claybourne Co., TN Number of children: 11 Sex: Male Burial: Slate Hill Baptist Cemetery, London, Laurel Co., KY (Note: he was in the 10th KY Rebel Mounted Infantry)

......................+[468] Martha Lucinda Asbury b: July 11, 1828 in Tazewell Co., VA m: February 16, 1848 in Whitesburg, Letcher Co., KY d: September 20, 1900 in Scott Co., VA Number of children: 11 Father: William Asbury Mother: Elizabeth Chaffins Sex: Female

....................10 [469] John Asbury Caudill b: March 26, 1849 in Letcher Co., KY d: May 30, 1912 in Ivan, Stephens Co., TX Sex: Male Burial: Veale's Creek Cemetery

....................+[470] Alice Reeves b: Abt. 1853 in KY? Sex: Female

....................10 [471] William Jesse Caudill b: December 28, 1850 in Whitesburg, Letcher Co., KY d: April 14, 1914 in Hobart, Kiowa Co., OK Sex: Male

....................10 [472] Samuel Houston Caudill b: March 29, 1853 in Whitesburg, Letcher Co., KY d: 1928 in OK? Sex: Male

....................10 [473] Stephen B. Caudill b: March 29, 1855 in Whitesburg, Letcher Co., KY d: in KY Sex: Male

....................10 [474] Margaret Caudill b: 1857 in Whitesburg, Letcher Co., KY d: May 1937 in Lovington, NM Sex: Female

....................10 [475] Rachel Caudill b: 1860 Sex: Female

....................10 [476] James Watson Caudill b: 1862 in Whitesburg, Letcher Co., KY d: December 24, 1945 in Hatch, Dona Ana Co., NM Sex: Male

....................10 [477] Evelyn Caudill b: 1865 Sex: Female

....................10 [165] Benjamin Franklin Caudill b: May 03, 1867 in Sparta, Alleghanney Co., NC d: 1952 in Clay Co., KY Number of children: 10 Sex: Male Burial: Clay Co., KY

..........................+[478] Lucy Benge House b: September 30, 1867 in Manchester, Clay Co., KY m: December 26, 1885 in Manchester, Clay Co., KY d: April 01, 1938 in OK Number of children: 10 Father: James House Mother: Elizabeth Benge Sex: Female Burial: Erick Cemetery, Oklahoma City, OK

......................11 [479] Lilly "Lizzie" Belle Caudill b: August 04, 1886 in Clay Co., KY d: August 22, 1945 Sex: Female

......................11 [480] Victor Cleveland Caudill b: October 28, 1889 in Clay Co., KY d: December 12, 1948 in Hot Springs, Sierra, NM Number of children: 4 Sex: Male Burial: Hot Springs, Sierra, NM

.............................+[481] Mae D. Baker b: December 29, 1893 in Sewal, Wayne Co., IA m: Abt. 1911 d: February 20, 1976 in Clovis, NM Number of children: 4 Father: B. F. Baker Mother: Minnie Ensminger Sex: Female Burial: Clovis, NM

.........................12 Juanita C. Caudill b: August 12, 1912 in Erick, OK d: March 09, 1976 in Clovis, Curry Co., NM Sex: Female

.............................+Casey Jones b: Abt. 1910 Sex: Male

.........................12 Frank B. Caudill b: Abt. 1914 d: September 02, 1994 Sex: Male

..........................12 Thurman Caudill b: April 03, 1916 d: June 24, 1995 in Pleasanton, CA Sex: Male

..........................12 Sanford Caudill b: December 10, 1917 in Beckham Co., OK d: July 02, 1993 in Tucumcari, or Clayton, or Albuquerque, NM Number of children: 3 Sex: Male Burial: National Cemetery, Santa Fe, NM

..............................+Mildred Milnes b: March 21, 1921 in OK m: February 23, 1940 in OK d: July 02, 1996 in Tucumcari, NM Number of children: 3 Father: Floyd Milnes Sex: Female

................................13 Kay Caudill, b: 1941 in Clovis, Curry Co., NM

................................13 Marshall Sanford Caudill, b: about 1943

................................13 Robert A. Caudill, b: abt 1945

......................11 [482] Grover Garrett Garrard Caudill b: March 02, 1891 in Pigeon Roost, Clay Co., KY d: October 30, 1948 in Washington Co., OR Sex: Male

......................11 [483] Minnie Dora Caudill b: April 25, 1893 in Clay Co., KY d: May 1976 in Oklahoma City, OK Sex: Female

......................11 [484] Henry Clay Caudill b: June 01, 1896 in Clay Co., KY d: August 04, 1931 in Erick, Beckham Co., OK Sex: Male

......................11 [485] Margaret Luinda Caudill b: September 1897 in Clay Co., KY Sex: Female

......................11 [486] Mayme Ellen Caudill b: June 11, 1899 in Clay Co., KY d: June 17, 1977 in Whittier, Los Angeles Co., CA Sex: Female

......................11 [487] Lucy Mae Caudill b: May 07, 1901 in KY d: August 1986 in Dalhart, TX Sex: Female

......................11 [488] Elizabeth Beatrice Caudill b: June 10, 1904 in Sayre, Beckham Co., OK d: April 18, 1995 in Minneapolis, MN Sex: Female

......................11 [489] Benjamin Kathleen Caudill b: October 07, 1907 in Sayre, Beckham Co., OK d: October 10, 1997 in Albuquerque, NM Sex: Female

....................2nd Wife of [165] Benjamin Franklin Caudill:

..........................+[490] Stella Louise Lovelace b: February 25, 1898 in KY m: Bet. 1917 - 1923 in NC d: December 1976 in Marana, AZ Father: Frank Lovelace Sex: Female

....................10 [491] Emery M. Caudill, Sr. b: April 07, 1869 in Sparta, Alleghanney Co., NC d: January 09, 1953 in Albuquerque, NM Sex: Male

....................10 [492] Elizabeth Caudill b: Abt. 1871 Sex: Female

..................9 [166] Samuel Patton Caudill b: December 29, 1831 in Perry/Letcher Co., KY d: October 29, 1907 in Letcher Co., KY? Sex: Male Burial: Caudill Cemetery, Letcher Co., KY

......................+[493] Letitia Meade b: 1835 in Russell Co., VA m: Abt. 1852 d: 1884 Sex: Female

..................2nd Wife of [166] Samuel Patton Caudill:

......................+[494] Mary Ann Greer b: Abt. 1837 in Scott Co., VA m: November 14, 1854 d: Abt. 1862 Sex: Female

..................3rd Wife of [166] Samuel Patton Caudill:

......................+[495] Sarah J. Hart b: Abt. 1875 m: Aft. 1854 in Letcher Co., KY Father: Hugh Hart Mother: Jane Adams Sex: Female

..................9 [496] Sarah L. Caudill b: October 23, 1834 in Whitesburg, Letcher Co., KY d: May 17, 1914 in Letcher Co., KY Sex: Female

..................9 [497] John Dixon Caudill b: October 06, 1836 in Sandlick or Whitesburg, Letcher Co., KY d: June 17, 1917 in Sandlick, Letcher Co., KY Sex: Male

......................+[498] Mary Ann Green b: November 25, 1838 in VA m: January 12, 1859 in Letcher Co., KY? d: June 23, 1920 in Sandlick, Letcher Co., KY Sex: Female (Note: Looking for her ancestors)

..................9 [499] David Jesse Caudill b: March 09, 1839 in Letcher Co., KY d: April 09, 1907 in Olive Hill, Carter Co., KY Sex: Male

..................9 [353] Nancy "Jane" Caudill, Caudell, b: November 05, 1840 in Whitesburg, Letcher Co., KY d: November 12, 1922 in London, Laurel Co., KY Number of children: 2 Sex: Female

Burial: Lincks Cemetery

........................+[352] John Henderson Craft b: December 20, 1834 in Millstone, KY m: October 11, 1855 in Letcher Co., KY d: September 13, 1920 in Larue, Laurel Co., KY Number of children: 2 Father: Joseph Craft Mother: Martha Irby Bates Sex: Male Burial: Lincks Cemetery

......................10 [354] John Dixon Craft b: April 12, 1856 in Craftsville, Letcher Co., KY d: December 20, 1945 in KY Number of children: ? Sex: Male

...........................+[355] Mary Elizabeth Webb b: July 11, 1861 in Letcher Co., KY m: September 13, 1879 d: November 25, 1956 Number of children: ? Father: Henry T. "Chunk" Webb Mother: Francis Elizabeth "Franky" Adams Sex: Female (Webb Note: Like all of the other Webb individuals in this tree, this Webb family descends from the same line as the country singers Loretta (Webb) Lynn and her sister Brenda Gail "Crystal Gale" Webb. Loretta was born April 14, 1935, in Butcher Hollow, Pike Co., KY; Crystal Gale was born January 9, 1951, in Paintsville, Johnson Co., KY)

......................11 [500] Nancy Catherine "Nannie" Craft b: February 08, 1882 in Letcher Co., KY d: August 06, 1913 in KY? Sex: Female

............................+[501] William Wash Webb b: October 1883 in KY Father: Nelson Robinette Webb Mother: Frances Catherine Spangler Sex: Male (Webb Note: Like all of the other Webb individuals in this tree, this Webb family descends from the same line as the country singers Loretta (Webb) Lynn and her sister Brenda Gail "Crystal Gale" Webb. Loretta was born April 14, 1935, in Butcher Hollow, Pike Co., KY; Crystal Gale was born January 9, 1951, in Paintsville, Johnson Co., KY)

......................10 [356] Martha A. Craft b: September 12, 1860 in Craftsville, KY d: September 16, 1951 in TN Number of children: 3 Sex: Female

...........................+[357] Noah Milburn Reynolds, Jr. b: December 15, 1855 in KY m: November 15, 1879 in Blountsville, TN d: April 30, 1923 in Mayo Clinic in TN Number of children: 3 Father: Noah Milburn Reynolds, Sr. Mother: Mary Chaney Stone Sex: Male

......................11 [502] John Henderson Reynolds b: Abt. 1880 Number of children: ? Sex: Male

............................+[503] Nancy Jane Caudill Craft b: Abt. 1882 Number of children: ? Sex: Female

......................11 [504] Christopher Columbus Reynolds b: Abt. 1883 Sex: Male

......................11 [505] Mary C. Reynolds b: November 06, 1885 in Letcher Co., KY d: September 14, 1955 in Whitley Co., KY Sex: Female

............................+[506] Woodson Hodge Brown b: October 24, 1881 in Clay Co., KY m: December 06, 1906 in Clay Co., KY Sex: Male

................9 [507] Elizabeth "Betty" Caudill b: August 22, 1842 in Letcher Co., KY Sex: Female Burial: Buffalo Cemetery, Sayre, OK

................9 [508] Joseph Caudill, twin b: 1844 d: 1848 Sex: Male

................9 [509] Nathaniel Caudill, twin b: 1844 d: 1848 Sex: Male

................9 [350] Polly Ann Caudill b: April 15, 1847 in Letcher Co., KY d: February 11, 1937 in Millstone, Letcher Co., KY Number of children: ? Sex: Female

......................+[349] Enoch "Chunk" A. Craft b: December 29, 1842 m: May 02, 1867 in Letcher Co., KY d: February 16, 1937 in Millstone, Letcher Co., KY Number of children: ? Father: Archelous Craft Mother: Letty Webb Sex: Male

......................10 [351] Nancy Craft b: January 1872 in Letcher Co., KY d: August 1872 in Letcher Co., KY Sex: Female

................9 [510] Watson Garrard Caudill b: June 17, 1849 in Whitesburg, Letcher Co., KY d: August 05, 1930 in Perry Co., KY Sex: Male

................8 [167] Benjamin E. Caudill, b: 1799 in Wilkes Co., NC d: February 27, 1851 in Salyersville, Magoffin Co., KY Number of children: 3 Sex: Male

......................+[168] Abigail Pennington, b: May 09, 1803 in Lee Co., VA d: 1887 in Salyersville, Magoffin Co., KY Number of children: 3 Father: William Pennington Mother: Abigail Caudill, Cordell, Sex: Female

...................9 [169] William Jackson "Jack" Caudill b: 1822 in Perry Co., KY Sex: Male Burial: Oil Springs, Johnson Co., KY

........................+[170] Rebecca Harris b: Abt. 1826 in Floyd Co., KY Sex: Female Burial: Oil Springs, Johnson Co., KY

...................9 [171] Abel Caudill, b: January 16, 1827 in Morgan Co., KY Number of children: ? Sex: Male

........................+[172] Phoebe Hitchcock b: November 28, 1827 in Floyd Co., KY m: October 28, 1846 in Johnson Co., KY Number of children: ? Sex: Female

........................10 [173] Jesse E. Caudill, b: September 07, 1847 in Johnson Co., KY d: September 14, 1890 Number of children: ? Sex: Male

..........................+[174] Elizabeth "Lizzie" Elam b: November 28, 1847 in MaGoffin Co., KY m: February 18, 1869 in Magoffin Co., KY Number of children: ? Sex: Female

........................11 [175] Abel Caudill, b: February 09, 1870 in MaGoffin Co., KY Sex: Male

..........................+[176] Elizabeth Bailey b: May 1876 in KY? Sex: Female

...................9 [177] Elizabeth Caudill b: 1833 in Perry Co., KY d: April 15, 1915 Number of children: ? Sex: Female

........................+[178] Noah May b: Abt. 1831 in Magoffin Co., KY Number of children: ? Sex: Male

.......................10 [179] Campbell J. May b: 1851 Number of children: ? Sex: Male

..........................+[180] Rebecca E. Adams b: 1852 Number of children: ? Father: Gilbert A. Adams Mother: Perlina Prater Sex: Female

.......................11 [181] Augustus Noah May b: 1876 d: 1944 Number of children: ? Sex: Male

..........................+[182] Sarah Elizabeth Cornett b: 1876 d: 1966 Number of children: ? Father: Russell Cornett, Mother: Ailey Amburgey Sex: Female

.................8 [511] Elizabeth "Betsy" C. Caudill, b: June 18, 1800 in Wilkes Co., NC d: October 11, 1881 in Letcher Co., KY Number of children: ? Sex: Female Burial: Watty Caudill Cemetery, at the mouth of Dry Fork, Letcher Co., KY

........................+[512] John Quincy Brown b: 1788 in Ireland m: 1814 d: November 19, 1872 in Letcher Co., KY Number of children: ? Sex: Male

.................9 [513] Sarah "Sallie" Brown b: April 12, 1815 in KY d: April 19, 1892 in Letcher Co., KY Number of children: 3 Sex: Female

........................+[514] Joseph Enoch Cornett, Judge b: April 28, 1814 in KY m: Abt. 1837 d: May 30, 1881 in Crown, Letcher Co., KY Number of children: 3 Father: William Jesse Cornett, Mother: Mary Ann Everage Sex: Male

......................10 [515] Samuel A. Cornett b: April 18, 1840 d: Abt. 1931 Number of children: 6 Sex: Male

...........................+[516] Alcyann Couch, 4th wife b: Abt. 1870 in Perry Co., KY? m: Abt. 1888 Number of children: 6 Father: Samuel Couch, ? Mother: Emaline Wooten, ? Sex: Female

......................11 [517] Granville Cornett b: Abt. 1889 Sex: Male

......................11 [518] Lucy Cornett b: Abt. 1891 Sex: Female

......................11 [519] Susan Cornett b: Abt. 1893 Sex: Female

......................11 [520] James Cornett b: Abt. 1895 Sex: Male

......................11 [521] Stephen Cornett b: Abt. 1897 Sex: Male

......................11 [522] Armine Cornett b: Abt. 1900 Sex: Female

......................10 [523] Elizabeth Ann 'Betty' Cornett b: Abt. 1842 Number of children: 4 Sex: Female

...........................+[524] Ira Stamper b: October 11, 1829 in Perry Co., KY m: April 26, 1876 in Letcher Co., KY d: February 05, 1910 in Rome, Douglas Co., MO Number of children: 4 Father: Isom Stamper Mother: Sarah Creech Sex: Male

......................11 [525] Mary Ann 'Polly' Stamper Sex: Female

......................11 [526] Neale Stamper Sex: Male

......................11 [527] Nancy Elizabeth Stamper Sex: Female

..................11 [528] Joseph Stamper Sex: Male

..................10 [529] Rachel Cornett b: 1846 in Dry Fork, Pike Co. (or Letcher Co.) , KY Sex: Female

..............8 [530] Nancy Caudill, b: June 18, 1804 Number of children: 2 Sex: Female

..................+[531] Randolph "Randall" Adams b: 1802 in Roaring River, Wilkes Co., NC d: December 23, 1872 in Cowan, Perry/Letcher Co., KY Number of children: 2 Father: John Hobbs Adams, Jr., Mother: Lydia "Letty" or "Lettie" Simpson Sex: Male

................9 [532] Lydia Adams b: Abt. 1825 Number of children: 10 Sex: Female

..................+[533] Robert Collins b: October 21, 1823 in Rockhouse Creek, Perry Co., KY m: Abt. 1850 d: November 27, 1883 Number of children: 10 Father: James Shepherd Collins Mother: Elizabeth Lewis Sex: Male

..................10 [534] Randolph Collins b: October 12, 1852 in Hazard, Perry Co., KY d: December 14, 1947 in Red Bluff, CA Sex: Male

........................+[535] Eliza Jane Turner b: Abt. 1854 in Letcher Co., KY m: January 18, 1872 Father: James Turner Mother: Sarah Bailey Sex: Female

..................10 [536] Nancy Collins b: December 15, 1855 in Colson, Letcher Co., KY d: February 06, 1918 in Colson, Letcher Co., KY Sex: Female

........................+[537] James Jasper "Babe" Collins b: December 25, 1852 in Letcher Co., KY m: July 31, 1873 in Letcher Co., KY d: September 06, 1876 in Letcher Co., KY Father: Eli Collins Mother: Mary Barrett Sex: Male

..................10 [538] James H. Collins b: July 18, 1857 in Rockhouse Creek, Letcher Co., KY d: September 01, 1942 Sex: Male

........................+[539] Nancy Sarah Breeding b: Abt. 1859 in Letcher Co., KY m: September 18, 1879 Father: John Breeding Mother: Elizabeth "Betty" Combs Sex: Female

..................10 [540] Sarah Collins b: May 04, 1859 in Rockhouse Creek, Letcher Co., KY d: May 15, 1859 in Letcher Co., KY Sex: Female

..................10 [541] Elijah Collins b: Abt. 1860 Sex: Male

..................10 [183] William Silas Collins b: April 21, 1865 d: December 15, 1937 in Letcher Co., KY Sex: Male

........................+[542] Nancy Hale b: 1862 Father: William Rowlette Hale Mother: Elizabeth Collins Sex: Female

..................2nd Wife of [183] William Silas Collins:

........................+[358] Martha E. Crase b: Abt. 1868 m: March 03, 1888 in Letcher Co., KY Father: James Crase Mother: Elizabeth Stallard Sex: Female

..................10 [360] Greenbury Collins b: February 26, 1868 d: May 03, 1924 Sex: Male

........................+[359] Christina Adams b: June 10, 1858 d: January 07, 1951 Father: Jesse "Colly Jesse" Adams Mother: Mary "Polly" Craft Sex: Female

................10 [543] Lucinda Collins b: Abt. 1872 Sex: Female

..................10 [544] Lorenzo Dow Collins b: January 20, 1875 in Rockhouse Creek, Letcher Co., KY d: December 13, 1949 Sex: Male

........................+[545] Nancy Ann Caudill b: Abt. 1877 in Letcher Co., KY m: February 04, 1897 Father: Watson Caudill Mother: Elizabeth Combs Sex: Female

..................10 [546] Eliza Collins b: 1879 Sex: Female

................9 [184] Watson E. "Watty" Adams b: April 1837 d: 1919 Number of children: 9 Sex: Male

........................+[547] Rosa "Rausey" Hogg b: 1842 m: 1860 Number of children: ? Father: Hiram "Courthouse Hiram" Hogg Mother: Melvina "Viney" Polly Sex: Female

..................10 [548] Henry C. Adams b: 1863 Sex: Male

........................+[549] Catherine Campbell b: September 1884 d: 1966 Father: John Henry Campbell Mother: Elizabeth Maggard Sex: Female

................2nd Wife of [184] Watson E. "Watty" Adams:

........................+[550] Minerva Collins b: January 13, 1846 m: October 16, 1881 in Letcher Co.,

KY Number of children: 8 Father: Nathaniel "Nat" Collins Mother: Nancy Branham-Smith Sex: Female

....................10 [551] Floyd Adams b: Abt. 1882 Sex: Male

....................10 [552] Boyd Adams b: Abt. 1883 Sex: Male

....................10 [553] Randall Adams b: March 19, 1884 Sex: Male

....................10 [554] Francis Adams b: September 28, 1885 Sex: Female

....................10 [555] Patton Adams b: Abt. 1886 Sex: Male

....................10 [556] Green Ison Adams b: March 10, 1887 d: September 19, 1951 Sex: Male

....................10 [557] Hattie Adams b: August 21, 1889 Sex: Female

....................10 [558] Elizabeth Adams b: Abt. 1891 Sex: Female

................8 [559] Easter (or Esther) Caudill, b: 1806 in Wilkes Co., NC d: Abt. 1887 in Letcher Co., KY Number of children: ? Sex: Female

....................+[560] Levi Eldridge b: August 1810 in Scott Co., VA d: 1877 in Rowan Co., KY Number of children: ? Sex: Male

................9 [185] Elizabeth "Betsy" Eldridge b: Abt. 1841 Number of children: 2 Sex: Female

........................+[186] William W. "Wild Bill" Caudill b: Abt. 1839 in NC d: June 22, 1920 in Wolfe Co., KY Number of children: 2 Father: Wilburn E. Caudill Mother: Nancy Caudill Sex: Male

....................10 [187] Martha Ann Caudill b: Abt. 1861 Number of children: ? Sex: Female

........................+[188] Enoch Everidge b: Abt. 1860 Number of children: ? Sex: Male

........................11 [189] Susan "Susie" Everidge b: August 15, 1885 in KY d: December 29, 1962 in Perry Co., KY Number of children: 9 Sex: Female

............................+[190] Hiram Combs b: May 07, 1882 d: April 29, 1962 Number of children: 9 Father: Benjamin Combs Mother: Matilda "Tilda" Combs Sex: Male

....................10 [25] Sarah Caudill b: September 1872 in Campton, KY Number of children: ? Sex: Female

............................+[24] John C. Caudill b: February 1868 in Harlan or Letcher Co., KY m: April 18, 1889 in Breathitt Co., KY Number of children: ? Father: Henry H. Caudill Mother: Susannah Back Sex: Male

........................11 [9] Cleveland Caudill b: June 1891 in Letcher Co., KY Sex: Male

............................+[8] Peggy Caudill b: April 1890 in Letcher Co., KY m: July 14, 1909 in Letcher Co., KY d: January 14, 1916 Father: William B. Caudill Mother: Susannah "Sukie" Caudill Sex: Female

................8 [561] Sarah "Sally" Caudill, b: 1810 in Wilkes Co., NC d: 1863 in Hazard, Letcher Co., KY Number of children: 9 Sex: Female

....................+[361] Moses "Rockhouse Moses" Adams b: July 18, 1808 in Letcher Co., KY m: July 20, 1825 in Hazard, Perry/Letcher Co., KY d: 1885 in Hazard, Letcher Co., KY Number of children: 12 Father: Stephen "Rockhouse Steve" Adams Mother: Ellendar "Nellie" Buntin, or Benton Sex: Male

................9 [562] Sarah Adams b: Abt. 1826 Sex: Female

................9 [563] Mary Adams b: Abt. 1827 in Rockhouse Creek, Floyd Co., KY d: in Letcher Co., KY Sex: Female

................9 [564] Green Adams b: Abt. 1828 in Hazard, Letcher Co., KY d: in Hazard, Letcher Co., KY Number of children: 4 Sex: Male

........................+[565] Nancy Maggard b: Abt. 1830 m: Abt. 1850 d: in Hazard, Letcher Co., KY Number of children: 4 Sex: Female

....................10 [566] Esther Adams b: March 1850 Sex: Female

........................+[567] S. S. Banks b: Abt. 1850 m: September 24, 1897 Sex: Male

....................10 [568] Martha Adams b: Abt. 1855 d: October 15, 1939 in Letcher Co., KY Sex: Female

........................+[569] Daugherty Adams b: Abt. 1850 Sex: Male

....................10 [570] Mary Ann "Polly" Adams b: Abt. 1860 Sex: Female

........................+[571] George M. Gilley b: Abt. 1850 m: January 20, 1896 in Letcher Co., KY

Sex: Male

......................10 [209] Sarah Adams b: 1874 in Rockhouse Creek, Letcher Co., KY d: November 11, 1940 in Rockhouse Creek, Letcher Co., KY Sex: Female

.............................+[208] Elijah Adams b: May 31, 1866 in Rockhouse Creek, Letcher Co., KY m: March 25, 1890 in Letcher Co., KY d: September 02, 1932 in Rockhouse Creek, Letcher Co., KY Father: Stephen Adams Mother: Ursula Ison Sex: Male

...................9 [572] Stephen Adams b: 1827 in Hazard, Perry/Letcher Co., KY d: April 11, 1902 in Hazard, Perry/Letcher Co., KY Number of children: 10 Sex: Male

..........................+[573] Ursula Ison b: January 10, 1825 in Hazard, Perry/Letcher Co., KY m: 1848 in Hazard, Perry/Letcher Co., KY d: April 11, 1904 in Letcher Co., KY Number of children: 10 Father: Gideon Ison Mother: Rachel Stamper Sex: Female

......................10 [574] Sarah Adams b: Abt. 1848 Sex: Female

......................10 [575] Rachel Adams b: 1849 in Letcher Co., KY d: December 09, 1929 in Knott Co., KY Sex: Female

.............................+[576] Frazier Adams b: March 01, 1841 in Perry Co., KY m: in Whitesburg, KY d: July 04, 1917 in Knott Co., KY Sex: Male

......................10 [577] Moses Adams b: Abt. 1850 Sex: Male

......................10 [578] Gideon Adams b: June 26, 1851 in Jeremiah, Letcher Co., KY d: April 17, 1927 in Jeremiah, Letcher Co., KY Number of children: 13 Sex: Male

.............................+[579] Sarah Blair b: 1849 in Whitesburg, Letcher Co., KY m: Bet. 1877 - 1878 in Jeremiah, Letcher Co., KY d: August 11, 1924 in Jeremiah, Letcher Co., KY Number of children: 13 Father: Hiram "Humpy" Blair Mother: Drusilla "Raillie" Craft Sex: Female

......................11 [192] Celia Ann Adams b: June 23, 1877 d: November 14, 1969 in Letcher Co., KY Number of children: 9 Sex: Female

.............................+[580] Solomon Banks b: September 07, 1856 in Letcher Co., KY m: December 16, 1896 d: September 05, 1936 in Colson, Letcher Co., KY Number of children: 7 Father: Samuel G. Banks Mother: Mary Frazier Sex: Male

......................2nd Husband of [192] Celia Ann Adams:

.............................+[581] Preston Blair b: Abt. 1880 m: Abt. 1900 Number of children: 4 Sex: Male

......................11 [582] Ursula "Usley" Adams b: Abt. 1878 Sex: Female Burial: Waynesburg, KY

......................11 [583] Annie Adams b: Abt. 1879 d: in Jeremiah, KY Number of children: 7 Sex: Female

.............................+[584] Jim Adams b: Abt. 1875 m: Abt. 1905 d: in Jeremiah, Letcher Co., KY Number of children: 7 Sex: Male

......................11 [585] Hiram Adams b: Abt. 1881 d: in Waynesburg, Lincoln Co., KY Number of children: 6 Sex: Male

.............................+[586] _____ Caudill b: Abt. 1885 m: Abt. 1905 d: in Waynesburg, Lincoln Co., KY Number of children: 6 Sex: Female (Note: looking for her ancestors)

......................11 [587] Fannie Adams b: Abt. 1885 d: in Jeremiah, KY Number of children: 7 Sex: Female Burial: Blair Branch, Letcher Co., KY

.............................+[588] William Adams b: Abt. 1885 m: Abt. 1905 in Jeremiah, Letcher Co., KY d: in Jeremiah, Letcher Co., KY Number of children: 7 Sex: Male

......................11 [195] Rebecca Adams b: Abt. 1887 d: in Waynesburg, KY Number of children: 8 Sex: Female

.............................+[10] Henry H. Cleveland Caudill b: April 20, 1887 in KY m: Abt. 1905 d: May 06, 1971 in Whitesburg, Letcher Co., KY Number of children: 18 Father: James William "Noah Jim" Caudill Mother: Lucinda Sumner Sex: Male Burial: Cleveland Caudill Cemetery, Caudill's Branch, Blackey, Letcher Co., KY

......................11 [206] Stephen B. Adams b: July 15, 1888 in Letcher Co., KY d: July 02, 1963 in Waynesburg, KY Number of children: ? Sex: Male

.............................+[589] Flora Banks b: Abt. 1890 m: Abt. 1910 d: February 17, 1963 Number of children: ? Sex: Female

.....................2nd Wife of [206] Stephen B. Adams:

...........................+[590] Minnie Blair b: November 20, 1892 in Letcher Co., KY m: 1924 d: May 13, 1982 in Waynesburg, Lincoln Co., KY Sex: Female

.....................11 [591] Judy Adams b: Abt. 1889 in Jeremiah, KY d: Abt. 1890 in Jeremiah, KY Sex: Female

.....................11 [592] Dan Adams b: 1897 in Jeremiah, Letcher Co., KY d: 1937 in Horsemill Point, KY Number of children: 6 Sex: Male

...........................+[593] Virgie Smith b: Abt. 1900 m: Abt. 1920 d: in Jeremiah, Letcher Co., KY Number of children: 6 Sex: Female

.....................11 [594] Frazier C. Adams, Sr. b: January 23, 1899 in Jeremiah, KY d: in Waynesburg, Lincoln Co., KY Number of children: 11 Sex: Male

...........................+[595] Melvina "Viney" Jent b: February 11, 1903 in Smithbough, Knott Co., KY m: October 03, 1920 in Smithbough, Knott Co., KY d: October 13, 2000 in Somerset, KY Number of children: 11 Father: Sylvester Jent, Gent, Mother: Lucinda "Cinda" Smith, Sex: Female Burial: Double Springs Cemetery, Cemetery Road, Waynesburg, KY

.....................11 [596] Ritter Adams b: December 02, 1902 d: 1967 in Waynesburg, KY Number of children: 11 Sex: Female Burial: Double Creek, KY

...........................+[597] George Calfee b: Abt. 1900 m: Abt. 1920 d: in Waynesburg, Lincoln Co., KY Number of children: 11 Sex: Male

.....................11 [598] Nancy Adams b: January 17, 1904 d: May 1928 Number of children: 6 Sex: Female

...........................+[599] Curtis Stamper b: October 17, 1898 m: 1923 d: January 1932 Number of children: 6 Sex: Male

.....................11 [600] John Adams b: 1919 in Jeremiah, KY d: in died in WW I in Germany Sex: Male Burial: Horsemill Point, KY

...................10 [601] Anna "Annie" Adams b: October 04, 1853 in Letcher Co., KY d: in Letcher Co., KY Sex: Female

...........................+[602] Stephen C. Hampton b: 1851 Sex: Male

.....................10 [603] Ester Adams b: January 18, 1855 in Letcher Co., KY d: January 26, 1929 Sex: Female

.....................10 [604] Ison Moses Adams b: July 28, 1859 in Letcher Co., KY d: in Martin Co., KY Sex: Male

...........................+[605] Mary A. "Polly" Elkins b: 1860 in VA m: 1878 in Whitesburg, KY d: in Martin Co., KY Sex: Female

.....................10 [606] Nancy Adams b: April 1860 in Letcher Co., KY d: 1901 Sex: Female

...........................+[607] Daniel E. Adams b: June 05, 1849 in Letcher Co., KY m: 1874 in Whitesburg, KY Sex: Male

.....................10 [608] John Adams b: October 06, 1864 in Letcher Co., KY d: April 26, 1933 Sex: Male

...........................+[609] Laurena Roark b: November 24, 1874 d: May 20, 1965 Sex: Female

.....................10 [208] Elijah Adams b: May 31, 1866 in Rockhouse Creek, Letcher Co., KY d: September 02, 1932 in Rockhouse Creek, Letcher Co., KY Sex: Male

...........................+[209] Sarah Adams b: 1874 in Rockhouse Creek, Letcher Co., KY m: March 25, 1890 in Letcher Co., KY d: November 11, 1940 in Rockhouse Creek, Letcher Co., KY Father: Green Adams Mother: Nancy Maggard Sex: Female

.................9 [610] Ellender Adams b: January 20, 1829 in Rockhouse Creek, Floyd Co., KY d: March 07, 1886 in Letcher Co., KY Sex: Female

...........................+[611] Preston Blair b: 1827 in Perry/Letcher Co., KY m: March 04, 1849 in Letcher Co., KY d: 1878 in Letcher Co., KY Sex: Male

.................9 [612] Nancy Adams b: 1834 in Letcher Co., KY d: April 23, 1900 in Magoffin Co., KY Sex: Female

........................+[613] George Adams b: 1832 in Pert Creek, Floyd Co., KY m: December 08, 1852 in Prestonburg, Floyd Co., KY d: 1876 in Magoffin Co., KY Sex: Male

..................9 [614] Esther Adams b: November 03, 1837 in Rockhouse Creek, Floyd Co., KY d: December 11, 1911 in Eolina, Perry/Letcher Co., KY Sex: Female

........................+[615] Martin D. Collier b: March 27, 1834 in Eolina, Perry/Letcher Co., KY m: 1856 in Whitesburg, KY d: March 12, 1901 in Eolina, Perry/Letcher Co., KY Sex: Male

..................9 [616] John C. Adams b: July 02, 1841 in Rockhouse Creek, Floyd Co., KY d: February 27, 1930 in Letcher Co., KY Number of children: 8 Sex: Male

........................+[617] Susanna Back b: December 18, 1845 in Letcher Co., KY m: July 02, 1867 in Letcher Co., KY d: September 13, 1926 in Letcher Co., KY Number of children: 8 Father: John Back Mother: Sarah _____? Sex: Female

....................10 [618] Susan Adams b: Abt. 1868 Sex: Female

....................10 [619] Henry Adams b: November 05, 1868 in Letcher Co., KY d: July 21, 1939 in Letcher Co., KY Sex: Male

...........................+[620] Amanda Combs b: Abt. 1870 m: January 03, 1892 in Whitesburg, KY d: 1910 in Letcher Co., KY Sex: Female

....................10 [621] Stephen Adams b: October 16, 1871 in Letcher Co., KY d: July 21, 1954 in Letcher Co., KY Sex: Male

...........................+[622] Ardelia Craft b: 1874 in Letcher Co., KY m: November 17, 1893 in Whitesburg, KY d: 1921 in Letcher Co., KY Sex: Female

....................10 [623] Moses Adams b: 1874 in Letcher Co., KY Sex: Male

...........................+[624] Elizabeth Jane Caudill b: Abt. 1875 m: 1895 Sex: Female

....................10 [625] Joseph Adams b: 1877 in Letcher Co., KY d: September 01, 1954 in Letcher Co., KY Sex: Male

...........................+[626] Rachel Craft b: Abt. 1880 m: 1910 in Whitesburg, KY Sex: Female

....................10 [627] Frances "Fanny" Adams b: November 1879 Sex: Female

...........................+[628] Creed Craft b: Abt. 1875 Sex: Male

....................10 [629] James M. Adams b: 1882 in Letcher Co., KY d: in Jeremiah, Letcher Co., KY Sex: Male

...........................+[630] Anna _____? b: Abt. 1885 m: in Whitesburg, KY Sex: Female

....................10 [631] William Adams b: June 27, 1885 in Letcher Co., KY d: June 06, 1970 in Letcher Co., KY Sex: Male

...........................+[632] Frances _____? b: Abt. 1890 m: in Whitesburg, KY d: in Letcher Co., KY Sex: Female

..................9 [210] Benjamin Adams b: 1843 in Rockhouse Creek, Letcher Co., KY Number of children: 8 Sex: Male

...........................+[633] Sarah Sally Maggard b: Abt. 1845 m: Abt. 1861 Father: Henry Maggard Mother: Mary "Polly" Stamper Sex: Female

..................2nd Wife of [210] Benjamin Adams:

...........................+[634] Lucinda "Cindy" Combs b: June 06, 1847 in Letcher Co., KY m: 1862 in Whitesburg, KY d: February 07, 1874 in Jeremiah, KY Number of children: 8 Father: John Wesley Combs, Mother: Polly (Mary) Hogg Sex: Female

....................10 [635] Isaac Adams b: Abt. 1863 in Letcher Co., KY Sex: Male

....................10 [636] Millie Adams b: Abt. 1865 Sex: Female

...........................+[637] Leonard Crocker b: Abt. 1865 m: 1896 in Whitesburg, KY Sex: Male

....................10 [638] Elizabeth Adams b: 1863 in Letcher Co., KY Sex: Female

...........................+[639] John Cook b: Abt. 1860 m: August 26, 1882 in Whitesburg, KY Sex: Male

....................10 [640] Shadrack Adams b: March 03, 1865 in Letcher Co., KY d: December 24, 1937 Sex: Male

...........................+[641] Susan Brown b: March 24, 1876 m: July 03, 1898 in Whitesburg, KY d: December 27, 1965 Sex: Female

....................10 [642] Marianne Adams b: October 10, 1867 in Letcher Co., KY d: August 20, 1947 Sex: Female

...........................+[643] Shade Combs b: December 22, 1859 m: January 29, 1885 in Whitesburg, KY d: January 27, 1940 Sex: Male

....................10 [644] James M. Adams b: 1868 Sex: Male

....................10 [645] William Adams b: 1870 Sex: Male

....................10 [211] General Adams b: January 29, 1874 in Letcher Co., KY d: 1959 Sex: Male

...........................+[212] Martha Caudill b: February 14, 1882 in Perry Co., KY m: January 29, 1902 d: July 28, 1957 Father: Henry R. Stephen Caudill Mother: Mary Branson Sex: Female

................8 [646] Lydia Caudill, b: July 19, 1816 Number of children: ? Sex: Female

................+[647] Nathaniel Woolery Cornett, b: 1811 d: 1899 Number of children: ? Father: William Jesse Cornett, Mother: Mary Ann Everage Sex: Male

..................9 [648] Pollyann Cornett, b: 1842 in Knott Co., KY Sex: Female

................8 [649] Jesse B. Caudill, b: November 10, 1818 in Perry Co., KY d: 1904 in Letcher Co., KY Number of children: 8 Sex: Male Burial: Watty Caudill Cemetery, at the mouth of Dry Fork, Letcher Co., KY

....................+[650] Mary "Polly" Back, Bach b: February 03, 1827 in Letcher Co.,? KY m: April 04, 1844 in Letcher Co., KY d: July 29, 1888 Number of children: 8 Father: Henry Back, Bach Mother: Susannah Maggard Sex: Female Burial: Watty Caudill Cemetery, at the mouth of Dry Fork, Letcher Co., KY

..................9 [213] Benjamin "Paw Paw" Caudill, b: 1846 in Letcher Co., KY d: Abt. 1927 Number of children: 2 Sex: Male

........................+[651] Sarah "Sallie" Brashear b: Abt. 1856 in Perry Co., KY Sex: Female (Note: Looking for her ancestors)

..................2nd Wife of [213] Benjamin "Paw Paw" Caudill, :

........................+[652] Terry Hampton b: 1847 in Letcher Co., KY m: 1868 in KY d: March 06, 1877 in Letcher Co., KY Number of children: 2 Father: Wilburn Hampton Mother: Phoebe Caudill Sex: Female Burial: Watty Caudill Cemetery, at the mouth of Dry Fork, Letcher Co., KY

....................10 [653] Polly Ann Caudill, b: May 1872 in KY Number of children: 4 Sex: Female

...........................+[654] Elhannon Jent, b: September 12, 1873 in Indian Bottom, Perry Co., KY m: Abt. 1895 in Perry or Letcher Co., KY d: May 05, 1947 in Scuddy, Perry Co., KY Number of children: 4 Father: John Jent, Ghent, Mother: Nellie or Nella or "Nell" Sumner, Sex: Male Burial: May 06, 1947 Sumner Cemetery, Perry Co., KY

........................11 [655] Sally Jent b: March 1896 Sex: Female

........................11 [656] John D. Jent b: June 1898 Sex: Male

........................11 [657] Phoebe Jent b: 1909 in KY Sex: Female

...........................+[658] Ira Combs b: 1901 in KY? Father: Richard Nicholas "Dick" Combs Mother: Nancy Martin Sex: Male

........................11 [659] Chester Jent, b: Abt. 1911 in VicCo., KY? Number of children: ? Sex: Male

...........................+[660] Oma Smith b: Abt. 1913 in VicCo., KY? Number of children: ? Father: Thomas "Tom" Smith, Mother: Vinabelle Smith, Sex: Female

....................10 [661] John D. Caudill b: July 29, 1875 in KY d: October 17, 1955 in Perry Co., KY Number of children: ? Sex: Male

...........................+[662] Martha (or Patsy) Polly b: August 10, 1878 in KY m: Abt. 1897 in KY d: October 31, 1949 Number of children: ? Sex: Female (Note: Looking for her ancestors)

........................11 [663] Enoch Caudill b: Abt. 1910 Number of children: ? Sex: Male

...........................+[664] Hazel McIntry b: Abt. 1912 m: February 11, 1933 Number of children: ? Sex: Female

..................9 [665] Susanna Caudill b: January 1850 d: February 27, 1920 Sex: Female Burial: Watty Caudill Cemetery, at the mouth of Dry Fork, Letcher Co., KY

........................+[666] Stephen Roberts b: Abt. 1848 Father: Preston Roberts Mother: Rebecca

Caudill Sex: Male

.................9 [214] John Maggard Caudill b: June 25, 1852 in Letcher Co., KY d: August 31, 1939 Number of children: ? Sex: Male

.........................+[667] Susanna Hampton b: Abt. 1861 d: June 30, 1877 Father: Wilburn Hampton Mother: Phoebe Caudill Sex: Female Burial: Watty Caudill Cemetery, at the mouth of Dry Fork, Letcher Co., KY

.................2nd Wife of [214] John Maggard Caudill:

.........................+[668] Polly Ann Morgan b: 1861 in Letcher Co., KY m: May 31, 1882 in Letcher Co., KY Number of children: ? Sex: Female (Note: Looking for ancestors)

....................10 [669] William H. Caudill b: January 02, 1893 in Letcher Co., KY d: September 25, 1963 in Elkhorn City, Pike Co., KY Number of children: ? Sex: Male

..........................+[670] Ollie Mae Sumner b: September 02, 1897 in Fusonia, Perry Co., KY m: March 23, 1917 in Perry Co., KY d: July 11, 1953 in Grundy, VA Number of children: ? Sex: Female

.......................11 [671] Edith Caudill b: January 31, 1919 in Cornettsville, Perry Co., KY d: 1999 in Perry Co., KY Number of children: ? Sex: Female

.............................+[672] Marcellus Combs b: September 05, 1916 in Allais, Perry Co., KY m: November 03, 1939 in Perry Co., KY d: March 10, 1988 in Hazard, Perry Co., KY Number of children: ? Father: Owen Combs Mother: Mahala Campbell Sex: Male

.................9 [673] Nancy C. Caudill b: December 09, 1853 d: January 06, 1915 Number of children: 5 Sex: Female Burial: Watty Caudill Cemetery, at the mouth of Dry Fork, Letcher Co., KY

.........................+[674] James Dixon Caudill b: December 13, 1854 d: May 04, 1938 Number of children: 5 Sex: Male Burial: Watty Caudill Cemetery, at the mouth of Dry Fork, Letcher Co., KY

....................10 [675] Watson Caudill b: February 08, 1878 d: December 1878 Sex: Male Burial: Watty Caudill Cemetery, at the mouth of Dry Fork, Letcher Co., KY

....................10 [215] Mary Caudill b: December 05, 1881 d: November 29, 1930 Sex: Female Burial: Watty Caudill Cemetery, at the mouth of Dry Fork, Letcher Co., KY

..........................+[676] Jeremiah P. Dixon b: Abt. 1880 Sex: Male

....................2nd Husband of [215] Mary Caudill:

..........................+[677] Joe Hawkins b: Abt. 1879 Sex: Male

....................10 [678] James Caudill b: February 10, 1890 d: September 19, 1899 Sex: Male Burial: Watty Caudill Cemetery, at the mouth of Dry Fork, Letcher Co., KY

....................10 [679] Rachel Caudill b: July 13, 1898 d: October 02, 1900 Sex: Female Burial: Watty Caudill Cemetery, at the mouth of Dry Fork, Letcher Co., KY

....................10 [680] Boyd Caudill b: November 22, 1898 d: December 22, 1919 Sex: Male Burial: Watty Caudill Cemetery, at the mouth of Dry Fork, Letcher Co., KY

.................9 [681] Watson "Watty" Caudill b: Abt. 1854 Number of children: ? Sex: Male

.........................+[682] Rachel Hampton b: March 23, 1852 d: December 25, 1881 Number of children: ? Father: Wilburn Hampton Mother: Phoebe Caudill Sex: Female Burial: Watty Caudill Cemetery, at the mouth of Dry Fork, Letcher Co., KY

....................10 [216] Jesse Wilburn Caudill b: Abt. 1876 Number of children: ? Sex: Male

..........................+[683] Rosanna Tyree b: Abt. 1878 d: July 14, 1899 Sex: Female Burial: Watty Caudill Cemetery, at the mouth of Dry Fork, Letcher Co., KY

....................2nd Wife of [216] Jesse Wilburn Caudill:

..........................+[684] Mary Miller b: Abt. 1879 Number of children: ? Sex: Female

.......................11 [685] unnamed Caudill b: June 14, 1901 d: June 14, 1901 Sex: Male Burial: Watty Caudill Cemetery, at the mouth of Dry Fork, Letcher Co., KY

.................9 [686] Henry Caudill, b: November 15, 1856 in Letcher Co., KY? d: March 07, 1899 Number of children: 2 Sex: Male

.......................+[687] Barilla Jones b: May 22, 1877 d: January 29, 1899 Number of children: 2 Sex: Female

....................10 [688] William M. Caudill, World War I Soldier b: April 27, 1896 d: July 12,

1966 Number of children: 2 Sex: Male Burial: Caudill Cemetery at Uz, Letcher Co., KY
...........................+[689] Etta B. Dixon b: September 10, 1899 d: September 08, 1938 Number
of children: 2 Father: James C. Dixon Mother: Evelyn Back, Bach Sex: Female
......................11 [690] Harold K. Caudill, b: Abt. 1910 Number of children: ? Sex: Male
...........................+[691] Dociphene Frazier b: Abt. 1915 Number of children: ? Father: Enoch
Flanery Frazier Mother: Sarah "Elizabeth" Boatright Sex: Female
......................11 [692] Helen M. Caudill b: August 23, 1935 d: September 09, 1935 Sex: Female
Burial: Caudill Cemetery at Uz, Letcher Co., KY
......................10 [693] Jesse Caudill b: July 21, 1898 d: November 25, 1935 Killed by his wife with
an axe Sex: Male
...........................+[694] Artie Cornett, b: Abt. 1900 Sex: Female (Note: Looking for ancestors)
..................9 [695] Easter Caudill, Johnny's 7th wife b: December 17, 1859 d: November 08, 1882
Sex: Female Burial: Watty Caudill Cemetery, at the mouth of Dry Fork, Letcher Co., KY
........................+[696] Johnny C. Brown b: Abt. 1820 Father: George W. Brown Mother:
Susanna Wells Sex: Male
..................9 [697] David J. Caudill b: December 21, 1860 d: September 15, 1882 Sex: Male
Burial: Watty Caudill Cemetery, at the mouth of Dry Fork, Letcher Co., KY
...............8 [698] Henry Caudill, b: Abt. 1820 Sex: Male
...............8 [699] Watson E. "Old Watty" Caudill, b: March 14, 1822 in Perry Co., KY d:
December 05, 1898 in Letcher Co., KY Number of children: 4 Sex: Male
.....................+[700] Elizabeth "Betty" Branham-Smith, b: March 19, 1827 in Perry Co., KY m:
Abt. 1846 in Perry Co., KY? Number of children: 4 Father: William "Billy" Branham-Smith Mother:
Elizabeth (Betty) Childers Sex: Female
..................9 [701] Polly Ann Caudill b: Abt. 1847 Sex: Female
..................9 [702] Rachel Caudill b: December 24, 1855 d: October 09, 1876 Sex: Female Burial:
Watty Caudill Cemetery, at the mouth of Dry Fork, Letcher Co., KY
..................9 [703] Martha Salina Caudill b: Abt. 1860 Number of children: ? Sex: Female
.......................+[704] Rudolphus "Dolph" A. Lafayette Draughn b: Abt. 1855 m: Abt. 1882
Number of children: ? Sex: Male (Note: looking for ancestors)
....................10 [705] _____ Draughn, ? b: Abt. 1895 Number of children: ? Sex: Male
...........................+[706] _____ _____? b: Abt. 1900 Number of children: ? Sex: Female
..................9 [709] Lucinda Caudill b: April 10, 1862 d: October 13, 1906 Number of children:
? Sex: Female Burial: Watty Caudill Cemetery, at the mouth of Dry Fork, Letcher Co., KY
.......................+[710] Steve Hall b: Abt. 1860 Number of children: ? Sex: Male
....................10 [711] Beckham Hall b: June 04, 1904 d: June 04, 1904 Sex: Male Burial: Watty
Caudill Cemetery, at the mouth of Dry Fork, Letcher Co., KY
...............8 [712] Walter E. Caudill, b: Abt. 1824 Sex: Male
...............8 [713] Fanny Caudill, b: Abt. 1826 Sex: Female
............7 [774] John Washington "Wash" Adams, b: Bet. 1780 - 1785 in Roaring River or
Wilkesboro, Wilkes Co., NC d: 1851 Number of children: ? Sex: Male Burial: (Not sure if John is the
Father of Sarah)
..................+[1154] _____ _____? , b: 1785 in NC or KY? m: 1803 in NC or KY? Number of
children: ? Sex: Female (Note: Looking for her full name & ancestors)
...............8 [714] Sarah "Sally" Adams, parents unknown h: 1807 in NC Number of children: 9 Sex:
Female (Note: Looking for her ancestors; I think her Father MAY be John Washington "Wash" Adams.
b. 1785 in NC)
.....................+[715] William B. "Buckie" Holbrook, Sr., b: 1809 in Floyd Co., KY m: Abt. 1826
in Floyd Co., KY Number of children: 9 Father: Randolph (or Randel) "Buck" Holbrook, Mother:
Elizabeth Nancy Rebecca Adams, Sex: Male
..................9 [716] Mary "Polly" Holbrook, b: 1827 in Perry Co., KY d: April 11, 1854 in Letcher
Co., KY Number of children: 2 Sex: Female
.......................+[717] Esquire "Squire" Bentley, b: 1821 in Letcher Co., KY m: October 24,

1850 in Letcher Co., KY Number of children: 2 Father: John Queller Bentley, Sr., Mother: Margaret "Peggy" Hamilton, Sex: Male

.....................10 [718] William Barlow "Barlow" Bentley b: March 1849 in KY Number of children: 13 Sex: Male

.........................+[719] Susannah Quillen b: September 20, 1857 in Letcher Co., KY m: September 19, 1872 in Letcher Co., KY d: February 14, 1926 Number of children: 13 Father: Richard Teaque Quillen Mother: Catherine Yonts Sex: Female (Note: some say she was born 9 22 1859) .

.....................11 [720] William D. Bentley b: 1874 in KY Sex: Male

.....................11 [721] Mary Bentley b: 1876 in KY Sex: Female

.....................11 [722] Polly Bentley b: November 1876 Sex: Female

.....................11 [723] Arminda "Armindy" Bentley b: December 1878 in KY Sex: Female

.....................11 [724] Squire Richard Bentley b: December 12, 1879 d: May 06, 1933 Number of children: 16 Sex: Male

............................+[725] Rosemond Fidel Hall b: Abt. 1880 Number of children: 16 Sex: Female

.....................11 [726] Benjamin Franklin Bentley b: June 1882 Number of children: ? Sex: Male

.....................11 [727] James M. Bentley b: May 1888 Sex: Male

.....................11 [728] Wiley A. Bentley b: July 1889 Sex: Male

.....................11 [729] Nancy J. Bentley b: March 1894 Sex: Female

.....................11 [730] Samantha Bentley b: Abt. August 1895 Sex: Female

.....................11 [731] Robert S. Bentley b: March 1896 Sex: Male

.....................11 [732] Sarah E. Bentley b: April 1898 Sex: Female

.....................11 [733] Ira J. Bentley b: 1902 Sex: Male

.....................10 [734] Sarah "Sally" Bentley, b: July 1852 in Letcher Co., KY d: Aft. 1920 in Pulaski Co., KY? Number of children: 3 Sex: Female

...........................+[735] William James Yonts, b: December 1845 in Letcher Co., KY m: March 18, 1870 in Letcher Co., KY d: Aft. 1920 in Pulaski Co., KY? Number of children: 3 Father: William Yonts, Jr., Yants, Mother: Nancy F. Ray, Sex: Male (Yonts Note: like the author and all of the other Yonts individuals in this tree, this family descends from Wilhelm Jans, born in 1714 in the town of Oberalben, Rheineland-Pfalz, Germany; Wilhelm died in 1778 in Rowan Co., NC)

........................11 [417] Esquire "Squire" Lincoln Yonts, Yantz, b: April 30, 1874 in Letcher Co., KY d: December 10, 1942 in Knoxville, TN Number of children: 9 Sex: Male Burial: Abt. December 13, 1942 Sharp Cemetery (Note: Letcher Co. Birth Records state that his middle initial was "F"). NOTE: Squire is the author's great-grandfather.

...........................+[736] Mary Frances Wright, b: January 27, 1872 in Upper Elkhorn Creek, Pike Co., KY ? m: April 23, 1890 in Letcher Co., KY d: April 12, 1950 in Neon, Hogg Hollow, Letcher Co., KY Number of children: 9 Father: William A. Wright, Mother: Arty (Artie or Arta) M. Potter, Sex: Female Burial: Abt. April 15, 1950 Yonts Cemetery, Craft Funeral Home, Neon, Letcher Co., KY. NOTE: Mary is the author's great-grandmother.

........................2nd Wife of [417] Squire Lincoln Yonts, Yantz, :

...........................+[737] Louise _____? b: Abt. 1880 m: December 1907 Sex: Female

........................3rd Wife of [417] Squire Lincoln Yonts, Yantz, :

...........................+[738] Alice _____? b: Abt. 1900 m: Aft. 1920 Sex: Female Burial: Sharp Cemetery

........................11 [739] Nancy Chaney Yonts b: April 15, 1878 in Letcher Co., KY d: November 20, 1927 in at her daughter's home in Wise, VA or Waynesburg, Lincoln Co., KY Number of children: 9 Sex: Female

...........................+[740] Archibald "Archie" Lincoln Meade b: 1874 in Letcher Co., KY m: August 06, 1895 in Neon, Letcher Co., KY Number of children: 9 Sex: Male

........................11 [418] Robert Grant Yonts b: May 04, 1883 in Letcher Co., KY d: September 13, 1964 Number of children: 15 Sex: Male

..............................+[741] Henrietta "Hennie" Ritter Holbrook b: December 05, 1881 in Letcher Co., KY? m: 1901 in Letcher Co., KY d: April 02, 1965 Number of children: 9 Father: Enoch A. Holbrook Mother: Nancy Evelyn Webb Sex: Female

.......................2nd Wife of [418] Robert Grant Yonts:

..............................+[742] Dorothy Pence b: Abt. 1890 in KY? m: Aft. 1922 Number of children: 6 Sex: Female

.................9 [743] Nancy Ann Holbrook b: 1831 Sex: Female

.................9 [744] Susannah Holbrook b: 1834 Sex: Female

.................9 [745] James E. Holbrook b: November 18, 1836 Number of children: 7 Sex: Male

.......................+[746] Tabitha Bentley b: 1843 Number of children: 7 Father: Daniel Bentley, Sr., Mother: Marinda (Brinkley?) Ramey (Note: Marinda descends from the same family line as country singer Patty (Ramey) Loveless, born January 4, 1957 in Pikeville, Pike Co., KY) Sex: Female

.....................10 [747] Mary E. "Polly" Holbrook b: 1867 Number of children: ? Sex: Female

...........................+[748] Noah "Paw" Bentley b: Abt. 1865 Number of children: ? Father: Benjamin Bentley Mother: Elizabeth E. "Patsy" Reynolds Sex: Male

.......................11 [749] Lincoln Bentley b: Abt. 1890 Number of children: ? Sex: Male

...........................+[750] Etta Bentley b: Abt. 1895 Number of children: ? Sex: Female

.....................10 [751] William B. Holbrook b: May 1869 Sex: Male

...........................+[752] Sarah Clark b: Abt. 1870 Sex: Female

.....................10 [753] John A. Holbrook b: April 1871 Sex: Male

...........................+[754] Lucinda Huff b: 1874 Sex: Female

.....................10 [755] Sarah M. Holbrook b: 1872 Sex: Female

.....................10 [756] Didamey Holbrook b: Abt. 1876 Sex: Female

.....................10 [757] Zilpha P. Holbrook b: 1879 Sex: Female

.....................10 [758] Gracie Holbrook b: 1889 Sex: Female

.................9 [759] William B. Holbrook, Jr. b: 1839 Sex: Male

.................9 [760] Randolph E. Holbrook b: 1841 Sex: Male

.................9 [761] Benjamin W. Holbrook b: 1845 Sex: Male

.................9 [762] Ransom T. Holbrook b: March 21, 1846 d: March 01, 1894 Number of children: 5 Sex: Male Burial: Bottom Fork, Letcher Co., KY

.......................+[763] Elizabeth Ann Hughes b: March 10, 1850 in Letcher Co., KY m: July 10, 1866 d: October 22, 1917 Number of children: 5 Father: John Hughes Mother: Matilda Bentley, (Note: Looking for her ancestors) Sex: Female Burial: Bottom Fork, Letcher Co., KY

.....................10 [764] John A. Holbrook b: Abt. 1865 Number of children: ? Sex: Male (Note: Looking for his ancestors)

...........................+[765] Mary Ann Stewart b: Abt. 1860 Number of children: ? Father: Thomas "Tom" Stewart Mother: Susannah Fleming Sex: Female

.......................11 [766] Gabriel Holbrook b: Abt. 1880 Number of children: ? Sex: Male

...........................+[767] Norma Sturgill b: Abt. 1880 in Pound, VA Number of children: ? Father: Gordon Sturgill Sex: Female

.....................10 [768] Sarah "Sally" Holbrook b: November 05, 1867 in Letcher Co., KY d: February 16, 1929 Sex: Female

...........................+[769] Wiley W. Quillen b: September 1861 in Letcher Co., KY m: November 30, 1882 in Letcher Co., KY d: 1938 Father: Richard Teague Quillen Mother: Catherine Yonts Sex: Male

.....................10 [770] Nancy "Nannie" Holbrook b: 1868 Sex: Female

.....................10 [771] Francis Holbrook b: 1880 Sex: Female

.....................10 [772] John A. Holbrook b: Abt. 1880 Sex: Male

.................9 [773] Doctor "Dock" Holbrook b: 1850 Sex: Male

..............2nd Wife of [774] John Washington "Wash" Adams, :

...................+[1155] Mary Polly Hall b: 1806 in Letcher Co., KY m: April 08, 1830 in Hazard, Perry Co., KY Sex: Female (Note: Looking for her ancestors)

.............3rd Wife of [774] John Washington "Wash" Adams:

....................+[1156] Jane M. Donnell b: 1789 m: July 29, 1845 in Greene Co., MO Sex: Female (Note: Looking for ancestors)

.............7 [1157] Esther H. Adams b: 1787 in Roaring River, Wilkes Co., NC d: 1836 Sex: Female

....................+[1158] William Williams b: Abt. 1780 m: Abt. 1804 Sex: Male

.............7 [1159] Nancy Adams b: 1788 in Roaring River, Wilkes Co., NC d: 1840 in Letcher Co., KY Sex: Female

....................+[1160] Charles Lewis b: Abt. 1775 m: Abt. 1804 in Wilkes Co., NC d: Aft. 1840 in IN? Father: George ? Lewis Mother: _____ _____? Sex: Male

..........6 Buckner Caudill b: Abt. 1754 in VA, KY, or NC? d: Abt. 1823 in Rowan Co., NC Number of children: ? Sex: Male

...............+Elizabeth? _____? b: Abt. 1756 in VA, KY, or NC? Number of children: ? Sex: Female

.............7 John Caudill, Caudle b: Abt. 1775 in VA? or KY? Number of children: 2 Sex: Male (Note: looking for ancestors; his Father's name was Buckner Caudle)

....................+Susannah Thomas b: Abt. 1778 in VA? or KY? m: Abt. 1797 Number of children: 2 Sex: Female

................8 Buckner Caudill, Caudle b: April 26, 1798 in Bourbon, KY, or Wayne Twp., Clermont Co., OH d: September 02, 1862 Sex: Male

......................+Harriet Hannah Thomas b: May 29, 1797 in KY, or Wayne Twp., Clermont Co., OH m: March 27, 1815 in KY or Clermont, OH d: June 10, 1861 Father: John Thomas Mother: Ruth Ann _____? Sex: Female

................8 John Caudill, Caudle b: Abt. 1818 in Madison Co., KY? Number of children: 8 Sex: Male

......................+Eliza Jane Agee, royal line b: Abt. 1840 in Madison Co., KY? m: March 16, 1863 in Madison Co., KY Number of children: 8 Father: James Agee, royal line Mother: Agnes Barnes, or Barnett Sex: Female (Note: Eliza and her descendants descend from European royalty)

..................9 James Caudill, Caudle b: 1863 Sex: Male

..................9 William Green Caudill, Caudle, royal line b: 1864 d: 1944 in Gratz, Owen Co., KY? Number of children: 4 Sex: Male Burial: Mount Minnish Cemetery, Gratz, Owen Co., KY

.........................+Maggie Goodrich b: Abt. 1865 d: 1928 in Gratz, Owen Co., KY? Number of children: 4 Sex: Female Burial: Mount Minnish Cemetery, Gratz, Owen Co., KY

....................10 Stella (Della) Caudill, Caudle b: Abt. 1892 Sex: Female

....................10 Catherine "Katie" Caudill, Caudle b: Abt. 1895 Sex: Female

....................10 Frances "Frank" Caudill, Caudle b: Abt. 1897 Sex: Male

....................10 [775] Anna Caudill, Caudle b: April 23, 1892 in Gratz, Owen Co., KY d: January 20, 1966 Number of children: 8 Sex: Female

.........................+Edgar Hume Parker b: Abt. 1890 met: in (Note: They did not marry) Number of children: ? Sex: Male (Note: looking for his ancestors)

......................11 Edgar D. Parker b: September 18, 1911 in Gratz, Owen Co., KY? d: May 1986 Number of children: ? Sex: Male

.............................+_____ _____? b: Abt. 1913 in Gratz, Owen Co., KY? d: March 2001 Number of children: ? Sex: Female

....................1st Husband of [775] Anna Caudill, Caudle:

.........................+Robert Doke b: Abt. 1900 d: March 21, 1955 Sex: Male

....................2nd Husband of [775] Anna Caudill, Caudle:

.........................+Omer Moore b: Abt. 1905 d: June 08, 1958 Sex: Male

....................3rd Husband of [775] Anna Caudill, Caudle:

.........................+Sim Bond, or Bonds b: Abt. 1890 in KY? d: January 13, 1940 Number of children: 7 Sex: Male

......................11 William Bond b: June 03, 1914 Sex: Male

......................11 Maggie Bond b: June 06, 1916 Sex: Female

......................11 Lillian Bond b: October 12, 1918 Sex: Female

.......................11 Eva Jessie Bond b: August 06, 1921 Sex: Female
.......................11 Marvin Bond b: September 28, 1923 Sex: Male
.......................11 Robert Lester Bond b: April 07, 1926 Sex: Male
.......................11 Eljay Bond b: February 23, 1930 Sex: Male
..................9 Fannie Caudill, Caudle b: 1867 Sex: Female
..................9 Harriet Caudill, Caudle b: 1869 Sex: Female
..................9 Charley Caudill b: 1872 Sex: Male
..................9 Robert Caudill b: 1875 Sex: Male
..................9 George Caudill b: 1876 Sex: Male
..................9 Florence Caudill b: 1878 Sex: Female
..........6 James Caudill b: Abt. 1756 Sex: Male
...............+Sarah Caudill b: Abt. 1758 Sex: Female (Note: Looking for her ancestors)
..........6 Absalom Caudill b: Abt. 1758 Sex: Male
...............+Elizabeth Hanes b: Abt. 1760 Sex: Female
..........6 Stephen Caudill b: Abt. 1760 Sex: Male
...............+Fannie Adams b: Abt. 1731 in Sussex, VA Father: Benjamin Adams, Mother: Nancy
Agnes _____? , Sex: Female
..........6 Mary Caudill b: Abt. 1762 in Lunenburg or Sussex Co., VA Number of children: 2 Sex:
Female Burial: Wilkes Co., NC
...............+Thomas Joynes b: Abt. 1760 in Wilkes Co., NC d: February 1835 Number of children:
2 Father: Ezekiel Joines Mother: _____ _____? Sex: Male
.............7 Major Joines b: April 24, 1793 in Wilkes Co., NC d: May 06, 1889 Sex: Male
...................+Sarah "Sally" Caudill b: October 05, 1801 m: April 24, 1825 d: June 05, 1886 Sex:
Female; Father: Jeremiah Caudill (b. Abt. 1799) Mother: Sally Jane Adams (b. 1787)
.............7 [777] Ezekiel Joines b: June 02, 1800 in Wilkes Co., NC d: May 08, 1893 in Wilkes Co.,
NC Sex: Male Burial: 1893 Joynes Family Cemetery, Abshers, Wilkes Co., NC
...................+[776] Pheroby Caudill b: 1805 in Wilkes Co., NC m: Abt. 1827 d: 1870 in Wilkes
Co., NC Father: Benjamin "Ben of Sussex" Caudill, Sr., Mother: Elizabeth Buckner, Sex: Female
Burial: 1870 Joynes Family Cemetery, Abshers, Wilkes Co., NC
..........6 Solomon Caudill b: Abt. 1765 Sex: Male
..........6 David Caudill b: Abt. 1767 Sex: Male
..........6 William "Old William" Caudill b: between 1749-1753 in Wilkes Co., NC Sex: Male
(Notes: it is my theory (Lochlainn) that William Caudill, the father of Jeremiah Caudill (b. abt. 1779)
is the same as "Old William" Caudill, son of Benjamin Caudill (b. 1730) and Elizabeth Buckner (b.
1728), and I've tentatively listed him as their son. I have no proof of this theory yet, but I'm sure that
these two branches will turn out to be closely connected and related)
............+ Elizabeth Pruitt b: 1757 in Wilkes Co., NC (Note: Looking for her ancestors)
...............7 Jeremiah Caudill b: Abt, 1779 in Wilkes Co., NC d: 1829
.................+ Sally Jane Adams b: December 26, 1787 in Wilkes Co., NC d: May 1858 Burial:
Traphill, Wilkes Co., NC (Note: looking for her ancestors)
....................8 Sarah Sally Caudill b: October 5, 1801 probably in Wilkes Co., NC d: June 5 1886
........................+ Major Joines b: April 24, 1793 in Wilkes Co., NC d: May 6 1889 m: April 24,
1825 Father: Thomas Joines/Joynes Mother: Mary Caudill (daughter of Benjamin Caudill, b. 1730,
and Elizabeth Buckner, b. 1728)
....................8 William Caudill/Cordell b: 1803 in Wilkes Co., NC d: 1890 in Blaine, Lawrence
Co., KY
........................+ Jane Wheeler b: 1805 in Wheeler's Ford, VA d: 1852 in Blaine, Lawrence Co.,
KY m: January 19, 1823 in Lawrence Co., KY Father: James Moses Wheeler Mother: Eleanor
Harrison
...........................9 Isom Caudill b: 1822
...........................9 Jeremiah H. Caudill b: 1824
...........................9 James Boone Caudill b: 1825

...........................9 Eleanor Caudill b: 1827

...........................9 Amos Caudill b: 1831

...........................9 Phoebe Caudill b: 1834 in NC of Lawrence Co., KY

...........................9 William Caudill b: 1837

...........................9 Jesse Caudill b: 1839

...........................9 Jane Elizabeth Caudill b: 1842

...........................9 Ralph Caudill/Cordial b: May 1844 in Lawarence Co., KY d: January 01, 1921

.............................+ Nancy Moore b: April 1845 in KY (Note: Looking for her ancestors)

.............................10 William Caudill b: February 6, 1869 in KY d: September 01, 1941

.............................+ Rita LeMaster b: 1876 in Johnson Co., KY m: June 22, 1892 Father: James "Red Beard" "Jim Sharp" LeMaster Mother: Sarah C. Scarberry

.................................11 Chester M. Caudill b: June 21, 1893 in Wilbur, Lawrence Co., KY

...........................9 Holly Caudill b: 1846

...........................9 Henry David Caudill b: 1856

...........6 Benjamin Caudill, Jr. b: Abt. 1772 Sex: Male

...........6 Jesse Caudill b: Abt. 1775 Sex: Male

...........6 John "Old John" Caudill b: Abt. 1777 Sex: Male

...........6 Ann Caudill b: Abt. 1781 Sex: Female

...........6 [776] Pheroby Caudill b: 1805 in Wilkes Co., NC d: 1870 in Wilkes Co., NC Sex: Female Burial: 1870 Joynes Family Cemetery, Abshers, Wilkes Co., NC

.................+[777] Ezekiel Joines b: June 02, 1800 in Wilkes Co., NC m: Abt. 1827 d: May 08, 1893 in Wilkes Co., NC Father: Thomas Joynes Mother: Mary Caudill Sex: Male Burial: 1893 Joynes Family Cemetery, Abshers, Wilkes Co., NC

.........5 Ann Caudill, b: Bet. 1730 - 1733 in Fairfax Co., VA d: 1803 in Roaring River, Wilkes Co., NC Number of children: 15 Sex: Female Burial: 1803 Roaring River, Wilkes Co., NC (Note: we are not sure who her parents are; looking for her ancestors; my theory is that her parents are Stephen James Caudill (d. 1759) and Mary Elizabeth "Betsy" Fields (b. 1698), since the time and place match up; thus she is placed here tentatively)

..............+John Hobbs "Old John of KY" Adams, Sr., b: Bet. 1727 - 1729 in Sussex (or Stafford Co.) , VA m: 1746 in Fairfax, Fairfax Co., VA d: January 29, 1815 in Floyd, KY or Roaring River, Wilkes Co., N.C. Number of children: 16 Father: Benjamin Adams, Mother: Nancy Agnes _____? , Sex: Male Burial: 1815 Webb Cemetery, Mayking, Letcher Co., KY

...........6 Jesse Adams, Sr., b: 1747 in Lewis Fork, Surry Co., NC d: Bef. 1781 in Lewis Fork, Wilkes Co., NC Number of children: 4 Sex: Male

.................+Jane Green b: Abt. 1740 in Wilkes Co., NC m: 1759 in Wilkes Co., North Carolina d: 1804 in Lewis Fork, Wilkes Co., NC Number of children: 4 Sex: Female (Note: Looking for her ancestors)

..............7 Jesse Adams, Jr., b: 1763 in Lewis Fork, Wilkes Co., NC d: 1805 Number of children: 2 Sex: Male

...................+_____ Green b: Abt. 1765 Number of children: 2 Sex: Female

................8 [926] William Green "Billy Grit" Adams, b: Bet. 1788 - 1790 in Lewis Fork, Wilkes Co., NC d: 1870 in Letcher Co., KY Number of children: 9 Sex: Male

.....................+[925] Mary Ann "Polly" Adams, b: 1788 in KY or Wilkes Co., NC m: October 29, 1809 in Letcher Co., KY d: 1845 in Letcher Co., KY Number of children: 9 Father: John Hobbs Adams, Jr., Mother: Lydia "Letty" or "Lettie" Simpson Sex: Female

..................9 [927] John Adams b: 1811 Sex: Male

........................+[928] Sarah Meadows b: 1815 d: December 26, 1856 Sex: Female

..................9 [929] Jesse G. Adams b: 1815 d: Aft. 1880 Sex: Male

........................+[930] Keziah Meadows b: 1827 d: Aft. 1880 Sex: Female

..................9 [931] Simpson (or Sampson) Adams b: 1818 in Jellico River, Whitley Co., KY d:

1910 in Pine Creek, Letcher Co., KY Number of children: 10 Sex: Male

..........................+[932] Sarah Webb b: 1825 d: 1897 Number of children: 10 Father: Benjamin Webb Mother: Jane "Jennie" "Jincy" Adams, Sex: Female (Webb Note: Like all of the other Webb individuals in this tree, this Webb family descends from the same line as the country singers Loretta (Webb) Lynn and her sister Brenda Gail "Crystal Gale" Webb. Loretta was born April 14, 1935, in Butcher Hollow, Pike Co., KY; Crystal Gale was born January 9, 1951, in Paintsville, Johnson Co., KY)

.....................10 [933] Jane Adams b: 1846 Sex: Female

.....................10 [934] Mary M. Adams b: 1849 Sex: Female

.....................10 [935] Lettie Adams b: 1853 d: 1925 Sex: Female

.....................10 [936] Lydia Adams, twin b: March 14, 1855 Sex: Female

.....................10 [937] Rachel Adams, twin b: 1855 Sex: Female

.....................10 [938] Benjamin Jackson Adams b: 1856 d: 1938 Sex: Male

.....................10 [939] Jason Adams b: 1860 Sex: Male

.....................10 [940] Enoch M. Adams b: 1863 Sex: Male

.....................10 [941] Spencer Adams b: 1866 Sex: Male

.....................10 [942] Simpson M. Adams b: 1869 d: 1889 Sex: Male

...................9 [943] William Green Adams b: January 21, 1820 in Jellico River, Whitley Co., KY d: June 29, 1862 in Pound River, Wise Co., VA Number of children: 9 Sex: Male

..........................+[944] Mary Webb b: March 14, 1818 m: April 25, 1840 d: February 05, 1899 Number of children: 9 Father: Benjamin Webb Mother: Jane "Jennie" "Jincy" Adams, Sex: Female (Webb Note: Like all of the other Webb individuals in this tree, this Webb family descends from the same line as the country singers Loretta (Webb) Lynn and her sister Brenda Gail "Crystal Gale" Webb. Loretta was born April 14, 1935, in Butcher Hollow, Pike Co., KY; Crystal Gale was born January 9, 1951, in Paintsville, Johnson Co., KY)

.....................10 [945] Benjamin Adams b: July 04, 1840 Sex: Male

.....................10 [946] Purthia Adams b: September 22, 1842 Sex: Female

.....................10 [947] Lydia Adams b: November 07, 1844 Sex: Female

..............................+[948] Jesse Collins b: Abt. 1840 Sex: Male

.....................10 [949] Sarah Adams b: May 05, 1850 Sex: Female

..............................+[950] Nelson Hampton b: Abt. 1845 Sex: Male

.....................10 [951] Lettie Jane Adams b: January 23, 1852 in Letcher Co., KY d: September 08, 1883 Sex: Female

.....................10 [952] Jane Adams b: May 10, 1853 Sex: Female

..............................+[953] Benjamin Abbott Adams b: Abt. 1850 m: October 09, 1864 in Letcher Co., KY Sex: Male

.....................10 [954] Miles Mayo Adams b: June 18, 1855 in Letcher Co., KY Sex: Male

.....................10 [955] Simpson E. Adams b: October 29, 1857 in Letcher Co., KY d: May 04, 1935 Sex: Male

.....................10 [956] Mary Ellen Adams b: May 27, 1861 in Letcher Co., KY d: September 1889 Number of children: ? Sex: Female

..............................+[957] Willis Kirk Collier b: 1859 d: 1944 Number of children: ? Sex: Male

..........................11 [958] Harrison Collier b: April 1889 Sex: Male

...................9 [778] Sarah "Sally" Adams, b: 1821 in Jellico River, Whitley Co., KY? d: 1886 in Letcher Co., KY? Number of children: 3 Sex: Female

..........................+[959] Elihu Brown b: 1835 Sex: Male

...................2nd Husband of [778] Sarah "Sally" Adams, :

..........................+[960] _____ Jones b: Abt. 1820 m: 1843 in Whitesburg, KY Sex: Male

...................3rd Husband of [778] Sarah "Sally" Adams, :

..........................+[961] Stephen "Shank Steve" Adams, b: August 25, 1804 in Elizabethton, Carter Co., TN m: 1844 in Letcher Co., KY d: Abt. 1875 Number of children: 4 Father: Moses Adams, Mother: Mary Garland Sex: Male

..................10 [779] John S. "Tobacco" Adams, b: Abt. 1845 in Letcher Co., KY d: 1925 Number of children: ? Sex: Male

..........................+[962] Margaret Adams, b: Abt. 1845 m: Abt. 1863 Father: George M. Adams, Mother: Sarah Frazier Sex: Female

..................2nd Wife of [779] John S. "Tobacco" Adams:

..........................+[963] Elizabeth Blair, parents unknown b: Abt. 1849 in Letcher Co., KY m: June 05, 1864 in Letcher Co., KY Number of children: ? Father: John Robinson Blair Mother: Elizabeth Harrison Sex: Female (Note: Looking for ancestors; her parents MAY be John Robinson Blair & Elizabeth Harrison)

....................11 [964] William R. Adams, b: Abt. 1870 in KY Number of children: ? Sex: Male

..............................+[965] Malinda Brashear b: October 28, 1873 in Viper, Perry Co., KY m: Abt. 1892 in Viper, Perry Co., KY d: May 01, 1941 Number of children: ? Father: Sampson Brashear Mother: Mary Ann Hall Sex: Female

..................3rd Wife of [779] John S. "Tobacco" Adams, :

..........................+[966] Mariah Green b: Abt. 1855 m: 1875 Sex: Female

..................10 [967] Lydia Adams b: Abt. 1847 in Letcher Co., KY Sex: Female

..................10 [780] Daugherty (Doherty?) Adams b: April 10, 1853 in Letcher Co., KY Sex: Male

..........................+[968] Jane Adams b: Abt. 1855 m: April 03, 1870 Sex: Female

..................2nd Wife of [780] Daugherty (Doherty?) Adams:

..........................+[969] Mahalia Collier b: Abt. 1860 m: 1881 Sex: Female

................9 [970] Mary "Polly" Adams b: 1823 Sex: Female

................9 [971] Spencer Adams b: February 19, 1826 in Jellico River, Whitley Co., KY d: March 21, 1905 in Letcher Co., KY Number of children: 8 Sex: Male

........................+[972] Celia Church b: 1827 m: March 19, 1844 Number of children: 8 Father: Joel Church Mother: Margaret Adams Sex: Female

..................10 [781] William Adams b: 1848 in Letcher Co., KY d: 1880 Sex: Male

..........................+[973] Leudemia Hubbard b: Abt. 1850 m: Abt. 1870 Sex: Female

..................2nd Wife of [781] William Adams:

..........................+[974] Ida Maggard b: Abt. 1855 m: Abt. 1880 Sex: Female

..................10 [975] Margaret Adams b: 1849 in Letcher Co., KY Sex: Female

..................10 [782] Samuel Simpson Adams b: December 27, 1852 in Mayking, Letcher Co., KY d: September 1928 Sex: Male

..........................+[976] Nancy Ann Collins b: Abt. 1855 m: Abt. 1870 Sex: Female

..................2nd Wife of [782] Samuel Simpson Adams:

..........................+[977] Elizabeth Roberts b: Abt. 1860 m: January 01, 1872 Sex: Female

..................10 [978] David Maggard Adams b: 1854 in Tilly, KY d: June 1939 in Halo, KY Sex: Male

..................10 [979] Joseph L. Adams, Rev. b: May 19, 1855 in Pine Creek, Letcher Co., KY d: March 14, 1905 Number of children: ? Sex: Male Burial: Adkins Graveyard, Adkins Branch, Letcher Co., KY

..........................+[980] Mary Jane Short b: May 01, 1854 in Wise Co., Va. at Short's Creek d: February 25, 1929 in KY? Number of children: ? Father: William Alfred Short Mother: Elizabeth "Betsy" Roman Davis Sex: Female Burial: Adkins Graveyard, Adkins Branch, Letcher Co., KY

....................11 [981] James Taylor Adams b: 1892 in Crafts Colley, KY d: September 03, 1954 in Big Laurel, VA Number of children: 7 Sex: Male

..............................+[982] Dicey Roberts b: Abt. 1894 Number of children: 7 Sex: Female

..................10 [983] Jesse Adams b: 1859 Sex: Male

..................10 [984] Annalas Adams b: 1859 Sex: Female

..................10 [985] John Adams b: 1861 in Pine Creek, Letcher Co., KY d: 1915 Sex: Male

..........................+[986] Annie Chisenhall b: Abt. 1865 Sex: Female

................9 [987] Ellender "Nellie" Adams b: 1829 Sex: Female

...................9 [988] Lydia Adams b: 1833 Sex: Female
................8 Nancy Adams, b: 1805 in NC or KY? Number of children: 5 Sex: Female
.......................+James Sumner b: 1805 Number of children: 5 Sex: Male (Note: Looking for his ancestors)
..................9 Levi Sumner b: Abt. 1825 Sex: Male
..................9 Polly Jane Sumner b: 1830 Sex: Female
.........................+Nimrod Kiser, Jr., Kizer b: Abt. 1824 in Russell Co., VA d: in Letcher Co., KY Father: Nimrod Kiser, Sr. Mother: Mary "Polly" Breeding Sex: Male
..................9 [330] Judah Sumner b: 1831 Number of children: 12 Sex: Female
.......................+[329] Isom Jesse Caudill, Sr., twin b: February 08, 1829 d: Abt. 1917 Number of children: 12 Father: William C. "Billy" Caudill, Mother: Mary Nancy "Nancy" Craft Sex: Male
.....................10 [331] Mary Caudill b: 1850 Sex: Female
...........................+[332] Enoch Campbell b: Abt. 1847 Sex: Male
.....................10 [333] Nancy Caudill b: August 07, 1852 Sex: Female
...........................+[334] Alexander Singleton b: Abt. 1850 Sex: Male
.....................10 [335] Isom Caudill, Jr. b: July 26, 1855 Sex: Male
.....................10 [336] George Henry Caudill b: 1855 Sex: Male
.....................10 [337] Elizabeth Caudill b: June 02, 1856 Sex: Female
...........................+[338] John Hall b: Abt. 1855 Sex: Male
.....................10 [339] Lucinda Caudill b: Abt. 1857 Sex: Female
.....................10 [340] Margaret E. Caudill b: 1861 Sex: Female
...........................+[341] William Young b: Abt. 1860 Sex: Male
.....................10 [342] Sarah Sally Caudill b: 1864 Sex: Female
.....................10 [343] Patty Caudill b: Abt. 1865 Sex: Female
.....................10 [344] William Caudill b: 1867 Sex: Male
...........................+[345] Mary J. Adams b: Abt. 1870 Sex: Female
.....................10 [346] Julia Ann Caudill b: 1870 d: Abt. 1934 Sex: Female
...........................+[347] Ezekial Brashear b: Abt. 1867 Sex: Male
.....................10 [348] Ellen Caudill b: 1875 Sex: Female
..................9 Stephen Sumner b: 1835 Number of children: ? Sex: Male
.......................+America Craft b: 1840 d: Abt. 1870 Number of children: ? Sex: Female
.....................10 [783] James Sumner b: May 1860 Sex: Male
...........................+Polly Ann Combs b: May 1866 Father: William Combs Mother: Susan Combs Sex: Female
.....................2nd Wife of [783] James Sumner:
...........................+Polly Ann Crase b: Abt. 1870 Sex: Female
..................9 Nellie or Nella or "Nell" Sumner, b: May 1849 in Perry Co., KY? Number of children: 10 Sex: Female
.......................+John Jent, Ghent, b: March 1850 in Indian Bottom, Letcher Co., KY? m: Abt. 1870 in KY? d: 1916 in Perry Co., KY? Number of children: 10 Father: Henry Jent, Mother: Amanda "Manda" Messer Sex: Male
.....................10 [654] Elhannon Jent, b: September 12, 1873 in Indian Bottom, Perry Co., KY d: May 05, 1947 in Scuddy, Perry Co., KY Number of children: 4 Sex: Male Burial: May 06, 1947 Sumner Cem., Perry Co., KY
...........................+[653] Polly Ann Caudill, b: May 1872 in KY m: Abt. 1895 in Perry or Letcher Co., KY Number of children: 4 Father: Benjamin "Paw Paw" Caudill, Mother: Terry Hampton Sex: Female
.....................11 [655] Sally Jent b: March 1896 Sex: Female
.....................11 [656] John D. Jent b: June 1898 Sex: Male
.....................11 [657] Phoebe Jent b: 1909 in KY Sex: Female
...........................+[658] Ira Combs b: 1901 in KY? Father: Richard Nicholas "Dick" Combs Mother: Nancy Martin Sex: Male

......................11 [659] Chester Jent, b: Abt. 1911 in VicCo., KY? Number of children: ? Sex: Male

...........................+[660] Oma Smith b: Abt. 1913 in VicCo., KY? Number of children: ? Father: Thomas "Tom" Smith, Mother: Vinabelle Smith, Sex: Female

....................2nd Wife of [654] Elhannon Jent:

...........................+Barbara Smith b: Abt. 1880 m: Aft. 1911 Sex: Female

....................10 James "Jim" Jent b: September 1875 Sex: Male

....................10 Nancy Jane Jent b: June 13, 1877 in Indian Bottom, Letcher Co.?, KY d: October 24, 1944 in Perry Co., KY Number of children: 11 Sex: Female Burial: Scuddy Cemetery, Perry Co., KY

...........................+John "Long John" Combs, b: September 1870 in Perry Co., KY m: Abt. 1895 d: April 13, 1953 in Scuddy, Perry Co., KY Number of children: 11 Father: Hannabill "Hanbill" Combs, Mother: Susan Williams Sex: Male Burial: Scuddy Cemetery, Perry Co., KY

......................11 Chester Combs b: Abt. 1896 Sex: Male

......................11 Grant Combs b: Abt. 1898 Sex: Male

......................11 Melda Combs b: Abt. 1900 Sex: Female

......................11 Shafter Combs b: March 22, 1900 Sex: Male

......................11 Nellie Combs b: Abt. 1902 Sex: Female

......................11 Richmond Combs b: Abt. 1904 Sex: Male

......................11 Roosevelt Combs b: Abt. 1906 Sex: Male

......................11 Allie Combs b: Abt. 1908 Sex: Female

......................11 Lonia B. Combs b: May 09, 1913 Sex: Female

......................11 Betty Combs b: May 11, 1915 Sex: Female

......................11 Verna Combs b: March 09, 1918 Sex: Female

....................10 Thomas Jent b: August 1879 in Indian Bottom, Letcher Co., KY? Number of children: ? Sex: Male

...........................+Susan "Susie" Sumner b: Abt. 1877 Number of children: ? Sex: Female

......................11 Noah Jent b: February 15, 1911 in Hazard, Perry Co., KY? d: June 1990 Number of children: 3 Sex: Male

...........................+Rellia or Rilla Rice b: March 15, 1916 in Leslie Co., KY d: October 09, 1999 in Chavies, Perry Co., KY Number of children: 3 Sex: Female Burial: Announced in Lexington Herald newspaper on Oct. 10, 1999.

....................10 Sarah Jent b: Abt. 1881 Sex: Female

....................10 William "Bill" Jent b: September 1884 Sex: Male

....................10 Elijah S. "Lige" Jent b: March 1887 Sex: Male

....................10 Hester A. Jent b: April 1889 Sex: Female

....................10 Robert E. Jent b: April 1891 Sex: Male

....................10 Melissa Jent b: November 1895 Sex: Female

.............7 Charles Adams b: 1769 d: 1841 Sex: Male

.............7 Matthew Adams b: 1774 Sex: Male

.............7 Stephen "Rockhouse Steve" Adams b: 1779 in Lewis Fork, Wilkes Co., NC d: 1845 in Jeremiah, Letcher Co., KY Number of children: 9 Sex: Male

...................+Ellendar "Nellie" Buntin, or Benton b: Abt. 1780 in Surry Co., NC (or England) m: 1797 in Wilkesboro, Wilkes Co., NC d: Bet. 1832 - 1845 in Perry/Letcher Co., KY Number of children: 9 Father: William Buntin Mother: Elinor _____? Sex: Female

................8 Jesse Adams, Sr. b: 1798 in Lewis Fork, Wilkes Co., NC Number of children: 4 Sex: Male

....................+Mary Mullins b: 1799 in TN m: 1819 Number of children: 4 Father: _____ Mullins Mother: Mary ? Mullins Sex: Female

...................9 Moses Adams b: 1819 in Rockhouse Creek, Letcher Co., KY Number of children: ? Sex: Male

........................+Margaret D. Bentley b: 1826 in Perry Co., KY m: August 26, 1848 in Letcher

Co., KY Number of children: ? Father: Solomon Bentley, Sr., Mother: Mary "Polly" Yonts, Sex: Female

.....................10 Mary A. Adams b: January 1850 Sex: Female

..................9 Jesse G. Adams, Jr. b: 1820 in Rockhouse Creek, Floyd Co., KY Number of children: 4 Sex: Male

..........................+Sarah _____? b: 1822 in Floyd Co., KY m: 1836 in Hazard, Perry/Letcher Co., KY Number of children: 4 Sex: Female

.....................10 Sena Adams b: 1837 Sex: Female

.....................10 Diana Adams, twin b: 1844 Sex: Female

.....................10 Mary Adams, twin b: 1844 Sex: Female

.....................10 Soloman Adams b: 1849 in Rockhouse Creek, Floyd Co., KY Sex: Male

............................+Jane Addington b: Abt. 1849 in Hazard, Letcher Co., KY m: January 14, 1865 in Hazard, Perry/Letcher Co., KY Sex: Female

..................9 Hiram "Bad Hiram" Adams b: Abt. 1823 Number of children: ? Sex: Male

..........................+Dianah Collins b: Abt. 1825 m: July 14, 1881 in Letcher Co., KY Number of children: ? Sex: Female

.....................10 Moses Adams b: Abt. 1882 Sex: Male

..................9 Mary Adams b: Abt. 1825 in Rockhouse Creek, Floyd Co., KY d: in Letcher Co., KY Number of children: 3 Sex: Female

..........................+_____ Adams b: Abt. 1825 m: Abt. 1850 Number of children: 3 Sex: Male

.....................10 Martha Adams b: Abt. 1850 Sex: Female

.....................10 Matilda Adams b: Abt. 1852 Sex: Female

.....................10 Rilda Adams b: Abt. 1855 Sex: Female

................8 [361] Moses "Rockhouse Moses" Adams b: July 18, 1808 in Letcher Co., KY d: 1885 in Hazard, Letcher Co., KY Number of children: 12 Sex: Male

.....................+Hannah Collins b: Abt. 1810 m: Abt. 1822 Sex: Female

...............2nd Wife of [361] Moses "Rockhouse Moses" Adams:

.....................+[561] Sarah "Sally" Caudill, b: 1810 in Wilkes Co., NC m: July 20, 1825 in Hazard, Perry/Letcher Co., KY d: 1863 in Hazard, Letcher Co., KY Number of children: 9 Father: Stephen A. Caudill, Rev. War Soldier, Mother: Sarah "Sally" Francis Adams, 2nd wife Sex: Female

..................9 [562] Sarah Adams b: Abt. 1826 Sex: Female

..................9 [563] Mary Adams b: Abt. 1827 in Rockhouse Creek, Floyd Co., KY d: in Letcher Co., KY Sex: Female

..................9 [564] Green Adams b: Abt. 1828 in Hazard, Letcher Co., KY d: in Hazard, Letcher Co., KY Number of children: 4 Sex: Male

..........................+[565] Nancy Maggard b: Abt. 1830 m: Abt. 1850 d: in Hazard, Letcher Co., KY Number of children: 4 Sex: Female

.....................10 [566] Esther Adams b: March 1850 Sex: Female

..........................+[567] S. S. Banks b: Abt. 1850 m: September 24, 1897 Sex: Male

.....................10 [568] Martha Adams b: Abt. 1855 d: October 15, 1939 in Letcher Co., KY Sex: Female

..........................+[569] Daugherty Adams b: Abt. 1850 Sex: Male

.....................10 [570] Mary Ann "Polly" Adams b: Abt. 1860 Sex: Female

..........................+[571] George M. Gilley b: Abt. 1850 m: January 20, 1896 in Letcher Co., KY Sex: Male

.....................10 [209] Sarah Adams b: 1874 in Rockhouse Creek, Letcher Co., KY d: November 11, 1940 in Rockhouse Creek, Letcher Co., KY Sex: Female

..........................+[208] Elijah Adams b: May 31, 1866 in Rockhouse Creek, Letcher Co., KY m: March 25, 1890 in Letcher Co., KY d: September 02, 1932 in Rockhouse Creek, Letcher Co., KY Father: Stephen Adams Mother: Ursula Ison Sex: Male

..................9 [572] Stephen Adams b: 1827 in Hazard, Perry/Letcher Co., KY d: April 11, 1902 in Hazard, Perry/Letcher Co., KY Number of children: 10 Sex: Male

..........................+[573] Ursula Ison b: January 10, 1825 in Hazard, Perry/Letcher Co., KY m: 1848 in Hazard, Perry/Letcher Co., KY d: April 11, 1904 in Letcher Co., KY Number of children: 10 Father: Gideon Ison Mother: Rachel Stamper Sex: Female

......................10 [574] Sarah Adams b: Abt. 1848 Sex: Female

......................10 [575] Rachel Adams b: 1849 in Letcher Co., KY d: December 09, 1929 in Knott Co., KY Sex: Female

.............................+[576] Frazier Adams b: March 01, 1841 in Perry Co., KY m: in Whitesburg, KY d: July 04, 1917 in Knott Co., KY Sex: Male

......................10 [577] Moses Adams b: Abt. 1850 Sex: Male

......................10 [578] Gideon Adams b: June 26, 1851 in Jeremiah, Letcher Co., KY d: April 17, 1927 in Jeremiah, Letcher Co., KY Number of children: 13 Sex: Male

.............................+[579] Sarah Blair b: 1849 in Whitesburg, Letcher Co., KY m: Bet. 1877 - 1878 in Jeremiah, Letcher Co., KY d: August 11, 1924 in Jeremiah, Letcher Co., KY Number of children: 13 Father: Hiram "Humpy" Blair Mother: Drusilla "Raillie" Craft Sex: Female

........................11 [192] Celia Ann Adams b: June 23, 1877 d: November 14, 1969 in Letcher Co., KY Number of children: 9 Sex: Female

.............................+[580] Solomon Banks b: September 07, 1856 in Letcher Co., KY m: December 16, 1896 d: September 05, 1936 in Colson, Letcher Co., KY Number of children: 7 Father: Samuel G. Banks Mother: Mary Frazier Sex: Male

........................2nd Husband of [192] Celia Ann Adams:

.............................+[581] Preston Blair b: Abt. 1880 m: Abt. 1900 Number of children: 4 Sex: Male

........................11 [582] Ursula "Usley" Adams b: Abt. 1878 Sex: Female Burial: Waynesburg, KY

........................11 [583] Annie Adams b: Abt. 1879 d: in Jeremiah, KY Number of children: 7 Sex: Female

.............................+[584] Jim Adams b: Abt. 1875 m: Abt. 1905 d: in Jeremiah, Letcher Co., KY Number of children: 7 Sex: Male

........................11 [585] Hiram Adams b: Abt. 1881 d: in Waynesburg, Lincoln Co., KY Number of children: 6 Sex: Male

.............................+[586] _____ Caudill b: Abt. 1885 m: Abt. 1905 d: in Waynesburg, Lincoln Co., KY Number of children: 6 Sex: Female (Note: looking for ancestors)

........................11 [587] Fannie Adams b: Abt. 1885 d: in Jeremiah, KY Number of children: 7 Sex: Female Burial: Blair Branch, Letcher Co., KY

.............................+[588] William Adams b: Abt. 1885 m: Abt. 1905 in Jeremiah, Letcher Co., KY d: in Jeremiah, Letcher Co., KY Number of children: 7 Sex: Male

........................11 [195] Rebecca Adams b: Abt. 1887 d: in Waynesburg, KY Number of children: 8 Sex: Female

.............................+[10] Henry H. Cleveland Caudill b: April 20, 1887 in KY m: Abt. 1905 d: May 06, 1971 in Whitesburg, Letcher Co., KY Number of children: 18 Father: James William "Noah Jim" Caudill Mother: Lucinda Sumner Sex: Male Burial: Cleveland Caudill Cemetery, Caudill's Branch, Blackey, Letcher Co., KY

........................11 [206] Stephen B. Adams b: July 15, 1888 in Letcher Co., KY d: July 02, 1963 in Waynesburg, KY Number of children: ? Sex: Male

.............................+[589] Flora Banks b: Abt. 1890 m: Abt. 1910 d: February 17, 1963 Number of children: ? Sex: Female

........................2nd Wife of [206] Stephen B. Adams:

.............................+[590] Minnie Blair b: November 20, 1892 in Letcher Co., KY m: 1924 d: May 13, 1982 in Waynesburg, Lincoln Co., KY Sex: Female

........................11 [591] Judy Adams b: Abt. 1889 in Jeremiah, KY d: Abt. 1890 in Jeremiah, KY Sex: Female

........................11 [592] Dan Adams b: 1897 in Jeremiah, Letcher Co., KY d: 1937 in Horsemill Point, KY Number of children: 6 Sex: Male

.............................+[593] Virgie Smith b: Abt. 1900 m: Abt. 1920 d: in Jeremiah, Letcher Co., KY Number of children: 6 Sex: Female

.......................11 [594] Frazier C. Adams, Sr. b: January 23, 1899 in Jeremiah, KY d: in Waynesburg, Lincoln Co., KY Number of children: 11 Sex: Male

.............................+[595] Melvina "Viney" Jent b: February 11, 1903 in Smithbough, Knott Co., KY m: October 03, 1920 in Smithbough, Knott Co., KY d: October 13, 2000 in Somerset, KY Number of children: 11 Father: Sylvester Jent, Gent, Mother: Lucinda "Cinda" Smith, Sex: Female Burial: Double Springs Cemetery, Cemetery Road, Waynesburg, KY

.......................11 [596] Ritter Adams b: December 02, 1902 d: 1967 in Waynesburg, KY Number of children: 11 Sex: Female Burial: Double Creek, KY

.............................+[597] George Calfee b: Abt. 1900 m: Abt. 1920 d: in Waynesburg, Lincoln Co., KY Number of children: 11 Sex: Male

.......................11 [598] Nancy Adams b: January 17, 1904 d: May 1928 Number of children: 6 Sex: Female

.............................+[599] Curtis Stamper b: October 17, 1898 m: 1923 d: January 1932 Number of children: 6 Sex: Male

.......................11 [600] John Adams b: 1919 in Jeremiah, KY d: in died in WW I in Germany Sex: Male Burial: Horsemill Point, KY

....................10 [601] Anna "Annie" Adams b: October 04, 1853 in Letcher Co., KY d: in Letcher Co., KY Sex: Female

...........................+[602] Stephen C. Hampton b: 1851 Sex: Male

....................10 [603] Ester Adams b: January 18, 1855 in Letcher Co., KY d: January 26, 1929 Sex: Female

....................10 [604] Ison Moses Adams b: July 28, 1859 in Letcher Co., KY d: in Martin Co., KY Sex: Male

...........................+[605] Mary A. "Polly" Elkins b: 1860 in VA m: 1878 in Whitesburg, KY d: in Martin Co., KY Sex: Female

....................10 [606] Nancy Adams b: April 1860 in Letcher Co., KY d: 1901 Sex: Female

...........................+[607] Daniel E. Adams b: June 05, 1849 in Letcher Co., KY m: 1874 in Whitesburg, KY Sex: Male

...............10 [608] John Adams b: October 06, 1864 in Letcher Co., KY d: April 26, 1933 Sex: Male

...........................+[609] Laurena Roark b: November 24, 1874 d: May 20, 1965 Sex: Female

....................10 [208] Elijah Adams b: May 31, 1866 in Rockhouse Creek, Letcher Co., KY d: September 02, 1932 in Rockhouse Creek, Letcher Co., KY Sex: Male

...........................+[209] Sarah Adams b: 1874 in Rockhouse Creek, Letcher Co., KY m: March 25, 1890 in Letcher Co., KY d: November 11, 1940 in Rockhouse Creek, Letcher Co., KY Father: Green Adams Mother: Nancy Maggard Sex: Female

.................9 [610] Ellender Adams b: January 20, 1829 in Rockhouse Creek, Floyd Co., KY d: March 07, 1886 in Letcher Co., KY Sex: Female

.......................+[611] Preston Blair b: 1827 in Perry/Letcher Co., KY m: March 04, 1849 in Letcher Co., KY d: 1878 in Letcher Co., KY Sex: Male

.................9 [612] Nancy Adams b: 1834 in Letcher Co., KY d: April 23, 1900 in Magoffin Co., KY Sex: Female

.......................+[613] George Adams b: 1832 in Pert Creek, Floyd Co., KY m: December 08, 1852 in Prestonburg, Floyd Co., KY d: 1876 in Magoffin Co., KY Sex: Male

.................9 [614] Esther Adams b: November 03, 1837 in Rockhouse Creek, Floyd Co., KY d: December 11, 1911 in Eolina, Perry/Letcher Co., KY Sex: Female

.......................+[615] Martin D. Collier b: March 27, 1834 in Eolina, Perry/Letcher Co., KY m: 1856 in Whitesburg, KY d: March 12, 1901 in Eolina, Perry/Letcher Co., KY Sex: Male

.................9 [616] John C. Adams b: July 02, 1841 in Rockhouse Creek, Floyd Co., KY d: February 27, 1930 in Letcher Co., KY Number of children: 8 Sex: Male

...................+[617] Susanna Back b: December 18, 1845 in Letcher Co., KY m: July 02, 1867 in Letcher Co., KY d: September 13, 1926 in Letcher Co., KY Number of children: 8 Father: John Back Mother: Sarah _____? Sex: Female

...................10 [618] Susan Adams b: Abt. 1868 Sex: Female

...................10 [619] Henry Adams b: November 05, 1868 in Letcher Co., KY d: July 21, 1939 in Letcher Co., KY Sex: Male

...................+[620] Amanda Combs b: Abt. 1870 m: January 03, 1892 in Whitesburg, KY d: 1910 in Letcher Co., KY Sex: Female

...................10 [621] Stephen Adams b: October 16, 1871 in Letcher Co., KY d: July 21, 1954 in Letcher Co., KY Sex: Male

...................+[622] Ardelia Craft b: 1874 in Letcher Co., KY m: November 17, 1893 in Whitesburg, KY d: 1921 in Letcher Co., KY Sex: Female

...................10 [623] Moses Adams b: 1874 in Letcher Co., KY Sex: Male

...................+[624] Elizabeth Jane Caudill b: Abt. 1875 m: 1895 Sex: Female

...................10 [625] Joseph Adams b: 1877 in Letcher Co., KY d: September 01, 1954 in Letcher Co., KY Sex: Male

...................+[626] Rachel Craft b: Abt. 1880 m: 1910 in Whitesburg, KY Sex: Female

...................10 [627] Frances "Fanny" Adams b: November 1879 Sex: Female

...................+[628] Creed Craft b: Abt. 1875 Sex: Male

...................10 [629] James M. Adams b: 1882 in Letcher Co., KY d: in Jeremiah, Letcher Co., KY Sex: Male

...................+[630] Anna _____? b: Abt. 1885 m: in Whitesburg, KY Sex: Female

...................10 [631] William Adams b: June 27, 1885 in Letcher Co., KY d: June 06, 1970 in Letcher Co., KY Sex: Male

...................+[632] Frances _____? b: Abt. 1890 m: in Whitesburg, KY d: in Letcher Co., KY Sex: Female

...................9 [210] Benjamin Adams b: 1843 in Rockhouse Creek, Letcher Co., KY Number of children: 8 Sex: Male

...................+[633] Sarah Sally Maggard b: Abt. 1845 m: Abt. 1861 Father: Henry Maggard Mother: Mary "Polly" Stamper Sex: Female

...................2nd Wife of [210] Benjamin Adams:

...................+[634] Lucinda "Cindy" Combs b: June 06, 1847 in Letcher Co., KY m: 1862 in Whitesburg, KY d: February 07, 1874 in Jeremiah, KY Number of children: 8 Father: John Wesley Combs, Mother: Polly (Mary) Hogg Sex: Female

...................10 [635] Isaac Adams b: Abt. 1863 in Letcher Co., KY Sex: Male

...................10 [636] Millie Adams b: Abt. 1865 Sex: Female

...................+[637] Leonard Crocker b: Abt. 1865 m: 1896 in Whitesburg, KY Sex: Male

...................10 [638] Elizabeth Adams b: 1863 in Letcher Co., KY Sex: Female

...................+[639] John Cook b: Abt. 1860 m: August 26, 1882 in Whitesburg, KY Sex: Male

...................10 [640] Shadrack Adams b: March 03, 1865 in Letcher Co., KY d: December 24, 1937 Sex: Male

...................+[641] Susan Brown b: March 24, 1876 m: July 03, 1898 in Whitesburg, KY d: December 27, 1965 Sex: Female

...................10 [642] Marianne Adams b: October 10, 1867 in Letcher Co., KY d: August 20, 1947 Sex: Female

...................+[643] Shade Combs b: December 22, 1859 m: January 29, 1885 in Whitesburg, KY d: January 27, 1940 Sex: Male

...................10 [644] James M. Adams b: 1868 Sex: Male

...................10 [645] William Adams b: 1870 Sex: Male

...................10 [211] General Adams b: January 29, 1874 in Letcher Co., KY d: 1959 Sex: Male

...................+[212] Martha Caudill b: February 14, 1882 in Perry Co., KY m: January 29,

1902 d: July 28, 1957 Father: Henry R. Stephen Caudill Mother: Mary Branson Sex: Female
................3rd Wife of [361] Moses "Rockhouse Moses" Adams:
......................+[784] Martha Ann "Patsy" Craft b: Abt. 1835 m: October 03, 1867 in Letcher Co.,
KY d: in Letcher Co., KY Number of children: 3 Father: William Craft Mother: Rachel Parker Sex:
Female
.................9 [785] Mary Adams b: 1867 in Letcher Co., KY Sex: Female
......................+[786] Creed Craft b: 1873 in Letcher Co., KY m: November 20, 1900 in
Whitesburg, KY Sex: Male
.................9 [787] Joseph Adams b: 1870 in Rockhouse Creek, Floyd Co., KY Sex: Male
......................+[788] Flora Tyree b: 1878 m: September 10, 1894 in Letcher Co., KY Sex:
Female
.................9 [789] Lucinda Adams b: 1878 in Letcher Co., KY Sex: Female
......................+[790] Robert E. Banks b: Abt. 1875 m: August 10, 1897 in Letcher Co., KY Sex:
Male
................8 Jane Bunton "Jennie" Adams b: 1810 in KY Number of children: 11 Sex: Female
......................+Edward Oliver "Ned" Polly b: April 1803 in Carter Co., TN m: April 28, 1825
in Perry Co., KY d: October 25, 1864 in Morgan Co., MO Number of children: 11 Father: Edward
Polly, Mother: Mary Agnes Mullins, Sex: Male
.................9 [460] Stephen Polly b: 1826 in Perry Co., KY Sex: Male
......................+[459] Nancy Adams b: Abt. 1830 m: August 25, 1848 in Letcher Co., KY
Father: George M. Adams, Mother: Henrietta Caudill, Sex: Female
.................9 Claborn Polly b: 1830 Sex: Male
.................9 Sarah Polly b: 1831 Sex: Female
.................9 David Polly b: 1833 Sex: Male
......................+Jane Kelsey b: Abt. 1835 m: November 11, 1860 Sex: Female
.................9 Cely M. "Patsy" Polly b: 1836 Sex: Female
.................9 Nancy Polly b: 1838 Sex: Female
.................9 John William Polly b: 1841 Sex: Male
.................9 Elizabeth Polly b: July 22, 1843 Sex: Female
.................9 Lucinda Polly b: 1846 Sex: Female
.................9 [791] Andrew Jackson "Drew" Polly b: June 1848 Sex: Male
......................+Sarah Elizabeth Kays b: 1858 Sex: Female
.................2nd Wife of [791] Andrew Jackson "Drew" Polly:
......................+Mary Ann Carroll b: Abt. 1860 Sex: Female
.................3rd Wife of [791] Andrew Jackson "Drew" Polly:
......................+Daisy Fletcher b: August 08, 1869 Sex: Female
.................9 Jane Polly b: 1850 Sex: Female
................8 [792] Ellender Adams b: 1813 in Rockhouse Creek, Floyd Co., KY Number of
children: 2 Sex: Female
......................+John Dickson b: Abt. 1810 m: Abt. 1830 Sex: Male
................2nd Husband of [792] Ellender Adams:
......................+Isaac Whitaker b: Abt. 1815 m: Abt. 1835 Number of children: 2 Sex: Male
.................9 John Whitaker b: Abt. 1835 Sex: Male
.................9 Stephen Whitaker b: Abt. 1840 Sex: Male
................8 Mary Polly Adams b: 1815 in Rockhouse Creek, Floyd Co., KY Number of children:
2 Sex: Female
......................+Isaac D. Stamper b: September 19, 1816 m: May 28, 1840 in Perry/Letcher Co.,
KY Number of children: 2 Father: William "Tater Bill" Stamper Mother: Emily "Millie" Polly Sex:
Male
.................9 John H. Stamper b: Abt. 1836 in Letcher Co., KY Sex: Male
......................+Nancy Hogg b: 1840 m: 1858 Father: Hiram "Courthouse Hiram" Hogg Mother:
Melvina "Viney" Polly Sex: Female

..................9 Daniel B. Stamper b: Abt. 1847 in Letcher Co., KY Sex: Male
.........................+Lucinda Hogg b: 1843 d: October 19, 1855 Father: Hiram "Courthouse Hiram" Hogg Mother: Melvina "Viney" Polly Sex: Female
................8 Stephen Adams b: 1816 in Rockhouse Creek, Floyd Co., KY Sex: Male
................8 Nancy Adams b: 1817 in Rockhouse Creek, Floyd Co., KY d: in Letcher Co., KY Number of children: ? Sex: Female
.......................+John Sumner b: Abt. 1815 m: December 29, 1838 d: 1879 in Letcher Co., KY Number of children: ? Sex: Male
..................9 Louisa Sumner b: Abt. 1839 Sex: Female
................8 Elijah Adams b: August 16, 1819 in Rockhouse Creek, Letcher Co., KY d: December 30, 1898 in Douglas Co., MO Number of children: ? Sex: Male
.......................+Mary (Polly) Branham-Smith b: December 08, 1821 m: April 09, 1840 d: 1912 Number of children: ? Father: William "Billy" Branham-Smith Mother: Elizabeth (Betty) Childers Sex: Female
..................9 Isaac Adams b: October 30, 1844 Sex: Male
................8 [797] Spencer Adams b: 1822 in Rockhouse Creek, Floyd Co., KY Number of children: 16 Sex: Male
.......................+Jane "Jenny" Amburgey b: August 11, 1821 d: November 26, 1912 Number of children: 2 Father: Ambrose Amburgey Mother: Rebecca Francis Sex: Female Burial: Ball Point at old Carr Church on Carr's Creek, Knott or Letcher Co., KY
..................9 Rebecca Adams b: February 18, 1841 Sex: Female
.......................+William B. Smith b: September 20, 1836 Sex: Male
..................9 [793] John B. Adams b: 1847 d: 1882 in Paintsville, KY Number of children: 8 Sex: Male
.......................+Jane Stumbo b: 1827 d: 1865 Sex: Female
..................2nd Wife of [793] John B. Adams:
.......................+[798] Cassandra "Cassie" Banks b: 1825 in Wilkes Co., NC d: 1870 Number of children: 14 Father: Johnson (or Jonathan) Banks Mother: Mary Ann Adams Sex: Female
..................3rd Wife of [793] John B. Adams:
.......................+Lucy Ann Hamilton b: January 19, 1852 in Scott Co., VA m: 1866 in Carr Creek, KY d: January 1916 in Knott Co., KY Number of children: 13 Father: Robert Schuyler Hamilton Mother: Malissa J. Wheatley Sex: Female
.....................10 Margaret Ellen Adams b: 1867 Number of children: 3 Sex: Female
...........................+Allen Martin b: Abt. 1865 m: Abt. 1885 Number of children: 3 Sex: Male
.......................11 John B. Martin b: Abt. 1885 Sex: Male
.......................11 Joseph Martin b: Abt. 1887 d: WFT Est. 1890-1989 Sex: Male
.......................11 Susan Martin b: Abt. 1890 Sex: Female
.....................10 Chamillous "Kay" Adams b: November 14, 1869 d: July 16, 1922 Number of children: 11 Sex: Male
...........................+Mary Hall b: February 25, 1880 m: August 16, 1902 d: March 29, 1951 Number of children: 11 Sex: Female
.......................11 Eddie Adams b: Private Sex: Female
...........................+Denver Tolliver b: Private m: Private Sex: Male
.......................11 [794] John B. Adams b: September 24, 1904 d: October 20, 1979 Number of children: 3 Sex: Male
...........................+Guliner Honeycutt b: Abt. 1905 m: Private Number of children: ? Sex: Female
.......................2nd Wife of [794] John B. Adams:
...........................+Brosa Pigman b: Private m: Private Number of children: 2 Sex: Female
.......................11 Elizabeth Adams b: Private Number of children: 10 Sex: Female
...........................+Ray King b: Private m: Private Number of children: 10 Sex: Male
.......................11 James Adams b: August 10, 1908 d: February 19, 1965 Number of children: ?

Sex: Male
..............................+Emma Blair b: Private m: Private Number of children: ? Sex: Female
.......................11 Hattie Adams b: Abt. 1910 Number of children: 9 Sex: Female
..............................+Lonnie Amburgey b: October 21, 1909 in Knott Co., KY m: July 31, 1936 d: February 15, 1997 in IN Number of children: 9 Father: William "Willie" Amburgey Mother: Minnie Cook Sex: Male
.......................11 Milliard Adams b: Private Number of children: 5 Sex: Male
..............................+Cherina Ferguson b: Private m: Private Number of children: 5 Sex: Female
.......................11 Luther Adams b: 1913 d: 1913 Sex: Male
.......................11 Lucy Adams b: Abt. 1920 Number of children: 2 Sex: Female
..............................+Curtis Venters b: 1917 m: Private d: 1948 Number of children: 2 Sex: Male
.......................11 Dartha Adams b: Private Number of children: 6 Sex: Female
..............................+Willis Mullins b: Private m: Private Number of children: 6 Sex: Male
.......................11 Harrison Adams b: Private Number of children: ? Sex: Male
..............................+Betty J. Rudolph b: Private m: Private Number of children: ? Sex: Female
.......................11 Woodrow Adams b: 1920 d: 1940 in Panama Sex: Male
.....................10 John Carlyle Adams b: November 07, 1871 in Pinetop, Knott Co., KY d: May 23, 1924 in Greeley, CO Number of children: 11 Sex: Male
..............................+Margarine "Margie" Huff b: July 11, 1875 in Mallet, Knott Co., KY m: January 05, 1899 in Carr Creek, Knott Co., KY d: June 05, 1978 in Denver, CO Number of children: 11 Sex: Female
.......................11 Lawrence Cornelious "Neil" Adams b: September 29, 1899 in Knott Co., KY d: June 27, 1932 in Greeley, CO Sex: Male
.......................11 James Claude Adams b: Abt. 1901 in Knott Co., KY d: March 17, 1933 in Colorado Number of children: ? Sex: Male
..............................+Helen Kennedy b: Abt. 1903 d: 1983 Number of children: ? Sex: Female
.......................11 Augusta Adams b: July 19, 1903 in Knott Co., KY d: August 18, 1967 in Colorado Number of children: 4 Sex: Female
..............................+Ralph Henry McGhee b: Private m: Private Number of children: 4 Sex: Male
.......................11 Masadore (Harry H) Adams b: March 03, 1905 in Pinetop, Knott Co., KY d: January 26, 1969 in Colorado Number of children: 4 Sex: Male
..............................+Eunice Pitts b: Private m: Private Number of children: 4 Sex: Female
.......................11 William Bert Adams b: October 18, 1907 in Pound, Wise Co., VA d: June 27, 1932 in Colorado Number of children: ? Sex: Male
..............................+Irene B. Hiatt b: Private m: Private Number of children: ? Sex: Female
.......................11 Kay Milwas Adams b: Private Sex: Female
.......................11 Everd Christopher Adams b: July 08, 1911 in Collinsville, OK d: November 11, 1967 in Colorado Sex: Male
..............................+Frieda Ann Steputis b: Private m: Private Sex: Female
.......................11 Viola Edith Adams b: Private Sex: Female
.......................11 [795] Mae Nola Adams b: Private Sex: Female
.......................+Walter Arther Steputis b: Private m: Private Sex: Male
.......................2nd Husband of [795] Mae Nola Adams:
..............................+Dwight Lee Wilkins b: Private m: Private Sex: Male
.......................11 Helen Alice Pauline Adams b: August 1917 in Davenport, Iowa d: December 18, 1918 in Greeley, Colorado Sex: Female
.......................11 Marjorie Ella Adams b: Private Sex: Female
..............................+Eli Lafayette Lants b: March 03, 1915 in Aurora, WV m: Private d: November 13, 1983 Sex: Male
.....................10 [796] Robert Lee Adams b: 1873 in Pinetop, Knott Co., KY Number of children: 18 Sex: Male
..............................+Susan King b: abt 1875, Number of children: 11 Sex: Female

....................11 Flora Adams b: Private Sex: Female
....................11 James Adams b: Private Sex: Male
....................11 Thomas Adams b: Private Sex: Male
....................11 Daniel Webster Adams b: Private Sex: Male
....................11 Estill Adams b: Private Sex: Male
....................11 Sidney Adams b: Private Sex: Male
....................11 Lucy Ellen Adams b: Private Sex: Female
....................11 Margaret Adams b: Private Sex: Female
....................11 Susan Adams b: Private Sex: Female
....................11 Tolbia Adams b: Private Sex: Male
....................11 Bertha Adams b: Private Sex: Female
...................2nd Wife of [796] Robert Lee Adams:
..........................+Magnolia Bentley b: Private m: Private Number of children: 7 Sex: Female
....................11 Garnet Adams b: Private Sex: Female
....................11 Grace Adams b: Private Sex: Female
....................11 John Adams b: Private Sex: Male
....................11 Robert Adams b: Private Sex: Male
....................11 Henry Adams b: Private Sex: Male
....................11 Jeanette Adams b: January 22, 1936 d: December 01, 1936 Sex: Female
....................11 Andrew Adams b: Private Sex: Male
...................10 James Adams b: 1874 Sex: Male
.........................+Alice Lloyd b: Abt. 1876 Sex: Female
...................10 Spencer Adams b: 1876 in Knott Co., KY Number of children: 12 Sex: Male
.........................+Margie McGuire b: 1884; d: 1933 Number of children: 12 Sex: Female
....................11 Pearl Frances Adams b: Private Sex: Female
....................11 Andy Adams b: 1903 d: 1904 Sex: Male
....................11 John B. Adams b: Private Sex: Male
....................11 Lucy Jane Adams b: 1907 in Sperling, KY d: July 27, 1979 Number of children:
? Sex: Female
.............................+Walter Weltmer Jenkins b: Private m: Private Number of children: ? Sex:
Male
....................11 Ethel Adams b: Private Sex: Female
....................11 Linvell Adams b: Private Sex: Male
....................11 Letha Adams b: Private Sex: Male
....................11 Leslie Adams b: Private Sex: Male
....................11 Deloris Adams b: Private Sex: Male
....................11 Lomer Howard Adams b: Private Sex: Male
....................11 Delmer Adams b: Private Sex: Male
....................11 Dorothy Adams b: Private Sex: Female
...................10 Anna Belle Adams b: 1878 d: Sex: Female
...................10 Ann Susan Adams b: April 20, 1882 in Knott Co., KY Number of children: 12
Sex: Female
...........................+William F. Strange b: Abt. 1880 Number of children: 12 Sex: Male (Note:
Looking for his ancestors)
....................11 Melissa Strange b: December 24, 1901 d: October 19, 1971 Sex: Female
....................11 Theo Violet Strange b: January 21, 1915 d: May 02, 1955 Sex: Female
....................11 Neal Preston Strange b: July 13, 1922 d: 1986 Sex: Male
....................11 Kedrick W. Strange b: January 23, 1925 d: February 11, 1926 Sex: Male
.................2nd Wife of [797] Spencer Adams:
....................+[798] Cassandra "Cassie" Banks b: 1825 in Wilkes Co., NC m: Abt. 1842 in (Note:
they may not have married) d: 1870 Number of children: 14 Father: Johnson (or Jonathan) Banks
Mother: Mary Ann Adams Sex: Female

...................9 [1090] Mary Ann Banks b: Abt. 1843 in KY Number of children: ? Sex: Female

.........................+[1091] Gideon Ison b: May 14, 1844 m: March 09, 1871 in Letcher Co., KY d: July 29, 1903 in Defeated Creek, KY Number of children: ? Father: Gideon Ison Mother: Rachel Stamper Sex: Male

......................10 [1092] Susan Ison b: December 15, 1871 in Letcher Co., KY Number of children: 2 Sex: Female

.............................+[1093] Kelly Hogg b: Abt. 1861 in Letcher Co., KY m: in Letcher Co., KY d: January 12, 1937 Number of children: 2 Father: Hiram Wesley Hogg Mother: Margaret Brashear Sex: Male

........................11 [1094] Virgie Hogg Sex: Female

........................11 [1095] Myrtle Hogg Sex: Female

...................9 [1096] Elijah Banks b: Abt. 1847 Sex: Male Burial: Banks Cemetery, Letcher Co., KY

..........................+[1097] Elizabeth Burton b: Abt. 1860 m: February 25, 1868 in KY? Sex: Female Burial: Banks Cemetery, Letcher Co., KY

...................9 [1098] Sarah Banks b: Abt. 1848 in KY Sex: Female

...................9 [1099] Ester Banks b: Abt. 1851 Sex: Female

...................9 [1100] Harrison Banks b: June 23, 1854 Sex: Male

..........................+[1101] Millie Combs b: January 01, 1863 m: Bet. 1877 - 1880 d: March 03, 1911 Father: John Wesley Combs, Mother: Polly (Mary) Hogg Sex: Female

...................9 [1102] Wesley Banks b: February 18, 1855 Sex: Male

...................9 [1103] Nancy Banks b: Abt. 1856 Sex: Female

...................9 [799] Lincoln "Link" Banks b: 1859 in Letcher Co., KY d: 1888 in Whitesburg, Letcher, Co., KY Number of children: 2 Sex: Male Burial: The Babe Isom Cemetery on Rockhouse Creek (Notes: Link was murdered by Jim Frazier; case was dismissed before trial)

..........................+[1104] Lucinda Breeding b: November 26, 1865 in Letcher Co., KY m: Abt. 1881 d: March 15, 1948 in Sackett, Letcher Co., KY Number of children: ? Father: John Breeding Mother: Elizabeth "Betty" Combs Sex: Female Burial: Ison Cemetery, Johnson Funeral Home, Hazard, Perry Co., KY

......................10 [1105] Malissie "Lissie" Breeding b: March 21, 1882 in Letcher Co., KY d: May 04, 1924 in Knott Co., KY Number of children: 6 Sex: Female Burial: The Seymore Amburgey Cemeter at Bath, Knott Co., KY

.............................+[1106] James Robert "Crick" Collins b: December 15, 1881 Number of children: 6 Father: James Wesley Collins Mother: Elizabeth "Liz" Amburgey Sex: Male

........................11 [1107] Lola Collins b: November 23, 1899 Sex: Female

........................11 [1108] Luly Collins b: January 18, 1902 Sex: Female

........................11 [1109] Lizzie Collins b: December 25, 1903 Sex: Female

........................11 [1110] Johnny L. Collins b: August 25, 1906 Sex: Male

........................11 [1111] Jimmy J. Collins b: April 03, 1908 Sex: Male

..........................11 [1112] Oma Lee Collins b: January 09, 1913 in Knott Co., KY d: June 12, 1994 in McRoberts, Letcher Co., KY Sex: Female Burial: Amburgey Cemetery, Knott Co., KY

............................+[1113] Hillard A. Collins b: Abt. 1910 Sex: Male

...................Partner of [799] Lincoln "Link" Banks:

..........................+[1114] Elizabeth "Liz" Amburgey b: June 24, 1857 in Whitesburg, Letcher, Co., KY met: Abt. 1883 in (Note: they did not marry) d: February 28, 1937 in Bath, Knott Co., KY Number of children: 4 Father: John Amburgey III Mother: Rachel Hall Sex: Female Burial: Seymour Amburgey Cemetery, Bath, Knott Co., KY (Note: some records state that she was born on January 7, 1857)

......................10 [1115] Maggie Banks b: June 28, 1884 in Knott (now Letcher) Co., KY d: January 11, 1960 in Clarksville, IN Number of children: 5 Sex: Female Burial: Clarksville, IN

..........................+[1116] Watson Collins b: April 17, 1887 in Letcher Co., KY d: May 20, 1972 in Isom, Letcher Co., KY Number of children: 5 Father: John "Long John" Collins Mother: Sarah

"Sally" Stacy Sex: Male Burial: Walnut Ridge Cemetery, Jeffersonville, IN

........................11 [1117] Norman Collins b: April 09, 1911 in Bath, Knott Co., KY d: November 05, 1994 Sex: Male Burial: Forest Lawn Memorial Pak, Glendale, CA

...............................+[1118] Lucille McCabe b: Abt. 1917 in Los Angeles, CA d: December 1990 in Los Angeles, CA Sex: Female

........................11 [800] Lava Collins b: March 04, 1913 in Bath, Knott Co., KY Number of children: 3 Sex: Female

...............................+[1119] Sonny Anderson b: Abt. 1910 Sex: Male

........................Partner of [800] Lava Collins:

...............................+[12] Delmer V. Caudill b: January 13, 1917 in Polly (Sandlick), Letcher Co., KY met: Abt. 1939 in (Note: they did not marry) d: January 06, 1985 in Hazard, Perry Co., KY Number of children: 9 Father: John Breckenridge "Johnny" Caudill Mother: Thursa Ann Mason Sex: Male Burial: Green Acres Cemetery, Ermine, KY (Note: resided in Ulvah, Letcher Co., KY at time of death)

........................2nd Husband of [800] Lava Collins:

...............................+[1120] Willard Gibson b: September 10, 1895 in Democrat, Letcher Co., KY m: Abt. 1945 d: November 21, 1959 in Colson, Letcher Co., KY Number of children: 15 Father: Anderson Gibson Mother: Lucinda Sexton Sex: Male Burial: Colson Cemetery, Colson, KY

........................11 [1121] Rachel Collins b: Abt. 1915 Sex: Female

........................11 [1122] Vada Collins b: Abt. 1917 Sex: Female

........................11 [801] Lilly Collins b: February 27, 1919 in SeCo., Letcher Co., KY d: March 24, 2003 in Hospital in New Albany, IN (lived in Clarksville, Clark Co., IN at time of death) Number of children: 4 Sex: Female

...............................+[802] William "Luther" Yonts b: March 19, 1906 in Neon, Letcher Co., KY m: April 27, 1940 in Camp Branch, Colson, Letcher Co., KY d: July 22, 1962 in Jeffersonville, Clark Co., IN Number of children: 4 Father: John Quiller Yonts Mother: Sarah Frances Collier Sex: Male Burial: Walnut Ridge Cemetery, Jeffersonville, IN (Yonts Note: like the author and all of the other Yonts individuals in this tree, this family descends from Wilhelm Jans, born in 1714 in the town of Oberalben, Rheineland-Pfalz, Germany; Wilhelm died in 1778 in Rowan Co., NC)

........................2nd Husband of [801] Lilly Collins:

...............................+[1123] John Henry "Buck" Coslow b: June 15, 1912 in Shelby Co., KY m: Aft. 1963 d: February 07, 1975 in Louisville, KY Sex: Male Burial: Walnut Ridge Cemetery, Jeffersonville, IN

..................9 [1124] Napoleon Bonaparte ("Boney"?) Banks b: February 17, 1860 Sex: Male

..................9 [1125] Cornelia Banks b: Abt. 1863 Sex: Male

..................9 [1126] William "Will" Banks b: Abt. 1864 in KY d: November 1918 in Whitesburg, Letcher Co., KY Sex: Male

........................+[1127] Usley (or Ulsey?) Ison b: 1867 m: June 12, 1883 Sex: Female (Note: looking for ancestors)

..................9 [1128] Irvin Banks b: March 16, 1866 in Letcher Co., KY d: December 25, 1937 in Letcher Co., KY Sex: Male

........................+[1129] Cornelia Combs b: October 24, 1870 in Letcher Co., KY m: April 29, 1886 in Letcher Co., KY? d: October 20, 1918 in Letcher Co., KY Father: John Combs Mother: Elizabeth "Betty" Breeding Sex: Female

..................9 [1130] James "Jim" Banks b: 1871 Sex: Male

..................9 [1131] Martha Banks b: 1873 Sex: Female

..........6 [803] John Hobbs Adams, Jr., b: 1747 in NC d: July 15, 1815 in Pine Creek, Floyd Co., KY Number of children: 12 Sex: Male Burial: Webb Cemetery, Mayking, Letcher Co., KY

................+[804] Nancy Ann "Ann" Caudill, b: 1752 in Sussex Co., VA m: August 10, 1768 in Loudoun Co., Virginia d: 1787 in Roaring River, Wilkes Co., NC Number of children: 3 Father: Benjamin "Ben of Sussex" Caudill, Sr., Mother: Elizabeth Buckner, Sex: Female

............7 [805] Elizabeth "Betsy" Adams b: Abt. 1770 in Loudon Co.,(or Lunenburg Co.) VA

Number of children: 11 Sex: Female (Note: looking for her ancestors; she is connected to Governor Owsley)

..................+[806] Archelous Craft, Sr., Rev. War Soldier b: December 25, 1749 in England (born on a ship en route from England to America) m: December 11, 1785 in Wilkes Co., NC d: November 08, 1853 in North Fork (of the KY River, 5 miles from the VA line) , Letcher Co., KY Number of children: 11 Father: _____ Craft Mother: _____ _____? Sex: Male (Note: he fought in the Rev. War)

................8 [237] Mary Nancy "Nancy" Craft b: 1784 in Harris Creek, Wilkes Co., NC d: July 27, 1877 in Letcher Co., KY Number of children: 14 Sex: Female

.....................+[7] William C. "Billy" Caudill, b: July 27, 1779 in Wilkes Co., NC m: Abt. 1804 d: July 27, 1880 in Letcher Co., KY Number of children: 14 Father: James "Jimmie" Caudill, Jr., Rev. War Soldier Mother: Mary A. Adams, Sex: Male

.................9 [238] Ellender Caudill b: Abt. 1805 Sex: Female

.................9 [239] Betsy Caudill b: Abt. 1806 Sex: Female

.................9 [240] Delilah "Lila" Caudill b: May 08, 1807 Sex: Female

.................9 [241] Isabel Caudill b: Abt. 1809 Sex: Female

.................9 [242] Mary Caudill b: March 10, 1811 in KY d: September 13, 1880 Number of children: 10 Sex: Female

.....................+[243] Joshua Mullins b: November 18, 1809 in Knox Co., KY d: February 15, 1900 in Letcher Co., KY Number of children: 10 Father: Joshua Mullins, Mother: Anna Robinson Sex: Male

....................10 [244] John Mullins b: December 26, 1834 Sex: Male

....................10 [245] Joseph M. Mullins b: June 19, 1834 Sex: Male

....................10 [246] Solomon Mullins b: 1838 Sex: Male

....................10 [247] Caleb Mullins b: 1840 Sex: Male

....................10 [248] Joshua Mullins b: 1842 Sex: Male

....................10 [249] Anna Mullins b: September 18, 1842 Sex: Female

...........................+[250] George Washington Adams b: September 02, 1839 in Letcher Co., KY d: 1943 in Washington Father: Moses "Smoot" Adams Mother: Rebecca (Roberts) Hall Sex: Male

....................10 [251] William Mullins b: 1846 Sex: Male

....................10 [252] Delilah Mullins b: Aft. 1846 Sex: Female

....................10 [253] Nancy Mullins b: Aft. 1847 Sex: Female

....................10 [254] James Henderson Mullins b: September 12, 1853 Sex: Male

.................9 [255] Rebecca "Becca" Caudill b: April 15, 1815 Sex: Female

.................9 [256] Elizabeth "Betsy" Caudill b: Abt. 1816 d: in Knox Co., KY Number of children: 12 Sex: Female

.....................+[257] Caleb Mullins b: 1810 in KY d: in KY Number of children: 12 Father: Joshua Mullins, Mother: Anna Robinson Sex: Male

....................10 [258] William Mullins b: 1834 Sex: Male

....................10 [259] Mary Mullins b: Abt. 1836 Sex: Female

....................10 [260] Ann Mullins b: Abt. 1838 Sex: Female

....................10 [261] Nancy Mullins b: Abt. 1838 Sex: Female

....................10 [262] Joab Mullins b: Abt. 1841 Sex: Male

....................10 [263] Sarah Mullins b: Abt. 1844 Sex: Female

....................10 [264] John Mullins b: Abt. 1847 Sex: Male

....................10 [265] Susan Mullins b: 1850 Sex: Female

....................10 [266] Hugh Mullins b: August 25, 1852 Sex: Male

....................10 [267] James K. Mullins b: September 03, 1856 Sex: Male

....................10 [268] Elizabeth Mullins b: 1860 Sex: Female

....................10 [269] Ann Mullins b: October 1868 Sex: Female

.................9 [218] Nancy Caudill b: Abt. 1817 in KY d: 1894 Number of children: 2 Sex: Female

.....................+[217] Wilburn E. Caudill b: Abt. 1812 in NC Number of children: 2 Father:

William Caudill Mother: Rachel Joines Sex: Male

.....................10 [186] William W. "Wild Bill" Caudill b: Abt. 1839 in NC d: June 22, 1920 in Wolfe Co., KY Number of children: 2 Sex: Male

.........................+[185] Elizabeth "Betsy" Eldridge b: Abt. 1841 Number of children: 2 Father: Levi Eldridge Mother: Easter (or Esther) Caudill, Sex: Female

.......................11 [187] Martha Ann Caudill b: Abt. 1861 Number of children: ? Sex: Female

.............................+[188] Enoch Everidge b: Abt. 1860 Number of children: ? Sex: Male

.......................11 [25] Sarah Caudill b: September 1872 in Campton, KY Number of children: ? Sex: Female

.............................+[24] John C. Caudill b: February 1868 in Harlan or Letcher Co., KY m: April 18, 1889 in Breathitt Co., KY Number of children: ? Father: Henry H. Caudill Mother: Susannah Back Sex: Male

.....................10 [18] Mary C. Caudill b: January 13, 1852 in Letcher Co., KY Number of children: ? Sex: Female

.............................+[17] Lewis E. Caudill b: March 05, 1855 in Letcher Co., KY m: January 13, 1852 in Letcher Co., KY Number of children: ? Father: Henry H. Caudill Mother: Susannah Back Sex: Male

.......................11 [19] Phoebe Caudill b: May 02, 1878 in Letcher Co., KY Number of children: 2 Sex: Female

.............................+[20] Levi S. Caudill b: December 22, 1875 in KY m: September 30, 1895 in Letcher Co., KY d: March 20, 1955 Number of children: 2 Father: Samuel B. Caudill Mother: Mary Ann "Polly" Eldridge Sex: Male

...................9 [270] James "Limber Jim" Caudill b: Abt. 1818 in Floyd Co., KY Number of children: 4 Sex: Male

.........................+[271] Elizabeth "Betsy" Mullins b: 1820 in KY d: 1899 Number of children: 4 Father: Joshua Mullins, Mother: Anna Robinson Sex: Female

.....................10 [272] Mary "Polly" Caudill b: 1840 Sex: Female

.............................+[273] Lewis Campbell b: 1830 Father: William C. Campbell Mother: Elizabeth Cornett, Sex: Male

.....................10 [274] Nancy Ann Caudill b: Abt. 1841 Number of children: ? Sex: Female

.............................+[275] Davis S. Fields b: Abt. 1840 Number of children: ? Sex: Male

.......................11 [276] William Fields b: December 22, 1861 in Letcher Co., KY d: 1938 in Whitley Co., KY Sex: Male

.............................+[277] Martha Brashear b: October 11, 1871 d: March 31, 1943 Father: James Nicholas Brashear, Jr. Mother: Elizabeth Pratt Sex: Female

.....................10 [27] William B. Caudill b: April 23, 1845 in Letcher Co., KY d: January 18, 1929 Number of children: ? Sex: Male (Note: William & Susannah were cousins)

.............................+[26] Susannah "Sukie" Caudill b: Abt. 1847 in KY m: February 28, 1867 in Letcher Co., KY d: August 14, 1925 Number of children: ? Father: Isom Caudill Mother: Elizabeth "Lizzie" Back, Bach Sex: Female (Note: Susannah & William were cousins)

.......................11 [8] Peggy Caudill b: April 1890 in Letcher Co., KY d: January 14, 1916 Sex: Female

.............................+[9] Cleveland Caudill b: June 1891 in Letcher Co., KY m: July 14, 1909 in Letcher Co., KY Father: John C. Caudill Mother: Sarah Caudill Sex: Male

.....................10 [14] Joshua M. Caudill b: June 23, 1850 in Letcher Co., KY d: March 22, 1941 Sex: Male

.............................+[13] Rhoda Caudill b: April 12, 1853 in Letcher Co., KY d: January 17, 1942 Father: Henry B. Caudill, twin, Mother: Margaret "Patsy" Campbell Sex: Female

...................9 [278] Sarah "Sally" Caudill b: July 29, 1823 d: April 13, 1884 Sex: Female

...................9 [279] Susannah Caudill b: April 18, 1825 in Perry Co., KY d: September 26, 1898 in Elk Creek, Letcher Co., KY Sex: Female Burial: Elder James Dixon Cemetery, Elk Creek, Letcher Co., KY

...................9 [280] William J. "Stiller Bill" Caudill b: July 05, 1827 in Letcher Co., KY d: November 26, 1908 Number of children: 16 Sex: Male

........................+[281] Nancy Dixon, Dickson b: April 19, 1830 in Letcher Co., KY m: February 07, 1847 in Letcher Co., KY d: December 31, 1899 Number of children: 16 Father: Thomas Dixon Mother: Susannah Proffitt Sex: Female

.....................10 [282] James William "Noah Jim" Caudill b: October 19, 1846 in Blackey, Letcher Co., KY d: August 14, 1911 Number of children: ? Sex: Male

..........................+[283] Lucinda Sumner b: January 28, 1850 in KY m: December 24, 1868 in Letcher Co., KY d: June 16, 1911 in KY Number of children: ? Father: John Sumner Mother: Nancy Hampton Sex: Female

.......................11 [10] Henry H. Cleveland Caudill b: April 20, 1887 in KY d: May 06, 1971 in Whitesburg, Letcher Co., KY Number of children: 18 Sex: Male Burial: Cleveland Caudill Cemetery, Caudill's Branch, Blackey, Letcher Co., KY

............................+[195] Rebecca Adams b: Abt. 1887 m: Abt. 1905 d: in Waynesburg, KY Number of children: 8 Father: Gideon Adams Mother: Sarah Blair Sex: Female

.......................2nd Wife of [10] Henry H. Cleveland Caudill:

............................+[284] Lucinda "Cinda" Watts b: April 20, 1886 m: May 11, 1911 in Letcher Co., KY d: October 22, 1963 in Letcher Co., KY Number of children: 10 Father: Allen Watts Mother: Elizabeth Brashear Sex: Female

.....................10 [285] Thomas D. Caudill b: December 26, 1848 in Letcher Co., KY Sex: Male

.........................+[286] Elizabeth Ann "Betsy" Pratt b: Abt. 1852 in Letcher Co., KY m: February 29, 1872 Father: John M. "Knock" Pratt Mother: Elizabeth Campbell Sex: Female

.....................10 [287] William J. "Miller Bill" Caudill b: May 27, 1850 in Letcher Co., KY d: December 11, 1924 Sex: Male Burial: Bill Caudill Cemetery, Blackey, Letcher Co., KY

.....................10 [288] John Caudill b: Abt. 1851 d: Abt. 1851 Sex: Male (Note: died in infancy)

.....................10 [289] Susannah Caudill b: February 20, 1853 in Letcher Co., KY d: November 23, 1941 in Perry Co., KY Sex: Female

.....................10 [290] Hiram W. Caudill b: Abt. September 20, 1853 in Letcher Co., KY d: December 20, 1913 Sex: Male

..........................+[291] Ester Banks b: April 08, 1853 in Letcher Co., KY d: September 25, 1905 Father: Harrison Banks Mother: Sarah Emeline Pridemore Sex: Female

.....................10 [292] Sarah Ann "Sally" Caudill b: January 22, 1855 d: March 02, 1930 Sex: Female

.....................10 [293] Nancy Jane Caudill b: October 05, 1856 d: January 06, 1929 Sex: Female

.....................10 [294] Isaac D. "Ike" Caudill b: February 17, 1859 in KY d: February 19, 1938 in Colson, or Roxanna, KY Sex: Male

.....................10 [295] Elizabeth "Betsy" Caudill b: Abt. 1860 in Letcher Co., KY d: Abt. 1927 Sex: Female

.....................10 [296] Jeremiah P. "Jerry" Caudill b: November 23, 1861 d: February 25, 1922 Sex: Male

.....................10 [297] George W. Caudill b: October 05, 1863 d: February 02, 1945 Sex: Male

.....................10 [298] Margaret Caudill b: August 25, 1865 d: September 21, 1939 Sex: Female

.....................10 [299] Henry Clay Caudill b: December 08, 1866 in Caudill Branch, Blackey, Letcher Co., KY d: September 06, 1938 in Red Star, KY Number of children: 5 Sex: Male Burial: Elmer Dixon Cemetery, Blackey, Letcher Co., KY

...........................+[300] Margaret Elizabeth "Maggie" Collins b: November 08, 1870 in Letcher Co., KY m: December 22, 1887 in Letcher Co., KY d: September 19, 1965 in Cincinnati, OH Number of children: 5 Father: Henry Powell Collins, Civil War Soldier Mother: Clarissa Ann "Clara" Bowman Sex: Female Burial: Elmer Dixon Cemetery, Blackey, Letcher Co., KY

.......................11 [301] Melissa Caudill b: 1890 d: August 10, 1964 in Nashville, TN Sex: Female Burial: Elmer Dixon Cemetery, Blackey, Letcher Co., KY

.......................11 [302] William Henry "Bill" Caudill b: 1892 d: February 25, 1950 Sex: Male

Burial: Elmer Dixon Cemetery, Blackey, Letcher Co., KY

...................11 [303] John Breckenridge "Johnny" Caudill b: January 21, 1894 in Camp Branch, Letcher Co., KY d: January 10, 1974 in Camp Branch, Letcher Co., KY Number of children: 9 Sex: Male Burial: George Caudill Cemetery, Blackey, Letcher Co., KY

.......................+[304] Thursa Ann Mason b: June 09, 1893 in Sandlick, Letcher Co., KY m: July 30, 1913 in McRoberts, Letcher Co., KY d: August 23, 1975 in Whitesburg, Letcher Co., KY Number of children: 9 Father: Tilghman (Tilton?) Howard Mason Mother: Cornelia "Kerneal" (Grant?) Kiser Sex: Female

......................11 [305] Louisa Caudill b: August 12, 1902 d: Abt. 1951 Sex: Female Burial: George Cemetery, Blackey, Letcher Co., KY

......................11 [306] Lavada Belle (Vada?) Caudill b: November 27, 1906 d: November 11, 1965 Sex: Female

....................10 [307] Martha Caudill b: May 10, 1868 in Lower Caudill Branch, Letcher Co., KY d: May 03, 1943 in Diablock, Perry Co., KY Sex: Female

....................10 [308] John Breckenridge Caudill b: March 11, 1870 in Letcher Co., KY d: February 24, 1947 in Stroud, Lincoln Co., OK Sex: Male (Note: resided in Chandler, OK, in 1938)

..................9 [309] Henry B. Caudill, twin, b: February 08, 1829 in Perry, Letcher Co., KY d: Abt. 1913 Number of children: 10 Sex: Male Burial: Felix York Cemetery, Viper, KY

.......................+[310] Margaret "Patsy" Campbell b: May 21, 1826 in Linefork, Perry/Letcher Co., KY m: February 15, 1849 in Letcher Co., KY Number of children: 10 Father: William C. Campbell Mother: Elizabeth Cornett, Sex: Female Burial: Felix York Cemetery, Viper, KY

....................10 [311] Elizabeth "Betty" Caudill b: August 29, 1850 in Letcher Co., KY d: September 05, 1904 Sex: Female

...........................+[312] Audley A. Cornett b: 1848 m: 1869 in Letcher Co., KY d: June 08, 1932 Sex: Male (Note: Looking for ancestors)

....................10 [313] Robert B. Caudill b: February 14, 1852 in Letcher Co., KY Sex: Male

...........................+[314] Elizabeth "Betty" Brashear b: December 05, 1856 in Perry Co., KY m: January 15, 1876 in Hazard, Perry Co., KY Father: Robert Samuel Brashear Mother: Sarah "Sally" Hall Sex: Female

....................10 [13] Rhoda Caudill b: April 12, 1853 in Letcher Co., KY d: January 17, 1942 Sex: Female

...........................+[14] Joshua M. Caudill b: June 23, 1850 in Letcher Co., KY d: March 22, 1941 Father: James "Limber Jim" Caudill Mother: Elizabeth "Betsy" Mullins Sex: Male

....................10 [315] Sarah "Sally" Caudill b: June 17, 1854 in Letcher Co., KY Sex: Female

...........................+[316] William "Bill" Young b: 1851 in Letcher Co., KY Father: Reece Young, Sr. Mother: Oriah R. "Ora" or "Arry" Ritchie Sex: Male

....................10 [317] Juda (Judy or Judah?) Caudill, b: March 1855 in Perry Co., KY Number of children: ? Sex: Female

...........................+[318] Jeremiah H. "Jerry" Combs b: 1859 in Perry Co., KY? Number of children: ? Father: Hiram Combs Mother: Mary Williams Sex: Male

......................11 [319] Daniel Combs b: Abt. 1892 in KY Number of children: ? Sex: Male

...........................+[320] Juda _____? b: Abt. 1900 in KY Number of children: ? Sex: Female

....................10 [321] Harriett Caudill b: 1859 in Letcher Co., KY Sex: Female

...........................+[322] Robert Hamilton b: Abt. 1855 Sex: Male

....................10 [323] William Hartley "Fuzzy Bill" Caudill b: Bet. 1860 - 1861 in Letcher Co., KY d: April 05, 1942 Sex: Male

...........................+[324] Cynthia Brashear b: September 02, 1858 in Perry Co., KY d: December 04, 1943 Sex: Female

....................10 [15] Lucretia "Lucy" Caudill b: Abt. 1864 in Perry Co., KY Sex: Female

...........................+[325] Jeptha Hamilton b: Abt. 1862 Sex: Male

....................2nd Husband of [15] Lucretia "Lucy" Caudill:

...........................+[326] Henry "Bud" Fields b: Abt. 1865 d: April 30, 1947 Sex: Male

....................10 [327] Polly Ann Caudill b: 1866 Sex: Female
....................10 [328] John Caudill b: 1869 Sex: Male
.................9 [329] Isom Jesse Caudill, Sr., twin b: February 08, 1829 d: Abt. 1917 Number of children: 12 Sex: Male
.....................+[330] Judah Sumner b: 1831 Number of children: 12 Father: James Sumner Mother: Nancy Adams, Sex: Female
....................10 [331] Mary Caudill b: 1850 Sex: Female
...........................+[332] Enoch Campbell b: Abt. 1847 Sex: Male
....................10 [333] Nancy Caudill b: August 07, 1852 Sex: Female
...........................+[334] Alexander Singleton b: Abt. 1850 Sex: Male
....................10 [335] Isom Caudill, Jr. b: July 26, 1855 Sex: Male
....................10 [336] George Henry Caudill b: 1855 Sex: Male
....................10 [337] Elizabeth Caudill b: June 02, 1856 Sex: Female
...........................+[338] John Hall b: Abt. 1855 Sex: Male
....................10 [339] Lucinda Caudill b: Abt. 1857 Sex: Female
....................10 [340] Margaret E. Caudill b: 1861 Sex: Female
...........................+[341] William Young b: Abt. 1860 Sex: Male
....................10 [342] Sarah Sally Caudill b: 1864 Sex: Female
....................10 [343] Patty Caudill b: Abt. 1865 Sex: Female
....................10 [344] William Caudill b: 1867 Sex: Male
...........................+[345] Mary J. Adams b: Abt. 1870 Sex: Female
....................10 [346] Julia Ann Caudill b: 1870 d: Abt. 1934 Sex: Female
...........................+[347] Ezekial Brashear b: Abt. 1867 Sex: Male
....................10 [348] Ellen Caudill b: 1875 Sex: Female
.................8 [807] Sarah "Sally" Craft b: Abt. 1786 in Letcher Co., KY? d: Abt. 1862 in Letcher Co., KY Sex: Female
.....................+[808] William Hammonds b: Abt. 1792 in NC m: April 12, 1812 in Floyd Co., KY d: Abt. 1862 in Letcher Co., KY Father: Joseph Hammonds Mother: Sarah _____? Sex: Male
.................8 [809] Ezekiel Craft b: Abt. 1788 Sex: Male
.................8 [810] James Craft b: Abt. 1790 in Wilkes Co., NC d: December 1879 in Wayne Co., KY Number of children: 10 Sex: Male
.....................+[811] Druscilla Hammonds b: Abt. 1790 in NC m: February 13, 1812 in Floyd Co., KY d: January 12, 1867 Number of children: 10 Father: Joseph Hammonds Mother: Sarah _____? Sex: Female
.................9 [812] Archibald Craft b: Abt. 1820 Sex: Male
...........................+[813] Lettishia "Lettie" Webb b: Abt. 1813 Father: Benjamin Webb Mother: Jane "Jennie" "Jincy" Adams, Sex: Female (Webb Note: Like all of the other Webb individuals in this tree, this Webb family descends from the same line as the country singers Loretta (Webb) Lynn and her sister Brenda Gail "Crystal Gale" Webb. Loretta was born April 14, 1935, in Butcher Hollow, Pike Co., KY; Crystal Gale was born January 9, 1951, in Paintsville, Johnson Co., KY)
.................9 [814] Archelous Craft b: Abt. 1814 in KY Number of children: 5 Sex: Male
...........................+[815] Letty Webb b: Abt. 1816 Number of children: 5 Sex: Female
....................10 [349] Enoch "Chunk" A. Craft b: December 29, 1842 d: February 16, 1937 in Millstone, Letcher Co., KY Number of children: ? Sex: Male
...........................+[350] Polly Ann Caudill b: April 15, 1847 in Letcher Co., KY m: May 02, 1867 in Letcher Co., KY d: February 11, 1937 in Millstone, Letcher Co., KY Number of children: ? Father: John Adams Caudill, Mother: Rachel Cornett, Sex: Female
....................11 [351] Nancy Craft b: January 1872 in Letcher Co., KY d: August 1872 in Letcher Co., KY Sex: Female
....................10 [816] Jane Craft b: Abt. 1846 Sex: Female
....................10 [817] Joseph Craft b: Abt. 1848 Sex: Male
....................10 [818] Benjamin Craft b: Abt. 1852 Sex: Male

..................10 [819] Wiley Craft b: Abt. 1855 Sex: Male

.................9 [820] Joseph Craft b: December 07, 1816 d: December 05, 1886 Number of children: 12 Sex: Male

........................+[821] Martha Irby Bates b: December 11, 1816 m: March 20, 1834 d: April 18, 1895 Number of children: 12 Father: John Wallis Bates, Sr., Sheriff Mother: Sarah Walthrop, or Waltrop Sex: Female

....................10 [352] John Henderson Craft b: December 20, 1834 in Millstone, KY d: September 13, 1920 in Larue, Laurel Co., KY Number of children: 2 Sex: Male Burial: Lincks Cemetery

...........................+[353] Nancy "Jane" Caudill, Caudell, b: November 05, 1840 in Whitesburg, Letcher Co., KY m: October 11, 1855 in Letcher Co., KY d: November 12, 1922 in London, Laurel Co., KY Number of children: 2 Father: John Adams Caudill, Mother: Rachel Cornett, Sex: Female Burial: Lincks Cemetery

.......................11 [354] John Dixon Craft b: April 12, 1856 in Craftsville, Letcher Co., KY d: December 20, 1945 in KY Number of children: ? Sex: Male

...........................+[355] Mary Elizabeth Webb b: July 11, 1861 in Letcher Co., KY m: September 13, 1879 d: November 25, 1956 Number of children: ? Father: Henry T. "Chunk" Webb Mother: Francis Elizabeth "Franky" Adams Sex: Female (Webb Note: Like all of the other Webb individuals in this tree, this Webb family descends from the same line as the country singers Loretta (Webb) Lynn and her sister Brenda Gail "Crystal Gale" Webb. Loretta was born April 14, 1935, in Butcher Hollow, Pike Co., KY; Crystal Gale was born January 9, 1951, in Paintsville, Johnson Co., KY)

.......................11 [356] Martha A. Craft b: September 12, 1860 in Craftsville, KY d: September 16, 1951 in TN Number of children: 3 Sex: Female

.............................+[357] Noah Milburn Reynolds, Jr. b: December 15, 1855 in KY m: November 15, 1879 in Blountsville, TN d: April 30, 1923 in Mayo Clinic in TN Number of children: 3 Father: Noah Milburn Reynolds, Sr. Mother: Mary Chaney Stone Sex: Male

....................10 [822] Sarah Craft b: Abt. 1836 Sex: Female

...........................+[823] Smith Mullins b: Abt. 1835 Sex: Male

....................10 [824] James W. Craft b: Abt. 1841 Sex: Male

....................10 [825] Martha Manerva Craft b: Abt. 1846 Sex: Female

...........................+[826] _____ Fouts, or Foote b: Abt. 1845 Sex: Male

....................10 [827] Mary Craft b: Abt. 1848 d: Aft. 1898 Sex: Female

...........................+[828] James Mullins b: Abt. 1845 d: Bef. 1898 Sex: Male

....................10 [829] Joseph Craft b: Abt. 1850 Number of children: ? Sex: Male

...........................+[830] Rasuea Bagwell b: March 29, 1850 in Grayson Co., VA m: September 02, 1869 in Letcher Co., KY Number of children: ? Sex: Female

.......................11 [415] Archie C. Craft, Jr. b: May 09, 1884 d: July 06, 1959 Number of children: 7 Sex: Male

.............................+[414] Lettie Dallas Wright b: January 08, 1894 in SeCo., KY m: November 05, 1919 in Letcher Co., KY d: April 04, 1974 Number of children: 7 Father: William S. Wright Mother: Letitia "Lettie/Moody" Bates Sex: Female Burial: Thorton, KY

....................10 [831] William Craft b: Abt. 1852 d: in Letcher Co., KY? Sex: Male

...........................+[832] _____ Sergeant b: Abt. 1855 m: in Letcher Co., KY d: in Letcher Co., KY? Sex: Female

....................10 [833] Eliza Craft b: Abt. 1854 in Letcher Co., KY Sex: Female

...........................+[834] John Christopher Reynolds b: Abt. 1851 in Scott Co., VA m: January 04, 1871 d: in SeCo., Letcher Co., KY Father: Noah Milburn Reynolds, Sr. Mother: Mary Chaney Stone Sex: Male

....................10 [835] Nancy Craft b: Abt. 1856 Sex: Female

...........................+[836] William Greer b: Abt. 1850 Sex: Male

....................10 [837] Morgan Craft b: Abt. 1868 Sex: Male

...........................+[838] Sallie _____? b: Abt. 1870 Sex: Female

.....................10 [839] Robert Craft b: Abt. 1870 Sex: Male

.....................10 [840] Drusilla Craft b: April 07, 1839 in Letcher Co., KY d: August 27, 1876 in Letcher Co., KY Number of children: 5 Sex: Female

...........................+[841] Stephen Nathaniel Reynolds b: Bet. 1838 - 1839 in Scott Co., VA d: Abt. June 1877 in Letcher Co., KY Number of children: 5 Father: Noah Milburn Reynolds, Sr. Mother: Mary Chaney Stone Sex: Male

.....................11 [842] Joseph Reynolds b: 1861 Sex: Male

.....................11 [843] Noah Christopher Reynolds b: February 08, 1864 Sex: Male

.....................11 [844] John C. Reynolds b: 1866 Sex: Male

.....................11 [845] Stephen Nathaniel Reynolds b: January 05, 1872 Sex: Male

.....................11 [846] Mary Chaney Reynolds b: May 1873 in Letcher Co., KY d: December 21, 1874 in Letcher Co., KY Sex: Female

.................9 [365] Mahala Craft b: Abt. 1818 Number of children: 13 Sex: Female

.......................+[364] Campbell C. Crase b: Abt. 1814 Number of children: 13 Father: Peter Crase, Mother: Annie Adams, Sex: Male

.....................10 [366] James Crase b: Abt. 1835 Number of children: 2 Sex: Male (Note: Not sure if James is the son of Campbell Crase & Mahala Craft)

...........................+[367] Elizabeth Stallard b: Bet. 1837 - 1841 m: December 04, 1856 in Letcher Co., KY Number of children: 2 Sex: Female

.....................11 [368] Hiram Monroe Crase b: March 16, 1866 Sex: Male

...........................+[369] Dicy Collins b: July 13, 1859 in Rockhouse Creek, Letcher Co., KY m: March 04, 1877 in Letcher Co., KY d: November 27, 1900 Father: William Sherman Collins Mother: Eliza Breeding Sex: Female

.....................11 [358] Martha E. Crase b: Abt. 1868 Sex: Female

...........................+[183] William Silas Collins b: April 21, 1865 m: March 03, 1888 in Letcher Co., KY d: December 15, 1937 in Letcher Co., KY Father: Robert Collins Mother: Lydia Adams Sex: Male

.....................10 [370] Peter C. Crase b: Abt. 1837 Sex: Male

.....................10 [371] Elizabeth Crase b: Abt. 1839 Sex: Female

.....................10 [372] Nehemiah Crase b: 1841 Number of children: 9 Sex: Male

...........................+[373] Mary Franklin b: February 1843 Number of children: 9 Sex: Female

.....................11 [374] Campbell M. Crase b: September 1861 Sex: Male

.....................11 [375] Elizabeth Crase b: Abt. 1866 Sex: Female

.....................11 [376] Lousia Crase b: Abt. 1868 Sex: Female

.....................11 [377] Frances Crase b: Abt. 1871 Sex: Male

.....................11 [378] Mantford L. Crase b: Abt. 1873 Sex: Male

.....................11 [379] Dora I. Crase b: Abt. 1875 Sex: Female

.....................11 [380] Cornelia Crase b: Abt. 1879 Sex: Male

.....................11 [381] Loly J. Crase b: Abt. 1883 Sex: Female

.....................11 [382] Malcolm Crase b: 1886 in Magoffin Co., KY d: 1932 in Magoffin Co., KY Number of children: 10 Sex: Male

...........................+[383] Lula LeMaster b: July 31, 1887 in Magoffin Co., KY d: June 1977 in Pike Co., OH Number of children: 10 Sex: Female

.....................10 [384] Pricilla Crase b: Abt. 1843 Sex: Female

.....................10 [385] Ciney M. Crase b: Abt. 1845 Sex: Unknown

.....................10 [386] Noah Crase b: August 1849 Sex: Male

.....................10 [387] Alfred W. Crase b: January 06, 1852 Sex: Male

.....................10 [388] Morgan Crase b: Abt. 1854 Sex: Male

.....................10 [389] Sarah Crase b: November 04, 1856 Sex: Female

.....................10 [390] Martha M. Crase b: Abt. 1860 Sex: Female

.....................10 [391] Frankie J. Crase b: May 06, 1861 Sex: Female

....................10 [392] Benjamin H. Crase b: June 1863 Sex: Male

..................9 [847] Elizabeth Craft b: Abt. 1820 Number of children: 8 Sex: Female

........................+[848] Jason L. Webb b: Abt. 1820 m: Abt. 1840 Number of children: 9 Father: Benjamin Webb Mother: Jane "Jennie" "Jincy" Adams, Sex: Male (Webb Note: Like all of the other Webb individuals in this tree, this Webb family descends from the same line as the country singers Loretta (Webb) Lynn and her sister Brenda Gail "Crystal Gale" Webb. Loretta was born April 14, 1935, in Butcher Hollow, Pike Co., KY; Crystal Gale was born January 9, 1951, in Paintsville, Johnson Co., KY)

....................10 [849] Nelson Webb b: Abt. 1840 Sex: Male

....................10 [850] Mahala Webb b: Abt. 1843 Sex: Female

....................10 [851] Archibald Webb b: Abt. 1845 Sex: Male

....................10 [852] Wiley W. Webb b: 1847 in Letcher Co., KY Sex: Male

..........................+[853] Nancy Adams b: March 07, 1847 in Smoot Creek, Letcher Co., KY d: September 25, 1925 Father: Isaac B. Adams Mother: Nancy Hayes Sex: Female

....................10 [854] Mary Webb b: Abt. 1849 Sex: Female

....................10 [855] Anna Webb b: Abt. 1851 Sex: Female

....................10 [856] Benjamin Webb b: Abt. 1855 Sex: Male

....................10 [857] Drusilla Webb b: Abt. 1857 Sex: Female

..................9 [397] Sarah "Sallie" Craft b: April 02, 1821 d: March 26, 1863 in Letcher Co., KY Number of children: 7 Sex: Female

........................+[396] John Isom Adams b: 1818 m: August 16, 1838 d: 1863 in (Note: Died trying to open an unexploded bomb to get at the gun powder inside) Number of children: 7 Father: Benjamin Adams, Mother: Nancy Holbrook, Sex: Male

....................10 [398] Benjamin Burford Adams b: 1840 Sex: Male

....................10 [399] James W. Adams b: 1842 Sex: Male

....................10 [400] Nancy Jane Adams b: 1845 Sex: Female

....................10 [401] Jesse Adams b: 1847 Sex: Male

....................10 [402] Joseph Simpson Adams b: 1851 Sex: Male

....................10 [403] Randolph N. Adams b: 1854 Sex: Male

....................10 [404] Archelous Adams b: 1858 Sex: Male

..................9 [858] Benjamin Craft b: Abt. 1824 Sex: Male

........................+[859] Jennifer "Jennie" Adams b: Abt. 1825 Sex: Female

..................9 [860] Nehemiah Craft b: Abt. 1826 Sex: Male

........................+[861] Artie Thornburg b: Abt. 1830 in Letcher Co., KY? Sex: Female

..................9 [862] Archelous Craft b: Abt. 1828 in Letcher Co., KY? d: 1897 in Letcher Co., KY Sex: Male

........................+[863] Nancy Polly b: Abt. 1830 in Letcher Co., KY? d: 1897 in Letcher Co., KY Sex: Female

..................9 [864] Stephen Craft b: Abt. 1830 Sex: Male

................8 [865] John William Craft b: Abt. 1792 Sex: Male

................8 [866] Stephen Craft b: Abt. 1794 Sex: Male

................8 [867] Simon Craft b: Abt. 1796 Sex: Male

................8 [868] Malinda Craft b: Abt. 1798 Sex: Female

................8 [869] Archaelous "Cheed" Craft, Jr. b: 1802 in Harris Creek, Wilkes Co., NC Number of children: 14 Sex: Male

........................+[870] Nancy Jane Polly b: 1805 in Carter Co., TN m: August 23, 1822 in Perry Co., KY d: Aft. 1880 in Letcher Co., KY Number of children: 14 Father: Edward Polly, Mother: Mary Agnes Mullins, Sex: Female

..................9 [871] Henry Craft b: 1825 Sex: Male

..................9 [872] Wiley Craft b: 1825 Sex: Male

..................9 [873] Elizabeth "Betsy" Craft b: 1831 Sex: Female

..................9 [874] Susanna Craft b: 1832 Sex: Female

..................9 [875] David K. Craft b: February 22, 1837 Sex: Male

..................9 [876] Henrietta Craft b: 1838 Sex: Female

..................9 [877] Serena Craft b: 1840 Sex: Female

..................9 [878] Melvina Jane "Viny" Craft b: 1842 Sex: Female

..................9 [879] Margaret Craft b: 1844 Sex: Female

..................9 [880] John P. Craft b: 1845 Sex: Male

..................9 [881] Martha Craft b: 1846 Sex: Female

..................9 [882] Joseph Wiley Craft b: May 1848 Sex: Male

..................9 [883] Edward Craft b: July 29, 1852 Sex: Male

..................9 [884] Mary "Polly" Craft b: 1828 in Perry Co., KY Number of children: 2 Sex: Female

.........................+[885] Jesse "Colly Jesse" Adams b: December 08, 1827 in Perry Co., KY m: July 24, 1845 in Letcher Co., KY d: January 18, 1912 in Letcher Co., KY Number of children: 2 Father: Stephen "Shank Steve" Adams, Mother: Elizabeth "Betsy" Whitaker Sex: Male

.....................10 [886] Cecilia "Celia" Adams b: May 20, 1852 in Letcher Co., KY Number of children: 2 Sex: Female

.........................+[887] James Taylor Addington b: October 19, 1850 in Russell Co., VA m: March 13, 1870 in Letcher Co., KY d: May 30, 1917 in Letcher Co., KY Number of children: 2 Father: John Addington Mother: Cora Lucinda Roberts Sex: Male

........................11 [888] Mary Elizabeth "Polly Ann" Addington b: September 15, 1869 in Crafts Colly (Ermine) , Letcher Co., KY Number of children: ? Sex: Female

............................+[889] William Basil Adkins, b: April 16, 1871 m: 1897 d: September 06, 1962 in Letcher Co., KY Number of children: ? Father: Peter Adkins, Mother: Louisa Ann Belcher Sex: Male Burial: Isom, Letcher Co., KY (Adkins Note: like the author and all of the other Adkins individuals in this tree and their descendants, this family descends from European royalty through Elizabeth Parker, born about 1697 in Charles City or Richmond, Henrico Co., VA. Elizabeth's husband was William Adkins/Atkinson, born March 28, 1689, in Charles City, Henrico Co. VA. Elizabeth is the proven 12th great-granddaughter of the King of England, Henry III, born October 1, 1206, in Winchester Castle, Hampshire Co., England)

.......................11 [890] Harvey Addington b: Abt. 1871 Number of children: 2 Sex: Male

............................+[891] Floria Collins b: November 24, 1883 in Lee Co., VA d: May 11, 1952 Number of children: 2 Father: James M. "Big Jimmer" Collins Mother: America Ann Bentley Sex: Female

.....................10 [359] Christina Adams b: June 10, 1858 d: January 07, 1951 Sex: Female

...........................+[360] Greenbury Collins b: February 26, 1868 d: May 03, 1924 Father: Robert Collins Mother: Lydia Adams Sex: Male

.................8 [892] William Craft b: Abt. 1807 d: 1898 in Letcher Co., KY Number of children: ? Sex: Male

.....................+[893] Rachel Parker b: Abt. 1800 Number of children: ? Sex: Female

..................9 [784] Martha Ann "Patsy" Craft b: Abt. 1835 d: in Letcher Co., KY Number of children: 3 Sex: Female

.......................+[361] Moses "Rockhouse Moses" Adams b: July 18, 1808 in Letcher Co., KY m: October 03, 1867 in Letcher Co., KY d: 1885 in Hazard, Letcher Co., KY Number of children: 12 Father: Stephen "Rockhouse Steve" Adams Mother: Ellendar "Nellie" Buntin, or Benton Sex: Male

.....................10 [785] Mary Adams b: 1867 in Letcher Co., KY Sex: Female

...........................+[786] Creed Craft b: 1873 in Letcher Co., KY m: November 20, 1900 in Whitesburg, KY Sex: Male

.....................10 [787] Joseph Adams b: 1870 in Rockhouse Creek, Floyd Co., KY Sex: Male

...........................+[788] Flora Tyree b: 1878 m: September 10, 1894 in Letcher Co., KY Sex: Female

.....................10 [789] Lucinda Adams b: 1878 in Letcher Co., KY Sex: Female

...........................+[790] Robert E. Banks b: Abt. 1875 m: August 10, 1897 in Letcher Co., KY

Sex: Male

.................8 [894] Charity Craft b: Abt. 1810 Sex: Female

.............7 [362] Stephen Adams, b: 1778 in NC d: 1858 in Morgan Co., KY Number of children: 10 Sex: Male

....................+[895] Mary "Polly" Holbrook b: Abt. 1785 in Rockhouse, Floyd Co., KY Father: Randolph Holbrook Mother: Elizabeth _____? Sex: Female

.............2nd Wife of [362] Stephen Adams, :

....................+[896] Mary "Mollie" Webb b: 1774 in NC m: Abt. 1798 in Wilkesboro, Wilkes Co., NC d: 1851 in Morgan Co., KY Number of children: 9 Father: James F. Webb, Sr., Soldier Mother: Elizabeth "Lettie" Jane Nelson (Nelson Note: Looking for Elizabeth's ancestors. I believe that she's part of the large Nelson clan from VA and NC, which spread out and migrated west into WV, TN, and KY in the 1830s. Like the author, the Judds [Naomi, Ashley, Wynonna], also descend from this family. The earliest known ancestor of this Nelson group is William "Old William" Nelson, born in 1747 in Prince Edward Co., VA, and died on August 9, 1834, in Hawkins Co., TN. Old William's wife was Rebecca Smith, born about 1757 in Stokes Co., NC. It's possible, in my opinion, that Elizabeth could be Old William's sister) Sex: Female (Webb Note: Like all of the other Webb individuals in this tree, this Webb family descends from the same line as the country singers Loretta (Webb) Lynn and her sister Brenda Gail "Crystal Gale" Webb. Loretta was born April 14, 1935, in Butcher Hollow, Pike Co., KY; Crystal Gale was born January 9, 1951, in Paintsville, Johnson Co., KY)

.............8 [897] Annie Adams, b: 1798 d: Abt. 1844 Number of children: 4 Sex: Female

......................+[363] Peter Crase, b: 1792 in Austusta Co., VA m: March 16, 1816 in Floyd (now Pike) Co., KY d: 1867 in Roxana, Letcher Co., KY Number of children: 13 Father: George Crase, Jr., Crace, Cress, Kress, Mother: Charity Morgan, Sex: Male

.................9 [364] Campbell C. Crase b: Abt. 1814 Number of children: 13 Sex: Male

.......................+[365] Mahala Craft b: Abt. 1818 Number of children: 13 Father: James Craft Mother: Druscilla Hammonds Sex: Female

....................10 [366] James Crase b: Abt. 1835 Number of children: 2 Sex: Male (Note: Not sure if James is the son of Campbell Crase & Mahala Craft)

...........................+[367] Elizabeth Stallard b: Bet. 1837 - 1841 m: December 04, 1856 in Letcher Co., KY Number of children: 2 Sex: Female

.......................11 [368] Hiram Monroe Crase b: March 16, 1866 Sex: Male

.............................+[369] Dicy Collins b: July 13, 1859 in Rockhouse Creek, Letcher Co., KY m: March 04, 1877 in Letcher Co., KY d: November 27, 1900 Father: William Sherman Collins Mother: Eliza Breeding Sex: Female

.......................11 [358] Martha E. Crase b: Abt. 1868 Sex: Female

.............................+[183] William Silas Collins b: April 21, 1865 m: March 03, 1888 in Letcher Co., KY d: December 15, 1937 in Letcher Co., KY Father: Robert Collins Mother: Lydia Adams Sex: Male

....................10 [370] Peter C. Crase b: Abt. 1837 Sex: Male

....................10 [371] Elizabeth Crase b: Abt. 1839 Sex: Female

....................10 [372] Nehemiah Crase b: 1841 Number of children: 9 Sex: Male

...........................+[373] Mary Franklin b: February 1843 Number of children: 9 Sex: Female

.......................11 [374] Campbell M. Crase b: September 1861 Sex: Male

.......................11 [375] Elizabeth Crase b: Abt. 1866 Sex: Female

.......................11 [376] Lousia Crase b: Abt. 1868 Sex: Female

.......................11 [377] Frances Crase b: Abt. 1871 Sex: Male

.......................11 [378] Mantford L. Crase b: Abt. 1873 Sex: Male

.......................11 [379] Dora I. Crase b: Abt. 1875 Sex: Female

.......................11 [380] Cornelia Crase b: Abt. 1879 Sex: Male

.......................11 [381] Loly J. Crase b: Abt. 1883 Sex: Female

.......................11 [382] Malcolm Crase b: 1886 in Magoffin Co., KY d: 1932 in Magoffin Co., KY

Number of children: 10 Sex: Male

...............................+[383] Lula LeMaster b: July 31, 1887 in Magoffin Co., KY d: June 1977 in Pike Co., OH Number of children: 10 Sex: Female

....................10 [384] Pricilla Crase b: Abt. 1843 Sex: Female

....................10 [385] Ciney M. Crase b: Abt. 1845 Sex: Unknown

....................10 [386] Noah Crase b: August 1849 Sex: Male

....................10 [387] Alfred W. Crase b: January 06, 1852 Sex: Male

....................10 [388] Morgan Crase b: Abt. 1854 Sex: Male

....................10 [389] Sarah Crase b: November 04, 1856 Sex: Female

....................10 [390] Martha M. Crase b: Abt. 1860 Sex: Female

....................10 [391] Frankie J. Crase b: May 06, 1861 Sex: Female

....................10 [392] Benjamin H. Crase b: June 1863 Sex: Male

................9 [898] Henry Crase b: July 1816 Sex: Male

................9 [899] Alfred Crase b: 1818 d: 1880 Sex: Male

................9 [900] Stephen M. Crase b: 1824 Sex: Male

..............8 [901] Daniel Adams b: July 16, 1799 in NC d: 1885 in Brainard, KY Sex: Male

....................+[902] Jane Stone b: Abt. 1800 m: 1818 in Floyd Co., KY Sex: Female

..............8 [903] Elizabeth "Betsy" Adams b: 1801 in NC Sex: Female

....................+[904] John Caudill b: Abt. 1798 m: 1819 in Prestonsburg, KY Sex: Male

..............8 [905] William "Uncle Billy" Adams b: Abt. 1802 d: 1881 Number of children: ? Sex: Male

....................+[906] Elizabeth Mullins b: Abt. 1805 Number of children: ? Sex: Female

................9 [907] Minerva Adams Number of children: ? Sex: Female

........................+[908] Thomas Reid Number of children: ? Sex: Male

....................10 [909] William Marion Reid Number of children: ? Sex: Male

........................+[910] Susan Prater Number of children: ? Sex: Female

....................11 [911] Ida Belle Reid Number of children: ? Sex: Female

........................+[912] Charles T. Hammond Number of children: ? Sex: Male

................8 [913] Gilbert Adams b: 1804 Sex: Male

....................+[914] Nancy Adams b: Abt. 1805 m: 1823 in Perry Co., KY Sex: Female

................8 [915] Francis Adams b: Abt. 1810 Number of children: ? Sex: Female

....................+[916] William Tolson Adams b: 1806 Number of children: ? Sex: Male

................9 [917] Gilbert A. Adams b: 1826 Number of children: ? Sex: Male

....................+[918] Perlina Prater b: Abt. 1830 Number of children: ? Sex: Female

....................10 [180] Rebecca E. Adams b: 1852 Number of children: ? Sex: Female

........................+[179] Campbell J. May b: 1851 Number of children: ? Father: Noah May Mother: Elizabeth Caudill Sex: Male

....................11 [181] Augustus Noah May b: 1876 d: 1944 Number of children: ? Sex: Male

........................+[182] Sarah Elizabeth Cornett b: 1876 d: 1966 Number of children: ? Father: Russell Cornett, Mother: Ailey Amburgey Sex: Female

................8 [393] Sarah "Sally" Adams b: March 21, 1813 in Rockhouse, Floyd Co., KY d: November 26, 1876 in Wolfe, KY Sex: Female

....................+[919] Blair May b: Abt. 1808 m: May 17, 1829 in Floyd, KY Sex: Male

................2nd Husband of [393] Sarah "Sally" Adams:

....................+[920] Daniel Conley b: Abt. 1809 in Rockhouse, Floyd Co., KY m: March 12, 1860 in KY? Sex: Male

................8 [420] Zilpha (Zelphia) Adams b: August 01, 1811 in Rockhouse Creek, Letcher Co., KY d: 1893 Number of children: 5 Sex: Female

....................+[419] Randolph Holbrook b: March 15, 1811 in Floyd Co., KY m: 1827 in Perry Co., KY Number of children: 5 Father: Randolph (or Randel) "Buck" Holbrook, Mother: Elizabeth Nancy Rebecca Adams, Sex: Male

................9 [421] Kelsey Holbrook b: April 05, 1829 Sex: Male

........................+[422] Rutha Mullins b: Abt. 1830 Sex: Female

...................9 [423] Nancy A. Holbrook b: 1830 in Floyd Co., KY Number of children: ? Sex: Female

.......................+[424] Richard Lee Spradling b: June 22, 1822 in Floyd Co., KY Number of children: ? Sex: Male

......................10 [425] Sarah Jane Spradling b: May 26, 1851 in Harrison Co., KY Number of children: ? Sex: Female

............................+[426] Reuben Porter Dennis b: June 04, 1848 in West Liberty, Morgan Co., KY Number of children: ? Sex: Male

.......................11 [427] Nancy Katherine Dennis b: July 05, 1870 in Hazel Green, KY Number of children: ? Sex: Female

..............................+[428] Jasper Bond Suiter b: September 06, 1872 in Wise Co., VA Number of children: ? Sex: Male

...................9 [429] Benjamin May Holbrook b: March 26, 1832 Number of children: 2 Sex: Male

........................+[430] Rhoda Bays Spradlin b: 1834 Number of children: 2 Sex: Female

.....................10 [394] Randolph Holbrook b: May 21, 1853 Number of children: 9 Sex: Male

...........................+[431] Virgie Bays b: Abt. 1851 Number of children: 9 Sex: Female

.......................11 [432] Adam Gus Holbrook b: Abt. 1877 Number of children: ? Sex: Male

........................+[433] Kate Miller b: 1876 Number of children: ? Sex: Female

.......................11 [434] Eva Jane Holbrook b: January 1880 Sex: Female

.........................+[435] Harrison Puckett b: Abt. 1875 Sex: Male

.......................11 [436] Jacob Holbrook b: March 07, 1882 Sex: Male

.........................+[437] Lisa Puckett b: Abt. 1886 Sex: Female

.......................11 [438] John A. Holbrook b: April 1885 Sex: Male

.........................+[439] Cynthia Prater b: Abt. 1889 Sex: Female

.......................11 [440] Samuel Holbrook b: Abt. 1887 Sex: Male

.......................11 [441] Jim Holbrook b: December 1887 Sex: Male

.........................+[442] Lethia Stone b: Abt. 1889 Sex: Female

.......................11 [443] Campbell May Holbrook b: June 16, 1890 Sex: Male

.......................11 [444] Virginia Maxine Holbrook b: Abt. 1891 Sex: Female

.......................11 [445] Elizabeth "Addie" Holbrook b: Abt. 1892 Sex: Female

.....................2nd Wife of [394] Randolph Holbrook:

..........................+[446] Sarah Shepherd b: 1852 Sex: Female

.....................10 [447] Harvey Trimble Holbrook b: June 21, 1879 Sex: Male

..........................+[448] Molly B. Hall b: Abt. 1880 Sex: Female

...................9 [449] Mary B. Holbrook b: 1837 Sex: Female

...................9 [450] Elizabeth Holbrook b: 1838 Sex: Female

................8 [921] Lucy Adams b: February 16, 1818 in Floyd Co., KY Sex: Female

.......................+[922] Lewis Patrick b: Abt. 1810 m: 1837 in Morgan Co., KY Sex: Male

.............3rd Wife of [362] Stephen Adams, :

....................+[923] Katherine T. Reid b: Abt. 1792 in VA m: March 11, 1853 in Morgan, KY Number of children: ? Sex: Female

................8 [924] Annie Adams b: Abt. 1855 Sex: Female

.............7 [395] Nancy Adams b: 1785 Sex: Female

...................+[7] William C. "Billy" Caudill, b: July 27, 1779 in Wilkes Co., NC d: July 27, 1880 in Letcher Co., KY Number of children: 14 Father: James "Jimmie" Caudill, Jr., Rev. War Soldier Mother: Mary A. Adams, Sex: Male

...........2nd Wife of [803] John Hobbs Adams, Jr., :

.................+Vinnie Bausell b: Abt. 1740 m: Abt. 1786 in Stafford Co., VA Number of children: ? Sex: Female

.............7 John Hobbs Adams, Jr. b: 1787 Sex: Male

...................+Nancy Caudill b: Abt. 1790 m: in Fairfax Co., VA Sex: Female

..........3rd Wife of [803] John Hobbs Adams, Jr., :

................+Lydia "Letty" or "Lettie" Simpson b: 1748 in Surrey Co. NC m: 1789 in Wilkesboro, Wilkes Co., N.C. d: 1845 in Floyd Co., or Pine Creek, Letcher Co., KY Number of children: 8 Father: Samuel Simpson Mother: Mary Swain Sex: Female

.............7 [925] Mary Ann "Polly" Adams, b: 1788 in KY or Wilkes Co., NC d: 1845 in Letcher Co., KY Number of children: 9 Sex: Female

...................+[926] William Green "Billy Grit" Adams, b: Bet. 1788 - 1790 in Lewis Fork, Wilkes Co., NC m: October 29, 1809 in Letcher Co., KY d: 1870 in Letcher Co., KY Number of children: 9 Father: Jesse Adams, Jr., Mother: _____ Green Sex: Male

...............8 [927] John Adams b: 1811 Sex: Male

......................+[928] Sarah Meadows b: 1815 d: December 26, 1856 Sex: Female

...............8 [929] Jesse G. Adams b: 1815 d: Aft. 1880 Sex: Male

......................+[930] Keziah Meadows b: 1827 d: Aft. 1880 Sex: Female

...............8 [931] Simpson (or Sampson) Adams b: 1818 in Jellico River, Whitley Co., KY d: 1910 in Pine Creek, Letcher Co., KY Number of children: 10 Sex: Male

......................+[932] Sarah Webb b: 1825 d: 1897 Number of children: 10 Father: Benjamin Webb Mother: Jane "Jennie" "Jincy" Adams, Sex: Female (Webb Note: Like all of the other Webb individuals in this tree, this Webb family descends from the same line as the country singers Loretta (Webb) Lynn and her sister Brenda Gail "Crystal Gale" Webb. Loretta was born April 14, 1935, in Butcher Hollow, Pike Co., KY; Crystal Gale was born January 9, 1951, in Paintsville, Johnson Co., KY)

..................9 [933] Jane Adams b: 1846 Sex: Female

..................9 [934] Mary M. Adams b: 1849 Sex: Female

..................9 [935] Lettie Adams b: 1853 d: 1925 Sex: Female

..................9 [936] Lydia (twin) Adams b: March 14, 1855 Sex: Female

..................9 [937] Rachel (twin) Adams b: 1855 Sex: Female

..................9 [938] Benjamin Jackson Adams b: 1856 d: 1938 Sex: Male

..................9 [939] Jason Adams b: 1860 Sex: Male

..................9 [940] Enoch M. Adams b: 1863 Sex: Male

..................9 [941] Spencer Adams b: 1866 Sex: Male

..................9 [942] Simpson M. Adams b: 1869 d: 1889 Sex: Male

...............8 [943] William Green Adams b: January 21, 1820 in Jellico River, Whitley Co., KY d: June 29, 1862 in Pound River, Wise Co., VA Number of children: 9 Sex: Male

......................+[944] Mary Webb b: March 14, 1818 m: April 25, 1840 d: February 05, 1899 Number of children: 9 Father: Benjamin Webb Mother: Jane "Jennie" "Jincy" Adams, Sex: Female (Webb Note: Like all of the other Webb individuals in this tree, this Webb family descends from the same line as the country singers Loretta (Webb) Lynn and her sister Brenda Gail "Crystal Gale" Webb. Loretta was born April 14, 1935, in Butcher Hollow, Pike Co., KY; Crystal Gale was born January 9, 1951, in Paintsville, Johnson Co., KY)

..................9 [945] Benjamin Adams b: July 04, 1840 Sex: Male

..................9 [946] Purthia Adams b: September 22, 1842 Sex: Female

..................9 [947] Lydia Adams b: November 07, 1844 Sex: Female

......................+[948] Jesse Collins b: Abt. 1840 Sex: Male

..................9 [949] Sarah Adams b: May 05, 1850 Sex: Female

......................+[950] Nelson Hampton b: Abt. 1845 Sex: Male

..................9 [951] Lettie Jane Adams b: January 23, 1852 in Letcher Co., KY d: September 08, 1883 Sex: Female

..................9 [952] Jane Adams b: May 10, 1853 Sex: Female

......................+[953] Benjamin Abbott Adams b: Abt. 1850 m: October 09, 1864 in Letcher Co., KY Sex: Male

..................9 [954] Miles Mayo Adams b: June 18, 1855 in Letcher Co., KY Sex: Male

..................9 [955] Simpson E. Adams b: October 29, 1857 in Letcher Co., KY d: May 04, 1935

Sex: Male

................9 [956] Mary Ellen Adams b: May 27, 1861 in Letcher Co., KY d: September 1889 Number of children: ? Sex: Female

......................+[957] Willis Kirk Collier b: 1859 d: 1944 Number of children: ? Sex: Male

....................10 [958] Harrison Collier b: April 1889 Sex: Male

..............8 [778] Sarah "Sally" Adams, b: 1821 in Jellico River, Whitley Co., KY? d: 1886 in Letcher Co., KY? Number of children: 3 Sex: Female

.....................+[959] Elihu Brown b: 1835 Sex: Male

...............2nd Husband of [778] Sarah "Sally" Adams, :

.....................+[960] _____ Jones b: Abt. 1820 m: 1843 in Whitesburg, KY Sex: Male

...............3rd Husband of [778] Sarah "Sally" Adams, :

.....................+[961] Stephen "Shank Steve" Adams, b: August 25, 1804 in Elizabethton, Carter Co., TN m: 1844 in Letcher Co., KY d: Abt. 1875 Number of children: 4 Father: Moses Adams, Mother: Mary Garland Sex: Male

................9 [779] John S. "Tobacco" Adams, b: Abt. 1845 in Letcher Co., KY d: 1925 Number of children: ? Sex: Male

.....................+[962] Margaret Adams, b: Abt. 1845 m: Abt. 1863 Father: George M. Adams, Mother: Sarah Frazier Sex: Female

................2nd Wife of [779] John S. "Tobacco" Adams, :

.....................+[963] Elizabeth Blair, parents unknown b: Abt. 1849 in Letcher Co., KY m: June 05, 1864 in Letcher Co., KY Number of children: ? Father: John Robinson Blair Mother: Elizabeth Harrison Sex: Female (Note: Looking for her ancestors; her parents MAY be John Robinson Blair & Elizabeth Harrison)

....................10 [964] William R. Adams, b: Abt. 1870 in KY Number of children: ? Sex: Male

...........................+[965] Malinda Brashear b: October 28, 1873 in Viper, Perry Co., KY m: Abt. 1892 in Viper, Perry Co., KY d: May 01, 1941 Number of children: ? Father: Sampson Brashear Mother: Mary Ann Hall Sex: Female

.....................11 Arlena Adams, b: 1894 in Perry Co., KY? d: November 04, 1919 in Viper, Perry Co., KY (died giving birth to a premature baby) Number of children: 2 Sex: Female

...........................+Robert May "Big May" Cornett b: June 28, 1888 in Jeff, Perry Co., KY m: Abt. 1913 in Perry Co., KY? d: May 02, 1970 in Viper, Perry Co., KY Number of children: 5 Father: Robert Cornett Mother: Sallie Combs, Sex: Male (Note: Looking for his ancestors)

................3rd Wife of [779] John S. "Tobacco" Adams, :

.....................+[966] Mariah Green b: Abt. 1855 m: 1875 Sex: Female

................9 [967] Lydia Adams b: Abt. 1847 in Letcher Co., KY Sex: Female

................9 [780] Daugherty (Doherty?) Adams b: April 10, 1853 in Letcher Co., KY Sex: Male

.....................+[968] Jane Adams b: Abt. 1855 m: April 03, 1870 Sex: Female

................2nd Wife of [780] Daugherty (Doherty?) Adams:

.....................+[969] Mahalia Collier b: Abt. 1860 m: 1881 Sex: Female

..............8 [970] Mary "Polly" Adams b: 1823 Sex: Female

..............8 [971] Spencer Adams b: February 19, 1826 in Jellico River, Whitley Co., KY d: March 21, 1905 in Letcher Co., KY Number of children: 8 Sex: Male

.....................+[972] Celia Church b: 1827 m: March 19, 1844 Number of children: 8 Father: Joel Church Mother: Margaret Adams Sex: Female

................9 [781] William Adams b: 1848 in Letcher Co., KY d: 1880 Sex: Male

.....................+[973] Leudemia Hubbard b: Abt. 1850 m: Abt. 1870 Sex: Female

................2nd Wife of [781] William Adams:

.....................+[974] Ida Maggard b: Abt. 1855 m: Abt. 1880 Sex: Female

................9 [975] Margaret Adams b: 1849 in Letcher Co., KY Sex: Female

................9 [782] Samuel Simpson Adams b: December 27, 1852 in Mayking, Letcher Co., KY d: September 1928 Sex: Male

.....................+[976] Nancy Ann Collins b: Abt. 1855 m: Abt. 1870 Sex: Female

..................2nd Wife of [782] Samuel Simpson Adams:

.........................+[977] Elizabeth Roberts b: Abt. 1860 m: January 01, 1872 Sex: Female

..................9 [978] David Maggard Adams b: 1854 in Tilly, KY d: June 1939 in Halo, KY Sex: Male

..................9 [979] Joseph L. Adams, Rev. b: May 19, 1855 in Pine Creek, Letcher Co., KY d: March 14, 1905 Number of children: ? Sex: Male Burial: Adkins Graveyard, Adkins Branch, Letcher Co., KY

.........................+[980] Mary Jane Short b: May 01, 1854 in Wise Co., Va. at Short's Creek d: February 25, 1929 in KY? Number of children: ? Father: William Alfred Short Mother: Elizabeth "Betsy" Roman Davis Sex: Female Burial: Adkins Graveyard, Adkins Branch, Letcher Co., KY

.......................10 [981] James Taylor Adams b: 1892 in Crafts Colley, KY d: September 03, 1954 in Big Laurel, VA Number of children: 7 Sex: Male

...........................+[982] Dicey Roberts b: Abt. 1894 Number of children: 7 Sex: Female

........................11 James Taylor "Jeems" Adams, Jr. Sex: Male

........................11 Spencer Adams b: Abt. 1920 Sex: Male

........................11 Simpson Adams Sex: Male

........................11 Naomi Adams Sex: Female

........................11 Virginia Adams Sex: Female

........................11 Lenora Adams Sex: Female

........................11 Eva Adams Sex: Female

..................9 [983] Jesse Adams b: 1859 Sex: Male

..................9 [984] Annalas Adams b: 1859 Sex: Female

..................9 [985] John Adams b: 1861 in Pine Creek, Letcher Co., KY d: 1915 Sex: Male

.........................+[986] Annie Chisenhall b: Abt. 1865 Sex: Female

................8 [987] Ellender "Nellie" Adams b: 1829 Sex: Female

................8 [988] Lydia Adams b: 1833 Sex: Female

.............7 Jane "Jennie" "Jincy" Adams, b: 1789 in NC d: 1863 in Letcher Co., KY Number of children: 10 Sex: Female

...................+Benjamin Webb b: 1785 in NC m: Abt. 1805 d: 1867 in Letcher Co., KY Number of children: 10 Father: James F. Webb, Sr., Soldier Mother: Elizabeth "Lettie" Jane Nelson (Nelson Note: Looking for Elizabeth's ancestors. I believe that she's part of the large Nelson clan from VA and NC, which spread out and migrated west into WV, TN, and KY in the 1830s. Like the author, the Judds [Naomi, Ashley, Wynonna], also descend from this family. The earliest known ancestor of this Nelson group is William "Old William" Nelson, born in 1747 in Prince Edward Co., VA, and died on August 9, 1834, in Hawkins Co., TN. Old William's wife was Rebecca Smith, born about 1757 in Stokes Co., NC. It's possible, in my opinion, that Elizabeth could be Old William's sister) Sex: Male (Webb Notes: Ben Webb was the first sheriff of Floyd Co., KY. Like all of the other Webb individuals in this tree, this Webb family descends from the same line as the country singers Loretta (Webb) Lynn and her sister Brenda Gail "Crystal Gale" Webb. Loretta was born April 14, 1935, in Butcher Hollow, Pike Co., KY; Crystal Gale was born January 9, 1951, in Paintsville, Johnson Co., KY)

................8 Pertaire Webb b: Abt. 1805 Sex: Female

......................+Isaac Adams b: Abt. 1800 Sex: Male

................8 Daniel Webb b: Abt. 1807 d: Abt. 1809 Sex: Male

................8 Nelson Webb b: Abt. 1809 d: Abt. 1811 Sex: Male

................8 [989] Enoch Adams "Captain Dutch" Webb, b: September 16, 1810 in KY Number of children: 13 Sex: Male

......................+Martha Lucas b: Abt. 1815 Sex: Female

................2nd Wife of [989] Enoch Adams "Captain Dutch" Webb, :

......................+Susannah L. Polly, b: 1812 in KY m: April 06, 1829 in Floyd Co., KY d: September 22, 1867 in Letcher Co., KY Number of children: 13 Father: Edward Polly, Mother: Mary Agnes Mullins, Sex: Female

..................9 Benjamin S. Webb b: Abt. 1830 Sex: Male

........................+Nancy Adams b: Abt. 1835 Father: George M. Adams, Mother: Mary "Polly" Hall Sex: Female

..................9 Jane "Jennie" Webb b: 1831 in Letcher Co., KY Number of children: ? Sex: Female

.........................+Randolph Holbrook b: 1836 in Perry Co., KY m: September 1848 in Letcher Co., KY Number of children: ? Father: Benjamin Holbrook, Mother: Nancy Jenkins Sex: Male

......................10 [991] Enoch A. Holbrook b: 1850 in Jenkins, Letcher Co., KY Number of children: 10 Sex: Male

...........................+[990] Nancy Evelyn Webb b: 1849 in Jenkins, Letcher Co., KY m: November 02, 1871 in Letcher Co., KY Number of children: 10 Father: Miles Mayo Webb Mother: Mary "Polly" Holbrook Sex: Female (Webb Note: Like all of the other Webb individuals in this tree, this Webb family descends from the same line as the country singers Loretta (Webb) Lynn and her sister Brenda Gail "Crystal Gale" Webb. Loretta was born April 14, 1935, in Butcher Hollow, Pike Co., KY; Crystal Gale was born January 9, 1951, in Paintsville, Johnson Co., KY)

......................11 [992] Miles Mayo (or Mahoe) Holbrook b: Abt. 1875 Number of children: ? Sex: Male

............................+[993] Flora Collins b: 1878 m: July 29, 1896 in Letcher Co., KY d: 1939 Number of children: ? Father: Henry Powell Collins, Civil War Soldier Mother: Clarissa Ann "Clara" Bowman Sex: Female

......................11 [994] William Oliver Holbrook b: Abt. 1877 Sex: Male

......................11 [995] Randall H. Holbrook b: Abt. 1879 Sex: Male

......................11 [996] Benjamin Holbrook b: Abt. 1881 Sex: Male

......................11 [741] Henrietta "Hennie" Ritter Holbrook b: December 05, 1881 in Letcher Co., KY? d: April 02, 1965 Number of children: 9 Sex: Female

...........................+[418] Robert Grant Yonts b: May 04, 1883 in Letcher Co., KY m: 1901 in Letcher Co., KY d: September 13, 1964 Number of children: 15 Father: William James (Madison?) Yonts, Mother: Sarah "Sally" Bentley, Sex: Male (Yonts Note: like the author and all of the other Yonts individuals in this tree, this family descends from Wilhelm Jans, born in 1714 in the town of Oberalben, Rheineland-Pfalz, Germany; Wilhelm died in 1778 in Rowan Co., NC)

......................11 [997] Jennie Holbrook b: Abt. 1883 Sex: Female

......................11 [998] Nancy Holbrook b: 1884 Sex: Female

......................11 [999] James Monroe Holbrook b: Abt. 1885 Sex: Male

......................11 [1000] Jesse P. Holbrook b: Abt. 1887 Sex: Male

......................11 [1001] Annanias Holbrook b: Abt. 1890 Sex: Unknown

..................9 Edward T. Webb b: November 17, 1832 d: May 09, 1925 Sex: Male

.........................+Betty Adams b: Abt. 1835 Sex: Female

..................9 Henry T. "Chunk" Webb b: June 15, 1836 in Perry Co., KY d: 1920 in Letcher Co., KY Number of children: 2 Sex: Male

...........................+Francis Elizabeth "Franky" Adams b: November 27, 1839 m: September 15, 1866 in Joesville, VA Number of children: 2 Sex: Female (Note: Looking for her ancestors)

......................10 [355] Mary Elizabeth Webb b: July 11, 1861 in Letcher Co., KY d: November 25, 1956 Number of children: ? Sex: Female

...........................+[354] John Dixon Craft b: April 12, 1856 in Craftsville, Letcher Co., KY m: September 13, 1879 d: December 20, 1945 in KY Number of children: ? Father: John Henderson Craft Mother: Nancy "Jane" Caudill, Caudell, Sex: Male

......................11 [500] Nancy Catherine "Nannie" Craft b: February 08, 1882 in Letcher Co., KY d: August 06, 1913 in KY? Sex: Female

...........................+[501] William Wash Webb b: October 1883 in KY Father: Nelson Robinette Webb Mother: Frances Catherine Spangler Sex: Male (Webb Note: Like all of the other Webb individuals in this tree, this Webb family descends from the same line as the country singers Loretta (Webb) Lynn and her sister Brenda Gail "Crystal Gale" Webb. Loretta was born April 14, 1935, in Butcher Hollow, Pike Co., KY; Crystal Gale was born January 9, 1951, in Paintsville, Johnson Co., KY)

....................10 Enoch F. Webb b: September 1865 in Letcher Co., KY d: June 06, 1947 Number of children: 2 Sex: Male

..........................+Laura Venters b: 1869 in VA m: October 07, 1886 d: Bef. 1960 Number of children: 2 Father: George Martin Venters Mother: Rhoda Cosby Branham Sex: Female

.......................11 Nancy Susan Webb b: October 1899 Sex: Female

.......................11 Kelly Webb b: September 30, 1908 d: February 1956 in Kona, Letcher Co., KY Number of children: 2 Sex: Male

..................9 Mary Ann "Pollyann" Webb b: Abt. 1838 Sex: Female

.......................+Henry Adams b: Abt. 1835 Sex: Male

..................9 Andrew L. Webb b: April 08, 1840 Sex: Male

.......................+Nancy Adams b: Abt. 1845 Sex: Female

..................9 Riley M. Webb b: July 04, 1843 Sex: Male

.......................+Hester Hackworth Sex: Female

..................9 Lettie Ann Webb b: Abt. 1844 in Letcher Co., KY Sex: Female

.......................+Richard Polly b: Abt. 1840 Sex: Male

..................9 Sarah Ann Webb b: January 28, 1848 Sex: Female

.......................+Peter Sprangler b: Abt. 1840 Sex: Male

..................9 David L. "Dutch" Webb b: July 1850 Sex: Male

.......................+Sarah Craft b: Abt. 1852 Sex: Female

..................9 Joseph Nelt Webb b: October 04, 1852 Sex: Male

..................9 Enoch Wiley "Dutch" Webb b: January 01, 1853 d: March 22, 1929 Number of children: 2 Sex: Male

.......................+Rachel Adams b: Abt. 1850 Number of children: 2 Sex: Female

....................10 Nannie Webb b: Abt. 1875 Number of children: ? Sex: Female

..........................+Joseph Frazier b: Abt. 1872 Number of children: ? Father: Solomon Frazier Mother: Sarah Fields Sex: Male

.......................11 Enoch Flanery Frazier b: Abt. 1895 Number of children: ? Sex: Male

..........................+Sarah "Elizabeth" Boatright b: Abt. 1897 Number of children: ? Father: Henry Clinton Boatright Mother: Doshie Adams Sex: Female

....................10 Willie George Webb b: December 04, 1891 in Letcher Co., KY d: April 08, 1978 Sex: Male

..........................+Elizabeth "Betty" Whitaker b: June 12, 1891 in Blackey, Letcher Co., KY m: August 31, 1913 d: October 11, 1967 Father: Alamander Whitaker Mother: Catherine Campbell Sex: Female

..................9 Nancy Ritter Webb b: 1856 Sex: Female

...............8 [813] Lettishia "Lettie" Webb b: Abt. 1813 Sex: Female

.......................+[812] Archibald Craft b: Abt. 1820 Father: James Craft Mother: Druscilla Hammonds Sex: Male

...............8 [944] Mary Webb b: March 14, 1818 d: February 05, 1899 Number of children: 9 Sex: Female

.......................+[943] William Green Adams b: January 21, 1820 in Jellico River, Whitley Co., KY m: April 25, 1840 d: June 29, 1862 in Pound River, Wise Co., VA Number of children: 9 Father: William Green "Billy Grit" Adams, Mother: Mary Ann "Polly" Adams, Sex: Male

..................9 [945] Benjamin Adams b: July 04, 1840 Sex: Male

..................9 [946] Purthia Adams b: September 22, 1842 Sex: Female

..................9 [947] Lydia Adams b: November 07, 1844 Sex: Female

.......................+[948] Jesse Collins b: Abt. 1840 Sex: Male

..................9 [949] Sarah Adams b: May 05, 1850 Sex: Female

.......................+[950] Nelson Hampton b: Abt. 1845 Sex: Male

..................9 [951] Lettie Jane Adams b: January 23, 1852 in Letcher Co., KY d: September 08, 1883 Sex: Female

..................9 [952] Jane Adams b: May 10, 1853 Sex: Female

........................+[953] Benjamin Abbott Adams b: Abt. 1850 m: October 09, 1864 in Letcher Co., KY Sex: Male

.................9 [954] Miles Mayo Adams b: June 18, 1855 in Letcher Co., KY Sex: Male

.................9 [955] Simpson E. Adams b: October 29, 1857 in Letcher Co., KY d: May 04, 1935 Sex: Male

.................9 [956] Mary Ellen Adams b: May 27, 1861 in Letcher Co., KY d: September 1889 Number of children: ? Sex: Female

........................+[957] Willis Kirk Collier b: 1859 d: 1944 Number of children: ? Sex: Male

....................10 [958] Harrison Collier b: April 1889 Sex: Male

...............8 [848] Jason L. Webb b: Abt. 1820 Number of children: 9 Sex: Male

.....................+Ludemia (Loudemia) Hubbard b: Abt. 1830 Number of children: ? Father: _____ Hubbard Mother: _____ Bowling, Bolling Sex: Female

.................9 Nehemiah Webb b: Abt. 1860 Sex: Male

...............2nd Wife of [848] Jason L. Web b:

.....................+[847] Elizabeth Craft b: Abt. 1820 m: Abt. 1840 Number of children: 8 Father: James Craft Mother: Druscilla Hammonds Sex: Female

.................9 [849] Nelson Webb b: Abt. 1840 Sex: Male

.................9 [850] Mahala Webb b: Abt. 1843 Sex: Female

.................9 [851] Archibald Webb b: Abt. 1845 Sex: Male

.................9 [852] Wiley W. Webb b: 1847 in Letcher Co., KY Sex: Male

........................+[853] Nancy Adams b: March 07, 1847 in Smoot Creek, Letcher Co., KY d: September 25, 1925 Father: Isaac B. Adams Mother: Nancy Hayes Sex: Female

.................9 [854] Mary Webb b: Abt. 1849 Sex: Female

.................9 [855] Anna Webb b: Abt. 1851 Sex: Female

.................9 [856] Benjamin Webb b: Abt. 1855 Sex: Male

.................9 [857] Drusilla Webb b: Abt. 1857 Sex: Female

...............8 Miles Mayo Webb b: June 27, 1822 in Millstone, KY d: September 20, 1912 Number of children: 2 Sex: Male

.....................+Mary "Polly" Holbrook b: February 13, 1826 d: October 23, 1892 Number of children: 2 Father: Benjamin Holbrook, Mother: Nancy Jenkins Sex: Female

.................9 [990] Nancy Evelyn Webb b: 1849 in Jenkins, Letcher Co., KY Number of children: 10 Sex: Female

........................+[991] Enoch A. Holbrook b: 1850 in Jenkins, Letcher Co., KY m: November 02, 1871 in Letcher Co., KY Number of children: 10 Father: Randolph Holbrook Mother: Jane "Jennie" Webb Sex: Male

....................10 [992] Miles Mayo (or Mahoe) Holbrook b: Abt. 1875 Number of children: ? Sex: Male

...........................+[993] Flora Collins b: 1878 m: July 29, 1896 in Letcher Co., KY d: 1939 Number of children: ? Father: Henry Powell Collins, Civil War Soldier Mother: Clarissa Ann "Clara" Bowman Sex: Female

.....................11 Arias K. Holbrook b: 1923 d: 1983 Sex: Male

..............................+Blanche Bowling, unknown line b: April 05, 1927 Sex: Female (Note: Looking for her ancestors)

....................10 [994] William Oliver Holbrook b: Abt. 1877 Sex: Male

....................10 [995] Randall H. Holbrook b: Abt. 1879 Sex: Male

....................10 [996] Benjamin Holbrook b: Abt. 1881 Sex: Male

....................10 [741] Henrietta "Hennie" Ritter Holbrook b: December 05, 1881 in Letcher Co., KY? d: April 02, 1965 Number of children: 9 Sex: Female

...........................+[418] Robert Grant Yonts b: May 04, 1883 in Letcher Co., KY m: 1901 in Letcher Co., KY d: September 13, 1964 Number of children: 15 Father: William James Yonts, Mother: Sarah "Sally" Bentley, Sex: Male (Yonts Note: like the author and all of the other Yonts individuals in this tree, this family descends from Wilhelm Jans, born in 1714 in the town of

Oberalben, Rheineland-Pfalz, Germany; Wilhelm died in 1778 in Rowan Co., NC)

...................11 Sarah Elvinse Yonts b: November 17, 1902 d: August 14, 1982 in KY 40489 Number of children: 2 Sex: Female

...........................+Roder Padgett b: June 12, 1901 Number of children: 2 Sex: Male

...................11 Nancy Chaney Yonts b: September 16, 1904 d: December 27, 1955 Number of children: 3 Sex: Female

...........................+Clayton Anderson b: Abt. 1900 Number of children: 3 Sex: Male

...................11 Squire Lincoln Yonts b: December 06, 1906 d: November 20, 1940 Number of children: 2 Sex: Male

...........................+Lena _____? b: August 24, 1904 Number of children: 2 Sex: Female

...................11 Bessie Jane Yonts b: November 09, 1908 d: November 24, 1979 in KY 40489 Number of children: 13 Sex: Female

...........................+Harve (Harvey?) Padgett b: May 23, 1902 Number of children: 13 Sex: Male

...................11 Margie Rene Yonts b: May 12, 1911 in Neon, KY d: August 14, 1984 in Fairfield, Ohio Number of children: 2 Sex: Female

...........................+Dennie Green Singleton b: June 02, 1906 in Waynesburg, KY m: May 11, 1933 d: May 29, 1987 in Fairfield, Ohio Number of children: 2 Father: William Singleton Mother: Mary _____? Sex: Male

...................11 Rosie Alverine Yonts b: August 23, 1913 d: May 09, 1914 Sex: Female

...................11 Enoch Jessie Morris Yonts, Sr. b: November 26, 1917 d: October 23, 1980 in Waynesburg, KY Number of children: 3 Sex: Male

...........................+Vernice Irvin b: November 08, 1923 Number of children: 3 Sex: Female

...................11 Laurie Ethel Yonts b: July 10, 1920 d: September 15, 1997 in Lexington, KY Number of children: 5 Sex: Female

...........................+Orville Padgett b: July 19, 1918 Number of children: 5 Sex: Male

...................11 Barbie Alice Yonts b: July 05, 1922 Number of children: 5 Sex: Female

...........................+James Weaver b: February 08, 1914 Number of children: 5 Sex: Male

...................10 [997] Jennie Holbrook b: Abt. 1883 Sex: Female

...................10 [998] Nancy Holbrook b: 1884 Sex: Female

...................10 [999] James Monroe Holbrook b: Abt. 1885 Sex: Male

...................10 [1000] Jesse P. Holbrook b: Abt. 1887 Sex: Male

...................10 [1001] Annanias Holbrook b: Abt. 1890 Sex: Unknown

...............9 Nelson Robinette Webb b: March 12, 1860 in KY Number of children: ? Sex: Male

...........................+Frances Catherine Spangler b: Abt. 1862 Number of children: ? Sex: Female

...................10 [501] William Wash Webb b: October 1883 in KY Sex: Male

...........................+[500] Nancy Catherine "Nannie" Craft b: February 08, 1882 in Letcher Co., KY d: August 06, 1913 in KY? Father: John Dixon Craft Mother: Mary Elizabeth Webb Sex: Female

...................2nd Wife of [501] William Wash Webb b:

...........................+Perlie Hall b: Abt. 1896 in Letcher Co., KY m: September 26, 1915 in Letcher Co., KY Father: David Hall Mother: Martha Brown Sex: Female

.............8 [932] Sarah Webb b: 1825 d: 1897 Number of children: 10 Sex: Female

...................+[931] Simpson (or Sampson) Adams b: 1818 in Jellico River, Whitley Co., KY d: 1910 in Pine Creek, Letcher Co., KY Number of children: 10 Father: William Green "Billy Grit" Adams, Mother: Mary Ann "Polly" Adams, Sex: Male

...............9 [933] Jane Adams b: 1846 Sex: Female

...............9 [934] Mary M. Adams b: 1849 Sex: Female

...............9 [935] Lettie Adams b: 1853 d: 1925 Sex: Female

...............9 [936] Lydia (twin) Adams b: March 14, 1855 Sex: Female

...............9 [937] Rachel (twin) Adams b: 1855 Sex: Female

...............9 [938] Benjamin Jackson Adams b: 1856 d: 1938 Sex: Male

...............9 [939] Jason Adams b: 1860 Sex: Male

...............9 [940] Enoch M. Adams b: 1863 Sex: Male

................9 [941] Spencer Adams b: 1866 Sex: Male

................9 [942] Simpson M. Adams b: 1869 d: 1889 Sex: Male

...............8 Wiley M. Webb b: October 30, 1827 Sex: Male

.....................+Elizabeth Polly b: Abt. 1830 Sex: Female

............7 Simpson Polly Adams b: Abt. 1790 Sex: Female

............7 [1002] Benjamin Adams, b: 1794 in Roaring Rv., Wilkes, N.C. d: November 11, 1855 in Letcher Co. KY Number of children: 4 Sex: Male

...................+[1003] Nancy Holbrook, b: 1799 in Roaring Rv., Wilkes, N.C. m: February 10, 1816 in Prestonburg, Floyd, KY d: Aft. 1870 in Letcher Co. KY Number of children: 4 Father: Randolph (or Randel) "Buck" Holbrook, Mother: Elizabeth Nancy Rebecca Adams, Sex: Female

...............8 [396] John Isom Adams b: 1818 d: 1863 in (Note: Died trying to open an unexploded bomb to get at the gun powder inside) Number of children: 7 Sex: Male

.....................+[397] Sarah "Sallie" Craft b: April 02, 1821 m: August 16, 1838 d: March 26, 1863 in Letcher Co., KY Number of children: 7 Father: James Craft Mother: Druscilla Hammonds Sex: Female

................9 [398] Benjamin Burford Adams b: 1840 Sex: Male

................9 [399] James W. Adams b: 1842 Sex: Male

................9 [400] Nancy Jane Adams b: 1845 Sex: Female

................9 [401] Jesse Adams b: 1847 Sex: Male

................9 [402] Joseph Simpson Adams b: 1851 Sex: Male

................9 [403] Randolph N. Adams b: 1854 Sex: Male

................9 [404] Archelous Adams b: 1858 Sex: Male

...............8 [1004] Jesse Adams, b: 1821 in Perry Co., KY d: in Letcher Co., KY Number of children: ? Sex: Male

.....................+[1005] Margaret Jenkins b: 1826 in Perry Co., KY m: August 20, 1846 in Letcher Co., KY d: October 09, 1882 in Letcher Co., KY Number of children: ? Father: William Jenkins Sex: Female

................9 [1006] Elizabeth Adams, b: Bet. November 1844 - 1845 in Letcher Co., KY Sex: Female

........................+[1007] Jesse S. Holbrook, b: February 06, 1837 in Perry Co., KY m: Abt. 1861 in Harlan, KY or Letcher Co., KY Father: Benjamin Holbrook, Mother: Nancy Jenkins Sex: Male Burial: Craft Cemetery, Millstone, KY?

...............8 [1008] Elizabeth Adams b: Abt. 1824 d: July 1880 Number of children: 9 Sex: Female

.....................+[1009] James Bates, Sr. b: Abt. 1823 in Letcher Co., KY, (Perry) m: February 26, 1843 in Letcher Co., KY d: April 11, 1864 Murdered in Letcher Co., KY during the Civil War Number of children: 9 Father: John Wallis Bates, Sr., Sheriff Mother: Sarah Walthrop, or Waltrop Sex: Male Burial: Kona KY, Bates Cem

................9 [1010] Henry C. Bates b: Abt. 1844 in Letcher Co., KY Sex: Male

........................+[1011] Rachel Lee b: Abt. 1840 in Russell Co., VA m: March 13, 1868 in Letcher Co., KY Sex: Female

................9 [1012] Sarah Bates b: Abt. 1846 Sex: Female

................9 [1013] Nancy Bates b: October 28, 1848 in Millstone, Letcher Co., KY d: September 10, 1927 in Beefhide, Letcher Co., KY Number of children: 12 Sex: Female Burial: Nancy Wright Cemetery, Beefhide, KY

........................+[1014] Andrew J. Wright, b: November 14, 1847 in Beefhide, Letcher Co., KY m: December 09, 1870 in Joel Wright's home?, Letcher Co., KY d: January 28, 1919 in Beefhide, Letcher Co., KY Number of children: 12 Father: Samuel W. Wright, Mother: Elizabeth "Betsy" Adams, Sex: Male Burial: Samuel W. Wright Cemetery, Beefhide, KY

.....................10 [405] Joel M. "Big Joel" Wright b: December 08, 1871 in Beefhide Creek, Beefhide, KY d: December 20, 1921 in Jenkins (Letcher Co.) , KY Number of children: 6 Sex: Male Burial: Nancy Wright Cemetery, Beefhide, KY

...........................+[1015] Cordelia Mullins b: Abt. 1871 in KY? m: February 24, 1892 Sex:

Female

....................2nd Wife of [405] Joel M. "Big Joel" Wright:

...........................+[1016] Susan Wright b: Abt. 1875 in KY? m: August 20, 1895 Sex: Female

....................3rd Wife of [405] Joel M. "Big Joel" Wright:

...........................+[1017] Mahala Sowards b: Abt. 1875 in KY? m: February 27, 1896 Number of children: 6 Sex: Female

......................11 Nancy Wright b: May 1898 Sex: Male

......................11 Adeline Wright b: November 18, 1899 Sex: Female

...........................+Frank Brown Sex: Male

......................11 Cora Wright b: Abt. 1904 Sex: Female

......................11 Sarah Wright b: Abt. 1906 Sex: Female

......................11 Johnson Wright b: Abt. 1907 Sex: Male

......................11 Edward Wright b: Abt. 1910 Sex: Male

....................10 [1018] Elizabeth Wright b: March 30, 1874 in Beefhide Creek, Beefhide, KY d: October 16, 1957 Number of children: 5 Sex: Female

...........................+[1019] Henry Blevins b: Abt. 1875 in KY? m: November 21, 1901 Number of children: 5 Sex: Male

....................10 [406] Eliza J. Wright b: December 13, 1875 in Beefhide Creek, Beefhide, KY d: January 10, 1946 in Norton, VA Sex: Female

...........................+[1020] Joe Willis b: Abt. 1875 in KY? Sex: Male

....................2nd Husband of [406] Eliza J. Wright:

...........................+[1021] Isaac "Ike" Mills b: Abt. 1875 in KY? m: October 04, 1900 Sex: Male

....................10 [1022] Sarah J. Wright b: November 16, 1877 in Beefhide KY d: May 02, 1920 in Burdine, Letcher Co., KY Number of children: 5 Sex: Female Burial: Burdine, Letcher Co., KY

...........................+[1023] William ("Willie") Blevins b: Abt. 1875 in KY? m: March 01, 1900 Number of children: 5 Sex: Male

....................10 [1024] Victoria Wright b: October 26, 1878 in Beefhide, KY d: December 11, 1940 in Letcher Co., KY Sex: Female Burial: Beefhide Creek, Beefhide, KY

...........................+[1025] Rathburn Burke b: November 12, 1859 m: April 18, 1922 d: May 13, 1942 Sex: Male

....................10 [1026] Margaret "Maggie" Wright b: August 06, 1880 in Beefhide, KY d: September 01, 1923 in Letcher Co., KY Number of children: 12 Sex: Female Burial: Nancy Wright Cemetery, Beefhide, KY

...........................+[1027] John Brown b: Abt. 1880 in KY? m: June 22, 1899 Number of children: 12 Sex: Male

....................10 [1028] William James Wright b: December 28, 1882 in Beefhide, KY d: April 15, 1940 in VA Number of children: 10 Sex: Male Burial: Nancy Wright Cemetery, Beefhide, KY

...........................+[1029] Elizabeth Mullins b: Abt. 1885 in KY? m: 1913 Number of children: 10 Sex: Female

....................10 [1030] Martha Josephine Wright b: November 18, 1884 in Beefhide, KY d: March 26, 1960 in VA Number of children: 8 Sex: Female Burial: Nancy Wright Cemetery, Beefhide, KY

...........................+[1031] John Wesley Ellison b: Abt. 1885 in KY? m: November 23, 1905 Number of children: 8 Sex: Male

....................10 [1032] John Wallis Wright b: February 06, 1887 in Beefhide, KY d: June 26, 1965 in Virginia Beach, VA Number of children: 10 Sex: Male Burial: Nancy Wright Cemetery, Beefhide, KY

...........................+[1033] Alka Mae Wright b: April 23, 1903 in Beefhide, KY m: November 05, 1919 d: October 19, 1986 in Virginia Beach, VA Number of children: 10 Father: Austin McJesse Wright Mother: Elizabeth Mullins Sex: Female Burial: Colonial Grove, Cemetery VA Beach, VA

......................11 Stella Nadina 'Poodie' Wright b: April 22, 1920 in Beefhide, KY Sex: Female

......................11 Icie Gertrude Wright b: January 07, 1922 in Beefhide, KY Sex: Female

......................11 Mona Estelle Wright b: November 10, 1924 in Beefhide, KY d: January 27,

1933 in Beefhide, KY Sex: Female Burial: Nancy Wreight, Cemetery Beefhide, KY

.......................11 Coleman Wallace Wright b: March 16, 1926 in Beefhide, KY Sex: Male

.......................11 Audrey Orbena Wright b: October 16, 1928 in Beefhide, KY Sex: Female

.......................11 Dorgan Pamela Wright b: April 14, 1931 in Beefhide, KY Sex: Female

.......................11 Billa Verne Wright b: January 24, 1934 in Beefhide, KY d: July 17, 1991 in Kettering, OH Sex: Male

.......................11 Marjorie Wright b: March 31, 1936 in Beefhide, KY Sex: Female

.......................11 Donald Ross Wright b: July 15, 1939 in Beefhide, KY d: March 18, 1977 Sex: Male

.......................11 James Webster Wright b: May 04, 1942 in Beefhide, KY Sex: Male

.....................10 [407] Etta Wright b: November 16, 1888 in Beefhide, Letcher Co., KY d: October 09, 1977 in Jenkins, Letcher Co., KY Sex: Female Burial: Nancy Wright Cemetery, Beefhide, Letcher Co., KY

...........................+[1034] T. O. Webb b: Abt. 1885 in KY? m: August 20, 1913 Sex: Male

.....................2nd Husband of [407] Etta Wright:

...........................+[1035] Lemuel Haynes b: Abt. 1890 in KY? m: September 21, 1915 Sex: Male

.....................10 [1036] Samuel Wright b: April 03, 1891 in Beefhide, KY d: May 18, 1936 in Beefhide, KY Number of children: 10 Sex: Male Burial: Nancy Wright Cemetery, Beefhide, KY

...........................+[1037] Ollie Bentley b: Abt. 1890 in KY? m: 1917 Number of children: 10 Sex: Female

.....................10 [1038] Ritter Wright, b: July 06, 1893 in Beefhide, KY d: September 15, 1953 in Fleming, KY Number of children: 5 Sex: Female Burial: Thornton Cem, Thornton, Letcher Co., KY

...........................+[1039] Jacob "Jake" Martin Adkins, b: March 24, 1893 in Greasy Creek, KY m: June 07, 1916 in Letcher Co., KY d: October 05, 1959 in Fleming, KY Number of children: 5 Father: Nelson Adkins, Mother: Malinda Robinson Sex: Male Burial: Thornton Cem, Thornton, Letcher Co., KY (Adkins Note: like the author and all of the other Adkins individuals in this tree and their descendants, this family descends from European royalty through Elizabeth Parker, born about 1697 in Charles City or Richmond, Henrico Co., VA. Elizabeth's husband was William Adkins/Atkinson, born March 28, 1689, in Charles City, Henrico Co. VA. Elizabeth is the proven 12th great-granddaughter of the King of England, Henry III, born October 1, 1206, in Winchester Castle, Hampshire Co., England)

.......................11 Nancy Irene Adkins b: May 13, 1918 in Beefhide KY Number of children: ? Sex: Female

...........................+James Howard May b: February 02, 1919 in Boone, N.C. m: June 07, 1940 d: January 27, 1955 in Memphis, TN. Number of children: ? Father: James Arthur May Mother: Dora Shirley Lewis Sex: Male Burial: Lansing, MI.

.......................11 James Martin Adkins b: March 19, 1921 in McRoberts KY d: July 10, 1977 in Benton IL Number of children: 8 Sex: Male Burial: Benton IL

...........................+Lillie Mae Stevens b: Abt. 1921 m: December 23, 1939 Number of children: 8 Sex: Female

.......................11 Roberta Adkins b: April 09, 1923 in McRoberts KY Number of children: 2 Sex: Female

...........................+Clyde Swanagin b: Abt. 1920 m: March 11, 1944 Number of children: 2 Father: G. Edward Swanagin Mother: Annie Yarber Sex: Male

.......................11 [1040] Mabel Hay Adkins b: June 18, 1925 d: April 30, 1986 Number of children: ? Sex: Female

...........................+_____ _____? b: Abt. 1925 m: October 24, 1945 Sex: Male

.......................2nd Husband of [1040] Mabel Hay Adkins:

...........................+Albert Henry Bostain b: Abt. 1925 m: October 24, 1945 Number of children: ? Sex: Male

.......................11 Billie Richard Adkins b: February 18, 1928 in Jenkins KY Number of children:

4 Sex: Male

............................+Bobby Jean Privett b: Abt. 1930 m: October 20, 1948 Number of children: 4 Sex: Female

.................9 [408] John W. 'Ringer' Bates b: November 23, 1852 in Letcher Co., KY d: November 24, 1932 Number of children: 7 Sex: Male

.....................+[1041] Mary Pigmon m: Abt. 1882 Number of children: 7 Sex: Female

...................10 [1042] Wlliam Bates b: Abt. 1883 d: August 16, 1959 Sex: Male

...................10 [1043] George Washington Bates b: 1884 in KY Sex: Male

...................10 [1044] James Bates b: 1886 in KY d: 1910 in Lexington, KY Sex: Male

...................10 [1045] Martin Van Bates b: 1888 d: 1904 in KY Sex: Male

...................10 [1046] Landis Dewey Bates b: December 25, 1890 in Knox Co., KY d: March 21, 1973 Sex: Male

.........................+[1047] Mary L. Hayes m: August 14, 1915 in Jenkins, KY Sex: Female

...................10 [1048] T. Monroe Bates b: 1892 in Pine Top, KY d: 1956 in Wise, VA Sex: Male

.........................+[1049] Edna Dale b: Abt. 1895 Sex: Female

...................10 [1050] Maggie Bates b: 1894 in Pine Top, KY Sex: Female

...............................+[1051] Christopher Columbus Tackett b: Abt. 1890 Sex: Male

.................2nd Wife of [408] John W. 'Ringer' Bates:

.........................+[1052] Elizabeth Gibson b: Abt. 1855 m: July 26, 1901 in Letcher Co., KY Sex: Female

.................9 [1053] Martha Bates b: January 19, 1855 in Letcher Co., KY Sex: Female

.................9 [1054] Letha Jane 'Jenny' Bates b: Abt. 1858 in Letcher Co., KY d: October 21, 1919 in Letcher Co., KY Sex: Female

.................9 [1055] Margaret Bates b: Abt. 1860 in Letcher Co., KY d: 1874 in Letcher Co., KY Sex: Female

.................9 [1056] James Bates, Jr. b: Abt. 1863 in Letcher Co., KY Sex: Male

.................9 [1057] Letitia "Lettie/Moody" Bates b: November 15, 1851 in Letcher Co., KY ? d: May 12, 1934 in Letcher Co., KY ? Number of children: 12 Sex: Female Burial: Thornton Cemetery, Letcher Co., KY

.........................+[1058] William S. Wright b: Bet. July 07 - 09, 1855 in Letcher Co., KY or Scott Co., VA m: April 12, 1872 in Letcher Co., KY d: January 30, 1900 in Boone Creek (Letcher Co.,?) , KY Number of children: 12 Father: Wilhelm "Bill" Luntz Mother: Sidney Wright Sex: Male Burial: Thornton Cem, Letcher Co., Ky

...................10 [1059] Nancy Wright b: April 25, 1873 in Baker, KY d: February 04, 1927 in Pikeville, KY Sex: Female

.........................+[412] James Johnson, Sr. b: Abt. 1870 m: April 26, 1888 in Letcher Co., KY Number of children: 4 Sex: Male

...................10 [409] Martha E. Wright b: December 12, 1874 in Seco or Baker, KY d: Bet. November 22, 1925 - 1926 in SeCo., KY Number of children: 4 Sex: Female Burial: Thornton Cemetery, Letcher Co., KY

.........................+[1060] _____ Pigman b: Abt. 1870 Sex: Male

.................2nd Husband of [409] Martha E. Wright:

.........................+[1061] _____ Bullard b: Abt. 1870 Sex: Male Burial: (Notes: not sure if he was her husband or not) .

.................3rd Husband of [409] Martha E. Wright:

.........................+[1062] William ("Willie") Venters b: April 09, 1874 in Jenkins, Letcher Co., KY m: July 31, 1893 in SeCo., Letcher Co , KY d: August 31, 1901 in Dunham, Jenkins, Letcher Co., KY Number of children: 4 Father: John Venters Mother: Mary Juliette Mullins Sex: Male Burial: Thornton Cemetery, Letcher Co., KY

.........................11 Lettie Venters b: May 1894 in Kona, KY d: March 22, 1923 in SeCo., KY Sex: Female

...............................+Tony Raniero b: Abt. 1890 in KY? Sex: Male

..................11 [1063] James Martin Venters b: June 09, 1896 in Kona, KY d: August 21, 1928 in SeCo., KY Sex: Male

..........................+Florence Evelyn Stanley b: April 18, 1900 in WV m: March 1916 in KY ? d: February 22, 1924 in SeCo., KY Sex: Female

..................2nd Wife of [1063] James Martin Venters:

..........................+Gertrude Lucas b: November 10, 1908 m: 1926 d: January 25, 1987 in Elkton, Maryland Sex: Female

..................11 Joseph Coleman Venters b: March 22, 1898 in Kona, KY d: March 02, 1984 in Holden, WV Sex: Male

..........................+Lillie Alice Mauk b: October 24, 1902 in LKline, KY m: November 02, 1920 in Holden, West Virginia d: April 18, 1990 in Huntington, WV Sex: Female

..................11 John Venters b: January 31, 1900 in Kona, KY d: September 25, 1944 Sex: Male

..........................+Carrie Lucas b: March 27, 1904 Sex: Female

..................10 [1064] Samuel Tilden Wright b: March 31, 1878 in Seco or McRoberts, KY d: April 27, 1974 in Letcher Co., KY Sex: Male Burial: Thornton Cemetery, Letcher Co., KY

..........................+[1065] Lydia Margaret Craft b: 1880 m: June 29, 1899 in Letcher Co., KY d: 1964 Sex: Female

..................10 [1066] Mary Wright b: April 04, 1880 in Letcher Co., KY d: March 1969 in Lexington, KY Sex: Female

..........................+[1067] William Wiley Craft b: Abt. 1880 in Letcher Co., KY ? m: 1897 in Letcher Co., KY Sex: Male

..................10 [1068] William Wright b: June 30, 1882 in Letcher Co., KY d: April 10, 1901 in SeCo., KY Sex: Male

..................10 [410] Theophalis Garret Wright b: Bet. May 15, 1884 - 1885 in Letcher Co., KY d: April 13, 1953 Sex: Male

..........................+[1069] Mandy _____? b: Abt. 1890 Sex: Female

..................2nd Wife of [410] Theophalis Garret Wright:

..........................+[1070] Carrie Blair b: Abt. 1885 in Letcher Co., KY ? m: August 30, 1907 in Letcher Co., KY Sex: Female

..................3rd Wife of [410] Theophalis Garret Wright:

..........................+[1071] Sylvia Hicks b: Abt. 1885 m: June 21, 1935 Sex: Female

..................10 [411] Joseph F. Wright b: July 01, 1886 in Baker, KY d: January 1975 in Russell, KY Number of children: 3 Sex: Male

..........................+[1072] Lillie Smallwood b: Abt. 1890 Number of children: 2 Sex: Female

..................11 Captain Wright Sex: Male

..................11 Garrett Wright Sex: Male

..................2nd Wife of [411] Joseph F. Wright:

..........................+[1073] Lilly Isom b: Abt. 1890 Number of children: ? Sex: Female

..................11 William T Wright b: Abt. 1910 in KY Sex: Male

..................10 [1074] John W. Wright b: April 09, 1888 d: December 30, 1945 Sex: Male

..........................+[1075] Arlena Mason b: Abt. 1890 Sex: Female

..................10 [1076] Nancy "Nan" Wright b: April 25, 1873 in Baker, KY d: February 04, 1927 in Pikeville, KY Number of children: 4 Sex: Female

..........................+[412] James Johnson, Sr. b: Abt. 1870 m: April 26, 1888 in Letcher Co., KY Number of children: 4 Sex: Male

..................11 Charley Johnson Sex: Male

..................11 William Johnson d: Abt. 1944 Sex: Male

..................11 James Johnson, Jr. Sex: Male

..................11 Ben Johnson Sex: Male

..................10 [1077] Henrietta "Ritter" Wright b: September 21, 1876 in Letcher Co., KY d: October 16, 1961 Number of children: 11 Sex: Female

..........................+[1078] L. Bert Tolliver b: Abt. 1870 in Letcher Co., KY ? m: July 12, 1894 in Letcher Co., KY d: Abt. 1934 Number of children: 11 Sex: Male

.....................11 Lettie Tolliver Sex: Female

...........................+Archibald Leach Sex: Male

.....................11 Verna Tolliver Sex: Female

.....................11 Melvin Tolliver Sex: Male

.....................11 Nannie Tolliver Sex: Female

.....................11 Arminta Tolliver b: Abt. 1895 Sex: Female

...........................+Henry Bates b: September 05, 1892 in Hindman, KY m: September 05, 1913 d: July 01, 1974 Father: Robert ("Robin") Bates Mother: Elizabeth Bentley Sex: Male

.....................11 Frona Tolliver Sex: Female

.....................11 George Tolliver Sex: Male

.....................11 Millard Tolliver Sex: Male

.....................11 Carrie Tolliver Sex: Female

.....................11 Ray Tolliver Sex: Male

.....................11 Joe Tolliver Sex: Male

....................10 [413] Benjamin Franklin Wright, Dr. b: March 12, 1891 in Whitaker, KY d: August 11, 1969 in Whitaker, KY Number of children: 3 Sex: Male Burial: SeCo., Ky

.........................+[1079] Scottie McClure b: Abt. 1895 Sex: Female

...................2nd Wife of [413] Benjamin Franklin Wright, Dr.:

.........................+[1080] Hazel Iris Adams b: Abt. 1895 Sex: Female

...................3rd Wife of [413] Benjamin Franklin Wright, Dr.:

...........................+[1081] Fanny Hall b: May 15, 1894 in Wise Co., VA d: April 03, 1940 in Letcher Co., KY ? Number of children: 3 Father: L. M. Hall Sex: Female Burial: Thornton Cemetery, Letcher Co., KY

.....................11 Edgar Allen P. Wright b: June 24, 1912 d: February 23, 1920 Sex: Male Burial: Thornton Cemetery, Letcher Co., KY

.....................11 Eva Irene Wright b: Abt. 1914 Sex: Female

.....................11 William Wright b: Abt. 1916 Sex: Male

....................10 [414] Lettie Dallas Wright b: January 08, 1894 in SeCo., KY d: April 04, 1974 Number of children: 7 Sex: Female Burial: Thorton, KY

.........................+[415] Archie C. Craft, Jr. b: May 09, 1884 m: November 05, 1919 in Letcher Co., KY d: July 06, 1959 Number of children: 7 Father: Joseph Craft Mother: Rasuea Bagwell Sex: Male

.....................11 [1082] Esta Craft b: January 14, 1913 in Letcher Co., KY d: 1991 in Pike Co., KY Number of children: 4 Sex: Female

...........................+[1083] Roy Conway b: 1906 d: 1950 in Pike Co., KY Number of children: 4 Sex: Male Burial: 1950 Thorton, KY

...................2nd Husband of [1082] Esta Craft:

...........................+[1083] Roy Conway b: 1906 m: May 27, 1933 in KY d: 1950 in Pike Co., KY Number of children: 4 Sex: Male Burial: 1950 Thorton, KY

.....................11 Garnett Craft b: July 19, 1914 in Letcher Co., KY Sex: Male

...........................+Mildred Daniels Sex: Female

.....................11 Morris Craft b: February 29, 1916 in Letcher Co., KY Sex: Male

...........................+Nila Kelly Sex: Female

.....................11 Narciassus Craft b: December 15, 1918 in Letcher Co., KY d: August 28, 1972 Sex: Female

...........................+Bernard Grubbs Sex: Male

.....................11 Letty June Craft b: December 15, 1918 in Letcher Co., KY d: November 11, 1960 Sex: Female

...........................+Theodore Cook b: Abt. 1915 Sex: Male

.....................11 William Craft b: November 28, 1923 in Letcher Co., KY d: January 29, 1944 Sex: Male

...........................+Margie _____? b: Abt. 1925 Sex: Female

.......................11 Wiley Jack Craft b: July 12, 1929 in Letcher Co., KY d: December 26, 1981 Sex: Male

...........................+Coleen Morgan Sex: Female

...............8 [416] Randolph "Randall" Adams b: November 30, 1834 in Perry Co., KY d: 1909 in Letcher Co., KY Number of children: ? Sex: Male Burial: Webb Cemetery, Mayking, Letcher, KY

.......................+[1084] Martha Hale b: 1841 in VA d: Bef. 1900 in Letcher Co., KY Number of children: ? Father: James Dickerson Hale Mother: Jane Grizzle Sex: Female

...................9 [1085] Martha "Mattie" Adams b: March 27, 1880 d: December 03, 1945 Sex: Female

.......................+[1086] Stephen Gilley b: Abt. 1875 Sex: Male

...............2nd Wife of [416] Randolph "Randall" Adams:

.......................+[1087] Louise Jenkins b: 1840 Sex: Female

...............3rd Wife of [416] Randolph "Randall" Adams:

.......................+[1088] Sarah Fields b: Abt. 1875 m: 1901 Sex: Female

.............7 Mary Ann Adams b: 1795 in Wilkes Co., NC d: September 17, 1872 in Letcher Co., KY Number of children: 5 Sex: Female

...................+Johnson (or Jonathan) Banks b: 1792 in Wilkes Co., NC m: February 23, 1814 in Wilkes Co., NC d: in Letcher Co., KY Number of children: 5 Father: John Gold Banks, Jr. Mother: Cassandra "Cassie" Bishop Sex: Male

...............8 John Goold Banks b: Abt. 1819 in Wilkes Co., NC Number of children: ? Sex: Male

.......................+Catherine Pence b: 1824 in Breathitt Co., KY m: 1844 Number of children: ? Father: Andrew Pence Mother: Rebecca Holland, Hollon Sex: Female

...................9 [1089] Andrew Banks b: Abt. 1845 Sex: Male

.......................+Rebecca Pelfrey b: Abt. 1850 d: 1874 Sex: Female

...............2nd Wife of [1089] Andrew Banks:

.......................+Ellen (Elander) Pelfrey b: Abt. 1852 m: Abt. 1875 Sex: Female

...............8 [798] Cassandra "Cassie" Banks b: 1825 in Wilkes Co., NC d: 1870 Number of children: 14 Sex: Female

.......................+[793] John B. Adams b: 1847 d: 1882 in Paintsville, KY Number of children: 8 Father: Spencer Adams Mother: Jane "Jenny" Amburgey Sex: Male

...............2nd Husband of [798] Cassandra "Cassie" Banks:

.......................+[797] Spencer Adams b: 1822 in Rockhouse Creek, Floyd Co., KY m: Abt. 1842 in (Note: they may not have married) Number of children: 16 Father: Stephen "Rockhouse Steve" Adams Mother: Ellendar "Nellie" Buntin, or Benton Sex: Male

...................9 [1090] Mary Ann Banks b: Abt. 1843 in KY Number of children: ? Sex: Female

.......................+[1091] Gideon Ison b: May 14, 1844 m: March 09, 1871 in Letcher Co., KY d: July 29, 1903 in Defeated Creek, KY Number of children: ? Father: Gideon Ison Mother: Rachel Stamper Sex: Male

...................10 [1092] Susan Ison b: December 15, 1871 in Letcher Co., KY Number of children: 2 Sex: Female

...........................+[1093] Kelly Hogg b: Abt. 1861 in Letcher Co., KY m: in Letcher Co., KY d: January 12, 1937 Number of children: 2 Father: Hiram Wesley Hogg Mother: Margaret Brashear Sex: Male

.......................11 [1094] Virgie Hogg Sex: Female

.......................11 [1095] Myrtle Hogg Sex: Female

...................9 [1096] Elijah Banks b: Abt. 1847 Sex: Male Burial: Banks Cemetery, Letcher Co., KY

.......................+[1097] Elizabeth Burton b: Abt. 1860 m: February 25, 1868 in KY? Sex: Female Burial: Banks Cemetery, Letcher Co., KY

...................9 [1098] Sarah Banks b: Abt. 1848 in KY Sex: Female

...................9 [1099] Ester Banks b: Abt. 1851 Sex: Female

...................9 [1100] Harrison Banks b: June 23, 1854 Sex: Male

........................+[1101] Millie Combs b: January 01, 1863 m: Bet. 1877 - 1880 d: March 03, 1911 Father: John Wesley Combs, Mother: Polly (Mary) Hogg Sex: Female

...................9 [1102] Wesley Banks b: February 18, 1855 Sex: Male

...................9 [1103] Nancy Banks b: Abt. 1856 Sex: Female

...................9 [799] Lincoln "Link" Banks b: 1859 in Letcher Co., KY d: 1888 in Whitesburg, Letcher, Co., KY Number of children: 2 Sex: Male Burial: The Babe Isom Cemetery on Rockhouse Creek (Notes: Link was murdered by Jim Frazier; case was dismissed before trial)

........................+[1104] Lucinda Breeding b: November 26, 1865 in Letcher Co., KY m: Abt. 1881 d: March 15, 1948 in Sackett, Letcher Co., KY Number of children: ? Father: John Breeding Mother: Elizabeth "Betty" Combs Sex: Female Burial: Ison Cemetery, Johnson Funeral Home, Hazard, Perry Co., KY

.......................10 [1105] Malissie "Lissie" Breeding b: March 21, 1882 in Letcher Co., KY d: May 04, 1924 in Knott Co., KY Number of children: 6 Sex: Female Burial: The Seymore Amburgey Cemeter at Bath, Knott Co., KY

...........................+[1106] James Robert "Crick" Collins b: December 15, 1881 Number of children: 6 Father: James Wesley Collins Mother: Elizabeth "Liz" Amburgey Sex: Male

.......................11 [1107] Lola Collins b: November 23, 1899 Sex: Female

.......................11 [1108] Luly Collins b: January 18, 1902 Sex: Female

.......................11 [1109] Lizzie Collins b: December 25, 1903 Sex: Female

.......................11 [1110] Johnny L. Collins b: August 25, 1906 Sex: Male

.......................11 [1111] Jimmy J. Collins b: April 03, 1908 Sex: Male

.......................11 [1112] Oma Lee Collins b: January 09, 1913 in Knott Co., KY d: June 12, 1994 in McRoberts, Letcher Co., KY Sex: Female Burial: Amburgey Cemetery, Knott Co., KY

..........................+[1113] Hillard A. Collins b: Abt. 1910 Sex: Male

...................Partner of [799] Lincoln "Link" Banks:

........................+[1114] Elizabeth "Liz" Amburgey b: June 24, 1857 in Whitesburg, Letcher, Co., KY m: Abt. 1883 in (Note: they did not marry) d: February 28, 1937 in Bath, Knott Co., KY Number of children: 4 Father: John Amburgey III Mother: Rachel Hall Sex: Female Burial: Seymour Amburgey Cemetery, Bath, Knott Co., KY (Note: some records state that she was born on January 7, 1857)

.....................10 [1115] Maggie Banks b: June 28, 1884 in Knott (now Letcher) Co., KY d: January 11, 1960 in Clarksville, IN Number of children: 5 Sex: Female Burial: Clarksville, IN

...........................+[1116] Watson Collins b: April 17, 1887 in Letcher Co., KY d: May 20, 1972 in Isom, Letcher Co., KY Number of children: 5 Father: John "Long John" Collins Mother: Sarah "Sally" Stacy Sex: Male Burial: Walnut Ridge Cemetery, Jeffersonville, IN

.......................11 [1117] Norman Collins b: April 09, 1911 in Bath, Knott Co., KY d: November 05, 1994 Sex: Male Burial: Forest Lawn Memorial Pak, Glendale, CA

.............................+[1118] Lucille McCabe b: Abt. 1917 in Los Angeles, CA d: December 1990 in Los Angeles, CA Sex: Female

.......................11 [800] Lava Collins b: March 04, 1913 in Bath, Knott Co., KY Number of children: 3 Sex: Female

............................+[1119] Sonny Anderson b: Abt. 1910 Sex: Male

...................Partner of [800] Lava Collins:

............................+[12] Delmer V. Caudill b: January 13, 1917 in Polly (Sandlick) , Letcher Co., KY m: Abt. 1939 in (Note: they did not marry) d: January 06, 1985 in Hazard, Perry Co., KY Number of children: 9 Father: John Breckenridge "Johnny" Caudill Mother: Thursa Ann Mason Sex: Male Burial: Green Acres Cemetery, Ermine, KY (Note: resided in Ulvah, Letcher Co., KY at time of death)

...................2nd Husband of [800] Lava Collins:

............................+[1120] Willard Gibson b: September 10, 1895 in Democrat, Letcher Co., KY m: Abt. 1945 d: November 21, 1959 in Colson, Letcher Co., KY Number of children: 15 Father: Anderson Gibson Mother: Lucinda Sexton Sex: Male Burial: Colson Cemetery, Colson, KY

.......................11 [1121] Rachel Collins b: Abt. 1915 Sex: Female

.....................11 [1122] Vada Collins b: Abt. 1917 Sex: Female

.....................11 [801] Lilly Collins b: February 27, 1919 in SeCo., Letcher Co., KY d: March 24, 2003 in Hospital in New Albany, IN (lived in Clarksville, Clark Co., IN at time of death) Number of children: 4 Sex: Female

...........................+[802] William "Luther" Yonts b: March 19, 1906 in Neon, Letcher Co., KY m: April 27, 1940 in Camp Branch, Colson, Letcher Co., KY d: July 22, 1962 in Jeffersonville, Clark Co., IN Number of children: 4 Father: John Quiller Yonts Mother: Sarah Frances Collier Sex: Male Burial: Walnut Ridge Cemetery, Jeffersonville, IN (Yonts Note: like the author and all of the other Yonts individuals in this tree, this family descends from Wilhelm Jans, born in 1714 in the town of Oberalben, Rheineland-Pfalz, Germany; Wilhelm died in 1778 in Rowan Co., NC)

.....................2nd Husband of [801] Lilly Collins:

...........................+[1123] John Henry "Buck" Coslow b: June 15, 1912 in Shelby Co., KY m: Aft. 1963 d: February 07, 1975 in Louisville, KY Sex: Male Burial: Walnut Ridge Cemetery, Jeffersonville, IN

.................9 [1124] Napoleon Bonaparte ("Boney"?) Banks b: February 17, 1860 Sex: Male

.................9 [1125] Cornelia Banks b: Abt. 1863 Sex: Male

.................9 [1126] William "Will" Banks b: Abt. 1864 in KY d: November 1918 in Whitesburg, Letcher Co., KY Sex: Male

.......................+[1127] Usley (or Ulsey?) Ison b: 1867 m: June 12, 1883 Sex: Female (Note: looking for ancestors)

.................9 [1128] Irvin Banks b: March 16, 1866 in Letcher Co., KY d: December 25, 1937 in Letcher Co., KY Sex: Male

.......................+[1129] Cornelia Combs b: October 24, 1870 in Letcher Co., KY m: April 29, 1886 in Letcher Co., KY? d: October 20, 1918 in Letcher Co., KY Father: John Combs Mother: Elizabeth "Betty" Breeding Sex: Female

.................9 [1130] James "Jim" Banks b: 1871 Sex: Male

.................9 [1131] Martha Banks b: 1873 Sex: Female

...............8 Harrison Banks b: October 01, 1825 in NC d: June 30, 1880 Number of children: 3 Sex: Male

.....................+Sarah Emeline Pridemore b: November 05, 1831 in Letcher Co., KY m: March 30, 1850 in Letcher Co., KY d: May 15, 1872 Number of children: 3 Sex: Female

.................9 Napolean Bonaparte "Boney" Banks b: Abt. 1852 Number of children: ? Sex: Male

.......................+Malissa Ison b: Abt. 1855 m: March 16, 1882 Number of children: ? Sex: Female

.....................10 Grant Banks b: Abt. 1885 Number of children: ? Sex: Male

...........................+Rausey Elizabeth Stallard b: Abt. 1890 m: May 30, 1911 Number of children: ? Sex: Female

.......................11 Harvey Astor Banks b: Abt. 1915 Number of children: ? Sex: Male

.............................+Cleta Pauline Richmond b: Abt. 1920 m: June 16, 1938 Number of children: ? Sex: Female

.................9 [291] Ester Banks b: April 08, 1853 in Letcher Co., KY d: September 25, 1905 Sex: Female

.......................+[290] Hiram W. Caudill b: Abt. September 20, 1853 in Letcher Co., KY d: December 20, 1913 Father: William J. "Stiller Bill" Caudill Mother: Nancy Dixon, Dickson Sex: Male

.................9 [1132] Sarah Banks b: February 18, 1859 in Letcher Co., KY d: August 1938 Number of children: 2 Sex: Female

.......................+[1133] Lewis Jesse Caudill b: July 08, 1857 in Letcher Co., KY m: March 18, 1875 in Letcher Co., KY Number of children: 2 Father: Isom Caudill Mother: Elizabeth "Lizzie" Back, Bach Sex: Male

.....................10 [1134] Wesley Caudill b: April 23, 1880 d: February 22, 1928 Number of children: ? Sex: Male

...........................+[1135] Hailey "Hade" Ison b: Abt. 1882 Number of children: ? Sex: Female

.......................11 [1136] Wendell Caudill b: Abt. 1898 Number of children: 3 Sex: Male Burial:

Caudill Cemetery at Uz, Letcher Co., KY
...........................+[1137] Muriel J. Dixon b: December 30, 1900 d: June 09, 1937 Number
of children: 3 Father: James C. Dixon Mother: Evelyn Back, Bach Sex: Female Burial: Caudill
Cemetery at Uz, Letcher Co., KY
..................10 [1138] Walter Caudill b: April 13, 1886 in Jeremiah, KY d: January 01, 1911 Sex:
Male
..........................+[1139] Hannah Ison b: 1886 in Letcher Co., KY m: November 01, 1907 in
Letcher Co., KY Sex: Female
................8 [1140] Samuel G. Banks b: Abt. 1826 in Adair, KY Number of children: 4 Sex: Male
......................+Mary "Polly" Frazier b: Abt. 1828 Father: Jonathan Frazier Mother: Elizabeth
"Betsy" Banks Sex: Female
................2nd Wife of [1140] Samuel G. Banks:
......................+Mary Frazier b: Abt. 1828 in KY m: October 08, 1848 in Letcher Co., KY
Number of children: 4 Father: Jonathan Frazier Mother: Elizabeth "Betsy" Banks Sex: Female
..................9 Susan Banks b: October 10, 1852 in Letcher Co., KY Sex: Female
..................9 [580] Solomon Banks b: September 07, 1856 in Letcher Co., KY d: September 05,
1936 in Colson, Letcher Co., KY Number of children: 7 Sex: Male
........................+Mary Back b: Abt. 1858 in KY m: September 18, 1884 Number of children: 2
Sex: Female
....................10 Susannah Banks b: June 1886 in Letcher Co., KY Sex: Female
..........................+John Niece b: Abt. 1884 m: April 04, 1912 Sex: Male
....................10 Nettie Banks b: February 1888 Sex: Female
.........................+Bill Niece b: Abt. 1886 m: December 30, 1907 Sex: Male
..................2nd Wife of [580] Solomon Banks:
.........................+Esther Eldridge b: Abt. 1868 m: October 08, 1891 Sex: Female
..................3rd Wife of [580] Solomon Banks:
........................+[192] Celia Ann Adams b: June 23, 1877 m: December 16, 1896 d: November
14, 1969 in Letcher Co., KY Number of children: 9 Father: Gideon Adams Mother: Sarah Blair Sex:
Female
....................10 [1141] Hettie Banks b: November 27, 1899 in Letcher Co., KY Sex: Female
..........................+[1142] Clinton Sexton b: Abt. 1887 Sex: Male
....................10 [1143] Juda Banks b: 1905 Sex: Male
....................10 [1144] L. C. "Lucky" Banks b: December 13, 1908 in Letcher Co., KY Sex: Male
..........................+[1145] Kathryn Sexton b: Abt. 1910 m: February 27, 1928 Sex: Female
....................10 [1146] Martha Banks b: March 26, 1914 Sex: Female
..........................+[1147] Wallace Sturgill b: Abt. 1912 m: June 04, 1935 Sex: Male
....................10 [1148] Robert "Bobby" Banks b: April 04, 1915 Sex: Male
..........................+[1149] Hoffa Sturgill b: Abt. 1917 m: April 07, 1932 Sex: Female
..................9 Hiram Banks b: Abt. 1858 Number of children: 2 Sex: Male
..................+Nancy _____? b: Abt. 1860 Number of children: 2 Sex: Female
....................10 Benton Banks b: Abt. 1879 Sex: Male
....................10 Polly Ann Banks b: April 1880 Sex: Female
..................9 Frazier Banks b: Abt. 1862 Sex: Male
...............8 Kizike Banks b: Abt. 1828 Sex: Female
............7 [531] Randolph "Randall" Adams b: 1802 in Roaring River, Wilkes Co., NC d: December
23, 1872 in Cowan, Perry/Letcher Co., KY Number of children: 2 Sex: Male
..................+[530] Nancy Caudill, b: June 18, 1804 Number of children: 2 Father: Stephen A.
Caudill, Rev. War Soldier, Mother: Sarah "Sally" Francis Adams, 2nd wife Sex: Female
................8 [532] Lydia Adams b: Abt. 1825 Number of children: 10 Sex: Female
......................+[533] Robert Collins b: October 21, 1823 in Rockhouse Creek, Perry Co., KY
m: Abt. 1850 d: November 27, 1883 Number of children: 10 Father: James Shepherd Collins Mother:
Elizabeth Lewis Sex: Male

..................9 [534] Randolph Collins b: October 12, 1852 in Hazard, Perry Co., KY d: December 14, 1947 in Red Bluff, CA Sex: Male

.......................+[535] Eliza Jane Turner b: Abt. 1854 in Letcher Co., KY m: January 18, 1872 Father: James Turner Mother: Sarah Bailey Sex: Female

..................9 [536] Nancy Collins b: December 15, 1855 in Colson, Letcher Co., KY d: February 06, 1918 in Colson, Letcher Co., KY Sex: Female

.......................+[537] James Jasper "Babe" Collins b: December 25, 1852 in Letcher Co., KY m: July 31, 1873 in Letcher Co., KY d: September 06, 1876 in Letcher Co., KY Father: Eli Collins Mother: Mary Barrett Sex: Male

..................9 [538] James H. Collins b: July 18, 1857 in Rockhouse Creek, Letcher Co., KY d: September 01, 1942 Sex: Male

.......................+[539] Nancy Sarah Breeding b: Abt. 1859 in Letcher Co., KY m: September 18, 1879 Father: John Breeding Mother: Elizabeth "Betty" Combs Sex: Female

..................9 [540] Sarah Collins b: May 04, 1859 in Rockhouse Creek, Letcher Co., KY d: May 15, 1859 in Letcher Co., KY Sex: Female

..................9 [541] Elijah Collins b: Abt. 1860 Sex: Male

..................9 [183] William Silas Collins b: April 21, 1865 d: December 15, 1937 in Letcher Co., KY Sex: Male

.......................+[542] Nancy Hale b: 1862 Father: William Rowlette Hale Mother: Elizabeth Collins Sex: Female

..................2nd Wife of [183] William Silas Collins:

.......................+[358] Martha E. Crase b: Abt. 1868 m: March 03, 1888 in Letcher Co., KY Father: James Crase Mother: Elizabeth Stallard Sex: Female

..................9 [360] Greenbury Collins b: February 26, 1868 d: May 03, 1924 Sex: Male

.......................+[359] Christina Adams b: June 10, 1858 d: January 07, 1951 Father: Jesse "Colly Jesse" Adams Mother: Mary "Polly" Craft Sex: Female

..................9 [543] Lucinda Collins b: Abt. 1872 Sex: Female

..................9 [544] Lorenzo Dow Collins b: January 20, 1875 in Rockhouse Creek, Letcher Co., KY d: December 13, 1949 Sex: Male

.......................+[545] Nancy Ann Caudill b: Abt. 1877 in Letcher Co., KY m: February 04, 1897 Father: Watson Caudill Mother: Elizabeth Combs Sex: Female

..................9 [546] Eliza Collins b: 1879 Sex: Female

................8 [184] Watson E. "Watty" Adams b: April 1837 d: 1919 Number of children: 9 Sex: Male

.......................+[547] Rosa "Rausey" Hogg b: 1842 m: 1860 Number of children: ? Father: Hiram "Courthouse Hiram" Hogg Mother: Melvina "Viney" Polly Sex: Female

..................9 [548] Henry C. Adams b: 1863 Sex: Male

.......................+[549] Catherine Campbell b: September 1884 d: 1966 Father: John Henry Campbell Mother: Elizabeth Maggard Sex: Female

................2nd Wife of [184] Watson E. "Watty" Adams:

.......................+[550] Minerva Collins b: January 13, 1846 m: October 16, 1881 in Letcher Co., KY Number of children: 8 Father: Nathaniel "Nat" Collins Mother: Nancy Branham-Smith Sex: Female

..................9 [551] Floyd Adams b: Abt. 1882 Sex: Male

..................9 [552] Boyd Adams b: Abt. 1883 Sex: Male

..................9 [553] Randall Adams b: March 19, 1884 Sex: Male

..................9 [554] Francis Adams b: September 28, 1885 Sex: Female

..................9 [555] Patton Adams b: Abt. 1886 Sex: Male

..................9 [556] Green Ison Adams b: March 10, 1887 d: September 19, 1951 Sex: Male

..................9 [557] Hattie Adams b: August 21, 1889 Sex: Female

..................9 [558] Elizabeth Adams b: Abt. 1891 Sex: Female

............7 Lydia "Lettie" Adams b: 1805 d: 1842 in Floyd Co., KY Sex: Female

.............7 Absalom Drury Adams b: 1809 in Perry Co., KY Sex: Male

..........6 [1150] Benjamin "Ben" Adams, Jr., b: 1749 in Fairfax Co., VA d: 1824 in Mayking, Perry (now Letcher) Co., KY Number of children: 5 Sex: Male. NOTE: Ben is the author's 6th great-grandfather.

..............+[1151] Henrietta "Henny" Caudill, b: 1753 in Sussex (Stafford) Co., VA. m: 1774 in Leesburg, Loudon Co., VA d: November 1836 in Mayking, Letcher Co., KY Number of children: 5 Father: Benjamin "Ben of Sussex" Caudill, Sr., Mother: Elizabeth Buckner, Sex: Female Burial: 1836 Letcher Co., KY. NOTE: Henny is the author's 6th great-grandmother.

.............7 [1152] Elizabeth Nancy Rebecca Adams, b: 1775 in Loudon Co., VA d: 1861 in Letcher Co., KY Number of children: 3 Sex: Female

.................+[1153] Randolph (or Randel) "Buck" Holbrook, b: Bet. 1770 - 1778 in Wilkes Co., NC m: 1795 in Wilkesboro, Wilkes Co. N.C. d: April 1847 in Mayking, Letcher Co., KY Number of children: 3 Father: John Henry Holbrook, Mother: Mary Elizabeth Hargis, Sex: Male

................8 [1003] Nancy Holbrook, b: 1799 in Roaring Rv., Wilkes, N.C. d: Aft. 1870 in Letcher Co. KY Number of children: 4 Sex: Female

.....................+[1002] Benjamin Adams, b: 1794 in Roaring Rv., Wilkes, N.C. m: February 10, 1816 in Prestonburg, Floyd, KY d: November 11, 1855 in Letcher Co. KY Number of children: 4 Father: John Hobbs Adams, Jr., Mother: Lydia "Letty" or "Lettie" Simpson Sex: Male

.................9 [396] John Isom Adams b: 1818 d: 1863 in (Note: Died trying to open an unexploded bomb to get at the gun powder inside) Number of children: 7 Sex: Male

......................+[397] Sarah "Sallie" Craft b: April 02, 1821 m: August 16, 1838 d: March 26, 1863 in Letcher Co., KY Number of children: 7 Father: James Craft Mother: Druscilla Hammonds Sex: Female

....................10 [398] Benjamin Burford Adams b: 1840 Sex: Male

....................10 [399] James W. Adams b: 1842 Sex: Male

....................10 [400] Nancy Jane Adams b: 1845 Sex: Female

....................10 [401] Jesse Adams b: 1847 Sex: Male

....................10 [402] Joseph Simpson Adams b: 1851 Sex: Male

....................10 [403] Randolph N. Adams b: 1854 Sex: Male

....................10 [404] Archelous Adams b: 1858 Sex: Male

.................9 [1004] Jesse Adams, b: 1821 in Perry Co., KY d: in Letcher Co., KY Number of children: ? Sex: Male

......................+[1005] Margaret Jenkins b: 1826 in Perry Co., KY m: August 20, 1846 in Letcher Co., KY d: October 09, 1882 in Letcher Co., KY Number of children: ? Father: William Jenkins Sex: Female

....................10 [1006] Elizabeth Adams, b: Bet. November 1844 - 1845 in Letcher Co., KY Sex: Female

.........................+[1007] Jesse S. Holbrook, b: February 06, 1837 in Perry Co., KY m: Abt. 1861 in Harlan, KY or Letcher Co., KY Father: Benjamin Holbrook, Mother: Nancy Jenkins Sex: Male Burial: Craft Cemetery, Millstone, KY?

.................9 [1008] Elizabeth Adams b: Abt. 1824 d: July 1880 Number of children: 9 Sex: Female

......................+[1009] James Bates, Sr. b: Abt. 1823 in Letcher or Perry Co., KY, m: February 26, 1843 in Letcher Co., KY d: April 11, 1864 Murdered in Letcher Co., KY during the Civil War Number of children: 9 Father: John Wallis Bates, Sr., Sheriff Mother: Sarah Walthrop, or Waltrop Sex: Male Burial: Kona KY, Bates Cemetery

....................10 [1010] Henry C. Bates b: Abt. 1844 in Letcher Co., KY Sex: Male

...........................+[1011] Rachel Lee b: Abt. 1840 in Russell Co., VA m: March 13, 1868 in Letcher Co., KY Sex: Female

....................10 [1012] Sarah Bates b: Abt. 1846 Sex: Female

....................10 [1013] Nancy Bates b: October 28, 1848 in Millstone, Letcher Co., KY d: September 10, 1927 in Beefhide, Letcher Co., KY Number of children: 12 Sex: Female Burial: Nancy Wright Cemetery, Beefhide, KY

...........................+[1014] Andrew J. Wright, b: November 14, 1847 in Beefhide, Letcher Co., KY m: December 09, 1870 in Joel Wright's home? , Letcher Co., KY d: January 28, 1919 in Beefhide, Letcher Co., KY Number of children: 12 Father: Samuel W. Wright, Mother: Elizabeth "Betsy" Adams, Sex: Male Burial: Samuel W. Wright Cemetery, Beefhide, KY

.......................11 [405] Joel M. "Big Joel" Wright b: December 08, 1871 in Beefhide Creek, Beefhide, KY d: December 20, 1921 in Jenkins, Letcher Co., KY Number of children: 6 Sex: Male Burial: Nancy Wright Cemetery, Beefhide, KY

...........................+[1015] Cordelia Mullins b: Abt. 1871 in KY? m: February 24, 1892 Sex: Female

.......................2nd Wife of [405] Joel M. "Big Joel" Wright:

...........................+[1016] Susan Wright b: Abt. 1875 in KY? m: August 20, 1895 Sex: Female

.......................3rd Wife of [405] Joel M. "Big Joel" Wright:

...........................+[1017] Mahala Sowards b: Abt. 1875 in KY? m: February 27, 1896 Number of children: 6 Sex: Female

.......................11 [1018] Elizabeth Wright b: March 30, 1874 in Beefhide Creek, Beefhide, KY d: October 16, 1957 Number of children: 5 Sex: Female

...........................+[1019] Henry Blevins b: Abt. 1875 in KY? m: November 21, 1901 Number of children: 5 Sex: Male

.......................11 [406] Eliza J. Wright b: December 13, 1875 in Beefhide Creek, Beefhide, KY d: January 10, 1946 in Norton, VA Sex: Female

...........................+[1020] Joe Willis b: Abt. 1875 in KY? Sex: Male

.......................2nd Husband of [406] Eliza J. Wright:

...........................+[1021] Isaac "Ike" Mills b: Abt. 1875 in KY? m: October 04, 1900 Sex: Male

.......................11 [1022] Sarah J. Wright b: November 16, 1877 in Beefhide KY d: May 02, 1920 in Burdine, Letcher Co., KY Number of children: 5 Sex: Female Burial: Burdine, Letcher Co., KY

...........................+[1023] William "Willie" Blevins b: Abt. 1875 in KY? m: March 01, 1900 Number of children: 5 Sex: Male

.......................11 [1024] Victoria Wright b: October 26, 1878 in Beefhide, KY d: December 11, 1940 in Letcher Co., KY Sex: Female Burial: Beefhide Creek, Beefhide, KY

...........................+[1025] Rathburn Burke b: November 12, 1859 m: April 18, 1922 d: May 13, 1942 Sex: Male

.......................11 [1026] Margaret "Maggie" Wright b: August 06, 1880 in Beefhide, KY d: September 01, 1923 in Letcher Co., KY Number of children: 12 Sex: Female Burial: Nancy Wright Cemetery, Beefhide, KY

...........................+[1027] John Brown b: Abt. 1880 in KY? m: June 22, 1899 Number of children: 12 Sex: Male

.......................11 [1028] William James Wright b: December 28, 1882 in Beefhide, KY d: April 15, 1940 in VA Number of children: 10 Sex: Male Burial: Nancy Wright Cemetery, Beefhide, KY

...........................+[1029] Elizabeth Mullins b: Abt. 1885 in KY? m: 1913 Number of children: 10 Sex: Female

.......................11 [1030] Martha Josephine Wright b: November 18, 1884 in Beefhide, KY d: March 26, 1960 in VA Number of children: 8 Sex: Female Burial: Nancy Wright Cemetery, Beefhide, KY

...........................+[1031] John Wesley Ellison b: Abt. 1885 in KY? m: November 23, 1905 Number of children: 8 Sex: Male

.......................11 [1032] John Wallis Wright b: February 06, 1887 in Beefhide, KY d: June 26, 1965 in Virginia Beach, VA Number of children: 10 Sex: Male Burial: Nancy Wright Cemetery, Beefhide, KY

...........................+[1033] Alka Mae Wright b: April 23, 1903 in Beefhide, KY m: November 05, 1919 d: October 19, 1986 in Virginia Beach, VA Number of children: 10 Father: Austin McJesse Wright Mother: Elizabeth Mullins Sex: Female Burial: Colonial Grove, Cemetery VA Beach, VA

.......................11 [407] Etta Wright b: November 16, 1888 in Beefhide, Letcher Co., KY d:

October 09, 1977 in Jenkins, Letcher Co., KY Sex: Female Burial: Nancy Wright Cemetery, Beefhide, Letcher Co., KY

.............................+[1034] T. O. Webb b: Abt. 1885 in KY? m: August 20, 1913 Sex: Male

.......................2nd Husband of [407] Etta Wright:

.............................+[1035] Lemuel Haynes b: Abt. 1890 in KY? m: September 21, 1915 Sex: Male

.......................11 [1036] Samuel Wright b: April 03, 1891 in Beefhide, KY d: May 18, 1936 in Beefhide, KY Number of children: 10 Sex: Male Burial: Nancy Wright Cemetery, Beefhide, KY

.............................+[1037] Ollie Bentley b: Abt. 1890 in KY? m: 1917 Number of children: 10 Sex: Female

.......................11 [1038] Ritter Wright, b: July 06, 1893 in Beefhide, KY d: September 15, 1953 in Fleming, KY Number of children: 5 Sex: Female Burial: Thornton Cem, Thornton, Letcher Co., KY

.............................+[1039] Jacob "Jake" Martin Adkins, b: March 24, 1893 in Greasy Creek, KY m: June 07, 1916 in Letcher Co., KY d: October 05, 1959 in Fleming, KY Number of children: 5 Father: Nelson Adkins, Mother: Malinda Robinson Sex: Male Burial: Thornton Cem, Thornton, Letcher Co., KY (Adkins Note: like the author and all of the other Adkins individuals in this tree and their descendants, this family descends from European royalty through Elizabeth Parker, born about 1697 in Charles City or Richmond, Henrico Co., VA. Elizabeth's husband was William Adkins/Atkinson, born March 28, 1689, in Charles City, Henrico Co., VA. Elizabeth is the proven 12th great-granddaughter of the King of England, Henry III, born October 1, 1206, in Winchester Castle, Hampshire Co., England)

.......................10 [408] John W. 'Ringer' Bates b: November 23, 1852 in Letcher Co., KY d: November 24, 1932 Number of children: 7 Sex: Male

.............................+[1041] Mary Pigmon m: Abt. 1882 Number of children: 7 Sex: Female

.......................11 [1042] Wlliam Bates b: Abt. 1883 d: August 16, 1959 Sex: Male

.......................11 [1043] George Washington Bates b: 1884 in KY Sex: Male

.......................11 [1044] James Bates b: 1886 in KY d: 1910 in Lexington, KY Sex: Male

.......................11 [1045] Martin Van Bates b: 1888 d: 1904 in KY Sex: Male

.......................11 [1046] Landis Dewey Bates b: December 25, 1890 in Knox Co., KY d: March 21, 1973 Sex: Male

.............................+[1047] Mary L. Hayes m: August 14, 1915 in Jenkins, KY Sex: Female

.......................11 [1048] T. Monroe Bates b: 1892 in Pine Top, KY d: 1956 in Wise, VA Sex: Male

.............................+[1049] Edna Dale b: Abt. 1895 Sex: Female

.......................11 [1050] Maggie Bates b: 1894 in Pine Top, KY Sex: Female

.............................+[1051] Christopher Columbus Tackett b: Abt. 1890 Sex: Male

.......................2nd Wife of [408] John W. 'Ringer' Bates:

.............................+[1052] Elizabeth Gibson b: Abt. 1855 m: July 26, 1901 in Letcher Co., KY Sex: Female

.......................10 [1053] Martha Bates b: January 19, 1855 in Letcher Co., KY Sex: Female

.......................10 [1054] Letha Jane 'Jenny' Bates b: Abt. 1858 in Letcher Co., KY d: October 21, 1919 in Letcher Co., KY Sex: Female

.......................10 [1055] Margaret Bates b: Abt. 1860 in Letcher Co., KY d: 1874 in Letcher Co., KY Sex: Female

.......................10 [1056] James Bates, Jr. b: Abt. 1863 in Letcher Co., KY Sex: Male

.......................10 [1057] Letitia "Lettie/Moody" Bates b: November 15, 1851 in Letcher Co., KY ? d: May 12, 1934 in Letcher Co., KY ? Number of children: 12 Sex: Female Burial: Thornton Cemetery, Letcher Co., KY

.............................+[1058] William S. Wright b: Bet. July 07 - 09, 1855 in Letcher Co., KY or Scott Co., VA m: April 12, 1872 in Letcher Co., KY d: January 30, 1900 in Boone Creek (Letcher Co.,?) , KY Number of children: 12 Father: Wilhelm "Bill" Luntz Mother: Sidney Wright Sex: Male

Burial: Thornton Cem, Letcher Co., Ky

........................11 [1059] Nancy Wright b: April 25, 1873 in Baker, KY d: February 04, 1927 in Pikeville, KY Sex: Female

.............................+[412] James Johnson, Sr. b: Abt. 1870 m: April 26, 1888 in Letcher Co., KY Number of children: 4 Sex: Male

........................11 [409] Martha E. Wright b: December 12, 1874 in Seco or Baker, KY d: Bet. November 22, 1925 - 1926 in SeCo., KY Number of children: 4 Sex: Female Burial: Thornton Cemetery, Letcher Co., KY

.............................+[1060] _____ Pigman b: Abt. 1870 Sex: Male

........................2nd Husband of [409] Martha E. Wright:

.............................+[1061] _____ Bullard b: Abt. 1870 Sex: Male (Notes: not sure if he was her husband or not) .

........................3rd Husband of [409] Martha E. Wright:

.............................+[1062] William "Willie" Venters b: April 09, 1874 in Jenkins, Letcher Co., KY m: July 31, 1893 in Seco., Letcher Co., KY d: August 31, 1901 in Dunham, Jenkins, Letcher Co., KY Number of children: 4 Father: John Venters Mother: Mary Juliette Mullins Sex: Male Burial: Thornton Cemetery, Letcher Co., KY

........................11 [1064] Samuel Tilden Wright b: March 31, 1878 in Seco or McRoberts, KY d: April 27, 1974 in Letcher Co., KY Sex: Male Burial: Thornton Cemetery, Letcher Co., KY

.............................+[1065] Lydia Margaret Craft b: 1880 m: June 29, 1899 in Letcher Co., KY d: 1964 Sex: Female

........................11 [1066] Mary Wright b: April 04, 1880 in Letcher Co., KY d: March 1969 in Lexington, KY Sex: Female

.............................+[1067] William Wiley Craft b: Abt. 1880 in Letcher Co., KY ? m: 1897 in Letcher Co., KY Sex: Male

........................11 [1068] William Wright b: June 30, 1882 in Letcher Co., KY d: April 10, 1901 in SeCo., KY Sex: Male

........................11 [410] Theophalis Garret Wright b: Bet. May 15, 1884 - 1885 in Letcher Co., KY d: April 13, 1953 Sex: Male

.............................+[1069] Mandy _____? b: Abt. 1890 Sex: Female

........................2nd Wife of [410] Theophalis Garret Wright:

.............................+[1070] Carrie Blair b: Abt. 1885 in Letcher Co., KY ? m: August 30, 1907 in Letcher Co., KY Sex: Female

........................3rd Wife of [410] Theophalis Garret Wright:

.............................+[1071] Sylvia Hicks b: Abt. 1885 m: June 21, 1935 Sex: Female

........................11 [411] Joseph F. Wright b: July 01, 1886 in Baker, KY d: January 1975 in Russell, KY Number of children: 3 Sex: Male

.............................+[1072] Lillie Smallwood b: Abt. 1890 Number of children: 2 Sex: Female

........................2nd Wife of [411] Joseph F. Wright:

.............................+[1073] Lilly Isom b: Abt. 1890 Number of children: ? Sex: Female

........................11 [1074] John W. Wright b: April 09, 1888 d: December 30, 1945 Sex: Male

.............................+[1075] Arlena Mason b: Abt. 1890 Sex: Female

........................11 [1076] Nancy "Nan" Wright b: April 25, 1873 in Baker, KY d: February 04, 1927 in Pikeville, KY Number of children: 4 Sex: Female

.............................+[412] James Johnson, Sr. b: Abt. 1870 m: April 26, 1888 in Letcher Co., KY Number of children: 4 Sex: Male

........................11 [1077] Henrietta "Ritter" Wright b: September 21, 1876 in Letcher Co., KY d: October 16, 1961 Number of children: 11 Sex: Female

.............................+[1078] L. Bert Tolliver b: Abt. 1870 in Letcher Co., KY ? m: July 12, 1894 in Letcher Co., KY d: Abt. 1934 Number of children: 11 Sex: Male

........................11 [413] Benjamin Franklin Wright, Dr. b: March 12, 1891 in Whitaker, KY d: August 11, 1969 in Whitaker, KY Number of children: 3 Sex: Male Burial: SeCo., Ky

...........................+[1079] Scottie McClure b: Abt. 1895 Sex: Female

......................2nd Wife of [413] Benjamin Franklin Wright, Dr.:

...........................+[1080] Hazel Iris Adams b: Abt. 1895 Sex: Female

......................3rd Wife of [413] Benjamin Franklin Wright, Dr.:

...........................+[1081] Fanny Hall b: May 15, 1894 in Wise Co., VA d: April 03, 1940 in Letcher Co., KY ? Number of children: 3 Father: L. M. Hall Sex: Female Burial: Thornton Cemetery, Letcher Co., KY

......................11 [414] Lettie Dallas Wright b: January 08, 1894 in SeCo., KY d: April 04, 1974 Number of children: 7 Sex: Female Burial: Thorton, KY

...........................+[415] Archie C. Craft, Jr. b: May 09, 1884 m: November 05, 1919 in Letcher Co., KY d: July 06, 1959 Number of children: 7 Father: Joseph Craft Mother: Rasuea Bagwell Sex: Male

..................9 [416] Randolph "Randall" Adams b: November 30, 1834 in Perry Co., KY d: 1909 in Letcher Co., KY Number of children: ? Sex: Male Burial: Webb Cemetery, Mayking, Letcher, KY

......................+[1084] Martha Hale b: 1841 in VA d: Bef. 1900 in Letcher Co., KY Number of children: ? Father: James Dickerson Hale Mother: Jane Grizzle Sex: Female

....................10 [1085] Martha "Mattie" Adams b: March 27, 1880 d: December 03, 1945 Sex: Female

..........................+[1086] Stephen Gilley b: Abt. 1875 Sex: Male

..................2nd Wife of [416] Randolph "Randall" Adams:

........................+[1087] Louise Jenkins b: 1840 Sex: Female

..................3rd Wife of [416] Randolph "Randall" Adams:

......................+[1088] Sarah Fields b: Abt. 1875 m: 1901 Sex: Female

................8 [715] William B. "Buckie" Holbrook, Sr., b: 1809 in Floyd Co., KY Number of children: 9 Sex: Male

......................+[714] Sarah "Sally" Adams, parents unknown b: 1807 in NC m: Abt. 1826 in Floyd Co., KY Number of children: 9 Father: John Washington "Wash" Adams, Mother: _____ _____? , Sex: Female (Note: Looking for her ancestors; I think her Father MAY be John Washington "Wash" Adams. b. 1785 in NC)

..................9 [716] Mary "Polly" Holbrook, b: 1827 in Perry Co., KY d: April 11, 1854 in Letcher Co., KY Number of children: 2 Sex: Female

........................+[717] Esquire "Squire" Bentley, b: 1821 in Letcher Co., KY m: October 24, 1850 in Letcher Co., KY Number of children: 2 Father: John Queller Bentley, Sr., Mother: Margaret ("Peggy") Hamilton, Sex: Male

....................10 [718] William Barlow "Barlow" Bentley b: March 1849 in KY Number of children: 13 Sex: Male

..........................+[719] Susannah Quillen b: September 20, 1857 in Letcher Co., KY m: September 19, 1872 in Letcher Co., KY d: February 14, 1926 Number of children: 13 Father: Richard Teague Quillen Mother: Catherine Yonts Sex: Female (Note: some say she was born 9- 22- 1859) .

....................11 [720] William D. Bentley b: 1874 in KY Sex: Male

......................11 [721] Mary Bentley b: 1876 in KY Sex: Female

......................11 [722] Polly Bentley b: November 1876 Sex: Female

......................11 [723] Arminda "Armindy" Bentley b: December 1878 in KY Sex: Female

......................11 [724] Squire Richard Bentley b: December 12, 1879 d: May 06, 1933 Number of children: 16 Sex: Male

...........................+[725] Rosemond Fidel Hall b: Abt. 1880 Number of children: 16 Sex: Female

....................11 [726] Benjamin Franklin Bentley b: June 1882 Number of children: ? Sex: Male

....................11 [727] James M. Bentley b: May 1888 Sex: Male

....................11 [728] Wiley A. Bentley b: July 1889 Sex: Male

....................11 [729] Nancy J. Bentley b: March 1894 Sex: Female

......................11 [730] Samantha Bentley b: Abt. August 1895 Sex: Female

......................11 [731] Robert S. Bentley b: March 1896 Sex: Male

......................11 [732] Sarah E. Bentley b: April 1898 Sex: Female

......................11 [733] Ira J. Bentley b: 1902 Sex: Male

......................10 [734] Sarah "Sally" Bentley, b: July 1852 in Letcher Co., KY d: Aft. 1920 in Pulaski Co., KY? Number of children: 3 Sex: Female

...........................+[735] William James Yonts, b: December 1845 in Letcher Co., KY m: March 18, 1870 in Letcher Co., KY d: Aft. 1920 in Pulaski Co., KY? Number of children: 3 Father: William Yonts, Jr., Yants, Mother: Nancy F. Ray, Sex: Male (Yonts Notes: Like the author and all of the other Yonts individuals in this tree, this family descends from Wilhelm Jans, born in 1714 in the town of Oberalben, Rheineland-Pfalz, Germany; Wilhelm died in 1778 in Rowan Co., NC)

......................11 [417] Esquire "Squire" Lincoln Yonts, Yantz, b: April 30, 1874 in Letcher Co., KY d: December 10, 1942 in Knoxville, TN Number of children: 9 Sex: Male Burial: Abt. December 13, 1942 Sharp Cemetery (Note: Letcher Co. Birth Records state that his middle initial was "F"). NOTE: Squire is the author's great-grandfather.

...........................+[736] Mary Frances Wright, b: January 27, 1872 in Upper Elkhorn Creek, Pike Co., KY ? m: April 23, 1890 in Letcher Co., KY d: April 12, 1950 in Neon, Hogg Hollow, Letcher Co., KY Number of children: 9 Father: William A. Wright, Mother: Arty (Artie or Arta) M. Potter, Sex: Female Burial: Abt. April 15, 1950 Yonts Cemetery, Craft Funeral Home, Neon, Letcher Co., KY. NOTE: Mary is the author's great-grandmother.

......................2nd Wife of [417] Squire Lincoln Yonts, Yantz, :

...........................+[737] Louise _____? b: Abt. 1880 m: December 1907 Sex: Female

......................3rd Wife of [417] Squire Lincoln Yonts, Yantz, :

...........................+[738] Alice _____? b: Abt. 1900 m: Aft. 1920 Sex: Female Burial: Sharp Cemetery

......................11 [739] Nancy Chaney Yonts b: April 15, 1878 in Letcher Co., KY d: November 20, 1927 in at her daughter's home in Wise, VA or Waynesburg, Lincoln Co., KY Number of children: 9 Sex: Female

...........................+[740] Archibald "Archie" Lincoln Meade b: 1874 in Letcher Co., KY m: August 06, 1895 in Neon, Letcher Co., KY Number of children: 9 Sex: Male

......................11 [418] Robert Grant Yonts b: May 04, 1883 in Letcher Co., KY d: September 13, 1964 Number of children: 15 Sex: Male

...........................+[741] Henrietta "Hennie" Ritter Holbrook b: December 05, 1881 in Letcher Co., KY? m: 1901 in Letcher Co., KY d: April 02, 1965 Number of children: 9 Father: Enoch A. Holbrook Mother: Nancy Evelyn Webb Sex: Female

......................2nd Wife of [418] Robert Grant Yonts:

...........................+[742] Dorothy Pence b: Abt. 1890 in KY? m: Aft. 1922 Number of children: 6 Sex: Female

..................9 [743] Nancy Ann Holbrook b: 1831 Sex: Female

..................9 [744] Susannah Holbrook b: 1834 Sex: Female

..................9 [745] James E. Holbrook b: November 18, 1836 Number of children: 7 Sex: Male

...........................+[746] Tabitha Bentley b: 1843 Number of children: 7 Father: Daniel Bentley, Sr., Mother: Marinda (Brinkley?) Ramey (Note: Marinda descends from the same family line as country singer Patty (Ramey) Loveless, born January 4, 1957 in Pikeville, Pike Co., KY) Sex: Female

......................10 [747] Mary E. "Polly" Holbrook b: 1867 Number of children: ? Sex: Female

...........................+[748] Noah (Paw) Bentley b: Abt. 1865 Number of children: ? Father: Benjamin Bentley Mother: Elizabeth E. "Patsy" Reynolds Sex: Male

......................11 [749] Lincoln Bentley b: Abt. 1890 Number of children: ? Sex: Male

...........................+[750] Etta Bentley b: Abt. 1895 Number of children: ? Sex: Female

......................10 [751] William B. Holbrook b: May 1869 Sex: Male

...........................+[752] Sarah Clark b: Abt. 1870 Sex: Female

......................10 [753] John A. Holbrook b: April 1871 Sex: Male

..........................+[754] Lucinda Huff b: 1874 Sex: Female

....................10 [755] Sarah M. Holbrook b: 1872 Sex: Female

....................10 [756] Didamey Holbrook b: Abt. 1876 Sex: Female

....................10 [757] Zilpha P. Holbrook b: 1879 Sex: Female

....................10 [758] Gracie Holbrook b: 1889 Sex: Female

..................9 [759] William B. Holbrook, Jr. b: 1839 Sex: Male

..................9 [760] Randolph E. Holbrook b: 1841 Sex: Male

..................9 [761] Benjamin W. Holbrook b: 1845 Sex: Male

..................9 [762] Ransom T. Holbrook b: March 21, 1846 d: March 01, 1894 Number of children: 5 Sex: Male Burial: Bottom Fork, Letcher Co., KY

..........................+[763] Elizabeth Ann Hughes b: March 10, 1850 in Letcher Co., KY m: July 10, 1866 d: October 22, 1917 Number of children: 5 Father: John Hughes Mother: Matilda Bentley, (Note: Looking for her ancestors) Sex: Female Burial: Bottom Fork, Letcher Co., KY

....................10 [764] John A. Holbrook b: Abt. 1865 Number of children: ? Sex: Male

..........................+[765] Mary Ann Stewart b: Abt. 1860 Number of children: ? Father: Thomas "Tom" Stewart Mother: Susannah Fleming Sex: Female

....................11 [766] Gabriel Holbrook b: Abt. 1880 Number of children: ? Sex: Male

..........................+[767] Norma Sturgill b: Abt. 1880 in Pound, VA Number of children: ? Father: Gordon Sturgill Sex: Female

....................10 [768] Sarah "Sally" Holbrook b: November 05, 1867 in Letcher Co., KY d: February 16, 1929 Sex: Female

..........................+[769] Wiley W. Quillen b: September 1861 in Letcher Co., KY m: November 30, 1882 in Letcher Co., KY d: 1938 Father: Richard Teaque Quillen Mother: Catherine Yonts Sex: Male

....................10 [770] Nancy "Nannie" Holbrook b: 1868 Sex: Female

....................10 [771] Francis Holbrook b: 1880 Sex: Female

....................10 [772] John A. Holbrook b: Abt. 1880 Sex: Male

..................9 [773] Doctor "Dock" Holbrook b: 1850 Sex: Male

................8 [419] Randolph Holbrook b: March 15, 1811 in Floyd Co., KY Number of children: 5 Sex: Male

....................+[420] Zilpha (Zelphia) Adams b: August 01, 1811 in Rockhouse Creek, Letcher Co., KY m: 1827 in Perry Co., KY d: 1893 Number of children: 5 Father: Stephen Adams, Mother: Mary "Mollie" Webb Sex: Female

..................9 [421] Kelsey Holbrook b: April 05, 1829 Sex: Male

....................+[422] Rutha Mullins b: Abt. 1830 Sex: Female

..................9 [423] Nancy A. Holbrook b: 1830 in Floyd Co., KY Number of children: ? Sex: Female

..........................+[424] Richard Lee Spradling b: June 22, 1822 in Floyd Co., KY Number of children: ? Sex: Male

....................10 [425] Sarah Jane Spradling b: May 26, 1851 in Harrison Co., KY Number of children: ? Sex: Female

..........................+[426] Reuben Porter Dennis b: June 04, 1848 in West Liberty, Morgan Co., KY Number of children: ? Sex: Male

....................11 [427] Nancy Katherine Dennis b: July 05, 1870 in Hazel Green, KY Number of children: ? Sex: Female

..........................+[428] Jasper Bond Suiter b: September 06, 1872 in Wise Co., VA Number of children: ? Sex: Male

..................9 [429] Benjamin May Holbrook b: March 26, 1832 Number of children: 2 Sex: Male

....................+[430] Rhoda Bays Spradlin b: 1834 Number of children: 2 Sex: Female

....................10 [394] Randolph Holbrook b: May 21, 1853 Number of children: 9 Sex: Male

..........................+[431] Virgie Bays b: Abt. 1851 Number of children: 9 Sex: Female

....................11 [432] Adam Gus Holbrook b: Abt. 1877 Number of children: ? Sex: Male

...........................+[433] Kate Miller b: 1876 Number of children: ? Sex: Female

......................11 [434] Eva Jane Holbrook b: January 1880 Sex: Female

...........................+[435] Harrison Puckett b: Abt. 1875 Sex: Male

......................11 [436] Jacob Holbrook b: March 07, 1882 Sex: Male

...........................+[437] Lisa Puckett b: Abt. 1886 Sex: Female

......................11 [438] John A. Holbrook b: April 1885 Sex: Male

...........................+[439] Cynthia Prater b: Abt. 1889 Sex: Female

......................11 [440] Samuel Holbrook b: Abt. 1887 Sex: Male

......................11 [441] Jim Holbrook b: December 1887 Sex: Male

...........................+[442] Lethia Stone b: Abt. 1889 Sex: Female

......................11 [443] Campbell May Holbrook b: June 16, 1890 Sex: Male

......................11 [444] Virginia Maxine Holbrook b: Abt. 1891 Sex: Female

......................11 [445] Elizabeth "Addie" Holbrook b: Abt. 1892 Sex: Female

....................2nd Wife of [394] Randolph Holbrook:

...........................+[446] Sarah Shepherd b: 1852 Sex: Female

....................10 [447] Harvey Trimble Holbrook b: June 21, 1879 Sex: Male

...........................+[448] Molly B. Hall b: Abt. 1880 Sex: Female

.................9 [449] Mary B. Holbrook b: 1837 Sex: Female

.................9 [450] Elizabeth Holbrook b: 1838 Sex: Female

.............7 [451] Sarah "Sally" Francis Adams, 2nd wife b: 1776 in Lunenburg Co., VA d: October 1842 in Letcher Co., KY Number of children: 13 Sex: Female

...................+[164] Stephen A. Caudill, Rev. War Soldier, b: 1763 in Lunenburg Co., VA (or NC?) m: 1790 in Wilkesboro, Wilkes Co., NC d: July 26, 1839 in Sandlick, Letcher Co., KY Number of children: 16 Father: James Caudill, Sr., Cordell, Coddill, Caudel Mother: Mary Yarborough, Yarbrough Sex: Male Burial: Watty Caudill Cemetery, Dry Fork, Letcher Co., KY (Note: fought in Revolutionary War, Kings Mountain & Cowpens)

................8 [452] Henrietta Caudill, b: 1792 in NC d: 1829 in Pert Creek, Letcher Co., KY Number of children: 6 Sex: Female

......................+[453] George M. Adams, b: September 16, 1800 in Elizabethton, Carter Co., TN m: February 25, 1820 in Prestonsburg, Floyd Co., KY d: October 25, 1869 in Taney Co., MO Number of children: 14 Father: Moses Adams, Mother: Mary Garland Sex: Male

...................9 [454] Sarah "Sallie" Adams b: 1821 Sex: Female

...................9 [455] Mary Adams b: 1825 Sex: Female

...................9 [456] John Adams b: Abt. 1826 Sex: Male

...................9 [457] Lydia Adams b: December 31, 1829 Sex: Female

.......................+[458] Edward Combs b: August 21, 1824 in Smoot Creek, Perry Co., KY d: May 17, 1911 Father: Shadrach "Old Shade" Combs, Jr., Mother: Martha Patsy Casebolt Sex: Male

...................9 [459] Nancy Adams b: Abt. 1830 Sex: Female

.......................+[460] Stephen Polly b: 1826 in Perry Co., KY m: August 25, 1848 in Letcher Co., KY Father: Edward Oliver "Ned" Polly Mother: Jane Bunton "Jennie" Adams Sex: Male

...................9 [461] Dianah Adams b: May 15, 1831 in Perry Co., KY d: June 06, 1873 Sex: Female

................8 [462] John Adams Caudill, b: January 01, 1798 in Wilkes or Ashe Co., NC d: May 10, 1873 in Letcher Co., KY Number of children: 14 Sex: Male

......................+[463] Rachel Cornett, b: February 10, 1807 in Bull Creek, Perry Co., KY m: March 20, 1824 in Perry Co., KY d: April 15, 1887 in Perry (Knott/Letcher) Co., KY Number of children: 14 Father: William Jesse Cornett, Mother: Mary Ann Everage Sex: Female

...................9 [464] William J. Caudill b: February 11, 1825 in Wilkes Co., NC d: January 11, 1899 in Rowan Co., KY Sex: Male

...................9 [465] Stephen Jacob Caudill b: November 18, 1826 in Perry Co., KY d: July 26, 1906 in Letcher Co., KY Sex: Male

...................9 [466] Mary A. Caudill b: August 04, 1828 d: December 31, 1839 Sex: Female

...................9 [467] Benjamin Everage Caudill, Civil War Col. b: January 11, 1830 in Whitesburg,

Perry/Letcher Co., KY d: February 11, 1889 in Claybourne Co., TN Number of children: 11 Sex: Male Burial: Slate Hill Baptist Cemetery, London, Laurel Co., KY (Note: he was in the 10th KY Rebel Mounted Infantry)

.........................+[468] Martha Lucinda Asbury b: July 11, 1828 in Tazewell Co., VA m: February 16, 1848 in Whitesburg, Letcher Co., KY d: September 20, 1900 in Scott Co., VA Number of children: 11 Father: William Asbury Mother: Elizabeth Chaffins Sex: Female

.....................10 [469] John Asbury Caudill b: March 26, 1849 in Letcher Co., KY d: May 30, 1912 in Ivan, Stephens Co., TX Sex: Male Burial: Veale's Creek Cemetery

..........................+[470] Alice Reeves b: Abt. 1853 in KY? Sex: Female

.....................10 [471] William Jesse Caudill b: December 28, 1850 in Whitesburg, Letcher Co., KY d: April 14, 1914 in Hobart, Kiowa Co., OK Sex: Male

.....................10 [472] Samuel Houston Caudill b: March 29, 1853 in Whitesburg, Letcher Co., KY d: 1928 in OK? Sex: Male

.....................10 [473] Stephen B. Caudill b: March 29, 1855 in Whitesburg, Letcher Co., KY d: in KY Sex: Male

.....................10 [474] Margaret Caudill b: 1857 in Whitesburg, Letcher Co., KY d: May 1937 in Lovington, NM Sex: Female

.....................10 [475] Rachel Caudill b: 1860 Sex: Female

.....................10 [476] James Watson Caudill b: 1862 in Whitesburg, Letcher Co., KY d: December 24, 1945 in Hatch, Dona Ana Co., NM Sex: Male

.....................10 [477] Evelyn Caudill b: 1865 Sex: Female

.....................10 [165] Benjamin Franklin Caudill b: May 03, 1867 in Sparta, Alleghanney Co., NC d: 1952 in Clay Co., KY Number of children: 10 Sex: Male Burial: Clay Co., KY

..........................+[478] Lucy Benge House b: September 30, 1867 in Manchester, Clay Co., KY m: December 26, 1885 in Manchester, Clay Co., KY d: April 01, 1938 in OK Number of children: 10 Father: James House Mother: Elizabeth Benge Sex: Female Burial: Erick Cemetery, Oklahoma City, OK

.......................11 [479] Lilly "Lizzie" Belle Caudill b: August 04, 1886 in Clay Co., KY d: August 22, 1945 Sex: Female

.......................11 [480] Victor Cleveland Caudill b: October 28, 1889 in Clay Co., KY d: December 12, 1948 in Hot Springs, Sierra, NM Number of children: 4 Sex: Male Burial: Hot Springs, Sierra, NM

.............................+[481] Mae D. Baker b: December 29, 1893 in Sewal, Wayne Co., IA m: Abt. 1911 d: February 20, 1976 in Clovis, NM Number of children: 4 Father: B. F. Baker Mother: Minnie Ensminger Sex: Female Burial: Clovis, NM

.......................11 [482] Grover Garrett Garrard Caudill b: March 02, 1891 in Pigeon Roost, Clay Co., KY d: October 30, 1948 in Washington Co., OR Sex: Male

.......................11 [483] Minnie Dora Caudill b: April 25, 1893 in Clay Co., KY d: May 1976 in Oklahoma City, OK Sex: Female

.......................11 [484] Henry Clay Caudill b: June 01, 1896 in Clay Co., KY d: August 04, 1931 in Erick, Beckham Co., OK Sex: Male

.......................11 [485] Margaret Luinda Caudill b: September 1897 in Clay Co., KY Sex: Female

.......................11 [486] Mayme Ellen Caudill b: June 11, 1899 in Clay Co., KY d: June 17, 1977 in Whittier, Los Angeles Co., CA Sex: Female

.......................11 [487] Lucy Mae Caudill b: May 07, 1901 in KY d: August 1986 in Dalhart, TX Sex: Female

.......................11 [488] Elizabeth Beatrice Caudill b: June 10, 1904 in Sayre, Beckham Co., OK d: April 18, 1995 in Minneapolis, MN Sex: Female

.......................11 [489] Benjamin Kathleen Caudill b: October 07, 1907 in Sayre, Beckham Co., OK d: October 10, 1997 in Albuquerque, NM Sex: Female

.....................2nd Wife of [165] Benjamin Franklin Caudill:

..........................+[490] Stella Louise Lovelace b: February 25, 1898 in KY m: Bet. 1917 - 1923 in NC d: December 1976 in Marana, AZ Father: Frank Lovelace Sex: Female

....................10 [491] Emery M. Caudill, Sr. b: April 07, 1869 in Sparta, Alleghanney Co., NC d: January 09, 1953 in Albuquerque, NM Sex: Male

....................10 [492] Elizabeth Caudill b: Abt. 1871 Sex: Female

..................9 [166] Samuel Patton Caudill b: December 29, 1831 in Perry/Letcher Co., KY d: October 29, 1907 in Letcher Co., KY? Sex: Male Burial: Caudill Cemetery, Letcher Co., KY

........................+[493] Letitia Meade b: 1835 in Russell Co., VA m: Abt. 1852 d: 1884 Sex: Female

..................2nd Wife of [166] Samuel Patton Caudill:

........................+[494] Mary Ann Greer b: Abt. 1837 in Scott Co., VA m: November 14, 1854 d: Abt. 1862 Sex: Female

..................3rd Wife of [166] Samuel Patton Caudill:

........................+[495] Sarah J. Hart b: Abt. 1875 m: Aft. 1854 in Letcher Co., KY Father: Hugh Hart Mother: Jane Adams Sex: Female

..................9 [496] Sarah L. Caudill b: October 23, 1834 in Whitesburg, Letcher Co., KY d: May 17, 1914 in Letcher Co., KY Sex: Female

..................9 [497] John Dixon Caudill b: October 06, 1836 in Sandlick or Whitesburg, Letcher Co., KY d: June 17, 1917 in Sandlick, Letcher Co., KY Sex: Male

........................+[498] Mary Ann Green b: November 25, 1838 in VA m: January 12, 1859 in Letcher Co., KY? d: June 23, 1920 in Sandlick, Letcher Co., KY Sex: Female (Note: Looking for her ancestors)

..................9 [499] David Jesse Caudill b: March 09, 1839 in Letcher Co., KY d: April 09, 1907 in Olive Hill, Carter Co., KY Sex: Male

..................9 [353] Nancy "Jane" Caudill, Caudell, b: November 05, 1840 in Whitesburg, Letcher Co., KY d: November 12, 1922 in London, Laurel Co., KY Number of children: 2 Sex: Female Burial: Lincks Cemetery

........................+[352] John Henderson Craft b: December 20, 1834 in Millstone, KY m: October 11, 1855 in Letcher Co., KY d: September 13, 1920 in Larue, Laurel Co., KY Number of children: 2 Father: Joseph Craft Mother: Martha Irby Bates Sex: Male Burial: Lincks Cemetery

....................10 [354] John Dixon Craft b: April 12, 1856 in Craftsville, Letcher Co., KY d: December 20, 1945 in KY Number of children: ? Sex: Male

...........................+[355] Mary Elizabeth Webb b: July 11, 1861 in Letcher Co., KY m: September 13, 1879 d: November 25, 1956 Number of children: ? Father: Henry T. "Chunk" Webb Mother: Francis Elizabeth "Franky" Adams Sex: Female (Webb Note: Like all of the other Webb individuals in this tree, this Webb family descends from the same line as the country singers Loretta (Webb) Lynn and her sister Brenda Gail "Crystal Gale" Webb. Loretta was born April 14, 1935, in Butcher Hollow, Pike Co., KY; Crystal Gale was born January 9, 1951, in Paintsville, Johnson Co., KY)

........................11 [500] Nancy Catherine "Nannie" Craft b: February 08, 1882 in Letcher Co., KY d: August 06, 1913 in KY? Sex: Female

...........................+[501] William Wash Webb b: October 1883 in KY Father: Nelson Robinette Webb Mother: Frances Catherine Spangler Sex: Male

....................10 [356] Martha A. Craft b: September 12, 1860 in Craftsville, KY d: September 16, 1951 in TN Number of children: 3 Sex: Female

...........................+[357] Noah Milburn Reynolds, Jr. b: December 15, 1855 in KY m: November 15, 1879 in Blountsville, TN d: April 30, 1923 in Mayo Clinic in TN Number of children: 3 Father: Noah Milburn Reynolds, Sr. Mother: Mary Chaney Stone Sex: Male

........................11 [502] John Henderson Reynolds b: Abt. 1880 Number of children: ? Sex: Male

...........................+[503] Nancy Jane Caudill Craft b: Abt. 1882 Number of children: ? Sex: Female

........................11 [504] Christopher Columbus Reynolds b: Abt. 1883 Sex: Male

........................11 [505] Mary C. Reynolds b: November 06, 1885 in Letcher Co., KY d:

September 14, 1955 in Whitley Co., KY Sex: Female

.............................+[506] Woodson Hodge Brown b: October 24, 1881 in Clay Co., KY m: December 06, 1906 in Clay Co., KY Sex: Male

...................9 [507] Elizabeth "Betty" Caudill b: August 22, 1842 in Letcher Co., KY Sex: Female Burial: Buffalo Cemetery, Sayre, OK

...................9 [508] Joseph Caudill, twin b: 1844 d: 1848 Sex: Male

...................9 [509] Nathaniel Caudill, twin b: 1844 d: 1848 Sex: Male

...................9 [350] Polly Ann Caudill b: April 15, 1847 in Letcher Co., KY d: February 11, 1937 in Millstone, Letcher Co., KY Number of children: ? Sex: Female

.........................+[349] Enoch "Chunk" A. Craft b: December 29, 1842 m: May 02, 1867 in Letcher Co., KY d: February 16, 1937 in Millstone, Letcher Co., KY Number of children: ? Father: Archelous Craft Mother: Letty Webb Sex: Male

......................10 [351] Nancy Craft b: January 1872 in Letcher Co., KY d: August 1872 in Letcher Co., KY Sex: Female

...................9 [510] Watson Garrard Caudill b: June 17, 1849 in Whitesburg, Letcher Co., KY d: August 05, 1930 in Perry Co., KY Sex: Male

................8 [167] Benjamin E. Caudill, b: 1799 in Wilkes Co., NC d: February 27, 1851 in Salyersville, Magoffin Co., KY Number of children: 3 Sex: Male

.......................+[168] Abigail Pennington, b: May 09, 1803 in Lee Co., VA d: 1887 in Salyersville, Magoffin Co., KY Number of children: 3 Father: William Pennington Mother: Abigail Caudill, Cordell, Sex: Female

...................9 [169] William Jackson "Jack" Caudill b: 1822 in Perry Co., KY Sex: Male Burial: Oil Springs, Johnson Co., KY

.........................+[170] Rebecca Harris b: Abt. 1826 in Floyd Co., KY Sex: Female Burial: Oil Springs, Johnson Co., KY

...................9 [171] Abel Caudill, b: January 16, 1827 in Morgan Co., KY Number of children: ? Sex: Male

.........................+[172] Phoebe Hitchcock b: November 28, 1827 in Floyd Co., KY m: October 28, 1846 in Johnson Co., KY Number of children: ? Sex: Female

......................10 [173] Jesse E. Caudill, b: September 07, 1847 in Johnson Co., KY d: September 14, 1890 Number of children: ? Sex: Male

............................+[174] Elizabeth "Lizzie" Elam b: November 28, 1847 in MaGoffin Co., KY m: February 18, 1869 in Magoffin Co., KY Number of children: ? Sex: Female

.........................11 [175] Abel Caudill, b: February 09, 1870 in MaGoffin Co., KY Sex: Male

...............................+[176] Elizabeth Bailey b: May 1876 in KY? Sex: Female

...................9 [177] Elizabeth Caudill b: 1833 in Perry Co., KY d: April 15, 1915 Number of children: ? Sex: Female

.........................+[178] Noah May b: Abt. 1831 in Magoffin Co., KY Number of children: ? Sex: Male

......................10 [179] Campbell J. May b: 1851 Number of children: ? Sex: Male

............................+[180] Rebecca E. Adams b: 1852 Number of children: ? Father: Gilbert A. Adams Mother: Perlina Prater Sex: Female

.........................11 [181] Augustus Noah May b: 1876 d: 1944 Number of children: ? Sex: Male

...............................+[182] Sarah Elizabeth Cornett b: 1876 d: 1966 Number of children: ? Father: Russell Cornett, Mother: Ailey Amburgey Sex: Female

...............8 [511] Elizabeth "Betsy" C. Caudill, b: June 18, 1800 in Wilkes Co., NC d: October 11, 1881 in Letcher Co., KY Number of children: ? Sex: Female Burial: Watty Caudill Cemetery, at the mouth of Dry Fork, Letcher Co., KY

......................+[512] John Quincy Brown b: 1788 in Ireland m: 1814 d: November 19, 1872 in Letcher Co., KY Number of children: ? Sex: Male

...................9 [513] Sarah "Sallie" Brown b: April 12, 1815 in KY d: April 19, 1892 in Letcher Co., KY Number of children: 3 Sex: Female

..........................+[514] Joseph Enoch Cornett, Judge b: April 28, 1814 in KY m: Abt. 1837 d: May 30, 1881 in Crown, Letcher Co., KY Number of children: 3 Father: William Jesse Cornett, Mother: Mary Ann Everage Sex: Male

.....................10 [515] Samuel A. Cornett b: April 18, 1840 d: Abt. 1931 Number of children: 6 Sex: Male

..........................+[516] Alcyann Couch, 4th wife b: Abt. 1870 in Perry Co., KY? m: Abt. 1888 Number of children: 6 Father: Samuel Couch, ? Mother: Emaline Wooten, ? Sex: Female

.....................11 [517] Granville Cornett b: Abt. 1889 Sex: Male

.....................11 [518] Lucy Cornett b: Abt. 1891 Sex: Female

.....................11 [519] Susan Cornett b: Abt. 1893 Sex: Female

.....................11 [520] James Cornett b: Abt. 1895 Sex: Male

.....................11 [521] Stephen Cornett b: Abt. 1897 Sex: Male

.....................11 [522] Armine Cornett b: Abt. 1900 Sex: Female

.....................10 [523] Elizabeth Ann 'Betty' Cornett b: Abt. 1842 Number of children: 4 Sex: Female

...........................+[524] Ira Stamper b: October 11, 1829 in Perry Co., KY m: April 26, 1876 in Letcher Co., KY d: February 05, 1910 in Rome, Douglas Co., MO Number of children: 4 Father: Isom Stamper Mother: Sarah Creech Sex: Male

.....................11 [525] Mary Ann 'Polly' Stamper Sex: Female

.....................11 [526] Neale Stamper Sex: Male

.....................11 [527] Nancy Elizabeth Stamper Sex: Female

.....................11 [528] Joseph Stamper Sex: Male

.....................10 [529] Rachel Cornett b: 1846 in Dry Fork, Pike or Letcher Co. , KY Sex: Female

...............8 [530] Nancy Caudill, b: June 18, 1804 Number of children: 2 Sex: Female

.......................+[531] Randolph "Randall" Adams b: 1802 in Roaring River, Wilkes Co., NC d: December 23, 1872 in Cowan, Perry/Letcher Co., KY Number of children: 2 Father: John Hobbs Adams, Jr., Mother: Lydia "Letty" or "Lettie" Simpson Sex: Male

.................9 [532] Lydia Adams b: Abt. 1825 Number of children: 10 Sex: Female

.......................+[533] Robert Collins b: October 21, 1823 in Rockhouse Creek, Perry Co., KY m: Abt. 1850 d: November 27, 1883 Number of children: 10 Father: James Shepherd Collins Mother: Elizabeth Lewis Sex: Male

.....................10 [534] Randolph Collins b: October 12, 1852 in Hazard, Perry Co., KY d: December 14, 1947 in Red Bluff, CA Sex: Male

...........................+[535] Eliza Jane Turner b: Abt. 1854 in Letcher Co., KY m: January 18, 1872 Father: James Turner Mother: Sarah Bailey Sex: Female

.....................10 [536] Nancy Collins b: December 15, 1855 in Colson, Letcher Co., KY d: February 06, 1918 in Colson, Letcher Co., KY Sex: Female

...........................+[537] James Jasper "Babe" Collins b: December 25, 1852 in Letcher Co., KY m: July 31, 1873 in Letcher Co., KY d: September 06, 1876 in Letcher Co., KY Father: Eli Collins Mother: Mary Barrett Sex: Male

.....................10 [538] James H. Collins b: July 18, 1857 in Rockhouse Creek, Letcher Co., KY d: September 01, 1942 Sex: Male

...........................+[539] Nancy Sarah Breeding b: Abt. 1859 in Letcher Co., KY m: September 18, 1879 Father: John Breeding Mother: Elizabeth "Betty" Combs Sex: Female

.....................10 [540] Sarah Collins b: May 04, 1859 in Rockhouse Creek, Letcher Co., KY d: May 15, 1859 in Letcher Co., KY Sex: Female

.....................10 [541] Elijah Collins b: Abt. 1860 Sex: Male

.....................10 [183] William Silas Collins b: April 21, 1865 d: December 15, 1937 in Letcher Co., KY Sex: Male

...........................+[542] Nancy Hale b: 1862 Father: William Rowlette Hale Mother: Elizabeth Collins Sex: Female

.....................2nd Wife of [183] William Silas Collins:

..........................+[358] Martha E. Crase b: Abt. 1868 m: March 03, 1888 in Letcher Co., KY Father: James Crase Mother: Elizabeth Stallard Sex: Female

....................10 [360] Greenbury Collins b: February 26, 1868 d: May 03, 1924 Sex: Male

..........................+[359] Christina Adams b: June 10, 1858 d: January 07, 1951 Father: Jesse "Colly Jesse" Adams Mother: Mary "Polly" Craft Sex: Female

....................10 [543] Lucinda Collins b: Abt. 1872 Sex: Female

....................10 [544] Lorenzo Dow Collins b: January 20, 1875 in Rockhouse Creek, Letcher Co., KY d: December 13, 1949 Sex: Male

..........................+[545] Nancy Ann Caudill b: Abt. 1877 in Letcher Co., KY m: February 04, 1897 Father: Watson Caudill Mother: Elizabeth Combs Sex: Female

....................10 [546] Eliza Collins b: 1879 Sex: Female

................9 [184] Watson E. "Watty" Adams b: April 1837 d: 1919 Number of children: 9 Sex: Male

..........................+[547] Rosa "Rausey" Hogg b: 1842 m: 1860 Number of children: ? Father: Hiram "Courthouse Hiram" Hogg Mother: Melvina "Viney" Polly Sex: Female

....................10 [548] Henry C. Adams b: 1863 Sex: Male

..........................+[549] Catherine Campbell b: September 1884 d: 1966 Father: John Henry Campbell Mother: Elizabeth Maggard Sex: Female

................2nd Wife of [184] Watson E. "Watty" Adams:

..........................+[550] Minerva Collins b: January 13, 1846 m: October 16, 1881 in Letcher Co., KY Number of children: 8 Father: Nathaniel "Nat" Collins Mother: Nancy Branham-Smith Sex: Female

....................10 [551] Floyd Adams b: Abt. 1882 Sex: Male

....................10 [552] Boyd Adams b: Abt. 1883 Sex: Male

....................10 [553] Randall Adams b: March 19, 1884 Sex: Male

....................10 [554] Francis Adams b: September 28, 1885 Sex: Female

....................10 [555] Patton Adams b: Abt. 1886 Sex: Male

....................10 [556] Green Ison Adams b: March 10, 1887 d: September 19, 1951 Sex: Male

....................10 [557] Hattie Adams b: August 21, 1889 Sex: Female

....................10 [558] Elizabeth Adams b: Abt. 1891 Sex: Female

................8 [559] Easter (or Esther) Caudill, b: 1806 in Wilkes Co., NC d: Abt. 1887 in Letcher Co., KY Number of children: ? Sex: Female

..........................+[560] Levi Eldridge b: August 1810 in Scott Co., VA d: 1877 in Rowan Co., KY Number of children: ? Sex: Male

................9 [185] Elizabeth "Betsy" Eldridge b: Abt. 1841 Number of children: 2 Sex: Female

..........................+[186] William W. "Wild Bill" Caudill b: Abt. 1839 in NC d: June 22, 1920 in Wolfe Co., KY Number of children: 2 Father: Wilburn E. Caudill Mother: Nancy Caudill Sex: Male

....................10 [187] Martha Ann Caudill b: Abt. 1861 Number of children: ? Sex: Female

..........................+[188] Enoch Everidge b: Abt. 1860 Number of children: ? Sex: Male

..........................11 [189] Susan "Susie" Everidge b: August 15, 1885 in KY d: December 29, 1962 in Perry Co., KY Number of children: 9 Sex: Female

..........................+[190] Hiram Combs b: May 07, 1882 d: April 29, 1962 Number of children: 9 Father: Benjamin Combs Mother: Matilda "Tilda" Combs Sex: Male

....................10 [25] Sarah Caudill b: September 1872 in Campton, KY Number of children: ? Sex: Female

..........................+[24] John C. Caudill b: February 1868 in Harlan or Letcher Co., KY m: April 18, 1889 in Breathitt Co., KY Number of children: ? Father: Henry H. Caudill Mother: Susannah Back Sex: Male

..........................11 [9] Cleveland Caudill b: June 1891 in Letcher Co., KY Sex: Male

..........................+[8] Peggy Caudill b: April 1890 in Letcher Co., KY m: July 14, 1909 in Letcher Co., KY d: January 14, 1916 Father: William B. Caudill Mother: Susannah "Sukie" Caudill Sex: Female

................8 [561] Sarah "Sally" Caudill, b: 1810 in Wilkes Co., NC d: 1863 in Hazard, Letcher Co., KY Number of children: 9 Sex: Female

.....................+[361] Moses "Rockhouse Moses" Adams b: July 18, 1808 in Letcher Co., KY m: July 20, 1825 in Hazard, Perry/Letcher Co., KY d: 1885 in Hazard, Letcher Co., KY Number of children: 12 Father: Stephen "Rockhouse Steve" Adams Mother: Ellendar "Nellie" Buntin, or Benton Sex: Male

..................9 [562] Sarah Adams b: Abt. 1826 Sex: Female

..................9 [563] Mary Adams b: Abt. 1827 in Rockhouse Creek, Floyd Co., KY d: in Letcher Co., KY Sex: Female

..................9 [564] Green Adams b: Abt. 1828 in Hazard, Letcher Co., KY d: in Hazard, Letcher Co., KY Number of children: 4 Sex: Male

........................+[565] Nancy Maggard b: Abt. 1830 m: Abt. 1850 d: in Hazard, Letcher Co., KY Number of children: 4 Sex: Female

.....................10 [566] Esther Adams b: March 1850 Sex: Female

...........................+[567] S. S. Banks b: Abt. 1850 m: September 24, 1897 Sex: Male

.....................10 [568] Martha Adams b: Abt. 1855 d: October 15, 1939 in Letcher Co., KY Sex: Female

...........................+[569] Daugherty Adams b: Abt. 1850 Sex: Male

.....................10 [570] Mary Ann "Polly" Adams b: Abt. 1860 Sex: Female

...........................+[571] George M. Gilley b: Abt. 1850 m: January 20, 1896 in Letcher Co., KY Sex: Male

.....................10 [209] Sarah Adams b: 1874 in Rockhouse Creek, Letcher Co., KY d: November 11, 1940 in Rockhouse Creek, Letcher Co., KY Sex: Female

...........................+[208] Elijah Adams b: May 31, 1866 in Rockhouse Creek, Letcher Co., KY m: March 25, 1890 in Letcher Co., KY d: September 02, 1932 in Rockhouse Creek, Letcher Co., KY Father: Stephen Adams Mother: Ursula Ison Sex: Male

..................9 [572] Stephen Adams b: 1827 in Hazard, Perry/Letcher Co., KY d: April 11, 1902 in Hazard, Perry/Letcher Co., KY Number of children: 10 Sex: Male

........................+[573] Ursula Ison b: January 10, 1825 in Hazard, Perry/Letcher Co., KY m: 1848 in Hazard, Perry/Letcher Co., KY d: April 11, 1904 in Letcher Co., KY Number of children: 10 Father: Gideon Ison Mother: Rachel Stamper Sex: Female

.....................10 [574] Sarah Adams b: Abt. 1848 Sex: Female

.....................10 [575] Rachel Adams b: 1849 in Letcher Co., KY d: December 09, 1929 in Knott Co., KY Sex: Female

...........................+[576] Frazier Adams b: March 01, 1841 in Perry Co., KY m: in Whitesburg, KY d: July 04, 1917 in Knott Co., KY Sex: Male

.....................10 [577] Moses Adams b: Abt. 1850 Sex: Male

.....................10 [578] Gideon Adams b: June 26, 1851 in Jeremiah, Letcher Co., KY d: April 17, 1927 in Jeremiah, Letcher Co., KY Number of children: 13 Sex: Male

...........................+[579] Sarah Blair b: 1849 in Whitesburg, Letcher Co., KY m: Bet. 1877 - 1878 in Jeremiah, Letcher Co., KY d: August 11, 1924 in Jeremiah, Letcher Co., KY Number of children: 13 Father: Hiram "Humpy" Blair Mother: Drusilla "Raillie" Craft Sex: Female

........................11 [192] Celia Ann Adams b: June 23, 1877 d: November 14, 1969 in Letcher Co., KY Number of children: 9 Sex: Female

...........................+[580] Solomon Banks b: September 07, 1856 in Letcher Co., KY m: December 16, 1896 d: September 05, 1936 in Colson, Letcher Co., KY Number of children: 7 Father: Samuel G. Banks Mother: Mary Frazier Sex: Male

........................2nd Husband of [192] Celia Ann Adams:

...........................+[581] Preston Blair b: Abt. 1880 m: Abt. 1900 Number of children: 4 Sex: Male

........................11 [582] Ursula "Usley" Adams b: Abt. 1878 Sex: Female Burial: Waynesburg, KY

........................11 [583] Annie Adams b: Abt. 1879 d: in Jeremiah, KY Number of children: 7 Sex:

Female

..............................+[584] Jim Adams b: Abt. 1875 m: Abt. 1905 d: in Jeremiah, Letcher Co., KY Number of children: 7 Sex: Male

........................11 [585] Hiram Adams b: Abt. 1881 d: in Waynesburg, Lincoln Co., KY Number of children: 6 Sex: Male

..............................+[586] _____ Caudill b: Abt. 1885 m: Abt. 1905 d: in Waynesburg, Lincoln Co., KY Number of children: 6 Sex: Female (Note: looking for her full name and ancestors)

........................11 [587] Fannie Adams b: Abt. 1885 d: in Jeremiah, KY Number of children: 7 Sex: Female Burial: Blair Branch, Letcher Co., KY

..............................+[588] William Adams b: Abt. 1885 m: Abt. 1905 in Jeremiah, Letcher Co., KY d: in Jeremiah, Letcher Co., KY Number of children: 7 Sex: Male

........................11 [195] Rebecca Adams b: Abt. 1887 d: in Waynesburg, KY Number of children: 8 Sex: Female

..............................+[10] Henry H. Cleveland Caudill b: April 20, 1887 in KY m: Abt. 1905 d: May 06, 1971 in Whitesburg, Letcher Co., KY Number of children: 18 Father: James William "Noah Jim" Caudill Mother: Lucinda Sumner Sex: Male Burial: Cleveland Caudill Cemetery, Caudill's Branch, Blackey, Letcher Co., KY

........................11 [206] Stephen B. Adams b: July 15, 1888 in Letcher Co., KY d: July 02, 1963 in Waynesburg, KY Number of children: ? Sex: Male

..............................+[589] Flora Banks b: Abt. 1890 m: Abt. 1910 d: February 17, 1963 Number of children: ? Sex: Female

........................2nd Wife of [206] Stephen B. Adams:

..............................+[590] Minnie Blair b: November 20, 1892 in Letcher Co., KY m: 1924 d: May 13, 1982 in Waynesburg, Lincoln Co., KY Sex: Female

........................11 [591] Judy Adams b: Abt. 1889 in Jeremiah, KY d: Abt. 1890 in Jeremiah, KY Sex: Female

........................11 [592] Dan Adams b: 1897 in Jeremiah, Letcher Co., KY d: 1937 in Horsemill Point, KY Number of children: 6 Sex: Male

..............................+[593] Virgie Smith b: Abt. 1900 m: Abt. 1920 d: in Jeremiah, Letcher Co., KY Number of children: 6 Sex: Female

........................11 [594] Frazier C. Adams, Sr. b: January 23, 1899 in Jeremiah, KY d: in Waynesburg, Lincoln Co., KY Number of children: 11 Sex: Male

..............................+[595] Melvina "Viney" Jent b: February 11, 1903 in Smithbough, Knott Co., KY m: October 03, 1920 in Smithbough, Knott Co., KY d: October 13, 2000 in Somerset, KY Number of children: 11 Father: Sylvester Jent, Gent, Mother: Lucinda "Cinda" Smith, Sex: Female Burial: Double Springs Cemetery, Cemetery Road, Waynesburg, KY

........................11 [596] Ritter Adams b: December 02, 1902 d: 1967 in Waynesburg, KY Number of children: 11 Sex: Female Burial: Double Creek, KY

..............................+[597] George Calfee b: Abt. 1900 m: Abt. 1920 d: in Waynesburg, Lincoln Co., KY Number of children: 11 Sex: Male

........................11 [598] Nancy Adams b: January 17, 1904 d: May 1928 Number of children: 6 Sex: Female

..............................+[599] Curtis Stamper b: October 17, 1898 m: 1923 d: January 1932 Number of children: 6 Sex: Male

........................11 [600] John Adams b: 1919 in Jeremiah, KY d: in died in WW I in Germany Sex: Male Burial: Horsemill Point, KY

....................10 [601] Anna "Annie" Adams b: October 04, 1853 in Letcher Co., KY d: in Letcher Co., KY Sex: Female

..............................+[602] Stephen C. Hampton b: 1851 Sex: Male

....................10 [603] Ester Adams b: January 18, 1855 in Letcher Co., KY d: January 26, 1929 Sex: Female

....................10 [604] Ison Moses Adams b: July 28, 1859 in Letcher Co., KY d: in Martin Co.,

KY Sex: Male

..............................+[605] Mary A. "Polly" Elkins b: 1860 in VA m: 1878 in Whitesburg, KY d: in Martin Co., KY Sex: Female

.....................10 [606] Nancy Adams b: April 1860 in Letcher Co., KY d: 1901 Sex: Female

..............................+[607] Daniel E. Adams b: June 05, 1849 in Letcher Co., KY m: 1874 in Whitesburg, KY Sex: Male

.....................10 [608] John Adams b: October 06, 1864 in Letcher Co., KY d: April 26, 1933 Sex: Male

..............................+[609] Laurena Roark b: November 24, 1874 d: May 20, 1965 Sex: Female

.....................10 [208] Elijah Adams b: May 31, 1866 in Rockhouse Creek, Letcher Co., KY d: September 02, 1932 in Rockhouse Creek, Letcher Co., KY Sex: Male

..............................+[209] Sarah Adams b: 1874 in Rockhouse Creek, Letcher Co., KY m: March 25, 1890 in Letcher Co., KY d: November 11, 1940 in Rockhouse Creek, Letcher Co., KY Father: Green Adams Mother: Nancy Maggard Sex: Female

...................9 [610] Ellender Adams b: January 20, 1829 in Rockhouse Creek, Floyd Co., KY d: March 07, 1886 in Letcher Co., KY Sex: Female

...........................+[611] Preston Blair b: 1827 in Perry/Letcher Co., KY m: March 04, 1849 in Letcher Co., KY d: 1878 in Letcher Co., KY Sex: Male

...................9 [612] Nancy Adams b: 1834 in Letcher Co., KY d: April 23, 1900 in Magoffin Co., KY Sex: Female

...........................+[613] George Adams b: 1832 in Pert Creek, Floyd Co., KY m: December 08, 1852 in Prestonburg, Floyd Co., KY d: 1876 in Magoffin Co., KY Sex: Male

...................9 [614] Esther Adams b: November 03, 1837 in Rockhouse Creek, Floyd Co., KY d: December 11, 1911 in Eolina, Perry/Letcher Co., KY Sex: Female

...........................+[615] Martin D. Collier b: March 27, 1834 in Eolina, Perry/Letcher Co., KY m: 1856 in Whitesburg, KY d: March 12, 1901 in Eolina, Perry/Letcher Co., KY Sex: Male

...................9 [616] John C. Adams b: July 02, 1841 in Rockhouse Creek, Floyd Co., KY d: February 27, 1930 in Letcher Co., KY Number of children: 8 Sex: Male

...........................+[617] Susanna Back b: December 18, 1845 in Letcher Co., KY m: July 02, 1867 in Letcher Co., KY d: September 13, 1926 in Letcher Co., KY Number of children: 8 Father: John Back Mother: Sarah _____? Sex: Female

.....................10 [618] Susan Adams b: Abt. 1868 Sex: Female

.....................10 [619] Henry Adams b: November 05, 1868 in Letcher Co., KY d: July 21, 1939 in Letcher Co., KY Sex: Male

..............................+[620] Amanda Combs b: Abt. 1870 m: January 03, 1892 in Whitesburg, KY d: 1910 in Letcher Co., KY Sex: Female

.....................10 [621] Stephen Adams b: October 16, 1871 in Letcher Co., KY d: July 21, 1954 in Letcher Co., KY Sex: Male

..............................+[622] Ardelia Craft b: 1874 in Letcher Co., KY m: November 17, 1893 in Whitesburg, KY d: 1921 in Letcher Co., KY Sex: Female

.....................10 [623] Moses Adams b: 1874 in Letcher Co., KY Sex: Male

..............................+[624] Elizabeth Jane Caudill b: Abt. 1875 m: 1895 Sex: Female

.....................10 [625] Joseph Adams b: 1877 in Letcher Co., KY d: September 01, 1954 in Letcher Co., KY Sex: Male

..............................+[626] Rachel Craft b: Abt. 1880 m: 1910 in Whitesburg, KY Sex: Female

.....................10 [627] Frances "Fanny" Adams b: November 1879 Sex: Female

..............................+[628] Creed Craft b: Abt. 1875 Sex: Male

.....................10 [629] James M. Adams b: 1882 in Letcher Co., KY d: in Jeremiah, Letcher Co., KY Sex: Male

..............................+[630] Anna _____? b: Abt. 1885 m: in Whitesburg, KY Sex: Female

.....................10 [631] William Adams b: June 27, 1885 in Letcher Co., KY d: June 06, 1970 in Letcher Co., KY Sex: Male

...........................+[632] Frances _____? b: Abt. 1890 m: in Whitesburg, KY d: in Letcher Co., KY Sex: Female

..................9 [210] Benjamin Adams b: 1843 in Rockhouse Creek, Letcher Co., KY Number of children: 8 Sex: Male

........................+[633] Sarah Sally Maggard b: Abt. 1845 m: Abt. 1861 Father: Henry Maggard Mother: Mary "Polly" Stamper Sex: Female

...................2nd Wife of [210] Benjamin Adams:

........................+[634] Lucinda "Cindy" Combs b: June 06, 1847 in Letcher Co., KY m: 1862 in Whitesburg, KY d: February 07, 1874 in Jeremiah, KY Number of children: 8 Father: John Wesley Combs, Mother: Polly (Mary) Hogg Sex: Female

.....................10 [635] Isaac Adams b: Abt. 1863 in Letcher Co., KY Sex: Male

.....................10 [636] Millie Adams b: Abt. 1865 Sex: Female

...........................+[637] Leonard Crocker b: Abt. 1865 m: 1896 in Whitesburg, KY Sex: Male

.....................10 [638] Elizabeth Adams b: 1863 in Letcher Co., KY Sex: Female

...........................+[639] John Cook b: Abt. 1860 m: August 26, 1882 in Whitesburg, KY Sex: Male

.....................10 [640] Shadrack Adams b: March 03, 1865 in Letcher Co., KY d: December 24, 1937 Sex: Male

...........................+[641] Susan Brown b: March 24, 1876 m: July 03, 1898 in Whitesburg, KY d: December 27, 1965 Sex: Female

.....................10 [642] Marianne Adams b: October 10, 1867 in Letcher Co., KY d: August 20, 1947 Sex: Female

...........................+[643] Shade Combs b: December 22, 1859 m: January 29, 1885 in Whitesburg, KY d: January 27, 1940 Sex: Male

.....................10 [644] James M. Adams b: 1868 Sex: Male

.....................10 [645] William Adams b: 1870 Sex: Male

.....................10 [211] General Adams b: January 29, 1874 in Letcher Co., KY d: 1959 Sex: Male

...........................+[212] Martha Caudill b: February 14, 1882 in Perry Co., KY m: January 29, 1902 d: July 28, 1957 Father: Henry R. Stephen Caudill Mother: Mary Branson Sex: Female

................8 [646] Lydia Caudill, b: July 19, 1816 Number of children: ? Sex: Female

.....................+[647] Nathaniel Woolery Cornett, b: 1811 d: 1899 Number of children: ? Father: William Jesse Cornett, Mother: Mary Ann Everage Sex: Male

................9 [648] Pollyann Cornett, b: 1842 in Knott Co., KY Sex: Female

...............8 [649] Jesse B. Caudill, b: November 10, 1818 in Perry Co., KY d: 1904 in Letcher Co., KY Number of children: 8 Sex: Male Burial: Watty Caudill Cemetery, at the mouth of Dry Fork, Letcher Co., KY

...................+[650] Mary "Polly" Back, Bach b: February 03, 1827 in Letcher Co.,? KY m: April 04, 1844 in Letcher Co., KY d: July 29, 1888 Number of children: 8 Father: Henry Back, Bach Mother: Susannah Maggard Sex: Female Burial: Watty Caudill Cemetery, at the mouth of Dry Fork, Letcher Co., KY

.................9 [213] Benjamin "Paw Paw" Caudill, b: 1846 in Letcher Co., KY d: Abt. 1927 Number of children: 2 Sex: Male

........................+[651] Sarah "Sallie" Brashear b: Abt. 1856 in Perry Co., KY Sex: Female (Note: Looking for her ancestors)

..................2nd Wife of [213] Benjamin "Paw Paw" Caudill, :

........................+[652] Terry Hampton b: 1847 in Letcher Co., KY m: 1868 in KY d: March 06, 1877 in Letcher Co., KY Number of children: 2 Father: Wilburn Hampton Mother: Phoebe Caudill Sex: Female Burial: Watty Caudill Cemetery, at the mouth of Dry Fork, Letcher Co., KY

.....................10 [653] Polly Ann Caudill, b: May 1872 in KY Number of children: 4 Sex: Female

...........................+[654] Elhannon Jent, b: September 12, 1873 in Indian Bottom, Perry Co., KY m: Abt. 1895 in Perry or Letcher Co., KY d: May 05, 1947 in Scuddy, Perry Co., KY Number of children: 4 Father: John Jent, Ghent, Mother: Nellie or Nella or "Nell" Sumner, Sex: Male Burial:

May 06, 1947 Sumner Cem., Perry Co., KY

..................11 [655] Sally Jent b: March 1896 Sex: Female

..................11 [656] John D. Jent b: June 1898 Sex: Male

..................11 [657] Phoebe Jent b: 1909 in KY Sex: Female

..........................+[658] Ira Combs b: 1901 in KY? Father: Richard Nicholas "Dick" Combs Mother: Nancy Martin Sex: Male

..................11 [659] Chester Jent, b: Abt. 1911 in VicCo., KY? Number of children: ? Sex: Male

.............................+[660] Oma Smith b: Abt. 1913 in VicCo., KY? Number of children: ? Father: Thomas "Tom" Smith, Mother: Vinabelle Smith, Sex: Female

...............10 [661] John D. Caudill b: July 29, 1875 in KY d: October 17, 1955 in Perry Co., KY Number of children: ? Sex: Male

.........................+[662] Martha (or Patsy) Polly b: August 10, 1878 in KY m: Abt. 1897 in KY d: October 31, 1949 Number of children: ? Sex: Female (Note: Looking for her ancestors)

..................11 [663] Enoch Caudill b: Abt. 1910 Number of children: ? Sex: Male

.........................+[664] Hazel McIntry b: Abt. 1912 m: February 11, 1933 Number of children: ? Sex: Female

.............9 [665] Susanna Caudill b: January 1850 d: February 27, 1920 Sex: Female Burial: Watty Caudill Cemetery, at the mouth of Dry Fork, Letcher Co., KY

..................+[666] Stephen Roberts b: Abt. 1848 Father: Preston Roberts Mother: Rebecca Caudill Sex: Male

.............9 [214] John Maggard Caudill b: June 25, 1852 in Letcher Co., KY d: August 31, 1939 Number of children: ? Sex: Male

..................+[667] Susanna Hampton b: Abt. 1861 d: June 30, 1877 Father: Wilburn Hampton Mother: Phoebe Caudill Sex: Female Burial: Watty Caudill Cemetery, at the mouth of Dry Fork, Letcher Co., KY

.............2nd Wife of [214] John Maggard Caudill:

..................+[668] Polly Ann Morgan b: 1861 in Letcher Co., KY m: May 31, 1882 in Letcher Co., KY Number of children: ? Sex: Female (Note: Looking for ancestors)

...............10 [669] William H. Caudill b: January 02, 1893 in Letcher Co., KY d: September 25, 1963 in Elkhorn City, Pike Co., KY Number of children: ? Sex: Male

.........................+[670] Ollie Mae Sumner b: September 02, 1897 in Fusonia, Perry Co., KY m: March 23, 1917 in Perry Co., KY d: July 11, 1953 in Grundy, VA Number of children: ? Sex: Female

..................11 [671] Edith Caudill b: January 31, 1919 in Cornettsville, Perry Co., KY d: 1999 in Perry Co., KY Number of children: ? Sex: Female

.........................+[672] Marcellus Combs b: September 05, 1916 in Allais, Perry Co., KY m: November 03, 1939 in Perry Co., KY d: March 10, 1988 in Hazard, Perry Co., KY Number of children: ? Father: Owen Combs Mother: Mahala Campbell Sex: Male

.............9 [673] Nancy C. Caudill b: December 09, 1853 d: January 06, 1915 Number of children: 5 Sex: Female Burial: Watty Caudill Cemetery, at the mouth of Dry Fork, Letcher Co., KY

..................+[674] James Dixon Caudill b: December 13, 1854 d: May 04, 1938 Number of children: 5 Sex: Male Burial: Watty Caudill Cemetery, at the mouth of Dry Fork, Letcher Co., KY

...............10 [675] Watson Caudill b: February 08, 1878 d: December 1878 Sex: Male Burial: Watty Caudill Cemetery, at the mouth of Dry Fork, Letcher Co., KY

...............10 [215] Mary Caudill b: December 05, 1881 d: November 29, 1930 Sex: Female Burial: Watty Caudill Cemetery, at the mouth of Dry Fork, Letcher Co., KY

.........................+[676] Jeremiah P. Dixon b: Abt. 1880 Sex: Male

...............2nd Husband of [215] Mary Caudill:

.........................+[677] Joe Hawkins b: Abt. 1879 Sex: Male

...............10 [678] James Caudill b: February 10, 1890 d: September 19, 1899 Sex: Male Burial: Watty Caudill Cemetery, at the mouth of Dry Fork, Letcher Co., KY

.....................10 [679] Rachel Caudill b: July 13, 1898 d: October 02, 1900 Sex: Female Burial: Watty Caudill Cemetery, at the mouth of Dry Fork, Letcher Co., KY

.....................10 [680] Boyd Caudill b: November 22, 1898 d: December 22, 1919 Sex: Male Burial: Watty Caudill Cemetery, at the mouth of Dry Fork, Letcher Co., KY

.................9 [681] Watson "Watty" Caudill b: Abt. 1854 Number of children: ? Sex: Male

.......................+[682] Rachel Hampton b: March 23, 1852 d: December 25, 1881 Number of children: ? Father: Wilburn Hampton Mother: Phoebe Caudill Sex: Female Burial: Watty Caudill Cemetery, at the mouth of Dry Fork, Letcher Co., KY

.....................10 [216] Jesse Wilburn Caudill b: Abt. 1876 Number of children: ? Sex: Male

..........................+[683] Rosanna Tyree b: Abt. 1878 d: July 14, 1899 Sex: Female Burial: Watty Caudill Cemetery, at the mouth of Dry Fork, Letcher Co., KY

....................2nd Wife of [216] Jesse Wilburn Caudill:

...........................+[684] Mary Miller b: Abt. 1879 Number of children: ? Sex: Female

.......................11 [685] unnamed Caudill b: June 14, 1901 d: June 14, 1901 Sex: Male Burial: Watty Caudill Cemetery, at the mouth of Dry Fork, Letcher Co., KY

.................9 [686] Henry Caudill, b: November 15, 1856 in Letcher Co., KY? d: March 07, 1899 Number of children: 2 Sex: Male

.......................+[687] Barilla Jones b: May 22, 1877 d: January 29, 1899 Number of children: 2 Sex: Female

.....................10 [688] William M. Caudill, World War I Soldier b: April 27, 1896 d: July 12, 1966 Number of children: 2 Sex: Male Burial: Caudill Cemetery at Uz, Letcher Co., KY

.......................+[689] Etta B. Dixon b: September 10, 1899 d: September 08, 1938 Number of children: 2 Father: James C. Dixon Mother: Evelyn Back, Bach Sex: Female

.....................11 [690] Harold K. Caudill, b: Abt. 1910 Number of children: ? Sex: Male

.............................+[691] Dociphene Frazier b: Abt. 1915 Number of children: ? Father: Enoch Flanery Frazier Mother: Sarah "Elizabeth" Boatright Sex: Female

.....................11 [692] Helen M. Caudill b: August 23, 1935 d: September 09, 1935 Sex: Female Burial: Caudill Cemetery at Uz, Letcher Co., KY

.....................10 [693] Jesse Caudill b: July 21, 1898 d: November 25, 1935; Killed by his wife with an axe Sex: Male

...........................+[694] Artie Cornett, b: Abt. 1900 Sex: Female (Note: Looking for her ancestors)

.................9 [695] Easter Caudill, Johnny's 7th wife b: December 17, 1859 d: November 08, 1882 Sex: Female Burial: Watty Caudill Cemetery, at the mouth of Dry Fork, Letcher Co., KY

.......................+[696] Johnny C. Brown b: Abt. 1820 Father: George W. Brown Mother: Susanna Wells Sex: Male

.................9 [697] David J. Caudill b: December 21, 1860 d: September 15, 1882 Sex: Male Burial: Watty Caudill Cemetery, at the mouth of Dry Fork, Letcher Co., KY

...............8 [698] Henry Caudill, b: Abt. 1820 Sex: Male

...............8 [699] Watson E. "Old Watty" Caudill, b: March 14, 1822 in Perry Co., KY d: December 05, 1898 in Letcher Co., KY Number of children: 4 Sex: Male

.....................+[700] Elizabeth "Betty" Branham-Smith, b: March 19, 1827 in Perry Co., KY m: Abt. 1846 in Perry Co., KY? Number of children: 4 Father: William "Billy" Branham-Smith Mother: Elizabeth "Betty" Childers Sex: Female

.................9 [701] Polly Ann Caudill b: Abt. 1847 Sex: Female

.................9 [702] Rachel Caudill b: December 24, 1855 d: October 09, 1876 Sex: Female Burial: Watty Caudill Cemetery, at the mouth of Dry Fork, Letcher Co., KY

.................9 [703] Martha Salina Caudill b: Abt. 1860 Number of children: ? Sex: Female

.......................+[704] Rudolphus "Dolph" A. Lafayette Draughn b: Abt. 1855 m: Abt. 1882 Number of children: ? Sex: Male (Note: looking for his ancestors)

.....................10 [705] _____ Draughn, ? b: Abt. 1895 Number of children: ? Sex: Male

...........................+[706] _____ _____? b: Abt. 1900 Number of children: ? Sex: Female

...................9 [709] Lucinda Caudill b: April 10, 1862 d: October 13, 1906 Number of children: ? Sex: Female Burial: Watty Caudill Cemetery, at the mouth of Dry Fork, Letcher Co., KY

.........................+[710] Steve Hall b: Abt. 1860 Number of children: ? Sex: Male

.....................10 [711] Beckham Hall b: June 04, 1904 d: June 04, 1904 Sex: Male Burial: Watty Caudill Cemetery, at the mouth of Dry Fork, Letcher Co., KY

.................8 [712] Walter E. Caudill, b: Abt. 1824 Sex: Male

.................8 [713] Fanny Caudill, b: Abt. 1826 Sex: Female

.............7 [774] John Washington "Wash" Adams, b: Bet. 1780 - 1785 in Roaring River or Wilkesboro, Wilkes Co., NC d: 1851 Number of children: ? Sex: Male (Not sure if John is the Father of Sarah)

...................+[1154] _____ _____? , b: 1785 in NC or KY? m: 1803 in NC or KY? Number of children: ? Sex: Female (Note: Looking for her full name & ancestors)

.................8 [714] Sarah "Sally" Adams, parents unknown b: 1807 in NC Number of children: 9 Sex: Female (Note: Looking for her ancestors; I believe her Father MAY be John Washington "Wash" Adams. b. 1785 in NC)

.......................+[715] William B. "Buckie" Holbrook, Sr., b: 1809 in Floyd Co., KY m: Abt. 1826 in Floyd Co., KY Number of children: 9 Father: Randolph (or Randel) "Buck" Holbrook, Mother: Elizabeth Nancy Rebecca Adams, Sex: Male

...................9 [716] Mary "Polly" Holbrook, b: 1827 in Perry Co., KY d: April 11, 1854 in Letcher Co., KY Number of children: 2 Sex: Female

.........................+[717] Esquire "Squire" Bentley, b: 1821 in Letcher Co., KY m: October 24, 1850 in Letcher Co., KY Number of children: 2 Father: John Queller Bentley, Sr., Mother: Margaret "Peggy" Hamilton, Sex: Male

...................10 [718] William Barlow "Barlow" Bentley b: March 1849 in KY Number of children: 13 Sex: Male

............................+[719] Susannah Quillen b: September 20, 1857 in Letcher Co., KY m: September 19, 1872 in Letcher Co., KY d: February 14, 1926 Number of children: 13 Father: Richard Teague Quillen Mother: Catherine Yonts Sex: Female (Note: some say she was born 9 22 1859) .

.......................11 [720] William D. Bentley b: 1874 in KY Sex: Male

.......................11 [721] Mary Bentley b: 1876 in KY Sex: Female

.......................11 [722] Polly Bentley b: November 1876 Sex: Female

.......................11 [723] Arminda ("Armindy") Bentley b: December 1878 in KY Sex: Female

.......................11 [724] Squire Richard Bentley b: December 12, 1879 d: May 06, 1933 Number of children: 16 Sex: Male

.............................+[725] Rosemond Fidel Hall b: Abt. 1880 Number of children: 16 Sex: Female

.......................11 [726] Benjamin Franklin Bentley b: June 1882 Number of children: ? Sex: Male

.......................11 [727] James M. Bentley b: May 1888 Sex: Male

.......................11 [728] Wiley A. Bentley b: July 1889 Sex: Male

.......................11 [729] Nancy J. Bentley b: March 1894 Sex: Female

.......................11 [730] Samantha Bentley b: Abt. August 1895 Sex: Female

.......................11 [731] Robert S. Bentley b: March 1896 Sex: Male

.......................11 [732] Sarah E. Bentley b: April 1898 Sex: Female

.......................11 [733] Ira J. Bentley b: 1902 Sex: Male

.....................10 [734] Sarah "Sally" Bentley, b: July 1852 in Letcher Co., KY d: Aft. 1920 in Pulaski Co., KY? Number of children: 3 Sex: Female

............................+[735] William James Yonts, b: December 1845 in Letcher Co., KY m: March 18, 1870 in Letcher Co., KY d: Aft. 1920 in Pulaski Co., KY? Number of children: 3 Father: William Yonts, Jr., Yants, Mother: Nancy F. Ray, Sex: Male (Yonts Note: Like the author and all of the other Yonts individuals in this tree, this family descends from Wilhelm Jans, born in 1714 in the town of Oberalben, Rheineland-Pfalz, Germany; Wilhelm died in 1778 in Rowan Co., NC)

.........................11 [417] Esquire "Squire" Lincoln Yonts, Yantz, b: April 30, 1874 in Letcher Co., KY d: December 10, 1942 in Knoxville, TN Number of children: 9 Sex: Male Burial: Abt. December 13, 1942 Sharp Cemetery (Note: Letcher Co. Birth Records state that his middle initial was "F"). NOTE: Squire Yonts is the author's great-grandfather.

.............................+[736] Mary Frances Wright, b: January 27, 1872 in Upper Elkhorn Creek, Pike Co., KY ? m: April 23, 1890 in Letcher Co., KY d: April 12, 1950 in Neon, Hogg Hollow, Letcher Co., KY Number of children: 9 Father: William A. Wright, Mother: Arty (Artie or Arta) M. Potter, Sex: Female Burial: Abt. April 15, 1950 Yonts Cemetery, Craft Funeral Home, Neon, Letcher Co., KY. NOTE: Mary is the author's great-grandmother.

.........................2nd Wife of [417] Squire Lincoln Yonts, Yantz, :

.............................+[737] Louise _____? b: Abt. 1880 m: December 1907 Sex: Female

.........................3rd Wife of [417] Squire Lincoln Yonts, Yantz, :

.............................+[738] Alice _____? b: Abt. 1900 m: Aft. 1920 Sex: Female Burial: Sharp Cemetery

.........................11 [739] Nancy Chaney Yonts b: April 15, 1878 in Letcher Co., KY d: November 20, 1927 in at her daughter's home in Wise, VA or Waynesburg, Lincoln Co., KY Number of children: 9 Sex: Female

.............................+[740] Archibald "Archie" Lincoln Meade b: 1874 in Letcher Co., KY m: August 06, 1895 in Neon, Letcher Co., KY Number of children: 9 Sex: Male

.........................11 [418] Robert Grant Yonts b: May 04, 1883 in Letcher Co., KY d: September 13, 1964 Number of children: 15 Sex: Male

.............................+[741] Henrietta "Hennie" Ritter Holbrook b: December 05, 1881 in Letcher Co., KY? m: 1901 in Letcher Co., KY d: April 02, 1965 Number of children: 9 Father: Enoch A. Holbrook Mother: Nancy Evelyn Webb Sex: Female

.........................2nd Wife of [418] Robert Grant Yonts:

.............................+[742] Dorothy Pence b: Abt. 1890 in KY? m: Aft. 1922 Number of children: 6 Sex: Female

.................9 [743] Nancy Ann Holbrook b: 1831 Sex: Female

.................9 [744] Susannah Holbrook b: 1834 Sex: Female

.................9 [745] James E. Holbrook b: November 18, 1836 Number of children: 7 Sex: Male

.........................+[746] Tabitha Bentley b: 1843 Number of children: 7 Father: Daniel Bentley, Sr., Mother: Marinda (Brinkley?) Ramey (Note: Marinda descends from the same family line as country singer Patty (Ramey) Loveless, born January 4, 1957 in Pikeville, Pike Co., KY) Sex: Female

.....................10 [747] Mary E. "Polly" Holbrook b: 1867 Number of children: ? Sex: Female

.........................+[748] Noah (Paw) Bentley b: Abt. 1865 Number of children: ? Father: Benjamin Bentley Mother: Elizabeth E. "Patsy" Reynolds Sex: Male

.........................11 [749] Lincoln Bentley b: Abt. 1890 Number of children: ? Sex: Male

.............................+[750] Etta Bentley b: Abt. 1895 Number of children: ? Sex: Female

.....................10 [751] William B. Holbrook b: May 1869 Sex: Male

.........................+[752] Sarah Clark b: Abt. 1870 Sex: Female

.....................10 [753] John A. Holbrook b: April 1871 Sex: Male

.........................+[754] Lucinda Huff b: 1874 Sex: Female

.....................10 [755] Sarah M. Holbrook b: 1872 Sex: Female

.....................10 [756] Didamey Holbrook b: Abt. 1876 Sex: Female

.....................10 [757] Zilpha P. Holbrook b: 1879 Sex: Female

.....................10 [758] Gracie Holbrook b: 1889 Sex: Female

.................9 [759] William B. Holbrook, Jr. b: 1839 Sex: Male

.................9 [760] Randolph E. Holbrook b: 1841 Sex: Male

.................9 [761] Benjamin W. Holbrook b: 1845 Sex: Male

.................9 [762] Ransom T. Holbrook b: March 21, 1846 d: March 01, 1894 Number of children: 5 Sex: Male Burial: Bottom Fork, Letcher Co., KY

.........................+[763] Elizabeth Ann Hughes b: March 10, 1850 in Letcher Co., KY m: July 10,

1866 d: October 22, 1917 Number of children: 5 Father: John Hughes Mother: Matilda Bentley, (Note: Looking for her ancestors) Sex: Female Burial: Bottom Fork, Letcher Co., KY

....................10 [764] John A. Holbrook b: Abt. 1865 Number of children: ? Sex: Male (Note: Looking for his ancestors)

...........................+[765] Mary Ann Stewart b: Abt. 1860 Number of children: ? Father: Thomas "Tom" Stewart Mother: Susannah Fleming Sex: Female

.....................11 [766] Gabriel Holbrook b: Abt. 1880 Number of children: ? Sex: Male

.............................+[767] Norma Sturgill b: Abt. 1880 in Pound, VA Number of children: ? Father: Gordon Sturgill Sex: Female

....................10 [768] Sarah "Sally" Holbrook b: November 05, 1867 in Letcher Co., KY d: February 16, 1929 Sex: Female

...........................+[769] Wiley W. Quillen b: September 1861 in Letcher Co., KY m: November 30, 1882 in Letcher Co., KY d: 1938 Father: Richard Teaque Quillen Mother: Catherine Yonts Sex: Male

....................10 [770] Nancy "Nannie" Holbrook b: 1868 Sex: Female

....................10 [771] Francis Holbrook b: 1880 Sex: Female

...................10 [772] John A. Holbrook b: Abt. 1880 Sex: Male

..................9 [773] Doctor "Dock" Holbrook b: 1850 Sex: Male

............2nd Wife of [774] John Washington "Wash" Adams, :

...................+[1155] Mary Polly Hall b: 1806 in Letcher Co., KY m: April 08, 1830 in Hazard, Perry Co., KY Sex: Female (Note: Looking for her ancestors)

............3rd Wife of [774] John Washington "Wash" Adams, :

...................+[1156] Jane M. Donnell b: 1789 m: July 29, 1845 in Greene Co., MO Sex: Female (Note: Looking for ancestors)

............7 [1157] Esther H. Adams b: 1787 in Roaring River, Wilkes Co., NC d: 1836 Sex: Female

...................+[1158] William Williams b: Abt. 1780 m: Abt. 1804 Sex: Male

............7 [1159] Nancy Adams b: 1788 in Roaring River, Wilkes Co., NC d: 1840 in Letcher Co., KY Sex: Female

...................+[1160] Charles Lewis b: Abt. 1775 m: Abt. 1804 in Wilkes Co., NC d: Aft. 1840 in IN? Father: George ? Lewis Mother: _____ _____? Sex: Male

..........6 Jacob Adams, b: 1753 Sex: Male

..........6 [1161] Spencer Adams, b: 1759 in Loudoun, VA d: October 12, 1830 in Selma, Dallas Co., AL Sex: Male

................+Nancy Irvin b: Abt. 1765 m: Aft. 1795 Sex: Female

..........2nd Wife of [1161] Spencer Adams, :

...............+Sarah Corbin b: Abt. 1761 m: February 10, 1796 in Pittsylvania, VA Sex: Female

..........6 [1162] Mary A. Adams, b: 1760 in Letcher Co., KY d: in Wilkes Co., NC Number of children: 11 Sex: Female

...............+[6] James "Jimmie" Caudill, Jr., Rev. War Soldier b: 1753 in Wilkes Co., NC m: February 09, 1785 in Wilkes Co., NC d: May 30, 1840 in Blackey, Letcher Co., KY Number of children: 12 Father: James Caudill, Sr., Cordell, Coddill, Caudel Mother: Mary Yarborough, Yarbrough Sex: Male Burial: Rockhouse Creek, Perry Co., KY (Note: fought in Revolutionary War, Kings Mountain & Cowpens)

............7 [7] William C. "Billy" Caudill, b: July 27, 1779 in Wilkes Co., NC d: July 27, 1880 in Letcher Co., KY Number of children: 14 Sex: Male

...................+[395] Nancy Adams b: 1785 Father: John Hobbs Adams, Jr., Mother: Nancy Ann "Ann" Caudill, Sex: Female

............2nd Wife of [7] William C. "Billy" Caudill, :

...................+[237] Mary Nancy "Nancy" Craft b: 1784 in Harris Creek, Wilkes Co., NC m: Abt. 1804 d: July 27, 1877 in Letcher Co., KY Number of children: 14 Father: Archelous Craft, Sr., Rev. War Soldier Mother: Elizabeth "Betsy" Adams Sex: Female

...............8 [238] Ellender Caudill b: Abt. 1805 Sex: Female

................8 [239] Betsy Caudill b: Abt. 1806 Sex: Female

................8 [240] Delilah "Lila" Caudill b: May 08, 1807 Sex: Female

................8 [241] Isabel Caudill b: Abt. 1809 Sex: Female

................8 [242] Mary Caudill b: March 10, 1811 in KY d: September 13, 1880 Number of children: 10 Sex: Female

......................+[243] Joshua Mullins b: November 18, 1809 in Knox Co., KY d: February 15, 1900 in Letcher Co., KY Number of children: 10 Father: Joshua Mullins, Mother: Anna Robinson Sex: Male

..................9 [244] John Mullins b: December 26, 1834 Sex: Male

..................9 [245] Joseph M. Mullins b: June 19, 1834 Sex: Male

..................9 [246] Solomon Mullins b: 1838 Sex: Male

..................9 [247] Caleb Mullins b: 1840 Sex: Male

..................9 [248] Joshua Mullins b: 1842 Sex: Male

..................9 [249] Anna Mullins b: September 18, 1842 Sex: Female

..........................+[250] George Washington Adams b: September 02, 1839 in Letcher Co., KY d: 1943 in Washington Father: Moses "Smoot" Adams Mother: Rebecca (Roberts) Hall Sex: Male

..................9 [251] William Mullins b: 1846 Sex: Male

..................9 [252] Delilah Mullins b: Aft. 1846 Sex: Female

..................9 [253] Nancy Mullins b: Aft. 1847 Sex: Female

..................9 [254] James Henderson Mullins b: September 12, 1853 Sex: Male

................8 [255] Rebecca "Becca" Caudill b: April 15, 1815 Sex: Female

................8 [256] Elizabeth "Betsy" Caudill b: Abt. 1816 d: in Knox Co., KY Number of children: 12 Sex: Female

......................+[257] Caleb Mullins b: 1810 in KY d: in KY Number of children: 12 Father: Joshua Mullins, Mother: Anna Robinson Sex: Male

..................9 [258] William Mullins b: 1834 Sex: Male

..................9 [259] Mary Mullins b: Abt. 1836 Sex: Female

..................9 [260] Ann Mullins b: Abt. 1838 Sex: Female

..................9 [261] Nancy Mullins b: Abt. 1838 Sex: Female

..................9 [262] Joab Mullins b: Abt. 1841 Sex: Male

..................9 [263] Sarah Mullins b: Abt. 1844 Sex: Female

..................9 [264] John Mullins b: Abt. 1847 Sex: Male

..................9 [265] Susan Mullins b: 1850 Sex: Female

..................9 [266] Hugh Mullins b: August 25, 1852 Sex: Male

..................9 [267] James K. Mullins b: September 03, 1856 Sex: Male

..................9 [268] Elizabeth Mullins b: 1860 Sex: Female

..................9 [269] Ann Mullins b: October 1868 Sex: Female

................8 [218] Nancy Caudill b: Abt. 1817 in KY d: 1894 Number of children: 2 Sex: Female

......................+[217] Wilburn E. Caudill b: Abt. 1812 in NC Number of children: 2 Father: William Caudill Mother: Rachel Joines Sex: Male

..................9 [186] William W. "Wild Bill" Caudill b: Abt. 1839 in NC d: June 22, 1920 in Wolfe Co., KY Number of children: 2 Sex: Male

..........................+[185] Elizabeth "Betsy" Eldridge b: Abt. 1841 Number of children: 2 Father: Levi Eldridge Mother: Easter (or Esther) Caudill, Sex: Female

....................10 [187] Martha Ann Caudill b: Abt. 1861 Number of children: ? Sex: Female

..........................+[188] Enoch Everidge b: Abt. 1860 Number of children: ? Sex: Male

......................11 [189] Susan "Susie" Everidge b: August 15, 1885 in KY d: December 29, 1962 in Perry Co., KY Number of children: 9 Sex: Female

..............................+[190] Hiram Combs b: May 07, 1882 d: April 29, 1962 Number of children: 9 Father: Benjamin Combs Mother: Matilda "Tilda" Combs Sex: Male

....................10 [25] Sarah Caudill b: September 1872 in Campton, KY Number of children: ? Sex: Female

..........................+[24] John C. Caudill b: February 1868 in Harlan or Letcher Co., KY m: April 18, 1889 in Breathitt Co., KY Number of children: ? Father: Henry H. Caudill Mother: Susannah Back Sex: Male

.....................11 [9] Cleveland Caudill b: June 1891 in Letcher Co., KY Sex: Male

..........................+[8] Peggy Caudill b: April 1890 in Letcher Co., KY m: July 14, 1909 in Letcher Co., KY d: January 14, 1916 Father: William B. Caudill Mother: Susannah "Sukie" Caudill Sex: Female

.................9 [18] Mary C. Caudill b: January 13, 1852 in Letcher Co., KY Number of children: ? Sex: Female

........................+[17] Lewis E. Caudill b: March 05, 1855 in Letcher Co., KY m: January 13, 1852 in Letcher Co., KY Number of children: ? Father: Henry H. Caudill Mother: Susannah Back Sex: Male

....................10 [19] Phoebe Caudill b: May 02, 1878 in Letcher Co., KY Number of children: 2 Sex: Female

..........................+[20] Levi S. Caudill b: December 22, 1875 in KY m: September 30, 1895 in Letcher Co., KY d: March 20, 1955 Number of children: 2 Father: Samuel B. Caudill Mother: Mary Ann "Polly" Eldridge Sex: Male

.....................11 [21] Benjamin "Bennie" Caudill b: Abt. 1902 Sex: Male

.....................11 [22] Howard Caudill b: Abt. 1915 Number of children: 11 Sex: Male

.............................+[23] Gladys Madden b: Abt. 1915 m: Abt. 1935 Number of children: 11 Father: Charles Madden Sex: Female

...............8 [270] James "Limber Jim" Caudill b: Abt. 1818 in Floyd Co., KY Number of children: 4 Sex: Male

.....................+[271] Elizabeth "Betsy" Mullins b: 1820 in KY d: 1899 Number of children: 4 Father: Joshua Mullins, Mother: Anna Robinson Sex: Female

.................9 [272] Mary "Polly" Caudill b: 1840 Sex: Female

........................+[273] Lewis Campbell b: 1830 Father: William C. Campbell Mother: Elizabeth Cornett, Sex: Male

.................9 [274] Nancy Ann Caudill b: Abt. 1841 Number of children: ? Sex: Female

........................+[275] Davis S. Fields b: Abt. 1840 Number of children: ? Sex: Male

....................10 [276] William Fields b: December 22, 1861 in Letcher Co., KY d: 1938 in Whitley Co., KY Sex: Male

.........................+[277] Martha Brashear b: October 11, 1871 d: March 31, 1943 Father: James Nicholas Brashear, Jr. Mother: Elizabeth Pratt Sex: Female

.................9 [27] William B. Caudill b: April 23, 1845 in Letcher Co., KY d: January 18, 1929 Number of children: ? Sex: Male (Note: William & Susannah were cousins)

.......................+[26] Susannah "Sukie" Caudill b: Abt. 1847 in KY m: February 28, 1867 in Letcher Co., KY d: August 14, 1925 Number of children: ? Father: Isom Caudill Mother: Elizabeth "Lizzie" Back, Bach Sex: Female (Note: Susannah & William were cousins)

....................10 [8] Peggy Caudill b: April 1890 in Letcher Co., KY d: January 14, 1916 Sex: Female

...........................+[9] Cleveland Caudill b: June 1891 in Letcher Co., KY m: July 14, 1909 in Letcher Co., KY Father: John C. Caudill Mother: Sarah Caudill Sex: Male

.................9 [14] Joshua M. Caudill b: June 23, 1850 in Letcher Co., KY d: March 22, 1941 Sex: Male

.......................+[13] Rhoda Caudill b: April 12, 1853 in Letcher Co., KY d: January 17, 1942 Father: Henry B. Caudill, twin, Mother: Margaret "Patsy" Campbell Sex: Female

...............8 [278] Sarah "Sally" Caudill b: July 29, 1823 d: April 13, 1884 Sex: Female

...............8 [279] Susannah Caudill b: April 18, 1825 in Perry Co., KY d: September 26, 1898 in Elk Creek, Letcher Co., KY Sex: Female Burial: Elder James Dixon Cemetery, Elk Creek, Letcher Co., KY

...............8 [280] William J. "Stiller Bill" Caudill b: July 05, 1827 in Letcher Co., KY d: November

26, 1908 Number of children: 16 Sex: Male

.......................+[281] Nancy Dixon, Dickson b: April 19, 1830 in Letcher Co., KY m: February 07, 1847 in Letcher Co., KY d: December 31, 1899 Number of children: 16 Father: Thomas Dixon Mother: Susannah Proffitt Sex: Female

...................9 [282] James William "Noah Jim" Caudill b: October 19, 1846 in Blackey, Letcher Co., KY d: August 14, 1911 Number of children: ? Sex: Male

.........................+[283] Lucinda Sumner b: January 28, 1850 in KY m: December 24, 1868 in Letcher Co., KY d: June 16, 1911 in KY Number of children: ? Father: John Sumner Mother: Nancy Hampton Sex: Female

.....................10 [10] Henry H. Cleveland Caudill b: April 20, 1887 in KY d: May 06, 1971 in Whitesburg, Letcher Co., KY Number of children: 18 Sex: Male Burial: Cleveland Caudill Cemetery, Caudill's Branch, Blackey, Letcher Co., KY

...........................+[195] Rebecca Adams b: Abt. 1887 m: Abt. 1905 d: in Waynesburg, KY Number of children: 8 Father: Gideon Adams Mother: Sarah Blair Sex: Female

.......................11 [196] Sarah Caudill b: Abt. 1905 Sex: Female

.............................+[197] _____ Neagle b: Abt. 1900 Sex: Male

.......................11 [198] Arthur Caudill b: Abt. 1907 Sex: Male

.......................11 [199] Mollie Caudill b: Abt. 1909 Sex: Female

.............................+[200] _____ Sanders b: Abt. 1905 Sex: Male

.......................11 [201] Cormie Caudill b: Abt. 1911 Sex: Female

.............................+[202] _____ Repass b: Abt. 1910 Sex: Male

.......................11 [203] Chester Caudill b: Abt. 1913 Sex: Male

.......................11 [204] Irene Caudill b: Abt. 1915 Sex: Female

.......................11 [205] Judy Caudill b: Abt. 1917 Sex: Female

.......................11 [194] Ida Caudill b: Abt. 1920 d: in Waynesburg, Lincoln Co., KY Sex: Female

.............................+[193] Coy Adams b: Abt. 1911 d: in Waynesburg, Lincoln Co., KY Father: Hiram Adams Mother: _____ Caudill Sex: Male

.....................2nd Wife of [10] Henry H. Cleveland Caudill:

...........................+[284] Lucinda "Cinda" Watts b: April 20, 1886 m: May 11, 1911 in Letcher Co., KY d: October 22, 1963 in Letcher Co., KY Number of children: 10 Father: Allen Watts Mother: Elizabeth Brashear Sex: Female

.......................11 [11] James W. Caudill b: February 21, 1912 in Blackey, Letcher Co., KY Number of children: 3 Sex: Male

.............................+[1163] Geneva Cornett b: December 1929 in Cumberland, KY m: June 08, 1946 in Whitesburg, Letcher Co., KY Number of children: 3 Father: Kip Cornett Mother: Alice Jackson Sex: Female

.......................2nd Wife of [11] James W. Caudill:

.............................+[1164] Tessa Mae Caudill b: May 16, 1913 in Roxana, Letcher Co., KY m: April 21, 1967 Father: Silas Caudill Mother: Martha Fields Sex: Female

.......................11 [1165] Watson Caudill b: October 23, 1913 in Letcher Co., KY d: May 10, 1953 in Perry Co., KY Sex: Male Burial: Cleveland Caudill Cemetery, Caudill's Branch, Blackey, Letcher Co., KY

.............................+[1166] Florence Mullins b: Abt. 1932 in Noble, KY m: May 06, 1952 in Letcher Co., KY Sex: Female

.......................11 [1167] Wesley Allen Caudill b: April 15, 1915 in Letcher Co., KY d: March 12, 1979 in Harlan Co., KY Sex: Male Burial: Cleveland Caudill Cemetery, Caudill's Branch, Blackey, Letcher Co., KY

.......................11 [1168] Callie Jane Caudill b: March 27, 1917 in Blackey, Letcher Co., KY Number of children: 3 Sex: Female

.............................+[1169] Howard Ison b: May 08, 1912 in Whitesburg, Letcher Co., KY m: December 06, 1945 in Whitesburg, Letcher Co., KY d: May 01, 1970 in Lexington, KY Number of children: 3 Father: Arch Ison Mother: Phoebe Lewis Sex: Male

........................11 [1170] Chester Caudill b: December 23, 1918 in Blackey, Letcher Co., KY d: November 11, 1988 in Whitesburg, Letcher Co., KY Number of children: 5 Sex: Male

..............................+[1171] Imogene Qualls b: January 13, 1924 in Centre, AL m: January 13, 1924 Number of children: 5 Father: William Qualls Mother: Bertha Hogue Sex: Female

........................11 [1172] Verna Caudill b: March 01, 1921 in Blackey, Letcher Co., KY Number of children: 2 Sex: Female

..............................+[1173] Wallace R. Ison b: June 02, 1924 in Blackey, Letcher Co., KY m: May 28, 1945 Number of children: 2 Father: May Ison Mother: Betty Adams Sex: Male

........................11 [1174] Herman Caudill b: April 23, 1923 Sex: Male

........................11 [1175] Vaxie Caudill b: January 16, 1925 in Letcher Co., KY d: October 24, 1980 in Hazard, Perry Co., KY Number of children: ? Sex: Female

..............................+[1176] Wade Whitehead b: March 12, 1921 m: November 25, 1950 d: August 10, 1975 in Perry Co., KY Number of children: ? Sex: Male

........................11 [1177] Rachel Caudill b: August 23, 1927 in Blackey, Letcher Co., KY Sex: Female

..............................+[1178] W. B. Watts b: February 09, 1937 in Hallie, KY Father: Pearl Watts Mother: Cinda Smith Sex: Male

........................11 [1179] Louetta Caudill b: May 08, 1929 Sex: Female

..............................+[1180] William C. "Hawk" Dixon b: May 12, 1927 m: April 12, 1949 Sex: Male

..................9 [285] Thomas D. Caudill b: December 26, 1848 in Letcher Co., KY Sex: Male

..........................+[286] Elizabeth Ann "Betsy" Pratt b: Abt. 1852 in Letcher Co., KY m: February 29, 1872 Father: John M. "Knock" Pratt Mother: Elizabeth Campbell Sex: Female

..................9 [287] William J. "Miller Bill" Caudill b: May 27, 1850 in Letcher Co., KY d: December 11, 1924 Sex: Male Burial: Bill Caudill Cemetery, Blackey, Letcher Co., KY

..................9 [288] John Caudill b: Abt. 1851 d: Abt. 1851 Sex: Male (Note: died in infancy)

..................9 [289] Susannah Caudill b: February 20, 1853 in Letcher Co., KY d: November 23, 1941 in Perry Co., KY Sex: Female

..................9 [290] Hiram W. Caudill b: Abt. September 20, 1853 in Letcher Co., KY d: December 20, 1913 Sex: Male

..........................+[291] Ester Banks b: April 08, 1853 in Letcher Co., KY d: September 25, 1905 Father: Harrison Banks Mother: Sarah Emeline Pridemore Sex: Female

..................9 [292] Sarah Ann "Sally" Caudill b: January 22, 1855 d: March 02, 1930 Sex: Female

..................9 [293] Nancy Jane Caudill b: October 05, 1856 d: January 06, 1929 Sex: Female

..................9 [294] Isaac D. "Ike" Caudill b: February 17, 1859 in KY d: February 19, 1938 in Colson, or Roxanna, KY Sex: Male

..................9 [295] Elizabeth "Betsy" Caudill b: Abt. 1860 in Letcher Co., KY d: Abt. 1927 Sex: Female

..................9 [296] Jeremiah P. "Jerry" Caudill b: November 23, 1861 d: February 25, 1922 Sex: Male

..................9 [297] George W. Caudill b: October 05, 1863 d: February 02, 1945 Sex: Male

..................9 [298] Margaret Caudill b: August 25, 1865 d: September 21, 1939 Sex: Female

..................9 [299] Henry Clay Caudill b: December 08, 1866 in Caudill Branch, Blackey, Letcher Co., KY d: September 06, 1938 in Red Star, KY Number of children: 5 Sex: Male Burial: Elmer Dixon Cemetery, Blackey, Letcher Co., KY

..........................+[300] Margaret Elizabeth "Maggie" Collins b: November 08, 1870 in Letcher Co., KY m: December 22, 1887 in Letcher Co., KY d: September 19, 1965 in Cincinnati, OH Number of children: 5 Father: Henry Powell Collins, Civil War Soldier Mother: Clarissa Ann "Clara" Bowman Sex: Female Burial: Elmer Dixon Cemetery, Blackey, Letcher Co., KY

........................10 [301] Melissa Caudill b: 1890 d: August 10, 1964 in Nashville, TN Sex: Female Burial: Elmer Dixon Cemetery, Blackey, Letcher Co., KY

........................10 [302] William Henry "Bill" Caudill b: 1892 d: February 25, 1950 Sex: Male

Burial: Elmer Dixon Cemetery, Blackey, Letcher Co., KY

.....................10 [303] John Breckenridge "Johnny" Caudill b: January 21, 1894 in Camp Branch, Letcher Co., KY d: January 10, 1974 in Camp Branch, Letcher Co., KY Number of children: 9 Sex: Male Burial: George Caudill Cemetery, Blackey, Letcher Co., KY

.........................+[304] Thursa Ann Mason b: June 09, 1893 in Sandlick, Letcher Co., KY m: July 30, 1913 in McRoberts, Letcher Co., KY d: August 23, 1975 in Whitesburg, Letcher Co., KY Number of children: 9 Father: Tilghman (Tilton?) Howard Mason Mother: Cornelia "Kerneal" (Grant?) Kiser Sex: Female

......................11 [1181] Denver Caudill b: October 20, 1914 in Letcher Co., KY Sex: Male Burial: Mason Cemetery, Letcher Co., KY

......................11 [1182] Dalma Caudill b: September 05, 1915 in Letcher Co., KY d: April 02, 2000 in Phoenix, AZ Number of children: 2 Sex: Female

...........................+[1183] Carl Thomas b: June 01, 1909 in Knott Co., KY d: February 1970 Number of children: 2 Father: Robert "Big Pop" Thomas Mother: Rosa "Big Mom" Collins Sex: Male

......................11 [12] Delmer V. Caudill b: January 13, 1917 in Polly (Sandlick) , Letcher Co., KY d: January 06, 1985 in Hazard, Perry Co., KY Number of children: 9 Sex: Male Burial: Green Acres Cemetery, Ermine, KY (Note: resided in Ulvah, Letcher Co., KY at time of death)

...........................+[1184] Mabel Breeding b: June 28, 1918 in Whitesburg, Letcher Co., KY m: December 17, 1934 in Letcher Co., KY Number of children: 8 Father: Brent Breeding Mother: Sarah Elizabeth "Lissie" Adams Sex: Female

......................Partner of [12] Delmer V. Caudill:

...........................+[800] Lava Collins b: March 04, 1913 in Bath, Knott Co., KY met: Abt. 1939 in (Note: they did not marry) Number of children: 3 Father: Watson Collins Mother: Maggie Banks Sex: Female

......................11 [1185] Dohina Caudill b: February 04, 1919 in Letcher Co., KY Sex: Female

......................11 [1186] Dale Caudill b: January 30, 1920 in Polly, Letcher Co., KY d: Abt. 1990 Sex: Male

......................11 [1187] Dana Caudill b: July 10, 1922 in WhitCo., Letcher Co., KY Sex: Female

......................11 [1188] Dorothy Caudill b: December 24, 1926 in Fleming, Letcher Co., KY Sex: Female

......................11 [1189] Della Mae Caudill b: June 09, 1928 in Campbranch, Letcher Co., KY Sex: Female

......................11 [1190] Danola "Dainy" Caudill b: July 26, 1933 d: July 31, 1933 Sex: Female Burial: Mason Cemetery, Letcher Co., KY

.....................10 [305] Louisa Caudill b: August 12, 1902 d: Abt. 1951 Sex: Female Burial: George Cemetery, Blackey, Letcher Co., KY

.....................10 [306] Lavada Belle (Vada?) Caudill b: November 27, 1906 d: November 11, 1965 Sex: Female

..................9 [307] Martha Caudill b: May 10, 1868 in Lower Caudill Branch, Letcher Co., KY d: May 03, 1943 in Diablock, Perry Co., KY Sex: Female

..................9 [308] John Breckenridge Caudill b: March 11, 1870 in Letcher Co., KY d: February 24, 1947 in Stroud, Lincoln Co., OK Sex: Male (Note: resided in Chandler, OK, in 1938)

...............8 [309] Henry B. Caudill, twin, b: February 08, 1829 in Perry, Letcher Co., KY d: Abt. 1913 Number of children: 10 Sex: Male Burial: Felix York Cemetery, Viper, KY

.........................+[310] Margaret "Patsy" Campbell b: May 21, 1826 in Linefork, Perry (Letcher) Co., KY m: February 15, 1849 in Letcher Co., KY Number of children: 10 Father: William C. Campbell Mother: Elizabeth Cornett, Sex: Female Burial: Felix York Cemetery, Viper, KY

..................9 [311] Elizabeth "Betty" Caudill b: August 29, 1850 in Letcher Co., KY d: September 05, 1904 Sex: Female

.........................+[312] Audley A. Cornett b: 1848 m: 1869 in Letcher Co., KY d: June 08, 1932 Sex: Male (Note: Looking for his ancestors)

..................9 [313] Robert B. Caudill b: February 14, 1852 in Letcher Co., KY Sex: Male

........................+[314] Elizabeth "Betty" Brashear b: December 05, 1856 in Perry Co., KY m: January 15, 1876 in Hazard, Perry Co., KY Father: Robert Samuel Brashear Mother: Sarah "Sally" Hall Sex: Female

...................9 [13] Rhoda Caudill b: April 12, 1853 in Letcher Co., KY d: January 17, 1942 Sex: Female

........................+[14] Joshua M. Caudill b: June 23, 1850 in Letcher Co., KY d: March 22, 1941 Father: James "Limber Jim" Caudill Mother: Elizabeth "Betsy" Mullins Sex: Male

...................9 [315] Sarah "Sally" Caudill b: June 17, 1854 in Letcher Co., KY Sex: Female

........................+[316] William "Bill" Young b: 1851 in Letcher Co., KY Father: Reece Young, Sr. Mother: Oriah R. "Ora" or "Arry" Ritchie Sex: Male

...................9 [317] Juda (Judy or Judah?) Caudill, b: March 1855 in Perry Co., KY Number of children: ? Sex: Female

........................+[318] Jeremiah H. "Jerry" Combs b: 1859 in Perry Co., KY? Number of children: ? Father: Hiram Combs Mother: Mary Williams Sex: Male

.....................10 [319] Daniel Combs b: Abt. 1892 in KY Number of children: ? Sex: Male

...........................+[320] Juda _____? b: Abt. 1900 in KY Number of children: ? Sex: Female

.....................11 [1191] Georgia Combs b: Abt. 1919 in KY Sex: Female

...................9 [321] Harriett Caudill b: 1859 in Letcher Co., KY Sex: Female

........................+[322] Robert Hamilton b: Abt. 1855 Sex: Male

...................9 [323] William Hartley "Fuzzy Bill" Caudill b: Bet. 1860 - 1861 in Letcher Co., KY d: April 05, 1942 Sex: Male

........................+[324] Cynthia Brashear b: September 02, 1858 in Perry Co., KY d: December 04, 1943 Sex: Female

...................9 [15] Lucretia "Lucy" Caudill b: Abt. 1864 in Perry Co., KY Sex: Female

........................+[325] Jeptha Hamilton b: Abt. 1862 Sex: Male

...................2nd Husband of [15] Lucretia "Lucy" Caudill:

........................+[326] Henry "Bud" Fields b: Abt. 1865 d: April 30, 1947 Sex: Male

...................9 [327] Polly Ann Caudill b: 1866 Sex: Female

...................9 [328] John Caudill b: 1869 Sex: Male

................8 [329] Isom Jesse Caudill, Sr., twin b: February 08, 1829 d: Abt. 1917 Number of children: 12 Sex: Male

........................+[330] Judah Sumner b: 1831 Number of children: 12 Father: James Sumner Mother: Nancy Adams, Sex: Female

...................9 [331] Mary Caudill b: 1850 Sex: Female

........................+[332] Enoch Campbell b: Abt. 1847 Sex: Male

...................9 [333] Nancy Caudill b: August 07, 1852 Sex: Female

........................+[334] Alexander Singleton b: Abt. 1850 Sex: Male

...................9 [335] Isom Caudill, Jr. b: July 26, 1855 Sex: Male

...................9 [336] George Henry Caudill b: 1855 Sex: Male

...................9 [337] Elizabeth Caudill b: June 02, 1856 Sex: Female

........................+[338] John Hall b: Abt. 1855 Sex: Male

...................9 [339] Lucinda Caudill b: Abt. 1857 Sex: Female

...................9 [340] Margaret E. Caudill b: 1861 Sex: Female

........................+[341] William Young b: Abt. 1860 Sex: Male

...................9 [342] Sarah Sally Caudill b: 1864 Sex: Female

...................9 [343] Patty Caudill b: Abt. 1865 Sex: Female

...................9 [344] William Caudill b: 1867 Sex: Male

........................+[345] Mary J. Adams b: Abt. 1870 Sex: Female

...................9 [346] Julia Ann Caudill b: 1870 d: Abt. 1934 Sex: Female

........................+[347] Ezekial Brashear b: Abt. 1867 Sex: Male

...................9 [348] Ellen Caudill b: 1875 Sex: Female

...............7 [1192] Sarah Elizabeth Caudill b: Abt. 1781 Sex: Female

.................+[1193] Benjamin Adams b: Abt. 1780 Sex: Male (Note: Looking for his ancestors)
............7 [1194] Sampson Caudill b: Abt. 1784 in Wilkes Co., NC Sex: Male
............7 [1195] Henry Caudill b: 1785 in Wilkes Co., NC d: June 18, 1856 in Letcher Co., KY Number of children: 5 Sex: Male
.................+[1196] Phoebe Jane Strailor b: 1794 in NC Number of children: 5 Sex: Female (Note: looking for ancestors)
...............8 [1197] Stephen Caudill b: Abt. 1810 in Wilkes Co., North Carolina Number of children: ? Sex: Male
.....................+[1198] Elizabeth "Betsy" Fields b: Abt. 1813 in KY m: November 21, 1833 Number of children: ? Sex: Female
.................9 [16] Henry R. Stephen Caudill b: February 22, 1837 d: March 02, 1910 Number of children: 2 Sex: Male
........................+[1199] Louisa Sumner b: Abt. 1833 in Perry Co., KY m: September 08, 1854 Sex: Female
.................2nd Wife of [16] Henry R. Stephen Caudill:
........................+[1200] Mary Branson b: Abt. 1860 in Perry Co., KY m: Abt. 1888 Number of children: 2 Sex: Female
.....................10 [212] Martha Caudill b: February 14, 1882 in Perry Co., KY d: July 28, 1957 Sex: Female
........................+[211] General Adams b: January 29, 1874 in Letcher Co., KY m: January 29, 1902 d: 1959 Father: Benjamin Adams Mother: Lucinda "Cindy" Combs Sex: Male
.....................10 [1201] Cro Carr Caudill b: December 09, 1891 in Middlesboro, Bell Co., KY d: June 25, 1951 in Harlan, Harlan or Letcher Co., KY Number of children: 4 Sex: Male Burial: Dianah Blair Cemetery, Letcher Co., KY
..........................+[1202] Martha Victoria Blair b: April 02, 1890 in Cowan, Letcher Co., KY m: Abt. 1915 d: June 16, 1976 in Lexington, Fayette Co., KY Number of children: 4 Father: Franklin "Dock" Blair, Doctor Mother: Dianah Day Sex: Female Burial: Dianah Blair Cemetery, Letcher Co., KY
........................11 [1203] Truman Caudill b: March 12, 1912 in Letcher Co., KY d: May 29, 1976 Sex: Male
.............................+[1204] Lovelle Frazier b: Abt. 1914 Sex: Female
.....................11 [1205] Henrietta Caudill b: July 17, 1914 Sex: Female
.....................11 [1206] James Caudill b: 1917 Sex: Male
.....................11 [1207] Harry M. Caudill, author & statesman b: 1922 d: 1990 in Letcher Co., KY Sex: Male (Note: Harry is the author of the fine book, *Slender is the Thread, Tales from a Country Law Office*)
..........................+[1208] Anne Frye b: March 06, 1924 in Harrison Co., KY m: December 15, 1946 Sex: Female
...............8 [105] Terry Caudill, b: Abt. 1812 in KY Number of children: 9 Sex: Female
.....................+[104] Matthew Caudill, Jr., b: Bet. 1801 - 1811 in Wilkes Co., NC m: April 16, 1829 in Perry/Letcher Co., KY Number of children: 9 Father: Matthew Caudill, Sr., Mother: Sarah H. Webb Sex: Male
.................9 [106] Henry M. "Dickie Henry" Caudill b: 1830 Sex: Male
.................9 [107] Phoebe Caudill b: 1832 Sex: Female
.....................+[108] Jeremiah Dixon b: 1827 Sex: Male
.................9 [109] Elizabeth "Betsy" Caudill b: December 25, 1835 Sex: Female
.................9 [110] Sarah Caudill b: 1844 Sex: Female
.....................+[111] Erasmus Bedwell b: Abt. 1840 Sex: Male
.................9 [112] Susan Caudill b: 1845 Sex: Female
.................9 [113] Rebecca Caudill b: 1846 Number of children: ? Sex: Female
.....................+[114] Benjamin Caudill b: 1842 in Letcher Co., KY m: October 28, 1867 in Letcher Co., KY Number of children: ? Sex: Male (Note: Looking for his ancestors)

.....................10 [115] Hiram Caudill b: Abt. 1870 in Letcher Co., KY Sex: Male

.................9 [116] William Caudill b: January 1848 Number of children: ? Sex: Male

.......................+[117] Sarah Sturgill b: Abt. 1845 Number of children: ? Sex: Female

.....................10 [118] George Washington Caudill, Sr. b: Abt. 1870 Number of children: ? Sex: Male

...........................+[119] Nannie Belle Stidham b: Abt. 1875 Number of children: ? Sex: Female

.....................11 [120] Emmett H. Caudill b: Abt. 1895 Number of children: ? Sex: Male

...........................+[121] Rena Vae Maggard b: Abt. 1900 Number of children: ? Sex: Female
(Note: Looking for ancestors)

.................9 [122] Nancy Ann Caudill, b: August 06, 1850 d: 1904 Number of children: ? Sex: Female

.......................+[123] Andrew Jackson Crase, b: 1847 d: 1938 Number of children: ? Father: Peter Crase, Mother: Rebecca Christian Sex: Male

.....................10 [124] Henry Peter Crase, b: 1886 d: 1981 Sex: Male

.................9 [125] Benjamin Caudill b: 1851 Sex: Male

...............8 [1209] Henry H. Caudill b: Abt. 1821 in Letcher Co., KY Number of children: 2 Sex: Male

.....................+[1210] Susannah Back b: Abt. 1830 in Harlan Co., KY m: October 03, 1846 Number of children: 2 Father: Henry Back, Bach Mother: Susannah Maggard Sex: Female

.................9 [17] Lewis E. Caudill b: March 05, 1855 in Letcher Co., KY Number of children: ? Sex: Male

.......................+[18] Mary C. Caudill b: January 13, 1852 in Letcher Co., KY m: January 13, 1852 in Letcher Co., KY Number of children: ? Father: Wilburn E. Caudill Mother: Nancy Caudill Sex: Female

.....................10 [19] Phoebe Caudill b: May 02, 1878 in Letcher Co., KY Number of children: 2 Sex: Female

...........................+[20] Levi S. Caudill b: December 22, 1875 in KY m: September 30, 1895 in Letcher Co., KY d: March 20, 1955 Number of children: 2 Father: Samuel B. Caudill Mother: Mary Ann "Polly" Eldridge Sex: Male

.....................11 [21] Benjamin "Bennie" Caudill b: Abt. 1902 Sex: Male

.......................11 [22] Howard Caudill b: Abt. 1915 Number of children: 11 Sex: Male

...........................+[23] Gladys Madden b: Abt. 1915 m: Abt. 1935 Number of children: 11 Father: Charles Madden Sex: Female

.................9 [24] John C. Caudill b: February 1868 in Harlan or Letcher Co., KY Number of children: ? Sex: Male

.......................+[25] Sarah Caudill b: September 1872 in Campton, KY m: April 18, 1889 in Breathitt Co., KY Number of children: ? Father: William W. "Wild Bill" Caudill Mother: Elizabeth "Betsy" Eldridge Sex: Female

.....................10 [9] Cleveland Caudill b: June 1891 in Letcher Co., KY Sex: Male

...........................+[8] Peggy Caudill b: April 1890 in Letcher Co., KY m: July 14, 1909 in Letcher Co., KY d: January 14, 1916 Father: William B. Caudill Mother: Susannah "Sukie" Caudill Sex: Female

...............8 [1211] Isom Caudill b: Abt. 1822 in Letcher Co., KY Number of children: 3 Sex: Male

.....................+[1212] Elizabeth "Lizzie" Back, Bach b: April 20, 1820 in KY Number of children: 3 Father: Henry Back, Bach Mother: Susannah Maggard Sex: Female

.................9 [1213] Samuel B. Caudill b: Abt. 1844 in KY Number of children: ? Sex: Male

.......................+[1214] Mary Ann "Polly" Eldridge b: Abt. 1847 in KY Number of children: ? Sex: Female

.....................10 [20] Levi S. Caudill b: December 22, 1875 in KY d: March 20, 1955 Number of children: 2 Sex: Male

...........................+[19] Phoebe Caudill b: May 02, 1878 in Letcher Co., KY m: September 30, 1895 in Letcher Co., KY Number of children: 2 Father: Lewis E. Caudill Mother: Mary C. Caudill

Sex: Female

......................11 [21] Benjamin "Bennie" Caudill b: Abt. 1902 Sex: Male

......................11 [22] Howard Caudill b: Abt. 1915 Number of children: 11 Sex: Male

............................+[23] Gladys Madden b: Abt. 1915 m: Abt. 1935 Number of children: 11 Father: Charles Madden Sex: Female

..................9 [26] Susannah "Sukie" Caudill b: Abt. 1847 in KY d: August 14, 1925 Number of children: ? Sex: Female (Note: Susannah & William were cousins)

.......................+[27] William B. Caudill b: April 23, 1845 in Letcher Co., KY m: February 28, 1867 in Letcher Co., KY d: January 18, 1929 Number of children: ? Father: James "Limber Jim" Caudill Mother: Elizabeth "Betsy" Mullins Sex: Male (Note: William & Susannah were cousins)

....................10 [8] Peggy Caudill b: April 1890 in Letcher Co., KY d: January 14, 1916 Sex: Female

...........................+[9] Cleveland Caudill b: June 1891 in Letcher Co., KY m: July 14, 1909 in Letcher Co., KY Father: John C. Caudill Mother: Sarah Caudill Sex: Male

..................9 [1133] Lewis Jesse Caudill b: July 08, 1857 in Letcher Co., KY Number of children: 2 Sex: Male

.......................+[1132] Sarah Banks b: February 18, 1859 in Letcher Co., KY m: March 18, 1875 in Letcher Co., KY d: August 1938 Number of children: 2 Father: Harrison Banks Mother: Sarah Emeline Pridemore Sex: Female

....................10 [1134] Wesley Caudill b: April 23, 1880 d: February 22, 1928 Number of children: ? Sex: Male

...........................+[1135] Hailey "Hade" Ison b: Abt. 1882 Number of children: ? Sex: Female

.......................11 [1136] Wendell Caudill b: Abt. 1898 Number of children: 3 Sex: Male Burial: Caudill Cemetery at Uz, Letcher Co., KY

...........................+[1137] Muriel J. Dixon b: December 30, 1900 d: June 09, 1937 Number of children: 3 Father: James C. Dixon Mother: Evelyn Back, Bach Sex: Female Burial: Caudill Cemetery at Uz, Letcher Co., KY

..................10 [1138] Walter Caudill b: April 13, 1886 in Jeremiah, KY d: January 01, 1911 Sex: Male

...........................+[1139] Hannah Ison b: 1886 in Letcher Co., KY m: November 01, 1907 in Letcher Co., KY Sex: Female

................8 [28] Benjamin Caudill, b: 1824 in Harlan Co., KY d: October 20, 1876 in Letcher Co., KY Number of children: 5 Sex: Male

....................+[1215] Mary Roark b: Abt. 1828 Sex: Female

................2nd Wife of [28] Benjamin Caudill, :

....................+[1216] Mary "Polly" Bowling, Bolling, b: Abt. 1826 in KY? m: January 04, 1849 in Letcher Co., KY Number of children: 5 Sex: Female (Note: Looking for her ancestors)

..................9 [1217] Rebecca Caudill b: 1850 d: 1935 Sex: Female

..................9 [1218] Sarah Caudill b: 1852 Sex: Female

..................9 [1219] Elizabeth Caudill b: 1853 Sex: Female

..................9 [1220] Dixon Caudill b: 1855 Sex: Male

..................9 [1221] Easter Caudill b: 1857 Sex: Female

............7 [1222] Thomas Caudill b: 1786 in Wilkes Co., NC Sex: Male

..................+[1223] Jane Caudill b: Abt. 1788 Sex: Female

............7 [161] Isom or Isham Caudill b: April 02, 1789 in Letcher Co., KY d: May 18, 1892 in Letcher Co., KY Number of children: ? Sex: Male

..................+[160] Elizabeth Caudill b: June 02, 1797 in GA m: October 02, 1814 in Franklin Co., Georgia d: May 18, 1892 Number of children: ? Father: Benjamin Caudill Mother: Sarah Humphries Sex: Female

................8 [162] James Caudill b: January 20, 1830 in GA Sex: Male

....................+[163] Mary "Polly" Fields b: April 1825 in KY m: 1850 Sex: Female

............7 [29] Sarah Elizabeth Caudill b: 1790 in Wilkes Co., NC d: April 30, 1881 in Lawrence

Co., KY, or Ordinary, Elliott Co., KY Number of children: 12 Sex: Female (Note: she and James were 2nd cousins)

..................+[36] James "Jimmie" Caudill, Jr. b: Bet. 1790 - 1800 in Wilkes Co., NC or GA? m: Abt. 1811 in Elliott Co., KY d: July 18, 1865 in Ordinary, Elliott Co., KY Number of children: 11 Father: James "Jimmie" Caudill, Jr., Rev. War Soldier Mother: Mary A. Adams, Sex: Male

................8 [37] Nancy Caudill b: Abt. 1812 in Letcher Co., KY? Sex: Female

......................+[38] James Roberts b: Abt. 1776 in SC m: Abt. 1841 in Letcher Co., KY d: Abt. 1867 in Perry Co., KY Sex: Male

................8 [39] William Riley "Red Bill" Caudill b: Abt. 1814 Number of children: 10 Sex: Male

......................+[40] Cynthia Ann (or Cynthy?) Combs, or Stacy b: Abt. 1820 m: 1835 in Breathitt Co., KY Number of children: 10 Father: Shadrack Combs, Sr. Mother: Rebecca Stacy Sex: Female

..................9 [41] Sarah Caudill b: Abt. 1835 Sex: Female

......................+[42] William Mullins b: Abt. 1835 Sex: Male (Note: Looking for his ancestors)

..................9 [43] Margaret Lou "Peggy" Caudill b: 1836 Sex: Female

..................9 [44] James Patterson Caudill b: 1843 Sex: Male

......................+[45] Sarah Frances Clagg b: Abt. 1845 Sex: Female

..................9 [46] Shadrack Thompson Caudill b: 1845 Sex: Male

..................9 [30] Kendrick ("Kinick"?) Caudill b: 1848 Sex: Male

......................+[47] Nancy Sarles b: Abt. 1850 Sex: Female

..................2nd Wife of [30] Kendrick ("Kinick"?) Caudill:

......................+[48] Martilla Back b: Abt. 1855 Sex: Female

..................9 [49] Emmaline Caudill b: 1850 in KY Sex: Female

......................+[50] Hughie Combs b: Abt. 1845 in KY m: 1879 in Boyd, KY Sex: Male Burial: (Looking for his ancestors)

..................9 [51] Mary Caudill b: August 13, 1853 Sex: Female

......................+[52] Asberry Back b: Abt. 1850 Sex: Male

..................9 [53] Louisa Jane Caudill b: 1854 Sex: Female

......................+[54] Talton Calhoun b: Abt. 1853 Sex: Male

..................9 [55] Manford May Caudill b: 1856 Sex: Male

......................+[56] Belle Elam b: Abt. 1858 Sex: Female

..................9 [57] William Breckenridge "Breck" Caudill b: 1859 Sex: Male

......................+[58] Elizabeth Taulbee b: Abt. 1860 Sex: Female

................8 [59] Sarah Elizabeth Caudill b: Abt. 1815 d: Abt. 1851 Sex: Female

................8 [60] Miriam Caudill b: Abt. 1818 Sex: Female

................8 [61] Electious Thompson Caudill b: October 1822 Sex: Female

................8 [62] Mary Caudill b: Abt. 1824 Sex: Female

................8 [63] Rebecca Caudill b: August 06, 1829 d: July 06, 1911 in Wolfe Co., KY Sex: Female

......................+[64] Thomas Tolson b: Abt. 1825 m: November 20, 1849 in Letcher Co., KY Sex: Male

................8 [65] Benjamin Caudill b: Abt. 1830 Sex: Male

................8 [66] Emmaline Caudill b: 1831 d: September 06, 1894 Number of children: 8 Sex: Female

......................+[67] James Young b: 1837 d: December 24, 1886 Number of children: 8 Sex: Male

..................9 [68] Sallie Young b: 1851 Sex: Female

..................9 [69] Thomas Young b: 1853 Sex: Male

..................9 [70] James Young b: 1855 Sex: Male

..................9 [71] Elizabeth "Betty" Young b: 1858 Sex: Female

..................9 [72] Brackton "Uncle Brack" Young b: March 1861 Sex: Male

..................9 [73] Elisha Young b: 1864 Sex: Male

..................9 [74] Mary Young b: May 01, 1868 Sex: Female

...................9 [75] Horace Greeley Young b: March 18, 1874 d: April 03, 1942 Sex: Male

..........................+[76] Louellen Fletcher b: March 03, 1877 d: December 16, 1911 Father: George Fletcher Mother: Jane Burkhart Sex: Female

.................8 [77] Elijah Caudill b: October 15, 1837 d: February 22, 1915 Sex: Male

.................8 [78] James Aaron Caudill b: March 21, 1841 d: August 24, 1930 Sex: Male

..............2nd Husband of [29] Sarah Elizabeth Caudill:

.......................+[31] Elijah Pennington b: May 12, 1812 in Lawrence Co., KY m: Abt. 1845 in Lawrence Co., KY d: December 18, 1878 in Lawrence Co., KY Number of children: ? Father: William Pennington Mother: Abigail Caudill, Cordell, Sex: Male

.................8 [32] Elijah Clarence Pennington b: January 01, 1849 in Lawrence Co., KY d: September 22, 1926 in Ordinary, Elliott Co., KY Number of children: ? Sex: Male

.........................+[33] Nancy Jane Barker b: April 15, 1859 in in what is now Elliott Co., KY m: March 27, 1880 in Sandy Hook, Elliott Co. KY d: February 24, 1940 in Elliott Co., KY Number of children: ? Father: John Barker Mother: Evaline Virginia Bowling Sex: Female

...................9 [34] Bracton Jayson Pennington b: August 13, 1883 in in what is now Elliott Co., KY Sex: Male

..........................+[35] Mary Jane Forest b: Abt. 1885 in Fayette Co. KY d: December 13, 1964 Father: Louis Forest Mother: Jemima Evans Sex: Female

..............7 [36] James "Jimmey" Caudill, Jr. b: Bet. 1790 - 1800 in Wilkes Co., NC or GA? d: July 18, 1865 in Ordinary, Elliott Co., KY Number of children: 11 Sex: Male

...................+[29] Sarah Elizabeth Caudill b: 1790 in Wilkes Co., NC m: Abt. 1811 in Elliott Co., KY d: April 30, 1881 in Lawrence Co., KY, or Ordinary, Elliott Co., KY Number of children: 12 Father: James "Jimmie" Caudill, Jr., Rev. War Soldier Mother: Mary A. Adams, Sex: Female (Note: she and James were 2nd cousins)

.................8 [37] Nancy Caudill b: Abt. 1812 in Letcher Co., KY? Sex: Female

.......................+[38] James Roberts b: Abt. 1776 in SC m: Abt. 1841 in Letcher Co., KY d: Abt. 1867 in Perry Co., KY Sex: Male

.................8 [39] William Riley "Red Bill" Caudill b: Abt. 1814 Number of children: 10 Sex: Male

.......................+[40] Cynthia Ann (or Cynthy?) Combs, or Stacy b: Abt. 1820 m: 1835 in Breathitt Co., KY Number of children: 10 Father: Shadrack Combs, Sr. Mother: Rebecca Stacy Sex: Female

...................9 [41] Sarah Caudill b: Abt. 1835 Sex: Female

..........................+[42] William Mullins b: Abt. 1835 Sex: Male (Note: Looking for his ancestors)

...................9 [43] Margaret Lou "Peggy" Caudill b: 1836 Sex: Female

...................9 [44] James Patterson Caudill b: 1843 Sex: Male

..........................+[45] Sarah Frances Clagg b: Abt. 1845 Sex: Female

...................9 [46] Shadrack Thompson Caudill b: 1845 Sex: Male

...................9 [30] Kendrick ("Kinick"?) Caudill b: 1848 Sex: Male

..........................+[47] Nancy Sarles b: Abt. 1850 Sex: Female

...................2nd Wife of [30] Kendrick ("Kinick"?) Caudill:

..........................+[48] Martilla Back b: Abt. 1855 Sex: Female

...................9 [49] Emmaline Caudill b: 1850 in KY Sex: Female

.......................+[50] Hughie Combs b: Abt. 1845 in KY m: 1879 in Boyd, KY Sex: Male Burial: (Looking for ancestors)

...................9 [51] Mary Caudill b: August 13, 1853 Sex: Female

..........................+[52] Asberry Back b: Abt. 1850 Sex: Male

...................9 [53] Louisa Jane Caudill b: 1854 Sex: Female

..........................+[54] Talton Calhoun b: Abt. 1853 Sex: Male

...................9 [55] Manford May Caudill b: 1856 Sex: Male

..........................+[56] Belle Elam b: Abt. 1858 Sex: Female

...................9 [57] William Breckenridge "Breck" Caudill b: 1859 Sex: Male

..........................+[58] Elizabeth Taulbee b: Abt. 1860 Sex: Female

.................8 [59] Sarah Elizabeth Caudill b: Abt. 1815 d: Abt. 1851 Sex: Female

...............8 [60] Miriam Caudill b: Abt. 1818 Sex: Female

...............8 [61] Electious Thompson Caudill b: October 1822 Sex: Female

...............8 [62] Mary Caudill b: Abt. 1824 Sex: Female

...............8 [63] Rebecca Caudill b: August 06, 1829 d: July 06, 1911 in Wolfe Co., KY Sex: Female

......................+[64] Thomas Tolson b: Abt. 1825 m: November 20, 1849 in Letcher Co., KY Sex: Male

...............8 [65] Benjamin Caudill b: Abt. 1830 Sex: Male

...............8 [66] Emmaline Caudill b: 1831 d: September 06, 1894 Number of children: 8 Sex: Female

......................+[67] James Young b: 1837 d: December 24, 1886 Number of children: 8 Sex: Male

.................9 [68] Sallie Young b: 1851 Sex: Female

.................9 [69] Thomas Young b: 1853 Sex: Male

.................9 [70] James Young b: 1855 Sex: Male

.................9 [71] Elizabeth "Betty" Young b: 1858 Sex: Female

.................9 [72] Brackton "Uncle Brack" Young b: March 1861 Sex: Male

.................9 [73] Elisha Young b: 1864 Sex: Male

.................9 [74] Mary Young b: May 01, 1868 Sex: Female

.................9 [75] Horace Greeley Young b: March 18, 1874 d: April 03, 1942 Sex: Male

........................+[76] Louellen Fletcher b: March 03, 1877 d: December 16, 1911 Father: George Fletcher Mother: Jane Burkhart Sex: Female

...............8 [77] Elijah Caudill b: October 15, 1837 d: February 22, 1915 Sex: Male

...............8 [78] James Aaron Caudill b: March 21, 1841 d: August 24, 1930 Sex: Male

............7 [1224] Stephen Caudill b: Abt. 1792 Sex: Male

............7 [1225] John Caudill b: 1793 in NC d: July 15, 1859 in Breathitt Co., KY Number of children: 2 Sex: Male

.................+[1226] Nancy Roberts b: 1805 in VA Number of children: 2 Father: Moses Roberts Mother: Polly King Sex: Female

...............8 [1227] Mary Polly "Maggie" Caudill, Caudle b: 1824 in Perry Co., KY Number of children: ? Sex: Female

......................+[1228] Cyrus Syra Combs, Sr., b: December 1821 in Perry Co., KY m: 1848 d: Aft. 1900 Number of children: 2 Father: Preston Combs, Sr., Mother: Nancy B. Stacy Sex: Male

.................9 [1229] _____ Combs b: Abt. 1860 Number of children: ? Sex: Male

......................+[1230] _____ _____? b: Abt. 1865 Number of children: ? Sex: Female

.................10 [1231] Judy Combs Sex: Female

...............8 [79] Tabitha Caudill, Caudle b: May 31, 1830 in Shoulder Blade, Clay Co., KY d: July 19, 1908 Number of children: ? Sex: Female

......................+[1232] Samuel Spicer b: Abt. 1830 in Clay Co., KY or Ashe Co., NC m: January 1852 in Breathitt Co., KY Number of children: ? Sex: Male

.................9 [1233] _____ Spicer b: Abt. 1860 Number of children: ? Sex: Unknown

.................10 [1234] _____ Spicer Number of children: ? Sex: Unknown

.................11 [1235] Lois Vincent Sex: Female

...............2nd Husband of [79] Tabitha Caudill, Caudle:

......................+[1236] Isham Arrowood b: 1826 in KY m: Abt. 1860 in Clay Co., KY Sex: Male

............7 [81] Jesse P. Caudill, Cordell b: April 24, 1795 in Wilkes or Alleghany Co., NC, some say Pocahantas, WV d: April 23, 1891 in Ashe or Alleghany Co., NC Number of children: 25 Sex: Male Burial: Family Cemetery on the Lonnie Edwards farm, two miles southeast of Whitehead, NC

.................+[1237] Sarah "Sary" Roberts, Roberds b: 1799 in Wilkes or Alleghany Co., NC m: October 11, 1817 in Wilkes or Alleghany Co., NC Number of children: 11 Father: Melachi Roberts Mother: Frances Simmons Sex: Female

...............8 [1238] Hugh Caudill b: 1817 in Alleghany Co., NC Number of children: 5 Sex: Male

......................+[1239] Elizabeth Blevins b: Abt. 1820 m: Abt. 1837 Number of children: 5 Sex:
Female
.................9 [1240] Sarah Caudill b: Abt. 1838 Sex: Female
.................9 [1241] Nancy J. Caudill b: Abt. 1840 Sex: Female
.................9 [1242] Thomas Jefferson Caudill b: Abt. 1842 Number of children: ? Sex: Male
.......................+[1243] Adeline Bowling, Bolling b: Abt. 1844 in Titusville, PA Number of
children: ? Sex: Female
....................10 [1244] Edward F. Caudill b: Abt. 1865 Number of children: ? Sex: Male
..........................+[1245] Virginia Rhoades b: Abt. 1867 Number of children: ? Sex: Female
....................11 [1246] Edward Thomas Lee Caudill b: Abt. 1888 Sex: Male
.................9 [1247] James Caudill b: Abt. 1844 Sex: Male
.................9 [1248] Enoch R. Caudill b: Abt. 1846 Number of children: ? Sex: Male
.......................+[1249] Rebecca _____? b: Abt. 1848 Number of children: ? Sex: Female
....................10 [1250] Hugh L. Caudill b: Abt. 1870 Sex: Male
...............8 [1251] James Robert Caudill b: November 10, 1818 in Ashe Co., NC d: November
07, 1887 in Alleghany Co., NC Number of children: 2 Sex: Male (Notes: owned slaves)
......................+[1252] Phoebe Louise Holloway b: April 10, 1818 d: December 31, 1879 Number
of children: 2 Father: Daniel Holloway Mother: Mary Woodruff Sex: Female
.................9 [80] James Franklin Caudill, Civil War Soldier b: May 10, 1845 in Alleghany Co., NC
d: June 08, 1921 Number of children: 13 Sex: Male (Note: His home is off of the Blue Ridge Parkway,
near Sparta, NC. At age 16, he joined the Confederate Army, served in Co. G, 45th NC Calvary. He
was wounded in the hip at Gatlinburg, TN)
......................+[1253] Catherine "Katie" Crouse b: Abt. 1847 m: Abt. 1860 Number of children:
2 Sex: Female
....................10 [1254] James Reeves Caudill b: September 26, 1861 Sex: Male
....................10 [1255] David Rufus Caudill b: June 05, 1865 Sex: Male
.................2nd Wife of [80] James Franklin Caudill, Civil War Soldier:
.......................+[1256] Elvira Koontz b: January 09, 1850 m: July 10, 1869 Number of children:
11 Sex: Female
....................10 [1257] Edwin E. Caudill b: February 06, 1871 Sex: Male
....................10 [1258] Frances Dona Caudill b: January 28, 1872 Sex: Female
....................10 [1259] Hillery Cleve Caudill b: April 22, 1874 Number of children: 12 Sex: Male
..........................+[1260] Celia Catherine Edwards b: Abt. 1875 Number of children: 12 Sex:
Female
....................11 [1261] Kyle Andrew Caudill b: Abt. 1895 Sex: Male
....................11 [1262] Charlie Caudill b: Abt. 1897 Sex: Male
....................11 [1263] Sherman Caudill b: Abt. 1899 Sex: Male
....................11 [1264] Kemp Caudill b: Abt. 1901 Sex: Male
....................11 [1265] Dean Caudill b: Abt. 1903 Sex: Male
....................11 [1266] Bertha Caudill b: Abt. 1905 Sex: Female
....................11 [1267] Ella Caudill b: Abt. 1907 Sex: Female
....................11 [1268] Zelma Caudill b: Abt. 1909 Sex: Female
....................11 [1269] Merle Caudill b: Abt. 1911 Sex: Male
....................11 [1270] Alma Caudill b: Abt. 1913 Sex: Female
....................11 [1271] Faye Caudill b: Abt. 1915 Sex: Female
....................11 [1272] Clay Caudill b: Abt. 1917 Sex: Male
....................10 [1273] James Benjamin Caudill b: November 23, 1875 Sex: Male
....................10 [1274] Robert C. Caudill b: July 27, 1877 Sex: Male
....................10 [1275] Phoebe L. Caudill b: July 08, 1879 Sex: Female
....................10 [1276] W. Vance Caudill b: April 03, 1881 Sex: Male
....................10 [1277] Nora Mae Caudill b: December 17, 1882 Sex: Female
....................10 [1278] Lula Elvira Caudill b: July 09, 1884 Sex: Female

...................10 [1279] Maude E. Caudill b: October 17, 1886 Sex: Female

...................10 [1280] Effie Geneva Caudill b: April 15, 1894 Sex: Female

.................9 [1281] Martha Elizabeth Caudill b: Abt. 1850 d: October 28, 1938 Number of children: ? Sex: Female Burial: The Joines Family Cem. Pine Swamp, NC

.....................+[1282] Richard Hayward Joines b: August 29, 1851 m: April 06, 1873 d: April 06, 1923 Number of children: ? Father: Ezekiel Joines Mother: Jane Crouse Sex: Male

...................10 [1283] Henry Clay Joines b: 1897 d: 1975 Sex: Male

.......................+[1284] Frona Caudill b: Abt. 1899 Sex: Female

.............8 [1285] Malachi Caudill, Caudle b: 1822 Number of children: ? Sex: Male

.....................+[1286] Martha French b: Abt. 1824 Number of children: ? Sex: Female

.................9 [1287] Amanda Biddie Caudill b: August 17, 1866 in Wise Co., VA Sex: Female

.............8 [1288] Biddy Caudill b: 1825 Sex: Female

.............8 [1289] Pherby (Ferba) Caudill b: 1828 in Ashe Co., NC d: 1916 in Alleghany Co., NC Number of children: 4 Sex: Female

.....................+[1290] Leander "Lee" Andrews, Anders b: Abt. 1826 m: Abt. 1846 Number of children: 4 Father: William Andrews Mother: Sarah Cheek Sex: Male

.................9 [1291] William Andrews b: 1849 Sex: Male

.................9 [1292] Sarah Jane Andrews b: March 08, 1852 in Ashe Co., NC d: December 26, 1921 in Alleghany Co., NC Sex: Female

.................9 [1293] Francis "Frankie" Andrews b: 1855 in Ashe Co., NC d: March 17, 1931 Sex: Female

.....................+[1294] James W. Crouse b: Abt. 1853 m: March 03, 1872 Sex: Male

.................9 [1295] Jessie F. Andrews b: 1847 in Ashe Co., NC d: 1924 in Alleghany Co., NC Sex: Male Burial: Antioch PBCC, Stratford Area

.....................+[1296] Elizabeth "Bettie" Sanders b: Abt. 1849 m: December 29, 1866 in Alleghany Co., NC d: in Alleghany Co., NC Sex: Female Burial: Antioch PBCC, Stratford Area

.............8 [1297] Frankie Caudill b: 1832 in Ashe Co., NC d: November 1919 Number of children: ? Sex: Female

.....................+[1298] Calvin Osborne b: Abt. 1830 Number of children: ? Sex: Male

.................9 [1299] Jesse Osborne b: 1847 Sex: Female

.............8 [1300] Jessie M. Caudill b: 1836 in Ashe Co., NC d: May 31, 1870 in Scott Co., VA Sex: Male

.....................+[1301] Ferelda Hensley b: 1841 m: 1855 Sex: Female (Note: Looking for her ancestors)

.............8 [1302] Andrew Jackson Caudill, Civil War Soldier b: 1837 in Ashe Co., NC d: 1862 Number of children: 2 Sex: Male (Note: he was in the 12th Reg. NC. Vol. in the Civil War. His Captain was Jesse F. Reeves)

.....................+[1303] Rosanna "Rowsey" Phipps b: Abt. 1839 m: January 03, 1856 Number of children: 2 Sex: Male

.................9 [1304] Mary J. Caudill b: 1857 Sex: Female

.................9 [1305] Candis Caudill b: 1859 Sex: Female

.............8 [1306] Nancy Caudill b: May 22, 1839 in Ashe Co., NC d: December 06, 1895 Sex: Female

.....................+[1307] Adam J. Waggoner, Wagoner, Wagner b: November 09, 1833 m: March 08, 1855 d: December 27, 1920 Father: Jacob Waggoner Mother: Annie Roberts Sex: Male Burial: New Hope Ch. Cem. Strafford, NC (Note: He was an Elder and a Primitive Baptist Minister)

.............8 [1308] Jeremiah "Jerry" Caudill b: 1841 in Ashe Co., NC Sex: Male

.....................+[1309] Mary Koontz b: Abt. 1843 Sex: Female

.............8 [1310] Jane Caudill b: 1841 in Ashe Co., NC Sex: Female

.............2nd Wife of [81] Jesse P. Caudill, Cordell:

.................+[1311] Lubidda "Biddy" Bledsoe b: April 10, 1828 in Letcher Co., KY m: June 25, 1842 in Ashe or Alleghany Co., NC d: August 08, 1904 Number of children: 14 Father: Tyrell

Bledsoe Mother: Nancy Reeves Sex: Female Burial: Family Cemetery on the Lonnie Edwards farm, two miles southeast of Whitehead, NC
................8 [1312] Jane Caudill b: 1842 in NC Sex: Female
................8 [1313] Isaac G. "Shade" Caudill b: October 08, 1843 in Whitehead, Ashe Co., NC Sex: Male
................8 [1314] Shadrack Caudill b: 1844 in NC Sex: Male
................8 [1315] Sarah E. Caudill b: December 20, 1845 in Ashe Co., NC d: March 28, 1910 in Alleghany Co., NC Number of children: ? Sex: Female Burial: Union Primitive Baptist Church Cemetery, Whitehead, NC
......................+[1316] John Whitehead b: December 17, 1848 in Ashe Co., NC m: February 10, 1867 d: September 27, 1938 Number of children: ? Sex: Male Burial: Pine Grove Cem. in Willow Springs, MO
..................9 [1317] James Pierce Whitehead b: August 08, 1884 in Alleghany Co., NC Sex: Male
........................+[1318] Christina Caudill b: Abt. 1886 m: June 02, 1909 in Alleghany Co., NC Sex: Female (Note: Looking for her ancestors)
................8 [1319] Matthew (or Mathis) Franklin Caudill b: April 28, 1848 in Ashe Co., NC Sex: Male
......................+[1320] Margaret Gentry b: Abt. 1850 m: September 25, 1867 Sex: Female
................8 [1321] Tyrell Robert Caudill b: November 20, 1850 in Ashe Co., NC d: October 24, 1918 in Whitehead Township, Alleghany Co. NC Number of children: 11 Sex: Male
......................+[1322] Nancy Caroline Fender b: April 02, 1853 in Ashe Co., NC m: March 07, 1869 in Alleghany Co. NC d: January 12, 1942 in Whitehead Township, Alleghany Co. NC Number of children: 11 Father: Allen Fender Mother: Nancy Edwards Sex: Female
..................9 [1323] Shade George Caudill b: January 02, 1870 in Whitehead, NC d: September 17, 1957 Number of children: 10 Sex: Male (Note: he was a Primitive Baptist Minister)
........................+[1324] Susan Martha Long b: April 14, 1866 in Alleghany Co., NC m: August 09, 1890 d: October 03, 1934 in Statesville, Iredell Co., NC Number of children: 10 Sex: Female
....................10 [1325] Jesse Reid Caudill b: 1900 d: 1985 Sex: Male
............................+[1326] Esther Ruth Lackey b: 1910 d: March 19, 201/02 Sex: Female
....................10 [1327] Helen Caudill b: Abt. 1891 Sex: Female
....................10 [1328] Robert Caudill b: Abt. 1893 Sex: Male
....................10 [1329] Mamie Caudill b: Abt. 1895 Sex: Female
....................10 [1330] George Caudill b: Abt. 1897 Sex: Male
....................10 [1331] Bayne Caudill b: Abt. 1902 Sex: Male
....................10 [1332] Edna Caudill b: Abt. 1904 Sex: Female
....................10 [1333] Stella Caudill b: Abt. 1906 Sex: Female
....................10 [1334] Eura Caudill b: Abt. 1908 Sex: Female
....................10 [1335] Emory Lipe Caudill b: Abt. 1910 Sex: Male
..................9 [1336] Nancy Catherine "Nannie" Caudill b: March 18, 1872 in Scotsville, NC d: March 04, 1956 Sex: Female
........................+[1337] Muncey H. Waddle b: Abt. 870 m: 1894 d: February 20, 1967 Sex: Male
..................9 [1338] Robert Franklin Caudill b: October 01, 1874 d: January 12, 1892 Sex: Male
..................9 [1339] Martha (Mattie) Ellen Caudill b: January 20, 1877 in Alleghany Co., NC d: April 02, 1946 in Fountain Green Hospital, Harford Co., MD Number of children: ? Sex: Female
........................+[1340] William Amadeus Greene b: December 31, 1877 in NC m: February 01, 1900 d: March 29, 1960 in Mt. Carmel, MD Number of children: ? Father: Solomon Green, Greene Mother: Sarah Green Sex: Male
....................10 [1341] James Hoyt Greene b: July 11, 1918 in Statesville, Falston Township, Iredel County, NC d: November 08, 1975 in Towson, Baltimore Co., MD Number of children: 2 Sex: Male
............................+[1342] Louise Christina Hausner b: July 27, 1919 d: October 09, 1994 Number of children: 2 Sex: Female

..................9 [1347] Candace Jane Caudill b: May 23, 1879 d: October 29, 1965 Number of children: ? Sex: Female

........................+[1348] Hiram Edwards b: Abt. 1877 m: June 15, 1898 in Alleghany Co., NC Number of children: ? Sex: Male

.....................10 [1349] Breece L. Caudill, (adopted) b: December 08, 1911 Sex: Unknown

..................9 [1350] Florence Alzenia Caudill b: January 07, 1882 d: March 10, 1959 Sex: Female Burial: Union Primitive Baptist Ch. Cem. Whitehead, NC

........................+[1351] Center Joshua Edwards b: 1873 d: 1951 Sex: Male Burial: Union Primitive Baptist Ch. Cem. Whitehead, NC

..................9 [82] Tyrell Oscar Caudill b: August 08, 1884 d: May 01, 1937 in Whitehead Township, Alleghany Co., NC Number of children: 7 Sex: Male

........................+[1352] Lou Choate b: Abt. 1886 m: December 21, 1910 Sex: Female

..................2nd Wife of [82] Tyrell Oscar Caudill:

........................+[1353] Hattie Maud Edwards b: August 10, 1893 m: March 1913 d: February 03, 1930 in Whitehead Township, Alleghany Co., NC Number of children: 7 Sex: Female

.....................10 [1354] Evelyn Caudill b: Abt. 1914 Sex: Female

.....................10 [1355] Louise Caudill b: Abt. 1916 Sex: Female

.....................10 [1356] Earl Caudill b: Abt. 1918 Sex: Male

.....................10 [1357] Bayne Caudill b: Abt. 1920 Sex: Male

.....................10 [1358] Edward Caudill b: Abt. 1922 Sex: Male

.....................10 [1359] Hubert Caudill b: Abt. 1924 Sex: Male

.....................10 [1360] Caery Caudill b: Abt. 1926 Sex: Female

..................9 [1361] Walter Cleveland Caudill, Senator & Dr. b: June 09, 1888 d: January 18, 1963 Number of children: ? Sex: Male Burial: (Notes: Was a member of the Virginia State Legislature 1936-1956 as a State Senator and also was Lt. Govenor of the State of VA. Along with his brother Estell and Dr. J. O. Woods, built St. Elizabeth Hospital, in Elizabeathion, TN.)

........................+[1362] Mary Ring Cornett b: Abt. 1890 m: June 30, 1920 d: September 29, 1964 Number of children: ? Sex: Female

.....................10 [1363] Carol Caudill b: Abt. 1921 Sex: Female

..................9 [1364] Estill Leftrage Caudill, Sr., Dr. b: October 23, 1890 d: September 03, 1977 in Giles Co., VA Number of children: 3 Sex: Male Burial: Memorial Presbyterian Church Cem.

........................+[1365] Flora Weatherly b: Abt. 1892 in VA m: Abt. 1912 d: February 27, 1966 in Giles Co., VA Number of children: 3 Sex: Female Burial: Memorial Presbyterian Church Cem.

.....................10 [1366] Mary Burns Caudill b: Abt. 1913 Sex: Female

.....................10 [1367] Estill Leftrage Caudill, Jr. b: Abt. 1915 Sex: Male

.....................10 [1368] Julian Tyrell Caudill b: Abt. 1917 Sex: Female

..................9 [1369] Munsey Edwin Caudill b: August 14, 1894 d: September 02, 1984 in Dallastown, PA Number of children: 2 Sex: Male

........................+[1370] Kate Tedder, Tudor b: Abt. 1895 Number of children: 2 Sex: Female

.....................10 [1371] Kyle Caudill b: Abt. 1915 Sex: Male

.....................10 [1372] Irene Caudill b: Abt. 1917 Sex: Female

..................9 [1373] Alta Blanche Caudill b: August 23, 1898 d: 1996 Sex: Female (Note: Lived at the Caudill Home Place, and still owns it.)

........................+[1374] Lonnie Edwards b: February 28, 1894 d: May 11, 1968 Sex: Male Burial: (Notes: Farmer in Alleghany Co. and was County Commissoner, 1952 and 1953)

.................8 [1375] Bledsoe E. "Bleth" Caudill b: May 17, 1853 in Ashe Co., NC d: December 23, 1921 Sex: Male

.....................+[1376] Margaret "Maggie" Douglas b: Abt. 1855 m: December 08, 1875 Sex: Female

.................8 [1377] Biddy Louisa Caudill b: 1856 in NC Sex: Female

.................8 [1378] Cynthia Jane Caudill b: September 11, 1858 in Ashe Co., NC d: May 06, 1922 Sex: Female

......................+[1379] Richard J. Fender b: Abt. 1856 m: November 24, 1886 Sex: Male

.................8 [1380] Candace S. Caudill b: December 19, 1861 in Alleghany Co., NC d: February 16, 1950 Sex: Female

......................+[1381] Thomas J. Shepherd b: Abt. 1859 m: July 13, 1889 Sex: Male

.................8 [1382] Virginia Ellen Caudill b: December 19, 1861 in Alleghany Co., NC d: February 16, 1950 Sex: Female

......................+[1383] Emery Floyd Poole b: Abt. 1860 m: February 04, 1892 in Alleghany Co., NC Sex: Male

.................8 [1384] Louisa B. Caudill b: Abt. 1863 in Ashe Co., NC d: October 29, 1907 Sex: Female

......................+[1385] Thomas Jefferson Mitchell b: Abt. 1860 m: September 24, 1876 Sex: Male

.................8 [1386] T. A. Caudill b: June 05, 1866 in Alleghany Co., NC d: June 05, 1866 in Alleghany Co., NC Sex: Male

.................8 [1387] George Thomas Caudill b: February 02, 1868 in Alleghany Co., NC d: July 19, 1937 Sex: Male

......................+[1388] Cornelia J. Choate b: Abt. 1870 m: February 14, 1887 Sex: Female

..........6 Frances "Franky" Adams, b: 1765 Sex: Female

..........6 Charles Adams, b: 1766 Sex: Male

..........6 Moses Adams, b: 1768 Sex: Male

..........6 Ann Adams, b: 1769 Sex: Female

..........6 William "Canebull" Adams, b: 1770 Sex: Male

..........6 Jane Adams, b: 1773 Sex: Female

..........6 Elizabeth A. Adams, b: 1775 in Loudon Co., VA d: 1861 in Letcher Co., KY Sex: Female

..........6 Sarah "Sally" Frances Adams, b: Bet. 1776 - 1779 in Loudon Co., VA d: October 1842 in Perry (or Letcher) Co., KY Sex: Female Burial: Watty Caudill Cemetery, Letcher Co., KY

..........6 Henry Adams, b: 1779 Sex: Male

........5 Isham or Isom Caudill, Cordell b: 1732 in Granville, VA Sex: Male

..............+Elizabeth _____? b: Abt. 1735 Sex: Female

........5 David Caudill b: 1734 in VA Sex: Male

........5 Edward Caudill b: Abt. 1736 in VA Sex: Male

........5 Henrietta Caudill b: 1738 in VA Sex: Female

........5 Zachariah Caudill, Sr., Cadle b: Abt. 1740 Number of children: ? Sex: Male

..............+_____ _____? b: Abt. 1742 Number of children: 1 Sex: Female

..........6 Zachariah Caudill, Jr., Cadle b: Abt. 1765 Sex: Male

The End

Center: Doris (Altizer) Caudill (on front book cover); right: Faro Caudill (on back book cover); left: their daughter Josie Lerlene Caudill. At the time this photograph was taken in 1940 the family was homesteading in a dugout house at Pie Town, New Mexico. Faro is a close cousin of the author. For Faro's family tree information see page 124. Photographer: Russell W. Lee (1903-1986).

The dugout home of Faro and Doris Caudill, Pie Town, New Mexico, 1940. Photographer: Russell W. Lee. Faro and Doris Caudill photos courtesy the Farm Security Administration and Office of War Information Photograph Collection.

APPENDIX E
Dixie Go Bragh!

I f you enjoyed *The Caudills* by Col. Seabrook, you may also be interested in helping to preserve our precious Southern culture, history, tradition, and heritage.[46]

Did you know that our wonderful and unique all-American South is fast disappearing? Yes, our multicultural Dixie traditions, language, symbols, heroes, flags, customs, foods, religious beliefs, ethics, history, heritage, music, and more, are under constant threat and attack, and are slowly but surely being exterminated by the uneducated, malicious, and ill-informed. Even our sacred Confederate cemeteries are vanishing—all due to ignorance, prejudice, and apathy.[47]

If you would like to learn more about this topic and what you can do to help, contact The League of the South. If you are a male consider joining the Sons of Confederate Veterans or the Military Order of Stars and Bars. If you are a female contemplate joining the United Daughters of the Confederacy or the Order of Confederate Rose.[48]

Because education is vital we recommend reading Lochlainn Seabrook's popular and outstanding book, *Everything You Were Taught About the Civil War is Wrong, Ask a Southerner!*, where you will get a crash course on the truth about Dixie, a truth that has been guilefully suppressed by the Left, the North, and the New South for 150 years. You will never look at the "Civil War" or the South the same way again.

Take up the banner. Get involved. Be pro-active. Future generations will thank you.

SEA RAVEN PRESS

---

46. *Dixie Go Bragh* is Gaelic Irish for the "South Forever."

47. For more on why preserving the American South and her culture and true history is so important see my books, *Confederate Monuments: Why Every American Should Honor Confederate Soldiers and Their Memorials*; *Rise Up and Call Them Blessed: Victorian Tributes to the Confederate Soldier, 1861-1901*; and *Victorian Confederate Poetry: The Southern Cause in Verse, 1861-1901*.

48. Do not be misled by anti-South individuals and groups who claim that these organizations are racist. They are quite the opposite: as organizations simply devoted to preserving Southern heritage, they are both multicultural and multiracial, possessing members of all races, from all fifty states. Remember: despite the false claims of Yankee myth, people of every race, color, and creed fought valiantly for the Confederacy during Lincoln's War, not just European-Americans. Today we Southerners are justly proud of our multiracial history and of the countless contributions made by the many different peoples who have called the South their home for the past 400 years.

Remembering Kentuckian & Southern Hero
JEFFERSON DAVIS

by Lochlainn Seabrook

When the "Civil War" is mentioned, most automatically think of the U.S. and Abraham Lincoln (1809-1865). This is historically inaccurate, for there were two republics and two presidents involved. In fact, here in Dixie, traditional Southerners are much more apt to think of the honorable and noble Jefferson Davis (1808-1889) than the dictator and war criminal Lincoln.

Born in Fairview, Christian (now Todd) County, Kentucky, Davis was to become the first and only President of the Confederate States of America.[49] Accurately predicting Lincoln's subversion of the U.S. Constitution after his minority win in the 1860 presidential election, the Southern states immediately began making plans to break away from the Union and form their own country. As such, eleven of them (and two provisional ones) began legally seceding from the United States of America in December 1860. These states were (in order of secession): South Carolina, Mississippi, Florida, Alabama, Georgia, Louisiana, Texas, Virginia, Arkansas, Tennessee, North Carolina, Missouri, and Kentucky (only parts of the last two states seceded).[50]

On February 18, 1861, at the new Confederate Capital in Montgomery, Alabama, the Confederacy elected Davis as its provisional president and Alexander Hamilton Stephens (1812-1883) as its provisional vice president.[51]

Shortly after, on March 11, 1861, the Confederate States of

---

49. I am cousins with both President Davis and his first wife, Sarah Knox Taylor (1815-1835). In May 1865, Sarah's brother, noted Confederate General Richard Taylor (1826-1879), also my cousin, surrendered the last Rebel forces east of the Mississippi River. Both Richard and Sarah were the children of U.S. President Zachary Taylor (1784-1850). For more on President Davis see my book, *The Quotable Jefferson Davis*.

50. For more on this topic see my book, *All We Ask is to be Let Alone: The Southern Secession Fact Book*.

51. For more on Vice President Stephens see my books, *The Alexander H. Stephens Reader* and *The Quotable Alexander H. Stephens*.

America (named after an early nickname for the U.S.A.),[52] drew up her own Constitution and proceeded with her plan for full and complete separation from the U.S.A. President Lincoln unlawfully threatened the newly created foreign republic—better known as the C.S.A.—while disregarding her constitutional power of states' rights (as tacitly laid out in the Ninth and Tenth Amendments).[53]

In response, President Davis sent a number of peace delegations to Washington, D.C. Tragically, all were ignored by Lincoln, inevitably setting the stage for war. Goaded on by the many America-hating socialists and communists in his administration and armies, this was obviously part of Lincoln's nefarious agenda to begin with.[54]

On April 12, 1861, as he later admitted, Lincoln taunted, then tricked, Davis into firing the first shot at the first battle (Fort Sumter, South Carolina) of the War for Southern Independence (incorrectly and duplicitously called the "Civil War" in the North). A bloody, illegal, and needless four years of horror followed, ending with the surrender of Confederate General Robert E. Lee (1807-1870) and his army at Appomattox, Virginia, on April 9, 1865.[55]

Though the Yanks won the war, they did not win the battle, for Lincoln utterly failed to either "abolish slavery" (which only finally ended in December 1865, with the ratification of the Thirteenth Amendment, eight months *after* he died),[56] or "preserve the Union," which the Founding

---

52. For more on this topic see my book, *Confederacy 101*.

53. For more on the topic of constitutional law see my books, *America's Three Constitutions: Complete Texts of the Articles of Confederation, Constitution of the United States of America, and Constitution of the Confederate States of America*; *The Articles of Confederation Explained: A Clause-by-Clause Study of America's First Constitution*; and *The Constitution of the Confederate States of America Explained: A Clause-by-Clause Study of the South's Magna Carta.*

54. For more on the radical far-left members of Lincoln's party see my book, *Abraham Lincoln Was a Liberal, Jefferson Davis Was a Conservative: The Missing Key to Understanding the American Civil War.*

55. General Lee is a cousin of mine. In 1870, observing the unnecessarily harsh and cruel treatment of the South by the North during so-called "Reconstruction" (1865-1877), Lee made it known that he sincerely regretted surrendering to "those people" (that is, Yankees). "I would have preferred to die at Appomattox with my brave men, my sword in this right hand," he told former Texas Governor Fletcher Stockdale. For more on General Lee see my books, *The Quotable Robert E. Lee*, and *The Old Rebel: Robert E. Lee as He Was Seen By His Contemporaries.*

56. We will note that Lincoln never originally intended to end (let alone disturb) slavery, as he himself said in his Inaugural Address in March 1861. Indeed, for the rest of his life he repeatedly asserted that the "Civil War" was not about slavery. To the contrary, Lincoln was a chief proponent of black colonization; that is of deporting all African-Americans out of the country, as he stated in his Second Annual Message to Congress on December 1, 1862. He even headed an Illinois chapter of the American Colonization Society. For more on Lincoln see my books, *Abraham Lincoln: The Southern View*; *Lincolnology*; *The Great Impersonator*; and *The Unquotable Abraham Lincoln.*

Fathers had intended to be *voluntary* (Lincoln made it *involuntary*).[57] Instead, the big government proponent widened an already existing, enormous cultural gap between the conservative South and the liberal North, one that will never be completely joined together. Indeed, the South continues to be a sharply distinct society with a richly unparalleled heritage of her own, one founded on the traditional principles of Old Europe.

However, due to her traditional values (which the North sees as "backward"), independent-mindedness ("uppityness"), and non-conformist attitude ("rebelliousness"), the South has been under increasing attack, from the very formation of the U.S. (in the 1770s) right into the present day, with each year bringing new signs of encroachment and oppression by the politically correct thought police (who want nothing more than for the leisurely agricultural South to become an exact replica of the fast-paced industrial North). Yankee-New South mythology continues to be accepted across the nation as "fact," reenforced by a progressive Northern-controlled media, educational system, and political body. Where will it end? Some, as Lincoln was, are committed to a complete obliteration of the South.

Our Southern culture is unique to America and is found nowhere else on earth. It is therefore something that all Americans, no matter what their race, religion, or political persuasion, should value and endeavor to protect. Davis certainly believed this, recording his thoughts on the matter for posterity in his brilliant work, *A Short History of the Confederate States of America* (which should be required reading in all American high schools).[58]

If you treasure America's Southern heritage, please do your part in helping to preserve it. There are many organizations dedicated to this cause (see Appendix E). Our early American Caudill ancestors, all who called Dixie their homeland, would have enthusiastically approved.

"All we ask is to be let alone."

JEFFERSON DAVIS
CONSERVATIVE PRESIDENT, C.S.A.

---

57. For more on this topic see my books, *All We Ask is to be Let Alone: The Southern Secession Fact Book*, and *Lincoln's War: The Real Cause, the Real Winner, the Real Loser*.
58. See my Sea Raven Press reprint of *A Short History of the Confederate States of America*.

DEAR ANCESTOR

Your tombstone stands among the rest, neglected and alone;
The name and date are chiseled out on polished, marbled stone.

It reaches out to all who care; it is too late to mourn;
You did not know that I exist; you died and I was born.

Yet each of us are cells of you in flesh, in blood, in bone;
Our blood contracts and beats a pulse entirely not our own.

Dear Ancestor, the place you filled one hundred years ago,
Spreads out among the ones you left who would have loved you so.

I wonder how you lived and loved, I wonder if you knew,
That someday I would find this spot, and come to visit you.

Author Unknown

BIBLIOGRAPHY

Ayto, John. *Dictionary of Word Origins*. New York, NY: Arcade, 1990.

Baring, Anne, and Jules Cashford. *The Myth of the Goddess: Evolution of an Image*. 1991. Harmondsworth, UK: Penguin, 1993 ed.

Boïelle, James. *Heath's French and English Dictionary*. Boston, MA: D. C. Heath and Co., 1903.

Briffault, Robert Stephen. *The Mothers: The Matriarchal Theory of Social Origins*. 1927. New York, NY: Macmillan, 1931 (single volume, abridged) ed.

Butler, Trent C. (ed). *Holman Bible Dictionary*. Nashville, TN: Holman Bible Publishers, 1991.

Campanelli, Pauline. *Ancient Ways: Reclaiming Pagan Traditions*. 1991. St. Paul, MN: Llewellyn, 1992 ed.

Campbell, Joseph. *The Masks of God: Primitive Mythology* (Vol. 1). 1959. Harmondsworth, UK: Arkana, 1991 ed.

Carlyon, Richard. *A Guide to the Gods: An Essential Guide to World Mythology*. New York, NY: William Morrown and Co., Inc., 1981.

Carroll, Mark. Personal correspondence.

Caudill, Delmerene. Personal correspondence.

Caudill, Harry M. *Slender is the Thread: Tales from a Country Law Office*. Lexington, KY: University Press of Kentucky, 1987.

Cirlot, J. E. *A Dictionary of Symbols* (Jack Sage, trans.). 1962. New York, NY: Philosophical Library, 1983 ed.

Constable, George (ed.). *Mysteries of the Unknown: Mystic Places*. Richmond, VA: Time-Life, 1987.

Cotterell, Arthur. *A Dictionary of World Mythology*. 1979. New York, NY: Oxford University Press, 1990 ed.

——. *The Macmillan Illustrated Encyclopedia of Myths and Legends*. New

York, NY: Macmillan, 1989.

Cross, Frank L., and Elizabeth A. Livingstone. *The Oxford Dictionary of the Christian Church*. 1957. London, UK: Oxford University Press, 1974 ed.

Domesday Book: A Survey of the Counties of England. Compiled by direction of King William I: Winchester, 1086. This edition: John Morris (gen. ed.), Chichester, UK: Phillimore and Co., 1984.

Dorward, David. *Scottish Surnames: A Guide to the Family Names of Scotland*. Glasgow, Scotland: Harper Collins, 1995.

Downing, Christine. *The Goddess: Mythological Images of the Feminine*. New York, NY: Crossroad, 1984.

Eisler, Riane. *The Chalice and the Blade: Our History, Our Future*. New York, NY: Perennial, 1987.

Eliade, Mircea. *Images and Symbols: Studies in Religious Symbolism* (Philip Mairet, trans.). 1952. Princeton, NJ: Mythos, 1991 ed.

Encyclopedia Britannica: A New Survey of Universal Knowledge. 1768. Chicago, IL/London, UK: Encyclopedia Britannica, 1955 ed.

Farmer, David Hugh. *The Oxford Dictionary of Saints*. 1978. Oxford, UK: Oxford University Press, 1992 ed.

Filmore, Charles. *Metaphysical Bible Dictionary*. Unity Village, MO: Unity School of Christianity, 1931.

Frazer, Sir James George. *The Golden Bough: A Study in Magic and Religion*. 1922. New York, NY: Collier, 1963 (abridged) ed.

——. *Folklore in the Old Testament: Studies in Comparative Religion, Legend, and Law*. New York, NY: Tudor, 1923 (abridged) ed.

Gimbutas, Marija Alseikaitė. *The Goddesses and Gods of Old Europe: Myths and Cult Images*. 1974. Berkeley, CA: University of California Press, 1992 ed.

——. *The Civilization of the Goddess: The World of Old Europe*. New York, NY: Harper Collins, 1991.

Glyn, Anthony. *The British: Portrait of a People*. New York, NY: G. P.

Putnam's Sons, 1970.

Graves, Robert. *The White Goddess: A Historical Grammar of Poetic Myth*. 1948. New York, NY: Noonday Press, 1991 ed.

———. *The Greek Myths*. 1955. Harmondsworth, UK: Penguin, 1992 combined ed.

Graves, Robert, and Raphael Patai. *Hebrew Myths: The Book of Genesis*. 1964. New York, NY: Anchor, 1989 ed.

Green, John Richard. *A Short History of the English People* (Vol. 1). London, UK: Macmillan and Co., 1892.

Farrell, Deborah, and Carole Presser. *The Herder Symbol Dictionary*. 1978. Wilmette, IL: Chiron, 1990 ed.

Hadas, Moses (ed.). *A History of Rome*. Garden City, NY: Doubleday, 1956.

Hall, Eleanor L. *The Moon and the Virgin: Reflections on the Archetypal Feminine*. New York, NY: Harper and Row, 1980.

Hall, John Richard Clark. *A Concise Anglo-Saxon Dictionary*. 1894. Toronto, Canada: University of Toronto Press (and the Medieval Academy of America), 1960 ed. (1996 imprint).

Hall, Manly P. *The Secret Teachings of All Ages*. 1925. Los Angeles, CA: Philosophical Research Society, 1989 ed.

Heer, Friedrich. *The Medieval World: Europe 1100-1350*. 1961. New York, NY: Mentor, 1962 ed.

Herm, Gerhard. *The Celts: The People Who Came Out of the Darkness*. New York, NY: St. Martin's Press, 1976.

Hodson, Geoffrey. *The Hidden Wisdom in the Holy Bible* (Vol. 2). 1967. Wheaton, IL: Quest, 1978 ed.

Johnston, Rev. James B. *Place-names of England and Wales*. London, UK: John Murray, 1915.

Jones, Gwyn. *A History of the Vikings*. 1968. Oxford, UK: Oxford University Press, 1984 ed.

Jones, Prudence, and Nigel Pennick. *A History of Pagan Europe*. London,

UK: Routledge, 1995.

Kettridge, J. O. *Kettridge's French-English Dictionary*. New York, NY: David McKay Co., n.d.

Larousse Encyclopedia of Mythology, New. 1959. London, UK: Hamlyn Publishing Group, 1976 ed.

Layton, Bentley. *The Gnostic Scriptures: Ancient Wisdom for the New Age*. 1987. New York, NY: Anchor, 1995 ed.

Littleton, C. Scott (ed). *Mythology: The Illustrated Anthology of World Myth and Storytelling*. London, UK: Duncan Baird, 2002.

MacLysaght, Edward. *The Surnames of Ireland*. 1985. Dublin, Ireland: Irish Academic Press, 1999 ed.

May, Barbara. Personal correspondence.

McArthur, Tom (ed.). *The Oxford Companion to the English Language*. Oxford, UK: Oxford University Press, 1992.

McKenzie, John L. *Dictionary of the Bible*. New York, NY: Collier, 1965.

Mills, A. D. *Oxford Dictionary of English Place-names*. 1991. Oxford, UK: Oxford University Press, 1998 ed.

Mollenkott, Virginia Ramey. *The Divine Feminine: The Biblical Imagery of God as Female*. New York, NY: Crossroad, 1993.

Monaghan, Patricia. *The Book of Goddesses and Heroines*. 1990. St. Paul, MN: Llewellyn, 1991 ed.

Montagu, Ashley. *The Natural Superiority of Women*. 1952. New York, NY: Collier, 1992 ed.

Myers, Philip Van Ness. *Ancient History*. 1904. Boston, MA: Ginn and Co., 1916 ed.

Neumann, Erich. *The Great Mother: An Analysis of the Archetype*. New York, NY: Pantheon, 1955.

Newall, Venetia. *The Encyclopedia of Witchcraft and Magic*. New York, NY: A and W Visual Library, 1974.

Norton-Taylor, Duncan. *The Emergence of Man: The Celts*. New York: Time-Life, 1974.

O'Brien, Arthur. *Europe Before Modern Times: An Ancient and Medieval History*. 1940. Chicago, IL: Loyola University Press, 1943 ed.

Olson, Carl (ed.). *The Book of the Goddess, Past and Present: An Introduction to Her Religion*. New York, NY: Crossroad, 1983.

Oxford English Dictionary, The (compact edition, 2 vols.). 1928. Oxford, UK: Oxford University Press, 1979 ed.

Patai, Raphael. *The Hebrew Goddess*. 1967. Detroit, MI: Wayne State University Press, 1990 ed.

Pennick, Nigel. *The Pagan Book of Days: A Guide to the Festivals, Traditions, and Sacred Days of the Year*. Rochester, VT: Destiny, 1992.

Raftery, Barry. *Pagan Celtic Ireland: The Enigma of the Irish Iron Age*. London, UK: Thames and Hudson, 1994.

Ramondino, Salvatore (ed.). *The New World Spanish-English and English-Spanish Dictionary*. New York, NY: Signet, 1969.

Reaney, P. H., and R. M. Wilson. *A Dictionary of English Surnames*. 1958. Oxford, UK: Oxford University Press, 1997 ed.

Reilly, Patricia Lynn. *A God Who Looks Like Me: Discovering a Woman-Affirming Spirituality*. New York, NY: Ballentine, 1995.

Riecke, Kay Caudill. Personal correspondence (contributors to Kay's genealogy: Janet and Emery Caudill, and Robert E. Caudill).

Rufus, Anneli S., and Kristan Lawson. *Goddess Sites: Europe*. New York, NY: Harper Collins, 1991.

Rule, Lareina. *Name Your Baby*. 1963. New York, NY: Bantam, 1978 ed.

Rutherford, Ward. *Celtic Mythology: The Nature and Influence of Celtic Myth—from Druidism to Arthurian Legend*. 1987. New York, NY: Sterling, 1990 ed.

Scarlett, James D. *Tartans of Scotland*. 1972. Cambridge, UK: The Lutterworth Press, 1996 ed.

Seabrook, Lochlainn. *Britannia Rules: Goddess-Worship in Ancient Anglo-Celtic Society - An Academic Look at the United Kingdom's Matricentric Spiritual Past*. Franklin, TN: Sea Raven Press, 1999.

——. *The Goddess Dictionary of Words and Phrases: Introducing a New Core Vocabulary for the Women's Spirituality Movement.* Franklin, TN: Sea Raven Press, 1999.

——. *The Book of Kelle: An Introduction to Goddess-Worship and the Great Celtic Mother-Goddess Kelle, Original Blessed Lady of Ireland.* 1999. Franklin, TN: Sea Raven Press, 2010 ed.

——. *The Blakeneys: An Entymological, Ethnological, and Genealogical Study: Unveiling the Mysterious Origins of the Blakeney Family and Name (With Additional Material on Blakeney Place-names, Blakeney Surname Variations, and the Surname Blake).* Franklin, TN: Sea Raven Press, 2000.

——. *Carnton Plantation Ghost Stories: True Tales of the Unexplained from Tennessee's Most Haunted Civil War House!* 2005. Franklin, TN: Sea Raven Press, 2008 ed.

——. *Abraham Lincoln: The Southern View - Demythologizing America's Sixteenth President* (Foreword by Clint Johnson). 2007. Franklin, TN: Sea Raven Press, 2009 ed.

——. *Princess Diana: Modern-Day Moon-Goddess - A Psychoanalytical and Mythological Look at Diana Spencer's Life, Marriage, and Death* (co-authored with Dr. Jane Goldberg). Franklin, TN: Sea Raven Press, 2008.

——. *The McGavocks of Carnton Plantation: A Southern History - Celebrating One of Dixie's Most Noble Confederate Families and Their Tennessee Home.* Franklin, TN: Sea Raven Press, 2008.

——. *Christmas Before Christianity: How the Birthday of the "Sun" Became the Birthday of the "Son."* Franklin, TN: Sea Raven Press, 2010.

——. *A Rebel Born: A Defense of Nathan Bedford Forrest - Confederate General, American Legend.* Franklin, TN: Sea Raven Press, 2010.

——. *The Way of Holiness: The Evolution of Religion—From the Cave Bear Cult to Christianity.* Franklin, TN: Sea Raven Press, unpublished manuscript.

——. *The Goddess Encyclopedia of Secret Words, Names, and Places.* Franklin, TN: Sea Raven Press, unpublished manuscript.

——. *Confederacy 101: Amazing Facts You Never Knew About America's Oldest Political Tradition.* Franklin, TN: Sea Raven Press, 2015.

——. *The Great Yankee Coverup: What the North Doesn't Want You To Know About Lincoln's War.* Franklin, TN: Sea Raven Press, 2015.

——. *Confederate Flag Facts: What Every American Should Know About Dixie's Southern Cross.* Franklin, TN: Sea Raven Press, 2015.

——. *Seabrook's Bible Dictionary of Traditional and Mystical Christian Doctrines.* Spring Hill, TN: Sea Raven Press, 2016.

——. *Abraham Lincoln Was a Liberal, Jefferson Davis Was a Conservative: The Missing Key to Understanding the American Civil War.* Spring Hill, TN: Sea Raven Press, 2017.

——. *All We Ask is to be Let Alone: The Southern Secession Fact Book.* Spring Hill, TN: Sea Raven Press, 2017.

——. *Confederate Monuments: Why Every American Should Honor Confederate Soldiers and Their Memorials.* Spring Hill, TN: Sea Raven Press, 2018.

——. *What the Confederate Flag Means to Me: Americans Speak Out in Defense of Southern Honor, Heritage, and History.* Spring Hill, TN: Sea Raven Press, 2021.

——. *Heroes of the Southern Confederacy: The Illustrated Book of Confederate Officials, Soldiers, and Civilians.* Spring Hill, TN: Sea Raven Press, 2021.

——. *Support Your Local Confederate: Wit and Humor in the Southern Confederacy.* Spring Hill, TN: Sea Raven Press, 2021.

——. *America's Three Constitutions: Complete Texts of the Articles of Confederation, Constitution of the United States of America, and Constitution of the Confederate States of America.* Spring Hill, TN: Sea Raven Press, 2021.

Sjöö, Monica, and Barbara Mor. *The Great Cosmic Mother: Rediscovering the*

Religion of the Earth. New York, NY: Harper and Row, 1987.

Skeat, Walter W. *A Concise Etymological Dictionary of the English Language*. 1882. New York, NY: Capricorn, 1963 ed.

Skelton, Robin, and Margaret Blackwood. *Earth, Air, Fire, Water: Pre-Christian and Pagan Elements in British Songs, Rhymes and Ballads*. Harmondsworth, UK: Arkana, 1990.

Smith, Lacey Baldwin. *This Realm of England: 1399 to 1688*. 1966. Lexington, MA: D. C. Heath and Co., 1983 ed.

Smith, Philip D. Jr. *Tartan For Me! Suggested Tartans for 13,695 Scottish, Scotch-Irish, Irish, and North American Names with Lists of Clan, Family and District Tartans*. Bruceton Mills, WV: Scotpress, 1990.

Stein, Diane. *The Goddess Book of Days*. 1988. Freedom, CA: Crossing Press, 1992 ed.

Stone, Merlin. *When God was a Woman*. San Diego, CA: Harvest, 1976.

——. *Ancient Mirrors of Womanhood: A Treasury of Goddess and Heroine Lore from Around the World*. 1979. Boston, MA: Beacon Press, 1990 ed.

Streep, Peg. *Sanctuaries of the Goddess: The Sacred Landscapes and Objects*. Boston, MA: Bullfinch Press, 1994.

Strong, James. *Strong's Exhaustive Concordance of the Bible*. 1890. Nashville, TN: Abingdon Press, 1975 ed.

Traupman, John C. *The New College Latin and English Dictionary*. 1966. New York, NY: Bantam, 1988 ed.

Trevelyan, George Macaulay. *History of England: Vol. 1, From the Earliest Times to the Reformation*. 1926. Garden City, NY: Anchor, 1952 ed.

——. *History of England: Vol. 2, The Tudors and the Stuart Era*. 1926. Garden City, NY: Anchor, 1952 ed.

Tripp, Edward. *The Meridian Handbook of Classical Mythology*. 1970. Harmondsworth, UK: Meridian, 1974 ed.

Valiente, Doreen. *An ABC of Witchcraft Past and Present*. New York, NY: St. Martin's Press, 1973.

Walker, Barbara G. *The Woman's Encyclopedia of Myths and Secrets*. San Francisco, CA: Harper and Row, 1983.

——. *The Crone: Woman of Age, Wisdom, and Power*. San Francisco, CA: Harper and Row, 1985.

——. *The Woman's Dictionary of Symbols and Sacred Objects*. San Francisco, CA: Harper and Row, 1988.

Warner, Ezra J. *Generals in Gray: Lives of the Confederate Commanders*. 1959. Baton Rouge, LA: Louisiana State University Press, 1989 ed.

Way, George, and Romilly Squire. *Scottish Clan and Family Encyclopedia*. Glasgow, Scotland: Harper Collins, 1994.

Webster's Biographical Dictionary. Springfield, MA: G. and C. Merriam Company, 1943.

Webster's Ninth New Collegiate Dictionary. 1898. Springfield, MA: Merriam-Webster, 1984 ed.

White, R. J. *The Horizon Concise History of England*. New York, NY: American Heritage, 1971.

Zimmerman, J. E. *Dictionary of Classical Mythology*. New York, NY: Bantam, 1964.

REAL HISTORY!

SEA RAVEN PRESS

Nashville, Tennessee

SOUTHERN BOOKS,

SEA RAVEN PRESS

FIVE-STAR BOOKS & GIFTS

From the Heart of the American South

SeaRavenPress.com

INDEX

MEET THE AUTHOR

NEO-VICTORIAN SCHOLAR LOCHLAINN SEABROOK, a descendant of the families of Alexander Hamilton Stephens, John Singleton Mosby, Edmund Winchester Rucker, and William Giles Harding, is a 7th generation Kentuckian and the most prolific pro-South writer in the world today. Known by literary critics as the "new Shelby Foote" and by his fans as the "Voice of the Traditional South," he is a recipient of the prestigious Jefferson Davis Historical Gold Medal. As a lifelong writer he has authored and edited books ranging in topics from history, politics, science, religion, and biography, to nature, music, humor, gastronomy, and the paranormal; books that his readers describe as "game changers," "transformative," and "life altering."

One of the world's most popular living historians, he is a 17th generation Southerner of Appalachian heritage who descends from dozens of patriotic Revolutionary War soldiers and Confederate soldiers from Kentucky, Tennessee, North Carolina, and Virginia. A proud member of the Sons of the Confederate Veterans, he is a true Renaissance Man. Besides being an accomplished and well respected author-historian and Bible authority, he is also a Kentucky Colonel, eagle scout, screenwriter, nature, wildlife, and landscape photographer, artist, graphic designer, songwriter (3,000 songs), film composer, multi-instrument musician, vocalist, session player, music producer, genealogist, former history museum docent, and a former ranch hand, zookeeper, and wrangler.

His (currently) 76 adult and children's books contain some 60,000 well-researched pages that have earned him accolades from around the globe. His works, which have sold on every continent except Antarctica, have introduced hundreds of thousands to vital facts that have been left out of our mainstream books. He has been endorsed internationally by leading experts, museum curators, award-winning historians, bestselling authors, celebrities, filmmakers, noted scientists, well regarded educators, TV show hosts and producers, renowned military artists, esteemed heritage organizations, and distinguished academicians of all races, creeds, and colors. Colonel Seabrook holds the world record for writing the most books on Southern icon Nathan Bedford Forrest: 12.

Of northern, western, and central European ancestry, he is the 6th great-grandson of the Earl of Oxford and a descendant of European royalty. His modern day cousins include: Johnny Cash, Elvis Presley, Lisa Marie Presley, Billy Ray and Miley Cyrus, Patty Loveless, Tim McGraw, Lee Ann Womack, Dolly Parton, Pat Boone, Naomi, Wynonna, and Ashley Judd, Ricky Skaggs, the Sunshine Sisters, Martha Carson, Chet Atkins, Patrick J. Buchanan, Cindy Crawford, Bertram Thomas Combs (Kentucky's 50th governor), Edith Bolling (second wife of President Woodrow Wilson), Andy Griffith, Riley Keough, George C. Scott, Robert Duvall, Reese Witherspoon, Lee Marvin, Rebecca Gayheart, and Tom Cruise.

A constitutionalist and avid outdoorsman and gun advocate, Colonel Seabrook is the author of the international blockbuster, *Everything You Were Taught About the Civil War is Wrong, Ask a Southerner!* He lives with his wife and family in beautiful historic Middle Tennessee, the heart of the Confederacy.

For more information on author Mr. Seabrook visit

LOCHLAINNSEABROOK.COM

SEA RAVEN PRESS · PURVEYOR OF FINE · BOOKS AND GIFTS · EST. 1995 ·

If you enjoyed this book you will be interested in Colonel Seabrook's popular related titles:

☛ VINTAGE SOUTHERN COOKBOOK: 2,000 DELICIOUS DISHES FROM DIXIE
☛ THE BLAKENEYS: AN ETYMOLOGICAL, ETHNOLOGICAL, & GENEALOGICAL STUDY
☛ THE MCGAVOCKS OF CARNTON PLANTATION: A SOUTHERN HISTORY
☛ ABRAHAM LINCOLN WAS A LIBERAL, JEFFERSON DAVIS WAS A CONSERVATIVE
☛ EVERYTHING YOU WERE TAUGHT ABOUT THE CIVIL WAR IS WRONG, ASK A SOUTHERNER!
☛ CONFEDERATE FLAG FACTS: WHAT EVERY AMERICAN SHOULD KNOW ABOUT DIXIE'S SOUTHERN CROSS

Available from Sea Raven Press and wherever fine books are sold

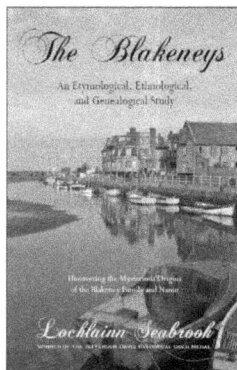

ALL OF OUR BOOK COVERS ARE AVAILABLE AS 11" X 17" COLOR POSTERS, SUITABLE FOR FRAMING

∞ **SeaRavenPress.com** ∞